SEATTLE IN THE

# SEATTLE TRANSFORMED

## *World War II to Cold War*

*Richard C. Berner*

CHARLES PRESS
Seattle, Washington

Copyright © 1999 Richard C. Berner

All Rights Reserved

Printed and Bound in the United States of America

No part of this book may reproduced or transmitted in any form of by any means, electronic or mechanical, photocopying, or by any information storage and retrieval system, without permission in writing from the author.

ISBN: 0-9629889-2-8

Printed by Thomson-Shore, Inc.

# TABLE OF CONTENTS

## PART 1

POLITICAL HISTORY OF THE 1940S:
AN INTRODUCTION — 2-16
    Trivialization of Politics: 1941 City Election — 11-13
    Trivialization, Part II: 1942 City Election — 14-16

EVACUATION AND INTERNMENT OF JAPANESE AMERICANS:
"THE DOMINATION OF POLITICS OVER LAW" — 18-42
    Introduction — 18-21
    Pearl Harbor Day — 21-28
    Movement Toward Evacuation — 28-32
    Tolan Committee Hearings — 32-35
    Evacuation Underway — 35-42

THE WARTIME ECONOMY — 44-106
    Introduction — 44-47
    Boeing's B-17s and B-29s — 55-57
    Composition of Workforce is Transformed — 47-54
    Comparative Wage Scales: Their Significance — 57-59
    Port of Embarkation — 59-60
    Getting To and From Work — 60-62
    Seattle's Congressional Liaison:
        Warren Magnuson — 62-63
    Energy for War — 64-67
    Transformation of Women's Roles — 68-79

| | |
|---|---|
| MILITARIZATION OF THE ECONOMY | 80-106 |
|     The Volunteerism Phase | 80-83 |
|     Implementation of OPA's Statutory Authority | 83-85 |
|     Implementation of Rationing, | |
|         Price and Rent Controls in the Seattle Area | 85-91 |
|     Rent Control and Housing | 91-95 |
|     Food Price Control and Rationing | 95-99 |
|     Boeing and Local 751 vs. WPB | 99-104 |
|     Salvage Drives | 104-106 |
| | |
| THE 1944 CITY ELECTIONS, CITY AND GENERAL | 107-112 |
| | |
| THE 1946 CITY ELECTION | 112-114 |

# PART 2

| | |
|---|---|
| SEATTLE CIVIC UNITY COMMITTEE | 118-134 |
|     INTRODUCTION | 118-124 |
|     RETURN OF THE JAPANESE | 124-130 |
|     THE CUC AND AFRICAN AMERICANS | 130-134 |
| | |
| RECREATION AND ENTERTAINMENT SCENE OF THE 1940S: A REVIEW | 136-151 |
|     GENERAL | 136-139 |
|     CLASSICAL MUSIC AND FINE ARTS DURING 1940s | 139-151 |
|     PEACE! | 151 |
| | |
| EDUCATION | 153-166 |
|     THE UNIVERSITY OF WASHINGTON: INDISPENSABLE TO CITY'S ADAPTATION TO MODERNITY | 153-161 |
|     SEATTLE PUBLIC SCHOOLS: VITAL COG IN WARTIME, TURN TOWARD FUTURE | 162-166 |

# PART 3

| | |
|---|---:|
| THE POSTWAR POLITICAL ECONOMY | 171-177 |
|     INTRODUCTION | 171-175 |
|     THE POSTWAR LABOR FORCE: | |
|         WHERE DID THE WOMEN GO? | 175-177 |
| | |
| RETURN TO CIVILIAN ECONOMY - ROLE OF OPA | 179-194 |
|     PHASING OUT OF OPA | 185-188 |
|     SEATTLE HOUSING IN EARLY POSTWAR PERIOD | 188-191 |
|     LABOR IN EARLY POSTWAR PERIOD | 191-194 |
| | |
| BOEING AND THE POSTWAR ECONOMY | 196-200 |
| | |
| 1948: LIBERALISM IN DISARRAY | 202-241 |
|     PRELUDE | 202-206 |
|     SEATTLE, THE NATION IN MICROCOSM? | 207-212 |
|     1948 CITY ELECTION | 212-214 |
|     THE GREAT BOEING STRIKE OF 1948 | 215-222 |
|     WATERFRONT STRIKE: CLASS COLLABORATION | |
|         DISPLACES ANTICOMMUNIST STRATEGY | 223-227 |
|     CANWELL HEARINGS ON THE UNIVERSITY OF WASHINGTON | |
|         AND SEATTLE REPERTORY PLAYHOUSE | 227-234 |
|     RESULTS OF THE 1948 GENERAL ELECTION | 234-235 |
|     THE UW'S TENURE COMMITTEE HEARINGS | 235-241 |
| | |
| 1950: END OF AN ERA? | 243-246 |
| | |
| POSTSCRIPT | 248-255 |
| | |
| ENDNOTES | 259-307 |
| | |
| INDEX | 311-327 |

*For Temy*

# ACKNOWLEDGEMENTS

From an examination of the sources cited it should be clear the holdings of the Manuscripts Collection and University Archives of the University of Washington Libraries have been indispensable for research on Seattle in the 1940s, just as they were for the two earlier volumes. The services and advice of Manuscript Curator Karyl Winn and her staff: Gary Lundell, Janet Ness, and Nan Cohen have been appreciated beyond measure.

The same can be said for Glenda Pearson, head of the Newspapers/Microfilm division and Terry Kato, together with their well trained student assistants who seem to spend much of their time troubleshooting on often idiosyncratic equipment that makes reading newspapers on microfilm a less painful undertaking than it would otherwise be.

Richard Engeman and Carla Rickerson of the Special Collections Division have been very helpful when called upon for use of the division's scrapbooks and photographs. Eleanor Chase and her Government Publications Division staff, principally Andrew Johnson and David Maack have rendered excellent service.

I am particularly indebted to Louis Fiset, Jane Sanders, and Richard S. Kirkendall for their critical readings of early chapter drafts. Louis Fiset's research on the Japanese evacuation includes transcriptions of taped interviews of many Nisei. His loan of these has made it possible to convey the impact at a more personal level on those experiencing this tragic violation of their constitutional rights. These interviews have been done in conjunction with his study of "Camp Harmony", the Puyallup Assembly Center, and publication of his *Imprisoned Apart: The World War II Correspondence of an Issei Couple*. Sally Kazama and Minnie and Henry Itoi lent encouragement and advice on the Japanese evacuation chapter, as did historian Roger Daniels, a leading authority on the evacuation and Asian American history.

It was natural to call upon Jane Sanders, author of the classic volume *Cold War on Campus* to critique the chapter "1948: Liberalism in Disarray". She is *the* civil liberties authority on this fateful postwar period in which the Cold War and McCarthyism took root. Any special merit to the chapter is due in some especially critical sections to her. Richard Kirkendall's profound knowledge of this historically reshaping period was then drawn upon for a review of that revision. To them I am grateful, hoping they will each recognize their contributions to the final result.

To Margaret Hall is owed a special debt: loyally, with dedication, Margaret labored through the entire manuscript, eliminating most use of the passive voice, correcting syntax, asking questions when meaning was unclear, and much more. All remaining shortcomings are my own.

Photographic historian Paul Dorpat is a treasure for all of us regional historians. His three volume *Now and Then* series picturing Seattle's transformation from village to metropolis is a gold mine of narrative and photographic detail not available anywhere else. Generous of his time and his photographic skills, he has been at my beck and call, shamefully to be exploited in fact.

Thanks to Van Diep for her work in laying out this volume.

Special appreciation is extended to Seattle Public Schools Archivist Eleanor Toews for guidance through its archival holdings. For material on the Civilian Wartime Commission - for which practically no archival records exist - City Archivist Scott Cline led me to sparse though excellent sources. At the Seattle Public Library Susan Rennels provided access to the rarely used scrapbook collection maintained by the CWC; these proved indispensable for documenting its work in coordinating all the volunteer groups operating in the city. Without these volunteers the city's support of the war effort would have been seriously handicapped.

Librarian Carolyn Marr made easy access to the superb photographic collection of the Museum of History and Industry, which also houses the Ladies Musical Club's scrapbooks. Boeing's archivist, Thomas Lubbersmunger guided me to ideal photographs in the enormous photography collection of the company. The staff of the Seattle Housing Authority proved very helpful at locating material in their files. Called upon also was Archivist Joyce Justice of the Regional Branch of the National Archives for help in locating material among its enormous holdings.

# PART 1

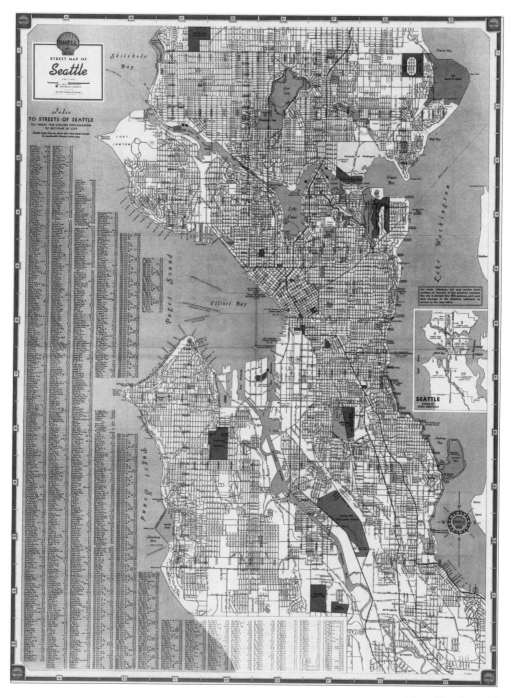

*Map of Seattle, 1946.*

# POLITICAL HISTORY OF THE 1940S: AN INTRODUCTION

Seattle's political history, as with other metropolitan areas along the Pacific Coast, was dramatically reshaped by the war and preparations for it. By 1941 mass unemployment of the 1930s had practically vanished, though not the memory of it. Men were drafted or moved into defense industry jobs. West Coast shipbuilding revived on a scale that superseded shipbuilding during World War I. West Coast shipbuilding was concentrated in the San Francisco Bay area, the Portland/Vancouver region, the Seattle-Tacoma industrial area, and the Puget Sound Naval Shipyard in Bremerton. Unique to this war was the emergence of the aircraft industry in the Los Angeles metropolitan complex, and in Seattle. The aircraft industry proved its strategic importance in modern warfare. It became the catalyst for postwar development presaging the postwar metamorphosis of the "military-metropolitan-industrial complex", concluding the steady militarization of the economy and its political/bureaucratic superstructure during the course of the war.

Federal relations with the nation's states and municipalities assumed critical importance during the Great Depression. Chronic unemployment existed on such an unprecedented scale that it lay beyond the capabilities of private charities and existing relief programs of states and municipalities. Federal intervention, then, began for all practical purposes in 1933 after the election of Franklin D. Roosevelt to the presidency. FDR instituted federal unemployment relief programs and public works projects to revive the economy - "pump priming". Roosevelt's administration implemented social reforms to buttress these efforts. Together, these reforms became known as the "New Deal". More federal intervention developed as a result of the defense buildup. The US became the "Arsenal of Democracy" during this period, 1940-1941. After Pearl Harbor production for war further extended federal penetration of the economy. Capitalist enterprise became wedded to federal assistance on such a scale as to make them largely inseparable in the future.

Organized labor, which became a political force before and during World War I, lost its political power when it lost bitter strikes in the early postwar period. Having won these vital strikes employers, nationwide, established their long sought instrument of dominance over labor, the open shop, known as the "American Plan". Not only was organized labor neutralized in terms of reaching out to unorganized sectors of the economy, - mainly in the mass production industries - but it no longer exercised political influence. When the Great Depression set in political disenchantment spread as President Hoover's measures to counter the nation's downward slide proved wholly inadequate, leading to the overwhelming victory of Franklin Roosevelt in 1932. One of Roosevelt's first legislative enactments was the National Industrial Recovery Act to underwrite the self-regulation of business. Included, however was a section 7a, which was intended to protect workers should they seek unionization on their own terms, not the employers' company unions or employer representation plans imposed during the early postwar period. Industry codes were formulated to implement the act, but trade associations dominated proceedings that led to their enactment. Section 7a proved a disappointing failure from labor's standpoint. When the Supreme Court ruled the NIRA unconstitutional in 1935 New York's Senator Robert Wagner stood ready with a labor bill which specifically protected labor organizing and bargaining rights: the National Labor Relations Act. By it the federal government took on the role of protecting workers who sought to form unions free from employer influence. Only then could collective bargaining proceed toward a mutually more equitable outcome. The National Labor Relations Board, with its regional boards, was set up to help guarantee this result. By its terms most of the employers' anti-union practices of the past were labeled "unfair" and illegal. This "Wagner Act" served as the labor's charter to organize. Organize it did, but the American Federation of Labor's failure to organize the mass production industries lent credibility to a movement within the AFL to establish unions on an industrial basis instead of perpetuating the AFL's crafts as its structural base. This result was not unexpected. Since the turn of the century there had been a running battle within the AFL between industrial and craft proponents. Out of this dissident movement emerged the Congress of Industrial Organizations in the fall of 1937. Under leadership of the United Mine Workers' president, John L. Lewis, the CIO began organizing the mass production industries: steel, automobile, rubber, electrical. United States Steel Corporation signed an agreement in 1937 with the United Steel Workers Union; General Motors fell in line, recognizing the United Automobile Workers Union; General Electric also signed a contract with the United Electrical Workers, then the Goodyear and the Firestone rubber companies conceded to the rubber workers union. The CIO had accumulated about four million members in the space of a year or so. Politically this meant a gathering in coalition that many, plus their families and sympathizers. Out of this movement the CIO emerged a loyal constituency dedicated to the New Deal programs, inherently liberal and reformist. Reflected in the formation of this New Deal coalition is a power to counter that of corporate America's political dominance, John K. Galbraith's concept of the "countervailing power". Above all elements in the coalition it was the CIO's organizational effectiveness at mobilizing the labor and ethnic vote which made it the main target of corporate power and its conservative congressional allies. [1]

While these events were unfolding in the midwest and northeastern states a brief look of the Seattle area will provide a somewhat different concurrent context. Here, mass production industries were largely absent. Being craft-oriented and primarily focused upon job protection, the unions affiliated with the Washington State Federation of Labor (WSFL) lost members during the 1920s and early 1930s. The general prosperity of the 1920s accounted for substantially all improvements for trade unionists, not aggressively organizing against the open shop.

Passivity with respect to organizing was common among these AFL unions. An exception in the Seattle area was the Teamsters union. Under the domineering leadership of Dave Beck it became the catalyst for whatever AFL organizing was done in the area. By 1925 the Teamsters dominated the Seattle Central Labor Council. In AFL unions rank and file involvement in union affairs, here as elsewhere, was actively discouraged by trade union officers. Through their own bureaucracies they dealt directly with those employers who chose to recognize the union as bargaining agent. Referral of a labor contract to the union membership for vote was the exception. The coastwide waterfront strike of 1934 is a case in point. When the International Longshoremen's Association on the West Coast struck the entire coast its national president Joe Ryan came West to make an agreement on his own authority. He and the shipowners' representative Roger Lapham concluded one. By tradition it seemed a done deal. However, San Francisco longshoreman Harry Bridges led the membership to insist on the original goals of the strike, and for a vote on the contract by the entire membership along the coast. They ignored the advice of Ryan and of the Teamster's Dave Beck, who represented Washington's governor Clarence Martin. The members overwhelmingly rejected the contract. The strike lasted 83 days, and was called off following the San Francisco general strike in July. Federal mediation won union recognition of the Pacific Coast division of the ILA. Control of the hiring hall by the union proved most critical. Formerly the employers controlled them. In arbitration the union won control. By 1937 the Pacific Coast locals joined the new CIO. In the Puget Sound area those ILA locals of Tacoma, Port Angeles, and Anacortes stayed with the AFL. On the Pacific Coast the ILA locals that followed Bridges into the CIO became the International Longshoremen's and Warehousemen's Union, the ILWU. Other maritime unions also joined the CIO. At this stage the CIO unions were subject to intense rank and file participation. [2]

Returning to the national scene, when the CIO had reached the height of its organizing drive, it was to experience a sharp reversal of fortune. Loss of strikes and lives against the Little Steel companies in summer of 1937 slowed down its original drive. Intervention by the New Deal administration on the side of the Little Steel strikers seemed called for but did not occur. That fall a recession set in that would not be relieved until 1940. Federal intervention with appropriate public relief programs was not reinforced by a timely infusion of deficit spending. Instead funding was cut back, deepening the recession. Strikes against the major meat packers were lost in 1939. Ford continued its stiff resistance, as did International Harvester. On the West Coast the Teamsters blocked the ILWU from extending its "march inland" among warehouse workers. Labor historian Nelson Lichtenstein concludes, "A year before Pearl Harbor, the CIO remained but a tentative and incomplete structure." [3]

CIO unions were noted for their volatility, due to the dynamism of its organizers at the local levels. From their direct contact with the rank and file and their grievances at the shop level they operated independently of CIO officialdom, such as it was. Leftists - including Communists - played the key role, inspiring whatever tactics seemed called for in gaining bargaining rights; they were further motivated to develop a mass political base that would sustain their gains. Dedication to this formidable task often meant risking life and limb. In proving indispensable at this early stage for organizing the Communists and leftists earned the CIO a reputation for being "Communist dominated", thereby the exposing the CIO to "Red-baiting". Under the aegis of the Cold War, Red-baiting would reach crescendo proportions...and political successes for its practitioners. Inasmuch as the CIO had challenged the AFL for its ineffectiveness at organizing, practically every CIO election victory meant a loss for the AFL. That these election outcomes were conducted under the auspices of the National Labor Relations Board converted the AFL into an opponent of the National Labor Relations Act (NLRA). The AFL often joined employers and many conservative legislators in the Red-baiting sequel. In Seattle employers accepted Dave Beck's version of unionism as their preferred alternative to the left wing waterfront unions, their trade associations joining with Beck in establishing controls for prices, checking "cutthroat competition", and avoiding strikes. [4]

Even before the Congress of Industrial Organizations was established the United Mine Workers' John L. Lewis geared up for the 1936 election, establishing Labor's Non-Partisan League (LNPL). Central to its agenda was defense of the New Deal and its recently enacted social reforms. As to the Wagner Act, it was the CIO's birth certificate. The CIO, thereby, became one of the critical components of the Roosevelt coalition in the process. It would remain so even after Lewis's personal defection in 1940. For this desertion from support of the New Deal Lewis was replaced as CIO president by Phillip Murray in November 1940. The LNPL operated through the

CIO's industrial union councils which were established for regions, states, and local operations. Locally, executive secretary of the Seattle IUC and of the Washington IUC was a Communist, Eugene Dennett. An anticommunist, Richard Francis, was CIO regional director, also its Washington state director. Several CIO locals, including Dennett's Inlandboatmen's Union, were members of the Washington Commonwealth Federation. The WCF had lost all but its left wing union affiliates during the 1939-1941 Nazi-Soviet Pact period. These affiliates were considered to be Communist-led, particularly for having followed the party's line during the pact period (September 1939-June 1941). When the WCF sought an alliance with the CIO during this period Francis rejected the proposal outright, asserting the CIO and "labor" have nothing in common with the WCF. He spoke for Lewis, who had just demoted Harry Bridges as western regional director of the CIO. Dennett was removed from his state CIO secretary position as part of this first CIO purge. If this purge would remove the red taint associated with CIO unions and satisfy its critics the answer is "no" - not as long as the CIO remained a vital component of the New Deal coalition. Indeed, the CIO had nowhere else to turn for protection. And the New Deal needed the CIO to mobilize the labor vote. It was in the mass production industries where the CIO was strongest, and where this vote was concentrated. Indicative of the distrust of the CIO in high places, Secretary of War Henry Stimson informed the national CIO office in 1941 that the War Department would use only "military labor battalions" to load and unload Army transports. The Army would have trouble enforcing Stimson's protocol on the West Coast because most of the outgoing cargo was military, and the ILWU controlled longshore hiring. [5]

The political framework within which labor-management relations were conducted was established during the defense buildup period when, under cover of "national defense", industrialists wanted to outlaw strikes and block further unionization. They counted upon congressional conservatives to help implement these objectives. For their part union leaders leaned toward accepting a "no strike" pledge providing measures were taken to protect the gains unions had recently achieved. Unions also wanted wage increases to compensate for the loss of purchasing power resulting from the rampant inflation of 1940 and early 1941. First FDR established a National Defense Advisory Committee (NDAC) in May 1940, chaired by William Knudsen of General Motors. FDR named CIO's Sidney Hillman as its labor division head. Then NDAC was replaced by the Office of Production Management in December 1940 with Hillman as co-director alongside Knudsen. This action, rather than defusing the CIO militants, led to the biggest strike wave since 1919. The strike at Allis-Chalmers required injection of the National Guard, while that at North American Aviation in Southern California resulted in the Army's intervention. [6]

The CIO leaders worried about repressive congressional legislation that might result from these strikes, which appeared out of control to congressional conservatives. Hillman suggested to FDR a tripartite mediation board for settling labor disputes. FDR, who was anxious to sustain defense production, created a National Defense Mediation Board March 1941 to implement a no-strike policy. After the German invasion of the USSR in June 1941 the CIO leadership declared it would no longer tolerate strikes. Prospective anti-labor legislation was stalled for the time being. Lichtenstein writes: "Deprived of the right to strike, and with many of the normal functions of the union leadership now assumed by government agencies, many unionists feared for the stability and integrity of their organizations." CIO leaders, in failing to gain recognition of the union shop as a pre-condition for employment, accepted instead a maintenance-of-membership formula by which an employee could withdraw from a union within fifteen days after a union agreement had been signed. Once the USSR became an ally even the union militants - more specifically the Communists and cohorts among them - declared to "win the war at any cost". Bureaucratization of the CIO moved a big step forward in the process. [7]

During the defense buildup period (September 1939-December 1941), but more emphatically during wartime, federal assistance was vital. Its help was essential for recruiting workers for the area's shipyards, foundries, fabricating plants, Boeing, business and governmental offices, and more. Women workers from the area and migrants primarily from within Washington and nearby states, proved indispensable to this effort. They proved fully capable at filling the traditional male jobs that had been vacated by White men who were drafted for military service. Employers were reluctant to employ women initially, and labor unions resisted admitting them to membership, and therefore, jobs. African Americans encountered even greater resistance. Women began entering the workforce in significant numbers by mid-1942; Blacks not until mid-1943. The region partook of the greatest inmigration in US history. Once here they had to be housed, provided with public transportation to their jobs, allocated their gas ration stamps for private transportation, provided with food ration books - all with federal assistance or under federal compulsion. Wages, rents, and prices became federally regulated, chiefly by the new Office of Price Administration. Complementing all these efforts and programs were volunteers recruited by the mayor's Civilian War Commission to conduct war bond and salvage drives, housing surveys, to supply and coordinate recreation activities for servicemen and women, to help operate nurseries and day care centers. Volunteers essentially filled the interstices not covered by more formal programs.

If all this manifested something new at the time the Japanese attacked Pearl Harbor on 7 December 1941, the fate of citizens of Japanese descent, Nisei, and their Issei parents was unprecedented. Issei and Nisei comprised the largest nonwhite population group in the city, approximately 7,000 people, slightly less than 2 percent of the population. They had been the largest nonwhite minority since the first decade of the century. A combination of wartime hysteria and a series of deceptions practiced by the leaders of the Army's Western Defense Command and War Department, the Japanese population was evacuated to concentration camps. By this federal collaboration - under the guise of "military necessity" - people of Japanese ancestry were deprived of their constitutional rights. Racism, pure and simple, underlay this entire process. Represented here was federal intervention in a wholly negative way, underwriting race as sufficient cause to exclude citizens (Nisei) and their resident alien parents of constitutional protections. The decision to evacuate the Nikkei (Issei and Nisei), along with the chronological local newspaper coverage, and responses of some Nikkei and proponents of evacuation are covered below.

Racism as traditionally enforced against African Americans continued during wartime, in Seattle as elsewhere. It was the Detroit race riot of 1943 that sparked the civic unity movement among major cities around the country, Seattle included. Their alleged object was to minimize interruption of war production, rather than resolving the "race problem". Most political, civic, and business leaders contended it was not a time for "social experimentation". Seattle's mayor William F. Devin, however, rather fully recognized the longterm volatility of the race issue. Devin established the Civic Unity Committee in February 1944. He appointed a committee composed of civic leaders who were comparably sensitive and committed to mitigating the growing tensions, not only in Black-White relations but also in dealing with the hostility being generated against the prospective return of the Japanese evacuees. The CUC played a critical role in paving the way for the peaceable return of the Japanese, and it proved much more activist in dealing with Black-White relations than has been accredited it.

Federal intervention of a more positive sort took place in the Columbia River Basin. By 1940 the electrical power generated at Grand Coulee and Bonneville dams provided the basis for linking other power lines in a regional power grid during the war, administered by the Bonneville Power Administration out of Portland. One outcome of this development was creation of the region's aluminum industry, which was vital to airplane production and metal fabricating plants. Another outcome was to supply power covertly to the Hanford project. The role of the BPA in relation to the state's public power movement, which was reaching maximum strength by 1940, is a different matter. How the BPA affected Seattle City Light's negotiations with Puget Sound Power and Light Company for its city plant, and negotiations between the Public Utility Districts and the same PSP&L and its private utility brethren, will be explored in some detail.

As noted above the most notorious violation of civil liberties during the war was directed at Japanese, citizen and resident alien alike. Despite passage of the Alien Registration Act ("Smith Act") in 1941, which ostensibly aimed to counter subversion, and passage of the War Labor Disputes Act ("Smith-Connally Anti-Strike Act") in 1943, civil liberties were comparatively unaffected during the war - certainly, when compared to their flagrant violation during World War I and its aftermath. Application of the Smith Act would assume critical importance after the war. The status of civil liberties was to abruptly change in 1946, when the growing tide of conservatism swept into Congress a Republican majority bent on dismantling New Deal programs. Washington state joined the conservative tide, similarly electing a majority of Republicans and conservative Democrats to the state legislature. For its support of New Deal programs the CIO became a primary target. President Roosevelt's reelection in 1944 was attributed to the role played by the CIO. The CIO here was less a specific target than it was in the upper midwest and northeast, although the ILWU and Harry Bridges and the International Woodworkers of America drew hostile fire. In Washington the state legislature launched an Un-American Activities Committee during the 1947 legislative session. The committee promptly prepared to investigate the left wing Washington Pension Union, the University of Washington, and the Seattle Repertory Playhouse. Concurrently the Cold War was taking shape. In the process, Popular Front liberals and anticommunist liberals, as well as Communists, were treated indistinguishably as subversives who ought to be banished from normal political and social discourse.

Transition to postwar was more deliberative than witnessed during the post-World War I period. Governmental agencies from federal to local levels began planning as early as mid-1944. Shipbuilding was expected to be sharply cutback, though not as abruptly and chaotically as after the first war. Boeing experienced cancellation of bomber contracts. An awakened citizenry mobilized to obstruct its worst effects, and the company gradually revived. The feminist potential, kindled for some women, went dormant after the war. Most women, who had been so vital to wartime production, returned to fill more traditional functions. Unexpected numbers of them, however, chose to remain in the workforce, even when it meant accepting something less than their work during the war. African Americans emerged as the largest nonwhite minority by war's end. Their leaders began pressuring liberal white sympathizers to join in efforts to integrate Blacks into the social fabric of the city and state.

In turning to the city's 1941 and 1942 elections Seattle's cultural and political insularity, its parochialism is pathetically demonstrated. A subtitle, "the trivialization of politics" seems fitting. Wartime was a transmutational experience.

## Trivialization of Politics:
## The 1941 City Election

When Seattle Mayor Arthur B. Langlie was elected governor in 1940 his departure to Olympia required a special election to fill his remaining eleven months in office. Fifteen candidates vied for the office in the February 1941 primaries. Most promised to continue the fine work of the past two years, although Langlie's promised reform of the police department had gone unfulfilled. He and two fellow city councilmen, who had won office as candidates of the conservative reformist New Order of Cincinnatus, previously had given up in frustration in 1935. The *P-I*'s city hall reporter, Carl Cooper, predicted the campaign would center upon police politics, since Police Chief William Sears's five year term was to expire in April. Cooper tabbed police court judge William F. Devin as heir to Langlie's support. Stressing the importance of solving the traffic problem, Devin led in the primaries, 7,000 votes ahead of County Auditor Earl Millikin, who warned: "selfish interests are seeking to gain control of city affairs".[8]

Millikin was a veteran Democratic party politician. Devin, on the other hand, was a relative political newcomer. Devin graduated from the UW law school in 1923, then joined Alfred Lundin's law firm (Lundin, a past Chamber of Commerce and Bar Association president), from which he was appointed police judge by Mayor Langlie. Millikin was well connected politically. He had direct lines to teachers, to labor unions, veterans groups, and sports followers. He had taught history and served as athletic director at Queen Anne High School in the 1920s, been a captain in the army reserve, was a past president of the Northwest Football League, and a founder of Local 200 of the American Federation of Teachers. Given this wide public exposure he was elected King County Auditor in 1934 and 1938, thereby potentially adding substantial numbers of county employees to his constituency. That he trailed Devin by 7,000 votes seems surprising, given their contrasting political experiences. Millikin was regarded as a competent elected official, to which the Municipal League's endorsement contributed more credibility. Even Langlie's political springboard, the New Order of Cincinnatus, threw its support to Millikin: "He is the one man in this campaign who has been endorsed by the Municipal League as well as labor. Not only is he a man of vision but also one of action." Stuart Whitehouse, the NOOC's chairman, noted that Devin's close association with the Chamber of Commerce's Industrial Council: [might] "prove embarassing...in our opinion". He pointed to the council's "attack on the picket lines in connection with the waterfront strike. Later...at the Fisher Flouring Mills."[9]

How to explain Millikin's miserable showing in the primaries? Howard MacGowan, a local New Dealer close to Congressman Warren Magnuson, offered "Maggie" the following credible analysis. "Millikin apparently had no campaign outlined for the finals. He did nothing for a week and few things became evident.

First a lot of Democrats were off Earl, especially the progressives. They were actually militant about it and some are right now in Devin's camp." His campaign made "no appeal to the progressives, and Earl didn't have much of a rep [sic] that way anyhow. He had never been much of a party man. In fact at the last convention he invited the entire progressive group to leave the party...[it] was no place for communists." Reference implied here, was to Hugh DeLacy, president of the left wing Washington Commonwealth Federation and former city councilman. In the campaign Dave Beck and the Teamsters provided the backbone of Millikin's support, and Devin made the most of it. Being Langlie's "heir" he also inherited Beck's enmity. But Beck was in a running battle with the leftist CIO unions for control of the regional labor movement, and he bitterly opposed the WCF. Clearly, Millikin's and Beck's political interests nicely coincided. What had been lacking in terms of Millikin's organization was compensated for by the entry of Beck and the Teamsters. [10]

While one cartoon pictured Devin as the "power trust's" (Puget Sound Power and Light) candidate, the campaigners focused on vice and the police. Devin linked Dave Beck and Joe Gottstein (owner of the Longacres racetrack) with Chief Sears as part of a vice ring. For this Devin earned fellow Republican and former congressman Ralph Horr's rebuke. Millikin picked up support from the Central Labor Council, which the Teamsters dominated. Devin won the endorsement of Leo Flynn, district organizer for the AFL (with whom Beck was in conflict), along with that of the plasterer's union. Millikin more than closed the gap, winning by more than 5,000 votes. According to MacGowan the odds figured by Green's tavern and cigar store (where bookie operations reputedly ran freely) favored Devin 10-7. When Millikin won MacGowan commented: "I think that both Earl and Torchy [Torrance] are going to do a lot of democratic cooperating from now on." The latter was closely associated with Emil Sick, owner of the Rainier Brewing Company, which the Teamsters protected. The Teamsters protected other "Western" beer companies from competition by refusing to transport "Eastern" beer. However, given the mere eleven months before the March 1942 election, it was apparent that this campaign was but a preliminary to that race. [11]

Who should Mayor Millikin nominate for police chief but Sears! Dave Beck cheered the nomination, pointing to "Sears' handling of the [police] in the unsuccessful plans of the Communists to picket the Boeing plants...His performance at Boeing's means more to...Seattle than any other thing he has handled in his entire administration..." Pointing to the absence of strikes recently, Beck continued: "I would say that right now capital and labor as they exist in Seattle could be a model for the entire United States." To his disappointment the City Council rejected the Sears nomination by a 5 to 4 vote. Quickly Millikin offered up former chief W.B. Kirtley. Then began a comedy that could have inspired Gilbert and Sullivan. Down with the flu, Millikin fled to Big Four Inn, in the Monte Cristo mountain area, to recover. With four council members opposed to Kirtley the absence of three would leave the council without a quorum, since one would have to serve as acting mayor and be without a vote. The council-four surprised the mayor by showing up at Big Four. Discussions with the mayor proved fruitless. When they all returned to the city or its environs each remained in hiding. Millikin indicated his availability should entrapment of some sort lead to a momentary quorum. After elapse of more than a week the mayor finally withdrew his Kirtley nomination, and offered up the name of police captain Herbert D. Kimsey, who won the council's unanimous approval.[12]

During this hiatus rumors floated in July that Seattle would be closed to soldiers unless the city brought vice under control. Acting mayor David Levine attempted a start while the above farce played out. King County sheriff William Severyns (a former Seattle chief in the 1920s, who had then been linked to police protection of vice and illegal liquor operations) threatened to clean up the city should Kimsey fail. Millikin met with the sheriff, promising cooperation of the Seattle police department, and assuring full cooperation to Fort Lewis's Colonel Robert Glass, and the command at Fort Lawton. To the murder of three persons at a speakeasy on 3 August Kimsey pleaded he had no money to hire undercover agents. The *Times*'s headline of 2 September, questioned the progress to date: "SPEAKS', GAMBLING FLOURISH AGAIN". The article indicated that although the newspaper's reporter could find the operations Chief Kimsey confessed "My men can't find them". Somewhat contrarily, he admitted they were operating, but: "If the city wants them shut up too, I'll do it". One week later neon lights advertising the speakesies were turned off. To this Kimsey denied any police department knowledge.[13]

All this play at governing ended abruptly on that fateful 7 December 1941, with the surprise attack on Pearl Harbor. The city's leaders then took their responsibilities more seriously. Whether wisely or compassionately in their actions is to be judged from the special chapter on the evacuation and internment of the Japanese. Be it noted here that Millikin was distrustful of the Issei and Nisei from the first. He warned them to be on good behavior. Later, he boasted of being the only public official to come out "flat-footedly" for evacuation of both categories of Japanese when the Tolan Committee held its hearings 28 February to 2 March 1942. Devin's attitude was not expressed, perhaps because his office was too far removed from making decisions on the issue. If, as alleged, Devin took his cues from Langlie, it should be noted that Governor Langlie hedged behind his constituents at the Tolan Committee's hearings, apparently unwilling to take responsibility for his personal opinions.[14]

## Trivialization, Part II: The 1942 Election

The *P-I*'s Ed Fussell wrote to Congressman Magnuson 18 February 1942, predicting victory in the primaries for Millikin and Devin, indicating: "Church and PTA people are blasting Millikin for all they are worth...Unions are lining up for him. The *Star* under new management has indicated no favoritism....Most everyone wants to get into an argument about what we should do with the resident Japs." *15*

In its "Forum for Candidates" the *P-I* published brief statements (250 words was the limit) of the two mayoral race finalists. Devin: "Labor, all of labor, should be given a fair break - not just one small group"; the police department must be fully reorganized; vice and gambling must be fought, "not merely because the army demands it." Millikin complained that Devin assigned civilian defense third place in importance, "with a Japanese submarine shelling the Coast off Santa Barbara...While enemy planes roar over Los Angeles...[and] the Second Interceptor Command here twice put Seattle on alert within a few days?" Millikin continued with a personal attack on Devin, without once mentioning what he would do if re-elected. *16*

"Beck Denies Labor Tries to Run Seattle" ran the P-I's front page column head on 4 March. Beck asserted: "We do not want to spend the next two years defending ourselves in bitter industrial warfare inspired by a prejudiced judge." To this Devin accused Beck and cohort Frank Brewster of "exercising control over the city and hope to stay in the saddle." In this portrayal of "labor" in the city's politics the reader should be aware that Beck had been at war with James Taylor, president of the State Federation of Labor and had withdrawn the Teamsters from the federation at this time. Beck clearly aspired to be the single voice of labor: "For more than a year before the war started the Teamsters Union adopted a rigid policy of no strikes, regardlesss of provocation, in any industry...affecting national defense." Devin alleged that Beck and *Washington Teamster* editor Lester Hunt had raced back to Seattle when Millikin's "backing had shrunk". Devin extended his critique by linking Beck with police corruption: for having cajoled Millikin to nominate Sears, who also "drew a salary from the race tracks" and alleging that Bobby Morris was appointed County Auditor (replacing Millikin) because "he was acceptable to the race tracks". *17*

In the closing days of the campaign Millikin raised the "fifth column" rumor before a Ballard audience, accusing Devin of ignoring the alleged threat: "Devin isn't afraid of the Japs; he's not too deeply worried". And when two Japanese were arrested during the first blackout they were released, and "No bench warrant was issued [by police judge Devin] for their arrest". Millikin cited other acts of Devin's leniency respecting Japanese during the period. At a forum in Meves Cafeteria on the 7th Millikin refused to shake hands with Devin, to which the *P-I* devoted a two-column headline on its front page. When the Municipal League adversely criticized the mayor Millikin labeled it a "nefarious" organization, accusing its president William Shannon (a consulting engineer for Puget Sound Power and Light and currently district manager of the priorities division of the War Production Board) of violating the Hatch Act. [18]

The election results showed how far Millikin had fallen out of favor in just a few months time. He lost by over 20,000 votes to Devin (63,892 to 43,541). It seems certain that Millikin's linkage with reputed "labor boss" Beck, his perceived tolerance of vice and gambling operations, the farce over the police chief appointment, and finally his pronounced racism with respect to the Japanese alienated substantial numbers of his former supporters. (Seattle's Church Council had been actively protecting the Japanese.) In the council race David Levine, Mike Mitchell, and Frank Laube were re-elected to three year terms. Publisher Frank McCaffrey defeated councilman Paul Revelle, who had "staunchly" defended Millikin, for a two year term. Hugh DeLacy finished in fourth place, more than 14,000 votes behind Laube. Not surprisingly DeLacy had been successfully Red-baited. DeLacy would rebound in the 1944 congressional race despite a comparable barrage at that time, when the US was allied with the USSR. [19]

Historian of the WCF, Albert Acena observed, "The Seattle electorate was monumentally indifferent" to the 1942 city election. While the primaries attracted about 30 percent of the registered voters, the final election managed to bring out another 20 percent. Acena attributed this to the proposed pay raises for police and firemen, plus the special school levy. He attributed Devin's huge 20,000 majority to a surge from property owners and the "business-connected" community. To this should be added the influence of the Church Council. [20]

One week before the 1942 city election the House Select Committee Investigating National Defense Migration, chaired by California's John Tolan, had conducted its Seattle hearings (28 February-2 March). The Tolan Committee met to to decide the fate of the American Japanese population, and its conduct directly affected the city election. From Pearl Harbor Day forward Millikin had repeatedly warned the local Japanese population to properly behave or pay the consequences (his behavior is covered in the following chapter on the evacuation). In the context of demoralizing newspaper headlines on the Pacific war, and proliferating front page reports of "roundups" and allegations of "fifth column" activities Millikin had accused judge Devin of being too tolerant of the Japanese, of ignoring the threat they posed for just remaining here in our midst. After the Tolan Committee hearings he boasted to one of his constituents that he was the only one who came out "flat-footedly" at the hearings urging their evacuation. Expecting to capitalize on the fears being generated by the press he had not only baited Devin unsuccessfully, but his tactic probably backfired, considering the basis of Devin's support among the church going public and the dread that many voters shared of the Teamsters union and the gambling and vice operations.

We can now turn to a detailed coverage of the Japanese evacuation as it transpired in Seattle and its environs.

# Evacuation and Internment of Japanese Americans: "The Domination of Politics Over Law"

### Introduction

Despite the growing tensions between Japan and the United States, no one could have been more shocked by the Japanese attack on Pearl Harbor than the Seattle Japanese population, resident aliens (Issei) and citizens (Nisei) alike. For at least fifty years these immigrants and their offspring had been assimilating American culture while confronting innumerable roadblocks along the way, obstacles rooted in race prejudice. Chinese immigrants were the first Asians to suffer discrimination ranging from random murders, mob violence, employment discrimination, anti-Chinese laws, and ultimately to Chinese exclusion legislation in 1882. Following mob violence against them in Tacoma and near Issaquah in fall 1885, Seattle's Chinese met the same fate, in February 1886. Driven from those communities, the Chinese were slow to return. Once the Chinese were made unwelcome and confined to Chinatown ghettoes as they dribbled back, Japanese were recruited by the Great Northern Railway for work extending its rail lines. The Japanese also provided cheap labor for lumber mills. Not content with just hiring out their labor, some among these new immigrants bought marginal farm land bypassed by the majority population. These lands and their produce provided supplementary, not competitive products. Some invested in city property - hotels, cafes and restaurants, small shops catering to Asian tastes primarily, but serving also blue collar clientele inhabiting the economically marginal districts where the Japanese were concentrated - Nihonmachi or Japantown. This district in Seattle extended from the Pioneer Square area uphill on Yesler Way to about 14th Avenue, merging south into Chinatown, but concentrated between 12th and 5th avenues. Today's Nippon Kan Theater near 7th and Yesler Way marks the approximate center of the district. Indicative of the characteristic small capital investment represented by their enterprises is a business survey conducted in 1935 by the Japanese Chamber of Commerce: the most important were hotels (183), groceries (148), dye works (94), Public Market stands (64), produce houses (57), gardeners (42), restaurants (36), barber shops (36), laundries (31), peddlers of fruit and vegetables (24).

Extended patriarchal families, often living in conjunction with their small shop, cafe or restaurant, or hotel were fairly normal. The Issei parents, being unschooled in English, necessitated that Japanese be the family's common language. To quote Bill Hosokawa, Issei also "controlled the purse strings". Children mainly began their education at Bailey-Gatzert elementary school on 12th Avenue two blocks south of Jackson Street. From there: on to Broadway High where about 400 youngsters were enrolled in 1940; or to Garfield High with only a slightly smaller number, or Franklin High where a significant yet smaller number matriculated. (One of the leaders in the Japanese community, James Y. Sakamoto, graduated from Franklin in 1920. He figures prominently in this narrative.) As students the Nisei were exceptional, aiming for the honor rolls and usually getting there: in 1937 three were class valedictorians, two salutatorians. It was at the three high schools where the Nisei often proved to be excellent athletes as well as fine students. It was also at the high schools where Nisei finally began to mesh with the majority community. The Nisei students encountered a largely positive experience all around, although there was little interracial mixing after school hours as students returned to their respective neighborhood enclaves, many Nisei youngsters to the Japanese Language School. Those who continued their education (about 400 were registered at the UW in 1940) usually discovered no advantage in the job market upon graduation. Practically no Caucasian employer would hire Japanese. Nisei with teaching certificates were denied appropriate employment in the Seattle public schools. Those who earned professional degrees in law or pharmacy or medicine could strike out on their own, but they practiced largely within the Asian community. An engineering education led in frustration to employment not in the US, but in Japan. Trade unions of the American Federation of Labor denied admission to nonwhites, thereby closing off most employment where the employer in those crafts was unionized. Under these conditions - reinforced by restrictive covenants barring house sales and renting to nonwhites in most neighborhoods - the Japanese inescapably became a tight knit community.

Few Japanese businessmen were admitted to the Seattle Chamber of Commerce, so they formed their own chamber. Given the large number of hotels a Japanese Hotel Owners Association was established to deal with their common problems. Nisei established their Japanese American Citizens League to inculcate perceived standards of Americanism for their generation; the JACL would take over leadership during the ensuing crisis. Churches flourished: Christianized Japanese congregations existed for Baptists, Methodists, Congregationalists, and Episcopalians, traceable to missionary work in Japan. Understandably, though, the largest

# ARROWS OF FIRES POINT TO SEATTLE

By Associated Press.

WASHINGTON, Wednesday, Dec. 10.—The War Department announced today that military and naval installations on Luzon, principal island of the Philippines, had been subjected to intermittent Japanese air attacks throughout the day, with particularly heavy attacks on the naval base at Cavite.

In its second communique of the war, the department said that initial Japanese attacks against the west coast of Luzon, north of San Fernando, were repulsed, with apparent heavy enemy losses, but the Japanese effected landings along the northern coast of the island.

The Japanese attacks, the department said, were in considerable strength and supported by heavy naval forces.

The department said no action has been reported in the Hawaiian Islands since the initial attack occurred December 7.

A search for fifth columnists on the west coast of Continental United States is being made, the department said, since Washington State Police last night found and extinguished near Port Angeles, Wash., a series of fires in the form of arrows pointed toward Seattle.

Steps to augment the defenses of both the east and west coasts began Sunday night, the communique said, when the department placed in effect plans which have materially strengthened the forces already stationed along the coasts.

(See Page 9, for communiques.)

---

The Navy public-relations office in Seattle said this afternoon it had heard "rumors" earlier today that fiery arrows pointing to Seattle had been seen on highways north of Seattle, but had not heard reports of arrows of flame near Port checked on rumors that a Japanese warship had been seen in the Strait of Juan de Fuca, but found that the ship was Canadian, the public relations office said.

Officers pointed out, however, that arrows outlined by flame "have been used in this war by fifth-columnist Japanese

*"Arrows of Fire", 10 December 1941, Seattle Times. On the strength of reports that such fire signals had been used by fifth-columnists in the Philippines to direct attacks there, the Seattle Naval public relations office checked out reports of "arrows on fire" near Port Angeles that pointed toward Seattle. The flames were the result of slash burning discovered by State Patrol officers.*

church was Buddhist; its largely Issei congregation had funded the construction of a new temple, completed in 1941. The Japanese Association of North America served largely as an immigrant aid society, linking those in need of help with the local consulate office and community agencies. Three vernacular newspapers kept them informed of events in the homeland. Of these Sakamoto's weekly *Japanese American Courier* was entirely in English while the *North American Times* and the *Great Northern Daily* included English sections and were practically the only domestic journalistic source for the Issei. Nisei, for the most part were inept in the Japanese language - despite schooling at the Japanese language school which most reportedly attended under parental duress - and read the local dailies as well as the *Courier* (circulation of about 10,000). [1]

## Pearl Harbor Day

On Pearl Harbor Day many Issei were quickly rounded up by the FBI and Immigration and Naturalization Service (INS) authorities, and abruptly transferred to the Immigration station where they remained for a short time then were moved to Fort Missoula, Montana, still under INS control. Under what authority had this roundup occurred? Since 1935 the Office of Naval Intelligence had been compiling a list of people in the Japanese community who might be suspected of spying for Japan or possibly be engaged in some subversive activity should any trouble with Japan break out. Included in this listing - the "ABC List" - were those conducting an import-export business with Japan, those working for the Japanese consulate, Japanese language teachers, Nisei children who were sent to Japan for their education - Kibei. By 9 December 116 of Seattle's Issei had been taken into INS custody - those deemed by presidential proclamation to be "dangerous to the public peace or safety of the United States". By mid-February 2,200 West Coast Japanese had been detained this way.

One prominent Issei transferred to Seattle's INS station was Iwao Matsushita, who with his wife of seven months, Hanaye, had arrived at Smith Cove, along with 233 other Japanese subjects mid-1919. Like so many other Japanese immigrants they planned to stay in the US long enough to save sufficient money to start them off to a more fruitful life upon return to the homeland, perhaps in five years. Though barred from obtaining citizenship many remained permanently. Having learned enough English to qualify for teaching English in Japan's high schools Matsushita hoped to enter the University of Washington soon. Meanwhile he took a job as a cook; then he and Hanaye managed a hotel in Chinatown before he finally caught on - because of his college education - with Mitsui and Company, a Tokyo-based trading company. There he remained in well paying positions, moving steadily upward until retiring in 1940. Always the teacher, he had served on the side as principal of the Japanese Language School. Assistant professor Eldon Griffin had wanted to introduce a Japanese language course at the UW. Griffin's friendship with Matsushita led to the latter's appointment, teaching a demonstration course without compensation in the extension division's evening classes in 1928. Unfortunantly this trial course did not lead to the hoped-for permanent position, so he stayed with Mitsui. Idled upon retiring from Mitsui, and restless, he took a job at the Japanese Chamber of Commerce compiling trade statistics. It was his misfortune that all of these professional/white collar employments qualified Matsushita for immediate transfer to INS custody. On the ABC list were names of about 2,000 Japanese aliens compiled by the FBI, Office of Naval Intelligence, and the INS. Matsushita had been anonymously reported to the FBI to be an "agent of a foreign principal". A knock on the Matsushita's front door sounded the evening of 7 December; he was hustled off to the immigration station. None who were rounded up knew what to expect; nor did their friends and families. While they waited only once-a-week family visits were allowed; conversations had to be in English; outgoing letters had to be in English, and were subject to INS censorship. He remained there eighteen days before being shipped off to Fort Missoula. Hanaye, in frail health, stayed in Seattle until she was evacuated to Minidoka, separated from Iwao for two years and thirty days, when at last INS authorities released him to join her at Minidoka. [2]

In the context of the surprise attack on Pearl Harbor, followed by Japanese advances toward the Philippines and in southeast Asia, special saliency was given rumors of spy activity, alleged signalling onshore to Japanese submarines off the coast; thirty enemy aircraft spotted over the Bay area. All such reports proved to be rumors, but they fed anxieties nonetheless. Samples locally: on 9 December the *P-I*'s front page blared: "COAST BLACKED OUT"...Mystery Planes Routed at S.F.". Next day the *Times*'s front page carried a two-column headline: "Arrows of Fire Pointed to Seattle". "Washington State Police last night found and extinguished near Port Angeles...a series of fires in the form of an arrow pointed toward Seattle." The Navy public relations office in Seattle lent credibility to this report by reporting "arrows outlined by flames have been used in this war by fifth-columnists...in the Philippines a few days ago". The *P-I* corrected the "arrows" report on the 11th, alleging, "The original disclosure came in a war department commumique issued in Washington, D.C. and it was confirmed by the Second Interceptor Command in Seattle." In fact assistant to the governor, Ross Cunningham (on loan from the *Times*) had earlier received information from the State patrolmen that two white men had set the fires while clearing some land and noticed their arrow shape. The *Times* offered no correction of its story. A steady stream of such rumors and stories were picked up by the Seattle dailies from notoriously biased/racist California newspapers and the Fourth Army's Western Defense Command headquarters at the Presidio in San Francisco. No attempt at verification seems to have been done by the local press before printing. The overall effect was to convey an impression the enemy was closing in and subversives everywhere were lending a helping hand. [3]

Removal of most of the influential Issei between 7 December and the 10th left a leadership void. There being no community organization prepared for such a role except the Japanese American Citizens League (JACL) its leadership stepped forward, arrogating to itself substantially all authority and leadership responsibilty. Most prominent was James Y. Sakamoto, a founder of the JACL, its national president 1936-1938. Upon his graduation in 1920 from Franklin High he formed the Seattle Progressive Citizens League to oppose enactment of the state's Anti-Alien Land Law. Feeling the need for an all-Engish newspaper for the local Japanese Sakamoto started *The Japanese American Courier* in 1928. First off he advocated reorganization of the league by some Nisei and sent lawyer/colleague Clarence Arai to Portland to form a chapter there. Inculcation of American values was the purpose, so that those of Japanese descent could contribute positively to American life. Along the West Coast other Nisei were thinking along the same lines. An inspirational meeting in April 1929 led to the JACL's founding in 1930. Though still a small organization at the time of Pearl Harbor no other organization existed to take responsibility. Writing for the 11 December *P-I* Sakamoto set the stage: "A word to the Nisei...[W]e will stand firm in our resolution that even if America 'disowns us' we will never disown America."

The following day the JACL formed an Emergency Defense Council to cooperate with federal and local defense agencies. Sakamoto was named its chairman. Committees were established for Red Cross drives; to round up volunteers for civil defense work; to handle hardship cases relating to loss of business financing, unemployment, food shortages, destitution, and demoralization; to promote sales of defense bonds and stamps; to work with the FBI in identifying potentially disloyal persons. Local JACL president Clarence Arai was also a reserve officer and became the self-appointed liaison with the FBI, a function that led some to suspect him of being responsible for some who were caught in the FBI's dragnet and for the early transfer of some dissidents from Camp Harmony, the Puyallup assembly center. Represented by this sequence of events was a generational shift in community leadership from the Issei to the Nisei. [4]

Relatively few Nisei were old enough to have assumed leadership roles. Some Nisei either helped found the Japanese-American Citizens League or joined soon after obtaining high school or college degrees. Their advantage over the Issei was their command of the English language and familiarity with American traditions and institutions, which they assimilated in their respective high schools and beyond.

While this transfer of leadership was developing within the Japanese community during the first two weeks after Pearl Harbor Day lives of individual families were being torn apart. Some simply cowered in their homes and in their often adjoining small shops, so uncertain were they about hostile reception awaiting them outside.

The Sugimoto family had a small grocery store next to the Tai Tung restaurant at 6th Avenue and King Street; they lived on the mezzanine level. Having the economic and social disadvantage for being a second son, Mr. Sugimoto migrated from Japan in 1905, and took jobs in Montana, Idaho, and Utah, in the course of which he picked up some command of English. Sugimoto used his command of English to help his fellow Issei in Seattle, to where he migrated about 1900. An Issei express company was adjacent to the store; Sugimoto used the company's equipment for buying his produce from Western Avenue merchants and that for three other grocers. Daughter Sharon [Aburano] helped out in the store. When Pearl Harbor Day abruptly intruded into their lives Sharon had been at a theater with friends outside Japantown when on the screen was suddenly flashed: "We are at war. Japan attacked Pearl Harbor". Immediately lights brightened. Sensing all eyes upon them "we all split for home". At home she found her parents looking very pale, depressed, fearful for knowing some of their Issei friends already had been rounded up by FBI agents. With reason. A sobbing Mrs. Sugimoto trundled downstairs to their tiny grocery store next morning telling her daughters father had been taken away earlier by FBI agents.

Kenji Okuda's father was among the earliest Japanese to migrate to the US, perhaps in the early 1890s, arriving in San Francisco, working in the grape fields and other farm work. He also acquired some command of English. Seeking more favorable opportunities he migrated to Seattle about 1900, becoming a labor contractor for the Great Northern Railway and running a cartage/transfer business on the side. He married a teacher of English for Japanese immigrants; she soon died and he remarried, then moved to near 9th Avenue and Pike Street. Kenji was born there in 1922; the family next moved to Beacon Hill where they remained until the evacuation. When Kenji heard the alarming news of the Pearl Harbor attack he took the streetcar directly to the UW, where he was an undergraduate and active in the YMCA. Talking first with his graduate student cousin he then walked to the YMCA where lively discussions were underway. Wanting the counsel of American Friends Service Committee director, Floyd Schmoe, Kenji travelled next to its office, just off campus. Schmoe was not there. Returning home for dinner there soon came a knock on the door where ominously stood an FBI agent, a sheriff deputy at his elbow. Asking to speak with Mr. Okuda they were invited in. A few minutes later two more agents came to the back door asking to look for documents. Granted permission - what else to do? - and finding the documents mostly in Japanese they asked to take them to the Immigration station for translation. There they took them and Mr. Okuda, who would soon find himself shipped off to Fort Missoula, along with many other Issei.

Unlike most immigrants, when Jim Akutsu's father had migrated to Seattle about 1905 he came with enough money to tide him over. Failing admission to the UW he took a janitorial job at Frederick and Nelsons, caught the eye of management, which encouraged him to start a shoe store in Chinatown. He did, the Golden Shoe Store on the corner of Jackson and Maynard streets. He soon established a successful shoe manufacturing business, shoe repair shop and retail outlets in other parts of town, which brought more amicable relationships with Caucasians for the family. Young Jim was even introduced to the famous Presbyterian leader Rev. Mark Matthews and public officials who might drop in. Father parlayed savings into real estate. Jim had graduated from Central school outside Japantown, a school with a broad ethnic composition drawn from children of first generation immigrants, except for race, no different from his own heritage. As an athlete at Broadway High he developed closest social ties with Caucasians. Upon graduating from Broadway in 1939 Jim entered the UW's civil engineering program under the friendly guidance of Professor Hiram Chittenden, Jr., whom he had met on one of his mountain hiking trips. He was determined on an engineering career in the US, not one in Japan as Nisei engineering graduates were advised to do. On Pearl Harbor Day soon after returning home from the university FBI agents asked for permission to enter, then directed "two or three" men who appeared from their dress to have been recruited from Skid Road, to search the house; the family was ordered to sit against a wall. Mr. Akutsu was hustled off to the Immigration station once the house was turned upside down in search of contraband. They kept him there for several weeks before shipping him off to Fort Missoula. Jim had noticed Clarence Arai's name on a document held by one of the agents, leading him to believe Arai had fingered his father. Apparently no effort was exerted by his influential Caucasian associates on behalf of his well connected father. The shoe plant, repair shop and store were all closed. Jim withdrew from the UW to deal with their real estate holdings. Later, when Jim was at Minidoka, an old hunched over man asked where the Akutsus lived; Jim failed to recognize his father, nor did father recognize him. So much disorientation had the evacuation upheaval wrought.

Shigeko Uno's brother had scheduled a dinner at a Japanese operated Chinese restaurant to celebrate his engagement. By dinner time guests assembled deep in gloom, ate and started downstairs for the exit, there, startled to meet FBI agents who were looking for Ed Ozawa, a worker employed by C.T. Takahashi, an exporter of scrap metal to Japan, who had been picked up that morning. Shortly FBI agents seized their dairy business books, ostensibly because Shigeko's sister was an Issei; but to carry on the business she had to have daily access to these business records. To do this she was required to get authorization from her attorney, Thomas Masuda, who had been jailed along with three others, initially charged with trading with the enemy. That assets of Issei operated businesses had been frozen added to their difficulties, forcing closure of their White River Dairy. [5]

In her autobiography, *Nisei Daughter*, Monica [Kazuko Itoi] Sone tells of her Pearl Harbor Day. She, her brother Henry and her little sister Sumiko were at choir practice preparing for a Christmas performance of Handel's *Messiah* when a tardy Chuck Mizumo burst into the chapel shouting, "Japan just bombed Pearl Harbor...in Hawaii! It's war!" As a known prankster Chuck's outburst was met with doubt from the choir director who urged him to take his choir place. Unmoved, he insisted they follow him downstairs to hear the news on the radio; most of the boys ran after Chuck, while the others stood catatonic not knowing what to make of it. When one of the girls broke the silence: "Do you think we'll be considered Japanese or American?" a boy resignedly answered, "We'll be Japs, same as always". Practice abruptly finished, Henry drove his sisters home in unaccustomed haste, arriving to find mother sunk, dazed, in her armchair. Henry tried comforting her, but she protested "it was bound to happen" the way events were unfolding. When Mr. Itoi arrived from their hotel he seemed skeptical, believing it just more propaganda. Not until evening, when he turned on his short wave radio to catch news from Japan, did he become convinced it was all true. The telephone kept wringing all this time. One caller, Taeko Tanabe, asked uncertainly if her mother was there. Three more times she phoned frantic to tell her mother that FBI agents had picked up their father. The house was searched, the agents anticipating a hoard of contraband and subversive material, given Mr. Tanabe's position as a newspaper editor. Mrs. Tanabe, herself, finally phoned reporting not only was Mr. Tanabe taken into custody, but "Messrs. Okayama, Higuchi, Sughira, Mori, Okada - we knew them all." [6]

Bill Hosokawa experienced Pearl Harbor Day and its immediate aftermath yet differently. He had graduated from Garfield High where he was on the editorial staff of the school's newspaper and played center on the football team. Over the advice of the UW's journalism dean that racial prejudice would probably bar him from a newspaper career Hosokawa stubbornly enrolled, became an editor on the school's *Daily*, did volunteer work on Sakamoto's *Courier* on the side, graduated, only to be thwarted in search for a job. He did find one finally at the Japanese Consulate, however, "[turning] their English into English". This proved a springboard to his first paying newspaper job: an English language edition of a Singapore newspaper. From there to working on the *Far Eastern Review* and the Shanghai *Times* he spent time at brief intervals in Japan witnessing war clouds abuilding. Taking advice from the US Consulate in Shanghai he returned to the US October 1941. On Pearl Harbor Day he found JACL president Clarence Arai "paralyzed" by the news, but Sakamoto anxious to set up a commitee to deal with the crisis and its affect on the Japanese community. As one to whom those in the community habitually turned for help when needed it just seemed natural that he would do so, and do it through JACL: the Emergency Defense Committee was born. Sakamoto appointed Hosokawa executive secretary, becoming "Jimmie's" "eyes" (Sakamoto was blind) and "ears", a vital link with those seeking help. First off they set up a register of names and addresses so that whereabouts of people and their status would be supplied to the fretful and dependent among them. Because Sakamoto had been popular among the city's journalists Hosokawa would prod them to do stories on happenings within the Japanese community. That sympathetic articles were frequently written, even after issuance of Executive Order 9066 (February 19, 1942) should probably be attributed to this store of goodwill Sakamoto had built up over the years. It was Hosokawa who prepared the pamphlet detailing Japanese contributions to the nation, which was submitted by Sakamoto to the hearings of the Tolan Committee subsequent to EO 9066. [7]

To see how the broader community was responding to the events of Pearl Harbor Day and the few days beyond an examination of the local newspaper coverage is perhaps the best available source.

On 8 December a blackout was ordered extending from the Canadian border to Roseberg, Oregon. Mayor Earl Millikin warned citizens to "remain calm" as he ordered police chief Herbert Kimsey to hire fifty more policemen. Six thousand air wardens went on active duty from Canada to California. Sakamoto was quoted that 8,000 "American-born Japanese will be 'first to uncover any saboteurs among the pro-Japanese elements'", thereby exposing the Issei to suspicion from the start. That day bank accounts of Japanese nationals were frozen, consequently confining most Nikkei businesses to operating with only the funds on hand and to whatever funds Nisei might have access to. FBI roundups were reported, the *P-I* tallying "upwards of fifty" in the Puget Sound area.

The chauvinistic American *Star* never uttered a word of sympathy for the Nikkei (all domestic Japanese) during the evacuation period. A Scripps owned newspaper, it had from its origins at the turn of the century considered itself to be the pro-labor voice and played the super-patriot during World War I. It quoted Millikin: "the Japanese must not congregate or make any utterance that could be used as grounds for reprisals". The *P-I* editorial of the 11th observed "Our Japanese"..."The saddest figures in Seattle today are the Nisei". Viewing the patriotic work of the EDC it alleged the "overwhelming majority" are loyal, continuing: "It is regrettable that a few instances of racial hostility are being reported." The *Star* of the 17th conjectured that a "camera fiend" seen taking pictures "far and wide" might be subversive because his last name was "Nomura", the very name of the Japanese ambassador, Admiral Nomura. "Rumor makes this kin...an important espionage figure."

On the 21st was reported the jailing of Thomas Masuda, Kenji Ito, Yoshima Osawa, and Charles "Ted" Takahashi on suspicion of trading with the enemy. A mass meeting was called on the 22nd of about 1,500 at the new Buddhist temple. Its purpose was to proclaim their Americanism. At the meeting Mayor Millikin alleged, "tolerance of the American people will be taxed to the limit...[Therefore] the good relations between us depend not only on your loyalty, but on your discretion as well". Singing of "God Bless America" closed the meeting. On the 28th Assistant US Attorney Gerald Shucklin was reported still preparing formal charges against the four men listed above. A *Times* editorial of 8 January cautioned readers: "There must be no incitement of groundless suspicion; no interuption of friendliness for any cause short of positive proof [of their guilt]."

Throughout December and January the three vernacular newspapers kept their readers in the Nikkei community uptodate on the volunteer work of the EDC. Convinced of the EDC's sincerity, Arthur Guild, director of the Municipal Defense Commission, invited the group to a meeting. He ambiguously acknowledged: "Most of the difficulties [being experienced by the Japanese community] seems to be economic with unemployment and failing business...The whole Japanese community will be judged by its worst members...[therefore, it should take responsibility] to see that each of its members is abiding by all the rules."

## Movement Toward Evacuation

While these shockwaves were reverberating through the Japanese communities here and elsewhere along the West Coast intense debate was occurring at the federal level that would decide the fate of all Nikkei. Two major issues had to be decided. One: which department should assume authority, Justice or the War

Department? Two: should the Nisei, as citizens, be differentiated from Issei, who were resident aliens?

Step-by-step authority would pass from Justice to the War Department. Not until the crisis required action under duress of "military necessity" would exclusive jurisdiction pass to the War Department. The key role was played by Lieutenant General John L. DeWitt who had been placed in charge of the Fourth Army at the Presidio in San Francisco in December 1939. His immediate staff strategist was Major (later "Colonel") Karl R. Bendetsen, a former counsel to the Washington Taxpayers Association. They worked closely with the Provost General Allen Gullion in Washington, D.C. in coordinating the War Department's strategy aimed at getting mass evacuation and internment under their control. How this evolved before "military necessity" was finally established in late February is beyond the scope of this book; however it is thoroughly covered in the following: Roger Daniels; *The Decision to Relocate the Japanese Americans*, Peter Irons, *Justice at War*, based on documentation obtained under the Freedom of Information Act which was not available to the US Supreme Court when it decided the internment cases; and the report by the Commission on Wartime Relocation and Internment of Civilians, *Personal Justice Denied*, which paved the way for redress and reparations in the late 1980s. [8]

Showing his hand early, DeWitt had sought "combat zone" status for a one hundred-mile strip along the coast and moving out "undesirables". FBI director J. Edgar Hoover advised this was impossible at this time, adding: "the army is getting a bit hysterical."

Not until after publication of Executive Order 9066 on 19 February 1942 did it become clear that Nisei would be evacuated along with those Issei not already transferred to Fort Missoula. Although intimations had been sensed that Nisei were to be included, only at the Tolan Committee hearings in Seattle from 28 February to 2 March did their fate become unmistakeable. Rumor mongering in the newspapers thenceforth gave way in emphasis to reporting on the ultimate mass evacuation. Their predominant tenor, while expressing some compassion, did so in the context of portraying the evacuees as good sports, spunkily putting up with all the harassment and dislocations the authorities could dish out.

Anxieties were running high, when an emergency meeting was called by the EDC for 16 January at the Buddhist temple, at which "do's and dont's of conduct under wartime restrictions" were to be explained by attorney William Mimbu. More than 500 people attended. Alarmed at the 21 January pronoucement of California Congressman Leland Ford urging placement of all Japanese in "concentration camps" Sakamoto protested this "would destroy all that we have built for more than one-half century." In promoting a broader acceptance of the idea of evacuation the *Star* on 28 January quoted the prediction of state American Legion commander Fred Fuecker that the state's legion would probably follow California's lead: Issei to be sent to "concentration camps". The *Times*, chimed in on the 29th by running an opinion column: "Kick Out Japs or Keep 'em Working? Seattleites

Argue". Next day the *Times* featured an article depicting local Japanese opposition to Ford's pronouncement, accompanied with photographs of volunteers working at JACL headquarters.

Playing on the fear of subversion the *Star* reported the jailing of Bainbridge Island Japanese and seizure of guns, cameras, maps, guns, and explosives all of which Assistant US Attorney Gerald Shucklin declared "illegal". News of "fifth column" raids in California flooded the dailies in early February, feeding a general uneasiness bordering for some on hysteria. On the 13th the *Star* announced the signing of the prestigious Walter Lippman to an opinion column leading off with: "Walter Lippman Answers What To Do With Japs On Coast" in which he emphasized the fifth column danger posed by their continued presence. On the 19th the state American Legion now advocated removal of all Japanese.

> On that fateful day President Roosevelt issued Executive Order 9066 authorizing the Secretary of War and Military Commanders "to prescribe military areas in such places and of such extent as he or the appropriate Military Commander may determine, from which any or all persons may be excluded..." Provost Marshall General Allen Gullion proceeded on the 20th to declare both Issei and Nisei were subject to exclusion from the declared military areas. Responsibility for drawing up an evacuation plan was assigned to Colonel Bendetsen. In his first draft resistance to the evacuation would be classed a felony. As such, violators could legally be shot. He was quickly overrruled, however, and violations were downgraded to misdemeanor status. Beginning 2 March a series of proclamations and regulations began pouring out. Proclamation 1 established Military Area 1 in the western halves of each coastal state and the southern half of Arizona. Area 2 listed 98 military "zones". Voluntary resettlement was offered to those choosing to move out immediately. This did not take into consideration that bank accounts had been frozen and few had contacts in the interior to serve as havens. That fewer than 10,000 Nikkei took advantage of the voluntary option helped DeWitt rationalize the need for a mass evacuation. On 21 March President Roosevelt signed Public Law 503 giving DeWitt full enforcement powers; these he assigned to Bendetsen. With alacrity the colonel began plans for locating the evacuees and constructing their facilities: two large reception centers at Manzanar and Parker in the Owens valley through which evacuees would be fed to any one of the several internment camps then under construction, each of which was planned to hold about 10,000 persons.[9]

Locally, as removal seemed increasingly apparent concern was diverted to fate of the truck garden crops growing in the hinterland. Seattle's Chamber of Commerce seemed to want the evacuation process slowed down until crops were harvested. Then came announcement of Executive Order 9066: "Roosevelt Order Permits Army To Oust Coast Japs". "Nipponese Born In U.S. Also Covered Under Edict". The *P-I* editorial of 21 February advised cooperation despite the expected "hardships" and "injustices". The *Star* practically ignored the president's order; instead it continued to play up the prospect of subversion with a front page headline: "STATE TO DISARM ALL JAPS", followed by a column head: "Seattle FBI Raids For Guns"...Gov. Arthur Langlie [orders] surrender of all firearms". Its slight reference to 9066 was only in relation to Langlie's order.

With Executive Order 9066 tensions grew apace. The *P-I*'s front page headline contributed: "FBI seizes 101 Japs Here", followed with a photograph and caption: "Taken Into Custody Here". On the 23rd, page 4, appeared the following:

"No sabotage Found Says FBI Director"

"American Civil Liberties Union Protests...Order"

"Idaho Farm Bureau Doesn't Want Japs"

Elsewhere, on the 24th the, *P-I* announced: "School Mothers Protest Japanese Office Girls". This was in reference to a group of four mothers in the city's Gatewood district (in West Seattle), where 20 young Japanese women had been hired to replace white clerks who had left for better paying defense jobs. Altogether 27 young Nisei women had been hired by the school district. Assistant superintendent Samuel Fleming objected to the mothers' group, contending Nisei, as citizens, had the same employment rights as whites. Superintendent Worth McClure proved less protective, however; he prohibited them from participating in air raid drills and sent their names to the FBI. The group of four then started a petition campaign the object of which was to force the firing of the Nisei. By threatening to withhold support for the upcoming school bond vote and requesting intervention by the Interceptor Command the mothers won out. Under these pressures and the wilting of McClure, Sakamoto convinced the women to resign . Their public statement "We take this step to prove our loyalty...We bear no ill will" was made despite their preference to stand up for their rights. Had the Civil Service Commission been consulted in this case it would have refused to permit their firing, as it did when City Light asked perimission on 24 February to fire its four Nisei employees. It chose to wait for federal authorization before taking action. In view of DeWitt's evacuation orders the commission granted this permission 20 March 1942; other Nisei municipal employees would soon be laid off; the UW fired 23. Their families in most cases, were thereby deprived of their last dependable source of income. [10]

Seeing the inevitability of evacuation the Itois, like their friends and compatriots, began making plans. Mr. Itoi, who had managed to catch up on his financial obligations and think of his childrens' future - Henry to medical school, Kazuko and Sumiko to do whatever they chose - but for now he had to look for someone to manage the hotel until war's end. Their friends the "Olsens" came to mind; they had managed the Camden apartment house, where many Japanese families resided. They had retired to Aberdeen, however, and compassionately expressed their sorrow at the Itoi's plight. Concerned, Marta and Karl Olsen paid a friendly visit the very next week. That was far short of accepting management however. Mr. Itoi finally was able to negotiate an agreement with the Bentley agency for them to hire a manager for the duration or until Mr. Itoi's management contract expired. Mr. Itoi proved one of the lucky few.

## The Tolan Committee Hearings

On 25 February the *P-I* trumpeted the coming of California Congressman John Tolan's Committee investigating national defense migration: "Alien Probe To Open Here On Sat"..."Evacuation of Japanese From NW Will Be Topic..." Tolan announced plans were being laid to remove "all Japanese, both American and foreign born...[but] There has to be some place for them to go...They should not be placed where there is timber or near power lines, [or near oil]..." That same day the *Star*'s headline ran: "SEATTLE ALIENS TO GO - TOLAN".

The hearings ran from Saturday 28 February to 2 March 1942. First to be heard was Governor Arthur B. Langlie. Expressing "safety" as the primary consideration, he predicted a drop in agricultural production of perhaps 20 percent. Being led to address the forest fire danger Langlie admitted to the possibility of sabotage should they not be evacuated, and while avoiding an opinion of his own he claimed, "Washington residents believe overwhelmingly that all enemy aliens should be evacuated immediately." In following the governor Mayor Earl Millikin conceded there had been no reports of sabotage and that of the 8,000 Japanese here probably 7,900 are loyal, "but the other 100 would burn this town down and let the Japanese planes come in and bring on something that would dwarf Pearl Harbor".

Tacoma's Mayor Harry Cain proved quite a contrast. He was careful to distinguish aliens from citizens and objected to depriving the latter of their constitutional protections, that we should assume their loyalty unless proved otherwise. Banker James Spangler expressed fear of mob violence being inflicted on the Japanese should they not be evacuated. Floyd Oles, president of the Washington Produce Packers Association in the Kent valley believed California propaganda he had received was "hysterical", and that selfish interests were promoting their evacuation. He felt confident that aliens under FBI supervision posed no threat to the public security.

In James Sakamoto's testimony the founding of the JACL and its purpose of inculcating American values was stressed, and that his *Japanese American Courier* conveyed those principles. Should there be an evacuation all of this work will have been for naught, setting back the JACL's program by at least 10 years. Tolan interrupted, telling Sakamoto that Japan has interned American citizens; therefore, just what does he suggest as the US alternative? When asked by Congressman Curtis how many "disloyal" Japanese had been reported to the FBI by the JACL Sakamoto replied the JACL locally and nationally had " 'turned in' people whom we thought should be checked into." This line of hostile questioning continued interposing as fact the fictions of sabotage and subversion by Hawaii's Japanese. Sakamoto protested Nikkei do not want to be sent to a safe place but instead want to contribute to the war effort. As documenation of the Japanese contributions to the US he submitted a report prepared by Bill Hosokawa.

When Orville Robertson testified for the Family Society of Seattle he indicated the society was preparing for welfare work among the Japanese in case of their evacuation, contributing as much to their well being as the society's resources permit. He expressed the hope that their loyalty be tested on an individual basis. Tolan responded "this is war" and our enemy "intern them all". Edward W. Allen, chair of the International Fisheries Commission, while conceding Japanese are the best fishermen in the world, alleged he "was not competent to speak [on the evacuation matter]." When Chamber of Commerce president D.K. McDonald testifed he was asked about their real estate holdings. McDonald reported the chamber had been looking into the matter, found the Japanese were "standing by and waiting", but that when they sought a person in whose judgment they had confidence they learned he had been picked up by the FBI. He confessed their fate is a matter for the Federal Government, not Seattle's. In the document submitted by the chamber concern was expressed about the prospective loss of farm commodity production should evacuation take place.

State Attorney General Smith Troy feared mob violence should Japanese remain; he concluded both alien and citizen alike should be evacuated "as quickly as possible". State Senator Mary Farquharson had been asked by some Issei to speak on their behalf. She objected to their being labeled "enemy aliens" because, from her knowledge of them they "have a very deep attachment" to the US, and shared a peace of mind that something few of them had experienced in Japan. She was quickly reminded by committee members that they had been sent out here by Congress to get fast action on this issue because the country could not be expected to fight a war on two fronts.

Floyd B. Schmoe was asked to outline the position of the American Friends Service Committee on the evacuation issue. Admitting the Friends had not yet taken a position Schmoe indicated the organization was profoundly concerned about their welfare. He contradicted the committee, when told the nation was at war and assumed that the AFSC supported its "successful prosecution"; Schmoe reminded the committee the AFSC was pacifist in orientation, and evacuation should be resorted to only as a "last resort".

Miller Freeman proved a more compatible witness. A perennial Japanophobe, publisher of the *Pacific Fisherman* and other trade journals he submitted the following: "...all Japanese, both alien and United States born, [should] be evacuated from the Pacific Coast States...and kept under strict control for the duration..." In questioning the loyalty of the Nisei Freeman asked "why have they taken no stand against the aggressions of Japan...in the past 10 years?...[nor] forced the closing of the Japanese language schools...[which are] part of its ambitious program to colonization of North and South America..."

Representing the Puget Sound chapter of the American Asociation of Social Workers June Purcell Guild, chair of its subcommittee on constitutional rights, presented their organization's statement of principles, adopted Thursday, 26 February: opposed "indiscriminate evacuation" of Issei and Nisei except under conditions of "military necessity" or "public safety" and only on a case by case basis; when and if evacuated their constitutional rights should be safeguarded and "careful plans" should be made upon their resettlement.

The Seattle (Downtown) Kiwanis Club resolved on 24 February that, "All enemy aliens and and all Japanese ought forthwith be removed from the Pacific slope". Representing the Washington Commonwealth Federation Terry Pettus referred to the recent grand jury indictments of attorneys Thomas Masuda and Kenji Ito for acting as agents of Japan when they opposed in public meetings the WCF's stand against shipment of scrap metals to Japan and opposed Senator Schwellenbach's resolution for embargoing Japan. He pronounced an emphatic "yes" for evacuation of both Issei and Nisei, though "as quickly as possible in a humane and orderly way...".

Rev. Harold V. Jensen, representing the Church Council of Seattle, submitted its statement, which observed the generally peaceful relationships between the local Japanese and the area communities in general during the difficult past two months. Consequently thoughtful consideration should be given to alternatives to mass evacuation, such as distinguishing the loyal from those whose loyalty is clearly suspect, and allowing the former to remain and take their chances. Should evacuation be judged militarily necessary then every consideration must be afforded them during resettlement. Tolan indicated the difficulty of doing so in light of responses from governors of 15 Westerrn states opposing resettlement there. Only Colorado's Governor Carr welcomed them. [11]

Repeatedly committee members spoke defensively that because the Axis powers interned Americans the US was justified in following their example. Was this war not one in defense of democratic principles? The committee members apparently dismissed the thought because "this was war!"

## Evacuation Underway

The Tolan Committee hearings brought sharp focus to the evacuation process, exposing points of view that hitherto had been partially closeted. The *Times* of 3 March carried what could be regarded as General DeWitt's marching orders quickening the pace of events: "Army Order Reveals Eventual Ouster of All Japs on Coast." On page 9: "Jap Families In Puyallup Valley Balk At Tilling", and "Some white people in the valley towns are making surveys of available labor." A group of Italian aliens offered to take over the County's "Willows" farm near Woodinville. Reminding readers of a fifth-column threat, on 4 March the *Times* front page noted "Areas Vital to Defense in Jap Hands"; District Attorney John Dockwiler noted that Japanese leases were held in "nearly every strategic region hereabouts." Further on Sakamoto cautioned Nikkei, "not to leave hastily". On the 6th the *Times* reported: "Whites Try To Buy Them Out At Low Price." By way of illustration Rev. Thomas Gill of the Catholic Charities wrote to the Tolan Committee on 16 March citing several instances of such offers and buyouts: the owner of two groceries valued at $4,000 each was offered $1,500 for both; valued at $2,500 the Pacific Cafe owner was offered $600; the Orpheum Hotel owner, who had purchased his lease for $12,000, offered to sell for $7,500 but was offered $4,000. A confidant reported to Gill 15 other hotel leasees being offered "abnormally low" bids. The Togo Realty Company was reported to have about fifty people "looking for bargains" and expecting to get them in due time. The same applied to "movable goods" and equipment.[12]

Indicative of the demoralizing pace of events, the Beppu brothers, who operated a fish tackle store, and clothing store owners Mits and George Kashiwagi, had had several ten-cents on the dollar offers for their businesses. At the Pike Place Public Market a produce shortage was reported because 95 percent of the vegetables offered there were Japanese grown, and 35 percent of the sellers were Nisei, "a requirement". The Uno family, owners of the White River Dairy, found a fair-minded buyer, the Alpine Dairy in the person of a Mr. Forrester.

Sharon Aburano recalled "a scramble for suitcases", but when it came for selecting what ought to be packed clues were few, rumors overabundant. Not knowing where the families were to be sent posed problems as to clothing; bedding would take too much space, but taking some was not out of the question. How to dispose of household property and for those with shops and stores, what about the goods and equipment in them? The Sugimotos sold what was on their store shelves for "a fraction" of their cost. Their store lessor promised to take care of everything. (When they returned after the war the store area had been taken over by neighboring Tai Tung restaurant for its expansion; the equipment was nowhere to be seen.) Sharon's brother was forced to sell his 1941 Dodge that had been given by a Filipino customer for payment of a debt, also at a token price. On evacuation day they just left the store as is. Her sister, a high school valedictorian and UW chemistry major transferred to Washington State College, a lucky one. [10]

Raising anxieties among Seattle area Japanese were reports on the 6 March of "Scores" of FBI raids in California. Their expectations were soon fulfilled here, as "New Raids Conducted In Seattle" was reported by the *Times* on the 7th's front page. "Roundup Not As Extensive as First; 250 Already in Custody on Suspicion of Subversive Activities". On the 9th was reported the arrest of 9 Japanese by the Army in connection with a railroad explosion near Port Townsend. Thomas Masuda's trial was announced for 5 May, and Kenji Ito's for 26 May; Masuda charged as an unregistered Japanese agent, Ito as an enemy agent.

A *Times* editorial of the 12 March advocated employing Japanese farmers, and on page 9 is a photograph set in a truck farm, capped: "Japs Register While Working", accompanied by an account of JACL members doing the registering, "so that they can keep in touch...when they are moved inland".

"Japs Here Plan Inland Empire Colony" was the *Times*'s front page headline of the 19th. "Nipponese Would Build Model City With U.S. Aid". Submitted by Sakamoto, he would not reveal the location, but he indicated "We are willing to put ourselves in voluntary exile." This innocent proposal was completely ignored by the authorities since their own plans were now in full swing.

Concern for the fate of Japanese-operated farms inspired the US Agriculture Department to open an office for its Federal Security Administration in Seattle on the 20th, "To Keep The Farms Going" by finding qualified farmers to take over.

> Nine days before the President signed P.L. 503 DeWitt already had assigned Bendetsen responsibility for evacuating "all persons of Japanese ancestry" from the West Coast. Work had begun on the two Owens Valley reception centers through which the evacuees would be processed for removal to the rural interior. On 16 March Bendetsen assigned two groups to select sites to serve as "Assembly Centers". By the 20th fifteen sites had been selected and orders were given the Army Engineers to erect housing for 100,000 evacuees. The job ahead was so large that DeWitt requested assistance from civilian agencies to help with the logistical operations. At Biddle's suggestion that a single agency be established in charge of the resettlement the President signed Executive Order 9102 creating the War Relocation Authority (WRA). It was to share authority with the War Department. Milton S. Eisenhower was appointed director. Bendetsen made it quickly known who was making the decisions. Bendetsen had DeWitt issue a

curfew order on 24 March ordering all enemy aliens and Nisei to remain in their homes from 8:00 P.M. to 6:00 A.M., and restricting their movements to within five miles radius from their homes or work places during non-curfew hours. DeWitt also issued the first of 108 "exclusion orders", directing fifty-four Japanese American families on Bainbridge Island (near the Bremerton Naval Base) to report to Manzanar by 30 March (the Puyallup Assembly Center was not yet ready to receive them). Fulfilling this "dress rehearsal" for those evacuations to follow, they were instructed to take only bedding, toilet articles, clothing, eating utensils, and those other possessions that could be carried in their arms. By this measure further "voluntary" migration became moot.

On 24 March attention was diverted to the Bainbridge Island Japanese, where they "Keep Working, Face Bill Collectors". Another article with photograph: "Soldiers Guard Bainbridge, Bar Jap Visitors To Island" as registration was being readied. Curfew was announced. The following day a three column article appeared with photographs on page 10 of the *Times*: "Bainbridge Japanese Wistful and Willing"..."Aliens Register to Leave Island on Monday". The *Star* front page story of the 26th began: "With face-saving smiles Bainbridge Island Japanese were registering at Anderson's store..." soldiers, photographed with fixed bayonets.

Meanwhile Walter Cline of the Farm Security Administration assured the public that details were being made to guarantee the evacuees would get a share from sales of their crops; all that was needed was White leasees. Tension was eased somewhat on page 3, where the *Times* of the 28th pictured the smiling faces of Mr. and Mrs. Robert Hosokawa accompanied by a touching story of their hastily assembled marriage, involving his quick trip to Willamette University to "kidnap" Toshi Yoshikawa before travel restrictions went into effect. The article listed several other crisis driven marriages.

On 30 March - despite the advance preparations - came the shocking reality as the Bainbridge Japanese assembled at the ferry dock for evacuation to Manzanar: "Tears, Smiles Mingle as Japs Bid Bainbridge Farewell" began the long, sympathetic front page account, continued on page 2 with photographs and thumbnail biographical sketches of some of the evacuees.

Some relief came with the announcement on 2 April that Kenji Ito was acquitted in the "first wartime trial of a Japanese". But on the following page appeared the painful news that Mrs. Tao Okumura, grieving over separation from her already interned husband, had committed suicide. Noted also was Nellie Woo, who was to be separated from her Chinese husband. On page 10: "Jap Students At U [*sic*] Transfer to Inland Schools" to beat the voluntary migration deadline. Sociologist Robert O'Brien, on leave from the UW, negotiated the transfer for students here and in Oregon; transportation and matriculation costs were to be borne by the federal government.

Store fronts of evacuees, boarded up before evacuation.

Fresh arrivals at Camp Harmony being oriented by former Garfield High and UW football player, Harry Yanagamachi, whose family owned an oyster farm on Willapa Bay. Buildings in the background are the horse stalls to which the evacuees were assigned.

The first group of Nikkei evacuated were from Bainbridge Island. They were ferried from the island, 30 March 1942. They are being conducted to a train bound for Manzanar, California. Seattle Nikkei soon followed, headed for Puyallup, "Camp Harmony".

Reminding readers of the Army's hard line, the *Times*'s front page of 4 April: "Army Will Not Relax Orders For Movement". The *Star*, which frequently gave the Japanophobe, Miller Freeman a podium, carried a front page story that day, headed: "Miller Freeman Outlines Program For American Japs".

The *Times*'s front page column head of the 11th turned to something new: "'Conshies' At U. of W. Are Led By Nisei Youth". About 250 persons attended a meeting at Eagleson Hall, sponsored by the Conscientious Objectors Group, formed by the Fellowship of Reconciliation, headed by engineering professor Burt Farquharson, and a Friends group led by Floyd Schmoe, on leave from the UW. Gordon Hirabayashi was named the troublesome Nisei. The American Legion blamed "aliens" for inciting the pacifists.

On the farm front the Farm Security Administration was giving advice "On How To Get Jap Property". A group of Filipinos from the Cannery Workers Union filed articles of incorporation on 13 April, to produce "Food For Victory", aimed at acquiring about 100 acres in the Kent valley and 60 acres near Riverton. On the 17th a group of Whites had applied to operate farms from "any area between Bothell and southern Pierce County as "Victory Farms". Profits, allegedly would be turned over to the FSA to be held in escrow. (It was estimated that in King County evacuees operated between 600 and 900 farms, and about 125 in Pierce County.) [13]

As the 20 April deadline drew near one hundred members of the JACL decided to set an example of "good Americanism". Sakamoto prepared a resolution which was unanimously adopted expressing appreciation for the government's "extraordinary measures under the circumstances to safeguard the comfort, safety and economic welfare of the persons due to be evacuated...JACL [goes] on record as indorsing cheerful and willing cooperation by the community with the government agencies in the carrying out of evacuation proceedings..."

The *Times* front page headline of the 21st punctuated the fateful day: "Japs Must Leave The City Next Week", as the areas to be evacuated were described in detail. Colonel Bendetsen left no doubt, with his announcement on the 23rd: "Japs Must Move Despite Crops"..."Military necessity must not be compromised. It is a stern taskmaster". The colonel informed Idaho Governor C.A. Clark that the Japanese would be settled within the Minidoka Reclamation Project to cultivate "its fertile soil". Those in the general community were advised to inquire with the local Wartime Civilian Control Administration should they interested in any of the farms being vacated. (*Times*, 24 April) On the 25th the *Times* reported: 'A majority of Seattle's Japanese, mostly smiling and jovial - as though resigned to the inevitable - ...began registering today at two centers for removal from their homes..." About 500 heads of families registered the first day, leaving but a "small handful" for tommorow. About 2,100 are expected to leave for Puyallup Assembly Center this week, about 350 in the first group; they will prepare the center for later arrivals.

"Farewell parties" were underway, though hardly of celebratory mood. By 29 April 1,600 more had been transferred there, but as of 3 May 2,000 more were still expecting to leave the city. On Sunday 10 May the *Times* reported that not until next Saturday would the last Japanese be cleared from the city. From there they would be moved to Minidoka to live in the tar papered barrack shelters being built by the Army Engineers. The WRA indicated: "They will be put to work to convert into farmland 68,000 acres of what is now sagebrush-covered waste adjoining the town of Eden..." Not quite the "fertile soil" previously advertized. (*Times*, 26 April, 3 May).

While Seattle's Nikkei were being transported to Puyallup one Nisei decided to resist the curfew order and he refused to register: that troublesome "conchie" leader at the UW, Gordon Hirabayashi. He had lived for his first three UW years at the University YMCA and had struck up many warm friendships with students and faculty. The role of the American Civil Liberties Union is instructive at this time; it had alerted it West Coast affiliates 2 March to identify prospective test cases. In Seattle State Senator Mary Farquharson served as the ACLU's official, as she had on a case by case basis in the 1930s with Irving Clark, Sr. As a friend of Hirabayashi, Farquharson simply took the initiative on her own when he was incarcerated. ACLU's Roger Baldwin observed: "In view of the fact that the Japanese have competent counsel [already] (Arthur Barnett) I think the only help we could render would be to issue a public statement of the facts, signed by a group of Seattle citizens who have investigated them on their own authority...There is also the opportunity of filing a brief in support of their claims in the courts and also conferring with government officials...We must leave it to you to determine what best can be done." Baldwin's ambivalence is traceable to the deep divisions within ACLU's board of directors on the fate of the Nisei and what to do with Communists among its leadership. Under these circumstances it took no time at all for Farquharson and Barnett of the Church Council to take charge of the Hirabayashi case.[14]

With Arthur Barnett of the Council of Churches Hirabayashi presented himself at the King County Sheriff's office, prepared protest statement in hand. He was quickly placed in a jail cell with Charles T. Takahashi (the scrap metal exporter); there he stayed for five months. Barnett, feeling he lacked adequate constitutional law experience, recruited Frank L. Walters to represent Hirabayashi. Walters filed his opinion 29 June, contending Hirabayashi's due process rights had been violated and that as a citizen his right to equal treatment before the law had also been negated. Foreshadowing his judicial stance when the trial began in October, Judge Lloyd Black overruled Walters' opinion on 15 September, citing threats of fifth-column activity as justification for incarceration, adding, to allow his right to

## EXILES LOAD LUGGAGE FOR TRIP TO PUYALLUP

Mrs. Haruo Fujino sits on a roll of luggage on the fender of the leading car in the evacuation caravan. Her husband, who was president of the Oriental Restaurant Workers' Union here, will be head waiter at the assembly center.

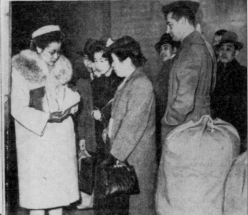

Martha Okuda, herself a prospective evacuee, aids in checking in Japanese as they board a bus at the evacuation assembly center at Puyallup. Miss Okuda is a staff member of the Family Society and U. of W. student from Oregon. She will be evacuated when she returns to her home state.

Japanese busily load their luggage into a truck as they prepare for their trek to the Puyallup assembly center. Baggage permitted is limited.

### City's Jap Evacuees Start 'Housekeeping' in Puyallup

Vanguard of the 2,000 Japanese who will be evacuated from two areas in Seattle by Friday arrived at their temporary home in Puyallup this afternoon and immediately began settling themselves in the community dwellings which have been built on the Puyallup Fair Grounds.

The first contingent of 500 men, women and children made the trip from Seattle in private automobiles and in buses chartered by the Army.

With the same efficiency which marked their departure from Seattle, the group took living quarters assigned to them and then began the hurried task of preparing the assembly center for the 1,500 more Japanese who will arrive within the next two days.

**Group Faces New Life**

The party was in high spirits for the most part as it left Seattle and the same attitude prevailed as the members stepped on the grounds which will be their home until they are transferred to resettlement centers east of the mountains.

The Japanese knew they were facing a new life and had seen their Seattle homes for the last time in a long while, but they accepted the situation cheerfully. They have no intimation as to where they next will be moved, other than the presumption they will be sent to the nearest resettlement center, the one being prepared on government land in Idaho.

While Seattle Japanese were in the process of moving, the Associated Press reported from San Francisco that the Army had ordered all Japanese removed from the city of Portland, Or., by next Tuesday noon. This is the first evacuation in Oregon. The Japanese in Portland will register tomorrow and Thursday. They will go to the assembly center recently completed on the Pacific International Livestock Exposition grounds. Portland has about 1,900 Japanese residents.

**Necessities Taken**

At 8 o'clock this morning the Seattle evacuees began to arrive at three pick-up points previously designated, taking with them those necessities which the Army had advised them to carry. These included, blankets, linen, silverware and dishes, extra clothing and personal necessities such as tooth brushes and razors.

Japanese who reported at Elliott Avenue and Virginia Street were the first to move to the meeting point in Beacon Avenue for the start to Puyallup.

Many friends, who will be evacuated later in the week, were on hand to bid the first contingent good-bye. Members of the crowd were in gay spirits. There was laughing and shouting and cheerful farewells. Children were in picnic mood and the departure was like the start of an excursion party.

At Lane Street and Eighth Avenue South, five buses were provided for 200 Japanese without other transportation. Here, also, everything was cheerfulness. Another group left from the third center in Spokane Street near 21st Avenue South, but it was a small one.

At Beacon Avenue and Alaska Street, where the caravan started toward Puyallup, the Japanese took their last look at Seattle "for the duration." There were no tears in evidence, only a few sad faces among the waving and smiling occupants of the many automobiles and buses.

**Girls Bid Youths Good-Bye**

Two white girls, in an automobile bearing a California license, were at the starting point to bid farewell to two Japanese youths. The youths sat in the girls' car until starting time came. Then they kissed the girls good-bye and joined the caravan.

Haru Fujino, former president of the Oriental Restaurant Workers' Association, Local 844, was among those who went to Puyallup today. He was accompanied by his family. Fujino said Local 844 had been dissolved because of the evacuation but would be reorganized when the war is over. He will become head waiter of the mess halls at the assembly center.

**Own Automobiles Used**

Vans were supplied for moving the evacuees' personal belongings. They are allowed to take their automobiles to Puyallup but must have made arrangements for their disposal after reaching there.

The Japanese themselves, under Army direction, are arranging all evacuation details. The removal was organized by the Japanese-American Citizens' League, headed by James Y. Sakamoto, editor of an English-language Japanese newspaper and the man who will be director of the assembly center for the Japanese. The evacuees who have self-government, which already has been organized.

Today's removal procedure went like clockwork, indicating that the later and larger evacuation will be accomplished with precision equal to that of a month ago when the Army removed 239 Japanese from Bainbridge Island. The Bainbridge Island Orientals were taken to the Manzanar relocation center in Owens Valley, Calif.

The Puyallup assembly center consisting of temporary barracks with central mess halls and built in 17 days, will accommodate 8,000. This will take care of all Japanese in Western Washington except those in the extreme southwestern portion, who probably will be taken to the Portland, Or., assembly center. The 200 Japanese to be evacuated from Alaska also will go to Puyallup.

Evacuation orders so far have not affected Japanese farmers in the Puget Sound area, except those on Bainbridge Island, but it was indicated these farmers soon would be removed by the urgent appeal today by the Washington State War Board of the United States Department of Agriculture for farmers to take over Japanese land.

### F. B. I. Begins Raids On California Japanese

SAN FRANCISCO, April 28.—(AP)—In its first big series of raids in Northern California this month, Federal Bureau of Investigation agents today moved concertedly against potentially dangerous Japanese aliens in 24 cities and towns in 16 counties.

More than 100 officers, including police and sheriff's deputies from 21 different law-enforcement agencies joined in the raids.

Nat J. L. Pieper, special agent in charge of the San Francisco F. B. I. office, said the raids were directed primarily against known members of Japanese nationalistic organizations.

### DON'T TOUCH IT; IT MAY EXPLODE!

A warning to civilians along the coasts of Washington and Oregon not to pick up or tamper with any strange metal objects washed up on the beaches was issued today by the 13th Naval District. The same suspicion should be directed to such objects on the shores of Puget Sound and off the Columbia River, the warning said.

Such objects, the Navy said, should not be tampered with until it is established by competent experts that they are not mines, bombs or other device capable of exploding.

No reports have been received as to the presence of floating enemy mines, either laid from submarines or dropped from planes, but "watchfulness is the best advice," the Navy said.

Finders of mines should report them immediately to the 13th Naval District headquarters by way of the nearest Naval activity, and under no circumstances should a bomb or mine be handled or moved except by trained Army or Navy

### Council Group O.K. Watchman at Dumps

The City Council public-safety committee today recommended passage an ordinance hiring laborer at $120 a month to guard fires under control at night at municipal garbage dumps.

The Army and Civilian Commission asked for a bi-nightly check on the fires so will not be beacons in case blackout.

"Exiles Load Luggage For Trip to Puyallup". Seattle Times, 28 April 1942.

due process would "endanger all of the constitutional rights of the whole citizenry".

While at the County jail Hirabayashi corresponded with Eleanor Ring, thanking her for her "moral suppport", recounting his appearance, handcuffed, before the Grand Jury. He reported to "Ellie" getting many letters "from the least expected sources", later, one from his distraught mother, who "sounds sort of proud of what I'm doing". [15]


After issuing the series of orders setting up the "evacuation centers" Milton Eisenhower tendered his resignation 13 June, admitting to the President that: "In democracy this [mass evacuation] is unquestionably sound and proper". Dillon S. Myer, an agronomist in the Soil Conservation Service, was named his replacement. Meanwhile successive evacuation orders were being issued, allowing one week to report to assigned assembly centers. The last order came on 7 June, but two days after the spectacular naval victory at Midway Island. Bendetsen's staff meticulously tallied 111,999 "persons of Japanese ancestry" having been place in relocation centers by 30 October 1942. The shacklike barracks located in remote desert areas, completely devoid of amenities, seemed more like an act of unprovoked vengeance imposed on innocent bystanders. Why the evacuees were not at least provided with something that simulated the comfort of homes seems inexplicable except for the racism that underlay decisions made by War Department authorities. Afterall, their incarceration was for the convenience of US authorities, authorities who knew the very falsehoods upon which their policy decisions had been based. Sadly, their extreme racist biases prevailed. One must turn to the "pro-slavery argument" of the pre-Civil War period for a close analogy.

# THE WARTIME ECONOMY

### INTRODUCTION

This complex chapter is introduced by providing a general framework of the wartime economy, the context within which other aspects are expanded upon in succeeding sections. For example, composition of the workforce was radically altered by the recruitment of women and African Americans on an unprecedented scale. Recruitment of women inevitably affected family and workplace relationships in myriad challenging ways, and inescapably the care of their children. Consequently a separate section is devoted to the "Transformation of Women's Roles".

African Americans were more slowly integrated into the workforce, though not in comparable numbers; but their introduction posed a unique set of problems associated with historically rooted racism that are dealt with in considerable detail in this first section in connection with their shipyard employment and working at Boeing. In Part 2 the consequences of their limited integration into the workforce is covered in the chapter on the Civic Unity Committee, which was a vital product of the nationwide civic unity committee movement generated by the race riots of 1943.

Price control and rationing, paralleled by volunteer mobilization, lay at the center of mobilization of the economy for war. In this general introduction section the wage scale discrepancy between the shipyards and Boeing is outlined; but its consequences are elaborated in a subsection on the Office of Price Administration (OPA): "Boeing and Local 751 vs. WPB", where the dynamics of price control at the local level are illustrated.

Historically states west of the Mississippi had been treated as a colony for Eastern investors. Their lock on private capital ventures oriented them to resource ex-traction in the West, primarily for the West's relatively unexploited forests and minerals. Puget Sound's economy had been colonized by San Francisco's lumber firms since the mid-19th century, a product of the those firms' West Coast migration after they decimated northeastern and midwestern forests. This dependency status changed dramatically during the Great Depression of the 1930s. Federal investments substituted for private capital on an unprecedented scale. But the purpose was radically different. The focus of federal concern was upon the problems of mass unemployment and relief, upon resettling bankrupted farmers, and on other related issues. Industrialization of the Pacific Coast states gradually took form under federal stimulus.

Augering an industrial future for Southern California, Puget Sound cities, and Portland was completion of the Hoover Dam on the Colorado River in 1936, accompanied by construction of the Bonneville Dam just forty miles upstream from Portland on the Columbia River, and the Grand Coulee Dam further upstream. Once the Northwest Power Pool was established during the war, under control of the Portland-based Bonneville Power Administration (BPA), the entire Pacific Northwest would be practically guaranteed electric power distribution at the lowest rates in the nation. These dams served a dual purpose: electric power generation and land reclamation. The BPA's first priority was supplying power to the nascent aluminum industry and the secretive Hanford project. After the war it would also act as the pumping station for irrigating the vast the Columbia River Basin Project. [1]

War production, finally, brought the nation and region out of the Great Depression. Clark Kerr of the University of Washington wrote in 1942: "No major industrial area in the United States during 1940 and 1941 felt the economic impact of the war more intensely than did the Seattle region". By August 1941 the relation of prime military contracts to the value of manufacturing products was five times greater than for the the nation as a whole. Seattle's military contracts were twice that for Los Angeles and four times that for San Francisco. Seattle's manufacturing labor force since 1939 had doubled by the end of 1941. The city seemed at last to have developed the manufacturing base it had sought since the turn of the century but had experienced only briefly from shipbuilding during World War I.

Shipbuilding proved a revitalizing force in the region's economy, preceding aircraft production in its effect. In the state overall eighty-eight shipyards operated, employing about 150,000 workers. The Kaiser shipyards in Vancouver and Vanport accounted for about half their employment. There were more than thirty shipyards in Seattle and Tacoma, another one a mere 20-minute ferry ride from Madison Park to Kirkland, and Bremerton's Navy Shipyard a one-hour ferry ride across the

Sound from Seattle. In the Puget Sound area substantially all contracts were for Army and Navy craft, mainly auxiliary types, excepting the Bremerton Navy Yard; there, destroyers and "baby flat-tops" were built to serve as convoy escorts.

The US Maritime Commission kept the Todd Shipbuilding Corporation's Tacoma yard at work as a model operation between the two wars. Todd established a new company in 1939, the Seattle-Tacoma Shipbuilding Corporation. In a conference with the "Admiral" Congressman Warren Magnuson and the Chamber of Commerce's Christy Thomas and John Underwood emerged with assurance that "destroyers would be built in Seattle and Tacoma". During the war the Seattle plant produced more than 20 destroyers, but its major work was in ship repair. Associated Shipbuilders was another major Seattle yard, specializing in Navy vessels. It turned out 26 ships in 1943, exceeding its quota in the process. Associated's labor force expanded from 195 yard workers and 53 office staff in 1941 to 7,657 employees in the yards and 468 in the offices by 1943. Many yards in the Lake Union basin turned out wooden craft for the Navy and commercial and fishing boats. Across Lake Washington, adjacent to the once sleepy rural town of Kirkland, the Navy refurbished the old Lake Washington Shipyard for building a variety of auxiliary crafts, and employing about 8,000 workers. The Bremerton Navy Yard employed about 30,000 workers mainly in repairing damaged Navy ships while building new ones. Overall, employment in the Puget Sound area's yards expanded phenomenally from 8,000 in 1940 to 92,000 by November 1943.

In the Seattle metropolitan area the number of manufacturing employees expanded from 34,709 in 1940 to 115,000 in 1943, comparable to growth of the area's manufacturing base during the first World War. Aircraft production, however, made a significant difference, representing the wave of the future. Two-thirds of the $1.5 billion in war contracts was for airplanes. Most of the rest was for shipbuilding.

While the major economic stimulus was felt first in shipbuilding the momentum spread elsewhere. Transportation equipment, mainly trucks and tanks at the Kenworth Trucks plant near Boeing and at Pacific Car and Foundry in nearby Renton, increased their employment from 6,300 to 40,500 during the same period. Boeing's employment roll shot up from about 4,000 in 1939 to 10,000 by mid-1941, to 20,000 that September, to 30,000 by December, and 40,000 by war's end. Housing construction to shelter the inmigrants and federal services absorbed most of the balance of federal expenditures. A ripple effect benefited the entire the region. City Light supplied electric ranges and water heaters to the 3,568 federally subsidized housing units built by the Seattle Housing Authority. The city's 27 foundries and pattern shops typically won sub-contracts, as did rolling mills, machine, sheet metal and fabricating plants. Seattle's department store sales registered the multiplier effects as their sales increased by 30 percent between 1940 and 1941; Tacoma's store sales jumped comparably by 32 percent. Civilian employment at federal operations at the Sand Point Naval Air Station and the Port of Embarkation added hundreds more jobs. Government supply contracts totalled $3,450,061,000 by 1944 in the three-counties area of King, Pierce, and Kitsap, where the Bremerton Navy Yard was located. Another $315 million went for plant expansions in Pierce and King counties.

The Navy Department, after the fall of France in June 1940, frantically handed out contracts. The Seattle Chamber of Commerce prepared a careful survey of its shipbuilding facilities for the Navy department, placing it near the head of the line for shipbuilding contracts. Winning the contracts was only a first step; to fulfill its obligations the City had to get the workers to the job sites along the south end of Elliott Bay. A viaduct on Spokane Street had to lift traffic above the railroad tracks, but the viaduct had yet to be built. The pressure on the city was intense because the Navy might cancel its contracts unless the the traffic problem could be solved. Mayor Earl Millikin assigned top priority to the project, urging Congressman Warren Magnuson to use his influence as a member of the House Naval Affairs Committee to move along the City's $1,200,000 application for viaduct funding. Not until January 1943 did the funding come through; how it came about is covered below in the section "Getting To and From Work". [2]

## COMPOSITION OF WORKFORCE IS TRANSFORMED

Workforce composition changed initially as men of militarily eligible age were steadily withdrawn from the Seattle civilian labor market. Gradually older men, then women, finally African Americans replaced the estimated 69,000 local men who joined the armed forces. Business firms, the Chamber of Commerce, and the War Manpower Commission actively recruited labor throughout the war. The three Pacific Coast states were the largest gainers among the western states: Washington's population grew by 37 percent during the 1940s to 2,368,963 people; California's expanded by 53.3 percent to over 10 million people; Oregon's by 39.6 percent to 1,521,311 people by 1950. The huge influx of immigrants from the Midwest and South converted Seattle into a more typical American city. [3]

Labor shortage overcame traditional resistance to the employment of women in typical "male" jobs, and to colored minorities. Labor unions - particularly the AFL craft unions - and employers both imposed barriers to their hiring. Gradually these restrictions were relaxed because of the tight labor market, and once male workers and employers realized their employment was probably only "for the duration".

Women became the most significant addition to the manufacturing workforce during the war. Nationally between 1940 and July 1944 six million women joined the workforce and their numbers did not level off until July 1945. The US Women's Bureau's study of their employment in ten war production areas found women more evenly distributed among the occupational fields in Seattle than in any of the nine other areas. Seattle women were drawn most heavily from households and schools in the general vicinity. Inmigrants constituted about one-third of the new entrants in the local labor market; of these 55 percent were women, and 40 percent of them were in the 15 to 29 age group. The Bureau noted in general that married women for the first time outnumbered single women in the workforce, and most of these married women were in the 35 to 44 age group. They and those in the next higher age range hoped to remain employed after the war. Nationwide the proportion of women employed in the war industries increased by 400 percent and those in general manufacturing increased by 110 percent. Men, who dominated office employment before the war, were largely replaced by women as the burgeoning bureaucracies in both the private and government sectors expanded exponentially; the Bureau singled out Seattle and San Francisco as areas where office employment increases were sharpest. [4]

Also of special significance to the workforce's composition were the African Americans who were drawn to the Puget Sound industrial area by the seemingly uncountable job opportunities available. Their numbers increased from 3,789 in 1940 to over 10,000 by war's end; they became the city's largest nonwhite minority by 1950, when their numbers reached 15,666. (Before their evacuation in spring of 1942 the Japanese had been the city's largest nonwhite minority since the turn of the century, numbering almost 7,000 in 1940 or slightly less than 2 percent of Seattle's population.)

A mere 171,000 Blacks lived west of the Mississippi River in 1940. Hoping to escape their oppression in the South about 620,000 Blacks moved westward where prospects of employment and freedom beckoned. Historian Gerald Nash noted their migration pattern: most traveled first to Los Angeles and branched out from there, depending upon job prospects. Because the Southern Pacific Railroad expected to hire them as section hands it offered them free transportation; consequently 340,000 Blacks migrated to California between spring 1942 and 1945. Blacks coming to the Pacific Northwest by 1945, and with those arriving from California, numbered 45,000. These Blacks came primarily to work in the shipyards of the Portland-Vancouver and Seattle-Tacoma-Bremerton areas. [5]

Despite the obvious need for more workers there lurked the serious question:

Just how many of the inmigrants could be absorbed by the region? Historian Karen Anderson observed their numbers overstressed the housing and municipal services to the point that importation of more labor slowed, forcing "a dramatic reversal in employers' policies. [Seattle] [w]omen who had been turned back just a few weeks or months before were not only hired, but also were being actively recruited." Initially women and Blacks were denied access to federally funded training programs, ostensibly because no demands for their employment were being placed with the US Employment Service. Ninety percent of placement requests in 1941 were for white men only. State Superintendent of Public Instruction, Pearl Wanamaker, overcame some employer resistance to employing women by opening enrollment in the State's vocational training schools in January 1942 to qualify women for aircraft production jobs. Blacks, for the time being, were still bypassed for such special consideration. The first thirty of these original women trainees began work at Boeing in April 1942. One survey of Boeing's problems concluded in desperation: "The only apparent solution is the employment of women, possibly to the extent of 50 percent." At that time women employed at Boeing offices outnumbered production workers by two to one. Five weeks later that ratio had been reversed. Women represented 26 percent of all employees at the company's Seattle plants by August 1942. Within the company's 14,435 women employees, however, by May 1943 only 3,062 fell into the semiskilled category, a mere 109 were found in the skilled ranks.

Shipyard training classes for women paralleled those for aircraft pre-employment training. Seattle area shipyards employed 10,000 women by 1943, but they were not evenly distributed. The proportion of women to men at Associated Shipbuilders, one of the newer yards, was 21 percent; at the Todd yards women constituted a mere 1.8 percent, and none were employed above the unskilled rank. Todd's closed shop agreement with Local 104 of the Boilermakers Union prevented job access for women. Local 104 had voted five to one against admitting women to membership. But, given the emergency Local 104 was overruled by the executive board of its parent international office in 1942. Women then found greater access to shipyard jobs and elsewhere once white male fears were assuaged by the thought, "It is only for the duration".

Trade unions rallied to protect their wage scales though, as women and African Americans moved into the white male dominated employment sector. Unions conceded "equal pay for equal work" in their contract negotiations, but male employees often evaded that formula through a number of loopholes allowed by the National War Labor Board. Cost-plus contracts, on the other hand, provided employers incentive to conform to the formula. On the other hand, women often accepted the lower paying, non-union clerical jobs because they could float in and out of employment for a variety of reasons, mainly associated with family responsibilities. The tight labor market enabled them to return to work with relative ease.

And the high pay scales in Seattle, San Francisco, and Detroit tended to pull up the pay scales in the lower paying occupations according to the Women's Bureau in its survey of the ten war industry centers.

Seattle's public schools responded variously to the stepped up demand for labor. Its curriculum and vocational training programs were adapted to factory employment. Of the enrollees at Edison Technical School almost one-third came from outside the school district; for them the State contributed $125,000 toward meeting their additional expense. Edison offered 52 occupational classes during 1941-1942 to 32,041 men and women; to another 33,000 in 1942-1943, bringing the total by then to about 150,000 trainees. The School Board anticipated the growing demand for pre-employment training and for upgrading skills and added more training facilities. The abandoned Rainier school, near 24th Avenue and South Jackson Street, was adapted for aircraft trades, shipyard training at the Interbay school. The Board also rented a three-story building, its largest facility, at 1516 Twelfth Avenue. Broadway High School signed up 917 trainees in 1942. By May 1943 ten training centers were operating. Women represented a growing proportion of the trainees as the war progressed.

Seattle's Public School's administration also revamped its curriculum to better phase students into the war economy. Early in 1942 the School Board announced "School Program Adjusted for Young Workers". Applied science courses were keyed to industrial employment upon the student's graduation. All nine high schools offered pre-flight courses; also map and blueprint reading. War propaganda themes permeated art courses. New syllabi were issued for standard courses; that for English and spelling attracted "national attention". Geography was taught as a "Postwar Fundamental", corresponding to the "One World" concept being propagated. Girls, at last, were allowed to enroll in "boys" classes such as one for auto mechanics. Minors received work permits, usually for jobs that released adults for higher level ones, as well as to simply extend their summertime employment. Faculty received professional credit for taking electricity courses to better prepare them for coaching their students in skills needed in the armed services and industry. Schooling in general mirrored the mobilization of the economy for war. [6]

African Americans moved more easily into shipyard jobs than into Boeing employment. Before the war Boeing had never employed Blacks. Sharing that bias, the Aero Mechanics Union, Local 751 of the International Association of Machinists refused to admit nonwhites to union membership. The labor shortage ultimately led to their employment at Boeing, but not until 1943 did their numbers achieve significance; 1,600 at the wartime peak. Even then Local 751 granted them a union work permit only, not membership. This meant Blacks could not accumulate seniority credits. Blacks found shipyard jobs because the new shipyards and those expanding chose to sign union contracts with the racially integrated Industrial Union of Maritime and Shipbuilding Workers of America, a Congress of Industrial Organizations (CIO) union, instead of the racist AFL's Local 104 of the Boilermakers Union.

The CIO's waterfront unions were racially integrated, a result of the great maritime strike of 1934, in which all the maritime unions joined together under leadership of Harry Bridges up and down the Pacific Coast in opposition to both the Waterfront Employers' Association and officers of AFL's International Longshoremens Association. Under Bridges' influence the Pacific Coast locals of the ILA joined the CIO when it was established in fall of 1937, becoming the International Longshoremen's and Warehousmens Union (the ILWU). Before 1934 Blacks had regularly been used by the Waterfront Employers' Association (WEA) as strikebreakers. With their former role in mind Blacks, during the war, were often caught between the shipowners and the ILWU because both the the WEA and Army Transport Service (ATS) distrusted the notoriously left-wing ILWU. Both wanted desperately to break the union and to have the popular Australian-born Bridges deported. Consequently the Waterfront Employers' Association and the ATS denied admission to "certain stevedores" to the ATS docks. In Oakland the ATS planned to train a "Negro Battalion" of 600 men to work their docks. Seattle unionists worried about the Oakland precedent because civil service employees were replacing longshoremen and warehousemen in Seattle; they expected another "colored battalion" of ATS trainees would take over their jobs. Threats to stall ATS shipments, however, forced the WEA and ATS to recognize the continued control of the hiring halls that the ILWU had won in 1934.

At Boeing, in 1940, Local 751 of the Aero Mechanics Union voted African Americans into the union, but the parent International Association of Machinists overturned their vote because its constitution barred nonwhites from membership. What began as a racial issue quickly expanded into a purge of Local 751's officers responsible for Blacks' short-lived admission to the union. Those officers were believed to be sympathetic to the CIO's policies of rank and file control of the unions and openness to nonwhite membership. Local 751's newspaper editor, Clifford Stone, accused the local's president Hugo Lundquist and business agent Barney Bader of being Communists or fellow travelers; worse, they might be seeking CIO affiliation. Lundquist and Bader were charged guilty of subversion and dual unionism. Local 751's charter was removed by the parent IAM office and it assumed direct authority over the local's affairs. Hearings began, in which about fifty other union members were screened under suspicion of subversion.

The CIO threat to the International Association of Machinists was serious at this time. The CIO organization drive among aircraft workers in Southern California was meeting with success. There, the aviation division of the United Automoblile Workers (UAW) had sent one of its most effective organizers, Wyndham Mortimer. In Southern California the Aeronautical Chamber of Commerce set the pattern of labor-management relations. The Chamber had set the entry level wage at the minimum standard set by the Walsh-Healy Minimum Wage Act, which was 50 cents per hour, amounting, after Social Security deduction, to a weekly pay of $19.40. After but three months in the region Mortimer won approval for a bargaining agent election in the Vultee aircraft plant from the National Labor Relations Board. The workers voted to affiliate with the United Automobile Workers, but when Vultee refused to negotiate Mortimer gained strike approval, not from the UAW, but from CIO president John L. Lewis. Fearful of incurring President Roosevelt's wrath and threat of a "labor draft", United Steel Workers (CIO) president Phillip Murray and FDR's labor confidant Sidney Hillman pressured Mortimer to order the Vultee workers back to work; he refused. The strikers won and the entry wage level was set at $.625 per hour, thereby upsetting the former fifty cents minimum at the other aircraft plants.

Mortimer then turned to organizing North American Aviation for his next target. Abruptly Mortimer was ordered to Seattle by UAW president R.J. Thomas just as he was succeeding at North American. In Seattle the situation was volatile, not promising. CIO leadership in Seattle was in some disarray as a result of recent purges in which a Communist Eugene Dennett was replaced as head of the State CIO by an anti-Communist Richard Francis. Francis denied the CIO had any membership drive in progress; instead he expressed satisfaction that Local 751 was the legitimate Boeing union and that he was not about to challenge it. This split in CIO leadership marked the first "open instance" of CIO intrusion at Boeing.

Local 751 claimed a membership of 9,100 at the time and was expecting a big increase as a result of Boeing's plan to increase its workforce to between 15,000 to 18,000. The so-called "Red trials" began in October 1940 and stretched into April 1941. The International Machinists' Union president Harvey Brown had replaced Hugo Lundquist and Barney Bader with Harry Bomber as president and Gary Cotton as business agent. Lundquist and Bader then proceeded to organize a "Save Our Union" group for potential CIO affiliation. President Brown hastened to Seattle for a membership meeting to be held in the Civic Auditorium Sunday 6 April 1941. The *Times* editorial of 4 April alleged it to be "one of the most important in Seattle's labor history", urging a big turnout: "too vital to the welfare of those men, too vital to the industrial welfare of Seattle, too vital to the dominant issue of the day - national defense - for those men to sit idly by".

Warming up for the Sunday meeting, Brown declared the Communist Party was responsible for the "strife and division" in the union. Local 751's new officers claimed a minority faction was trying to foment a strike. The much heralded meeting drew a bare 2,000 members. Of these less than 1,100 voted, although it is unclear from the *Times*'s reporting what the issues were. On at least one item, Harvey Jackins - who, previously had allegedly been beaten by "goons" - was cleared of charges by a vote of 634 to 451. Dissension and unruliness at the meeting continued the earlier five-month long pattern, leading Brown to suspend Local 751's charter. He later rationalized: "to halt the meeting until the membership agrees to recognize the union's duly appointed officers." This meant, only those appointed by Brown, not anyone elected by vote of the membership. Rank and file participation in union operations was not a standard operating procedure in AFL unions.

Some CIO sympathizers at the meeting were singled out for beatings afterward. Charges against twelve of the attackers were filed on the 8th with King County prosecuting attorney, B. Gray Warner. While contending he would not take sides Warner advised: "This office will not tolerate violence or any other illegal act which holds up national defense..." This line of reasoning led him to let the cases drift along without serious attention, inasmuch as the victims seemed to him the ones who might be holding up national defense.

Meanwhile A.E. Harding, head of the CIO's Seattle Industrial Union Council, at the request of the UAW, had CIO members distribute about 10,000 copies of their *Aircraft Organizer*. When William Muirhead of the Local 751 grievance committee tried to stop the distribution he and others were attacked. State CIO director Richard Francis continued to disclaim knowledge of any CIO organizing campaign at the plant, although he acknowledged: "[T]he U.A.W. has had organizers here previously, but they never consulted with me." In any case Francis confessed to his inability to do anything to prohibit them from such activity. At the same time Harry Bridges was encountering opposition from members of the Seattle ILWU; he accused them of a "lack of cooperation, trickery, misleadership, and a violation of contract." Francis would soon blame Bridges for all the dissension. By this diversion Francis made communism the issue, which was the reason alleged by the FBI's in seeking Bridges's deportation.

One result of the attack on Muirhead and the others was, according to him: "This fight did more than all we could yell at them for a year...I've been amazed at the activity around union headquarters today [Saturday, 12 April], offers of help and stuff." Then the UAW's big guns swept into town: Richard Frankensteen, national director of the UAW's aviation division, arrived on the 16th to direct the organizing drive. To this Local 751 officers announced formation of "national defense squads" in every Boeing shop, fifteen men to a squad. Other CIO leaders soon appeared: Wyndham Mortimer and Lewis Michener, CIO's West Coast regional director. There now seemed no mistaking a serious organizing drive was underway. Lundquist and Bader scheduled a Sunday meeting for the Civic Auditorium. Quickly the Seattle Central Labor Council officers met with city authorities to prevent use of the facility. They succeeded. Mayor Millikin denied its use after being convinced "Communists would dominate the meeting". Next, the Fire Department condemned the "Fishermen's Hall" when Mortimer had substituted that building for the meeting. Police Chief William Sears reinforced these obstructive tactics by sending a force of thirty policemen to the Boeing plant to reinforce the national defense squads already there. Playing upon the alleged communist threat County Prosecutor Warner emerged from a meeting with Millikin to announce: "I am advised that Communist elements in both the A.F. of L. and the C.I.O. have joined together at this time for the purpose of disrupting legitimate labor and its relations with Boeing's...for the express purpose of disrupting and slowing down the aircraft industry..." Warner pointed to the "lessening of sabotage" at the plant following the "purge" of Communists. He threatened criminal charges should picket lines be set up. Later, when Millikin nominated Sears to succeed himself as police chief, with Dave Beck's support, Beck praised Sears for his police handling of CIO pickets: "His performance at Boeing's means more to...Seattle than any other thing he has handled in his entire administration." When Mortimer applied to the National Labor Relations Board for an election at Boeing the Board refused to process the petition. Faced with this alliance of forces against it and divisions within the CIO, its organizing drive dissipated. Only in the shipyards did the CIO win Seattle affiliates during the war, and they would prove ephemeral during the downturn in shipbuilding after the war.

The internal struggle described above within Local 751 had been triggered by the question of African American employment at Boeing. The company had never hired them and when the issue came up Boeing officials blamed the union for the absence of Blacks on the payroll. Confronted with the persistently high labor turnover, however, Boeing cautiously hired two Black women in 1942, one as a stenographer, the other as a sheet metal worker. By July 1943 the company had 329 Blacks on its payroll, 280 of them women. Equally resistant about working alongside African Americans Local 751 protected its White members by restricting Blacks from union membership, extracting dues from them, and issuing them work permits instead. Not until 1948 were Blacks admitted to full union status, which gave them seniority rights and less likely in the future to be "last hired, first fired". Indicative of the prejudice encountered among fellow employees is a cartoon in the 15 April 1943 *Aero Mechanic* portraying a Southern Black, hat in hand, applying for a job, and being told about stabilizers: "Stable Lizers? Yas Suh! Ah sho knows 'bout dem'". Inset at the top of the cartoon is a Black sweeping out a stable. [7]

*Workers engaged in cabin control assembly for the B-17 "Flying Fortress".*

## Boeing's B-17s and B-29s

Boeing had designed the B-17 "Flying Fortress" in 1935 and hoped to recoup from financial losses it had suffered on two other models, the Model 247 and P-26 army pursuit planes. Its B-17 design had impressed GHQ Air Force commander Frank Andrews and General Henry "Hap" Arnold because it fitted in with their planning for a strategic bombing capability. Should they be influential Boeing could turn a profit. Decisive, however, was the legal proviso that denied a manufacturers' property rights in those designs for military aircraft. This meant Boeing's design could be allocated to any qualified producer, including those in Southern California, which was known as "the white spot of the open shop". Antiunionism was militantly enforced there by Douglas Aircraft, the Southern California Aircraft Industry, and the Los Angeles business establishment. When Boeing received a contract for thirteen B-17s in January 1936 it sought to stabilize its workforce by agreeing with the nascent Local 751 for a closed shop, an end to jurisdictional disputes, and the highest wage scale in the industry. In return Local 751 pledged not to strike. For its part its parent body, the International Association of Machinists, promised to stage an organizing drive in Southern California to bring their wage scales in line with that at Boeing. This would take wages out of competition.

Life *magazine*, 29 May 1944, featured "5000th Fortress"... "Seattle Plant No. 2 Sets Record".

The snag here, was that the IAM Grand Lodge was still resisting efforts to organize aircraft workers on an industrial, instead of a craft basis. This opened the door to CIO organizers because CIO unions extended jurisdiction over a whole industrial plant regardless of crafts within. [8]

Air Corps Chief of Staff General Oscar Westover opposed B-17 purchase, but when he was killed in an airplane accident General Hap Arnold succeeded Westover. Army Chief of Staff George C. Marshall also believed in the importance of strategic bombing. Once President Roosevelt saw the fearsome buildup of German air power he allied with proponents Arnold and Marshall. When Secretary of War Harry Woodring resisted even sending Great Britain ten B-17s after the fall of Poland in September 1939 FDR fired him, clearing the way for large scale B-17 production. [9]

While waiting for B-17 orders Boeing began planning for a long range bomber, establishing a special department to come up with the design. Upon receiving an "Urgent" letter dated 5 February inviting interested parties to submit in one-month's time a bomber capable of ranging 5,333 miles at high altitude, capable of high speed, Boeing quickly expanded it special department to 1,900 employees headed by the renowed test pilot Edmund "Eddie" Allen. Allied disasters, climaxing with the fall of France in June 1940 sped up B-17 orders, and the Army also requested from Congress 990 B-29 bombers for which designing was still in progress. Bickering and carping about the Boeing design among the contestants ended when Boeing's Wellwood Beall convinced the Army to accept the Boeing design. Budgeted at $3 billion, construction contracts were parcelled out to four companies: Bell at Marietta, Martin at Omaha, Boeing in both its Wichita and Renton plants. The first B-29 came of the Boeing-Wichita assembly line in June 1943. By March 1944 the 175th superfortress emerged, but sat waiting for parts and modifications. Under intense pressure to meet a new 10 April deadline the first one flew on the last day of March, headed for India by way of North Africa. A fleet of them followed. They were destined for the Pacific theater, not for Europe. By March 1945 Renton's B-29 production was running at a six-planes clip per day. Orders for 5,092 B-29s were abruptly cancelled in September. Seattle's portion of the B-29 workforce was cut drastically from 35,000 to a slight 6,000. That in Wichita fell from 16,000 to only 1,500. Altogether 3,974 B-29s were built, 1,119 by the Renton plant. In Seattle about 7,000 B-17s had come off the assembly lines.[10]

### COMPARATIVE WAGE SCALES: THEIR SIGNIFICANCE

Passing reference was made to the aircraft industry in Southern California and to the CIO organizing drive there. Wage scales their industry set bore a direct relation to those at Boeing. An examination of the Southern California aircraft industry will show how it affected Boeing's union relationships.

Boeing's wage scale stood the highest in the industry, but it lagged far below shipyard scales. In part this discrepancy is attributable to the fact that shipyards had historically been thoroughly unionized, resulting in firmly established wage scales which were already in place when the shipbuilding industry revived in 1940. From the above examination of aircraft industry wage structures it is clear that unionization in the industry was barely in progress. And, despite its relatively high wage scales at Boeing, the company faced a steady hemorrhaging of its skilled and semi-skilled workers. They left Boeing primarily for the shipyards. Its labor turnover hovered around 100 percent, reaching even 130 percent by some estimates. The War Manpower Commission's Paul McNutt judged Boeing had to hire 150,000 workers per year just to maintain a workforce of 30,000. In recognition of this general flight of skilled and semi-skilled workers from lower to higher paying jobs elsewhere in the economy, but especially from aircraft production to other jobs, President Roosevelt issued an executive order establishing the 48 hour work week. The order took effect in thirty-one cities, including Seattle, immediately on 31

March 1943. To control the migration of workers from job to job a certificate from the War Manpower Commission was required henceforth. In the Seattle-Tacoma industrial area this meant Boeing might be better able to hold onto its workers. FDR's executive order was issued, however, at the most contentious stage of negotiations that had begun in July 1942 for bringing wage scales in the aircraft industry more in line with those of shipyards in particular. This contest, in which the even lower wage scales of the Southern California Aircraft Industry served as a magnet to which the War Labor Board seemed attracted, is covered below as a case study in the chapter on the Office of Price Administration ("Boeing and Local 751 vs. WPB"). [11]

In dealing with national labor supply problems a congressional committee conducted hearings on "congested areas". The committee knew from ugly rumors something of what it would find. The committee went about its business, abetted by the FBI, the War Manpower Commission, War Production Board, and the Navy. Wide coverage by the Seattle press and Kirkland's *Eastside Journal* contributed to the growing mood of resentment as the evidence mounted. Paul McNutt, head of the War Manpower Commission, pointedly made the connection between overmanning at the shipyards and the labor turnover at Boeing in a nationwide radio address of 20 August: "more Flying Fortresses were lost in Seattle last month due to manpower shortages and missed schedules than were lost over Hamburg". Boeing had been unable to meet its production schedules during the summer of 1943 due to manpower shortages. At the urging of the War Production Board the Seattle Chamber of Commerce established a Flying Fortresses committee which pleaded with clubs and churches to press upon area business firms to release as many of their workers as possible. Concurrently the company experienced a loss of 800 workers while the Lake Washington Shipyard was asking with innocent audacity for 1,800 more workers! [12]

An open letter to Commandant of the Thirteenth Naval District Admiral Frank Fletcher, by Robert Frank in his *Eastside Journal*, reported loafing on the job and mismanagement at the Lake Washington Shipyard. He estimated the yard was overmanned by at least 10 percent. The *P-I* reprinted his letter as well as news of a shipyard investigation initiated by the War Production Board supporting Frank's allegations. The *P-I* urged a "Diversion of Labor from the Lake Yard". In her study of the Lake Washington Shipyard historian Lorraine McConaghy indicates that both Congressman Magnuson, who headed the local hearing, and A.F. Hardy, state director of the War Manpower Commission, found all area yards equally afflicted. Hardy claimed 16,000 men could be released from area yards for employment elsewhere without impeding construction of the Navy's ships. Magnuson added that West Coast yards in general could absorb cutbacks of 20 percent without affecting production. [13]

There was blame all around: the Navy came under fire for overall supervisory neglect, indecision, and endless change orders. The Boilermakers Union Local 104 accused McNutt and Hardy of trying to direct workers to Boeing, while it deflected blows aimed at managememt. Shop stewards at the Kirkland yard attacked the *P-I*. Meanwhile Local 104 relaxed its work rules so that workers in one job classification could be diverted as necessary to other functions when their own job was caught up. In the fallout Rear Admiral Edward L. Cochrane conducted his own investigations, and essentially concurred with all the negative allegations. He, then replaced Admiral Fletcher with Rear Admiral S.A. Taffinder. The US Attorney brought fraud charges against Lake Union Dry Dock, Associated Shipbuilders, and Puget Sound Bridge and Drydock from information gathered by the FBI. Shipyard workforces were reduced by at least 10 percent; Boeing was allowed to raise its wage scales retroactively to an entry level of 82 cents per hour, still short of the shipyards' 95 cents base, but this timed with the start of B-29 production at the Renton plant. [14]

## The Port of Embarkation

Supplying Alaska became the primary mission of Seattle shipping during World War II. The Seattle Army Quartermaster Supply Depot was reduced after World War I to supplying the Army's minimal needs in Alaska. The depot was subordinated to the Army Transport Service in performing this function; it, in turn, was subordinated to the San Francisco Depot. Its modest operations were transformed by the sudden buildup of military facilities in Alaska after the fall France in June 1940.

The Army Transport Service (ATS) purchased the Pacific Terminals property in January 1941 to serve as the embarkation area. Port of Embarkation historian Vernon Carstensen reported, "In February Seattle had become the home port of transportation carrying supplies to Alaska". The depot also geared up to supply the Fort Lewis District, which enbraced Oregon and idaho. Commercial warehouse space was rented while construction of the Quartermaster warehouse was being completed. Beginning modestly with the departure in October 1940 of five ATS ships, by April 1941 more military freight was moving out of Seattle than from San Francisco. During the summer fifteen ships headed north. To meet the ATS need for more staging facilities it bought in June the adjacent Ford assembly plant. By August the operation earned the "Seattle Port of Embarkation" designation and was granted independence from San Francisco.

Civilians performed almost all clerical and warehouse work in the depot. The peak employment at any one time was 2,942 in April 1943. Turnover was heavy due to the relatively low pay. Overall 7,500 people worked there during the war, and about 4,500 of them quit in that period. Women comprised a growing proportion of the workforce, about two women to three men at the peak period.

Army troop buildup after November 1941 sent Depot personnel scouring locally, seeking out suppliers of cold weather clothing, sleeping bags and other equipment. That such sources for this gear had been in business since the Klondike gold rush days meant an enormous expansion of their operations and a further boon to the economy. [15]

To spur war production the Army and Navy issued "E" awards to industrial plants that achieved outstanding production levels. Although a comprehensive list of Seattle "E" firms is not readily available my calculations indicate no more than ten such awards were given in 1942 and 1943. In January 1943 the Webster-Brinkley Company and the Austin Company won their "E"s; the latter was the first construction company winner on the Pacific Coast. Western Gear, a gear and parts producer, won an "E" in February. Pacific Huts won "praise" if not an "E" from the War Manpower Commission and the Army for its work in building houses for overseas troops. Chemical plant operator I.F. Laucks won an "E" in May, as did a Boeing Ground Crew Training School for its training program. Whether the "E" served as an incentive is unclear, but it must have been satisfying to both employers and employees, particularly for these relatively small operations who won them. [16]

### Getting To and From Work

Seattle was about to phase out its old streetcar trolley system with trackless electric trolleys on its main routes, supplemented by diesel buses on feeder lines. Completion date was set for February 1941. New lines were started. As a concession to West Seattleites one line directly connected West Seattle to the Ravenna district a few blocks north of the University of Washington. For old times sake people could ride two No. 19s on their fateful journey, in the the company of a noisy automobile escort, to the Fremont car barn, now the Red Hook Brewery building. The steel rails were dug up and recycled. The debt acquired by the City, when it purchased the street railway in 1919 from the Puget Sound Traction, Power and Light Company, had been at the center of the city's politics for over two decades. The company had leveraged the debt obligations to acquire its publicly-owned competitor, City Light. In that it failed, as did City Light in its attempt to buy out PSP&L. This street railway conversion project had been undertaken in August 1939 with a $10 million loan from the Reconstruction Finance Corporation. While the end of an era was marked in taking the City's street railway's debt out of politics, the entry of the Bonneville Power Administration signified the start of a new one. [17]

Throughout the war the new trolleys were overcrowded. Automobile ride sharing, which was promoted by some large scale employers, provided some relief. Staggering of work shifts helped to somewhat modify pressures on the system. Grocery stores remained open til 7 PM to accomodate women shoppers and downtown office workers. However, when the Office of Defense Transportation learned that only two-thirds of the city's employers were complying with the programs the city was threatened in mid-1942 "to expect no more equipment for its public transportation system" unless it solved the problem. A comparable threat had faced the city during World War I. Currently, only Boeing, the shipyards, and a majority of wholesale warehouses had complied. Mayor Devin promised to "put teeth" into enforcement should that be necessary. Kenneth B. Colman, chair of the War Production Transport Commission, did his best to discourage Monday night shopping by limiting the number of trackless trolleys available at night; he encouraged shoppers to car pool instead. Gasoline rationing complicated the issue; if gas rations were cut the public transportation system would be overwhelmed, he warned. The rubber shortage further compounded the transport problem. Tire retreading came into vogue. By mid-1944 the tire shortage for passenger cars was relieved, though not for the heavier duty tires required by commercial vehicles. Over the course of the war the public learned the value of a public transportation system; Seattle's was carrying 100 percent of its capacity and 200 percent of what it was designed for, and that it could carry no more than what it was doing. [18]

Concentration of industry in the southern reaches of the city - Boeing, the shipyards, foundries, flour mills - placed special emphasis on getting a viaduct over Spokane street. At street level north-south railroad track crossings interfered with bumper-to-bumper east-west traffic. The Works Progress Administration and the US transportation commissioner promised assistance in early 1941, but funds had to be approved by the Army, Navy, the Defense Commission, finally by the War Production Board. The City Council set applications in motion: $160,000 from WPA, $340,000 from the Bureau of Public Roads, and $250,000 from the railroads. Meanwhile the City showed its good intentions by paving streets on Harbor Island. Not until December 1941 did the money come through: $968,000. MacRae Brothers, a Seattle firm, won the contract. Construction was halted, however, by the need for steel. The City's steel application, as well as others for steel, had been rejected by the War Production Board. There was simply not enough steel to go around. City engineers, however, decided there was sufficient steel to complete the west end of the viaduct, nearest West Seattle. They proceeded with that phase and prepared to use wood instead of steel wherever feasible, at least as a temporary measure. To the cheers of West Seattleites, who had pleaded for decades for such a viaduct, the west end part of the project was formally opened 18 January 1942. [19]

Meanwhile intense lobbying by Mayor Devin, City Councilman Robert Jones, the Chamber of Commerce, the Harbor Island area shipyards, Boeing, the Metal Trades Council, and Congressman Magnuson led to upgrading the priority rating for completion of the project. Magnuson's key position on the Naval Affairs Committee helped because the Navy department's approval was crucial for getting the requisite steel allocations. That about 30,000 workers from the shipyards and Boeing, just a few blocks to the south, crowded onto the streets at shift-change times, where they might stall at the railroad crossings, clearly dramatized Seattle's traffic plight. Finally approval came from the WPB's governmental division whose head was a former liberal congressional sidekick of Magnuson's, Maury Maverick. The viaduct received priority rating, which assured access to the needed construction materials through October 1943. Work quickly moved ahead and the viaduct was completed January 1944. [20]

Shipyard workers from both Bremerton and Kirkland overflowed their shipbuilding bases, seeking lodging in Seattle's own overwhelmed facilities as they ferried back and forth: to and from Elliott Bay to Bremerton by an augmented ferry fleet and to and from the Madison Park ferry dock and Kirkland.

### SEATTLE'S CONGRESSIONAL LIAISON: WARREN G. MAGNUSON

Throughout the 1940s Warren Magnuson played a key role in securing legislation and removing bureaucratic bottlenecks favoring Seattle and the state. In Washington, D.C. he worked closely with the Seattle Chamber of Commerce's representative, John Underwood. Magnuson moved to Seattle in 1925, entered the University of Washington, supported by taking odd jobs, including one as an ice deliveryman, for which he joined the Teamsters Union. This probably brought him into early contact with Dave Beck. Upon graduation he entered law school and met the aspiring Democratic party leader Scott Bullitt, who took him under his wing. Bullitt introduced Magnuson to Democratic party politics by appointing him a delegate to the party's 1928 state convention where the party came out against prohibition and for support of the State Grange's public utility district bill. Magnuson had arrived in Seattle when a momentous charter revision fight had been in progress from 1923 to 1926. The fate of City Light's control and its Skagit River dam project was at stake. He must have learned then about the fundamentals of the decades-long fight between City Light and Puget Sound Power and Light Company, as well of the Municipal League's stalwart defense of City Light and its superintendent James D. Ross. Midway through the charter fight the sensational trial of Seattle's most famous bootlegger, Roy Olmstead, took place. Magnuson must have learned, then, much about Seattle's shadier politics and police corruption. After campaigning hard in Bullitt's race for governor and for presidential candidate Al Smith Magnuson was offered the Municipal League's secretaryship. Step-by-step he moved into Democratic party politics,

Warren Magnuson on short leave from Navy to Congress. He later resisted the return of the Japanese evacuees. At the top of a constituent letter protesting the return of the evacuees Magnuson pencilled his response: "Pronto. Answer tell her my long opposition to Japs shot at them." He seemed not to distinguish enemy Japanese from Nikkei. See endnote 13 in chapter on the Japanese evacuation.

just as the party was redefining its goals as a more urban-based party. Emboldened by the political contacts that came his way Magnuson ran for state representative in 1932 and handily won. As but one of the many new faces in the legislature Magnuson soon gained influence among those seeking remedial social legislation, so desperately needed at the bottom of those Great Depression days. He also promoted a bill allowing pari-mutuel betting and development of the Longacres racetrack, thus tying him to the racetrack crowd referred to above in coverage of the city elections of 1941, 1942, and 1944. With his winning personality he expanded the range of his political contacts almost exponentially. His sights next landed him in the 1934 race for King County Prosecuting Attorney, which he won so overwelmingly that he attained a real leadership recognition in the party. His performance and contacts made as county prosecutor led to his keynote speakership appointment at the raucous 1936 state Democratic party convention. In the course of his progress Magnuson joined the Washington Commonwealth Federation when the WCF supported the New Deal and the Popular Front. Congressman Marion Zioncheck's wild behavior and uncertainty about running for reelection caused Magnuson, with Teamster support, to declare for the seat. Zioncheck's suicide sealed the contest. Magnuson won another huge victory. When World War II broke out Magnuson was fully prepared to do all that a congressman could do for his constituency, as touched upon throughout this history.[21]

## Energy for War

Thrust into the war mobilization effort was energy supply. How much was already available, and from what other sources? How was the required economic expansion to be fueled? The answer seemed clear for this region: hydroelectric power. City Light had completed the first stage of construction on its third Skagit River dam in 1940. The huge demand for more electric power won authorization in 1942 from the War Production Board and the Federal Works Agency to raise this dam another 180 feet - named Ross Dam for the late City Light superintendent, James D. Ross. Power being generated at Grand Coulee Dam and the Bonneville Dam was being integrated by the Bonneville Power Administration into a single power grid, which was only beginning to be tapped.

Meanwhile City Light and several of the Public Utility Districts in western Washington were negotiating with Puget Sound Power and Light (PSP&L) for its electrical properties. They were frustrated at every turn. (City Light had initiated negotiations with PSP&L in 1934, when private utilities were in desperate financial straits.) Failing to get PSP&L to negotiate a "fair price" for its properties, the Whatcom County PUD commissioners chose the condemnation route. Although a jury set a value of $5 million, PSP&L insisted on $7 million, while the PUD commissioners insisted $3 million was adequate. The state Supreme Court upheld the jury award and upon appeal the Ninth Circuit Court also upheld the jury award in October. The US Supreme Court refused to hear the next appeal. However, the jury had attached a critical condition to its award: the PUD had to pay interest on the award up to the time of its acquisition. This put the price out of bounds for the PUD unless it could get legislation passed to alter the condemnation award. Governor Arthur B. Langlie, a known supporter of PSP&L, vetoed the corrective bill passed by the 1943 legislature. City Light superintendent Eugene Hoffman concluded: "We, here in Seattle, want an overall purchase plan to buy out [PSP&L] and distribute the property to the PUDs and cities." [22]

The State Grange's effort to allow the BPA to buy out the private utilities was lost in the flood of events turned loose by the attack on Pearl Harbor. City Light put to one side its proposal to buy PSP&L's city properties under these circumstances. Instead, City Light proposed on 20 March 1942 a "Cooperative Plan of Operation" to PSP&L, "to more efficiently meet emergencies created by the present war." City Light suggested freezing contracts, sharing power lines, and limiting competition. City Light had previously renewed its intertie agreement with Tacoma, and had contracted with the BPA for power interchange up to 200,000 kilowatts capacity. It also agreed to an intertie with PSP&L for exchange up to 30,000 kw capacity. City Light drew the line on cooperation, however, when the Federal Power Commission urged the utility to raise Ross Dam to 1,600 feet above sea level. Hoffman reminded the agency that it had already agreed, under pressure from the

BPA and War Production Board, to raise it to the height of 495 feet (1,525 feet above sea level). He judged it too much of "a gamble [to sell] surplus power to other utilities...[Because the City cannot control its rates] it must consider at all times the competition provided by the private utilities, whose position seems to be getting stronger instead of weaker...The City cannot take the chance of going broke." [23]

The private power companies now had the opportunity to tap into the Grand Coulee-Bonneville power grid as a result of wartime needs. Private power companies could thus undermine the public power preference clause required by the Water Power Act of 1920. The Langlie administration and the private utilites jointly proposed interconnection with the BPA's power grid. The State Grange leaders pointed to the endless obstructions imposed by the private power companies, and their opposition to federal dams on the Columbia before the war. Grange leaders countered with their proposal for a federal buyout of the private utilities. Given the war emergency the War Production Board settled the matter 30 September 1942 by ordering the "interconnection and integration of power systems' operations...As a result thereof, all resources, both privately and publicly owned, as well as industrial systems, were [to be] integrated through the Northwest Power Pool operations." PSP&L followed up in October 1943 by signing a one-year contract with the BPA for power. It did so annually thereafter, while continuing to press for long-term contracts. One effect of the power pool's operations was the general improvement of the financial positions of the private utilities, which had suffered so badly during the Great Depression. Indicative of their revival with federal help, was the complaint registered in the PUD Commissioner's newsletter of 20 March 1944, in which the BPA's flow charts showed the BPA "is supplying to the private utilities in the power pool nearly ten times as much as the private companies are supplying to the pool. Moreover [BPA] replaces the power private companies deliver over our lines and pay a mutually agreed price for the privilege of transmitting the power over their lines." The NWPP would continue beyond war's end due to the shortage of generating capacity in the region at that time. [24]

PSP&L's strategy of opposition to buyouts by any of the PUDs and City Light had been to refuse piecemeal acquisition by the prospective purchasers. The Whatcom County condemnation case inhibited individual PUDs from pursuing the same route alone. However, condemnation suits by three county PUDs (Thurston, Cowlitz, and Lewis counties) were in process and the company was stalling on Snohomish County PUD negotiations. BPA administrator Paul Raver handled their negotiations and had proposed formation of a non-profit corporation to undertake the purchase with funding assistance from the Reconstruction Finance Corporation. Federal Loan Administrator Jesse Jones, an opponent of public power, rejected such a loan. Raver then proceeded to set up a non-profit corporation to negotiate a joint purchase on behalf of BPA, City Light, and sixteen PUDs which had condemnation suits in process.

Raver assumed that the war had artificially stimulated the company's business, and City Light's Hoffman wrote: "it seemed to be the consensus of...those present that the pre-war figures would give a better foundation on which to build a purchase plan." PSP&L's Frank McLaughlin was never informed of this unstated assumption and would have rejected it out of hand, as he did when the offering price of $90 million was made 18 March 1944. McLaughlin insisted the figure should be closer to $130 million.

Meanwhile a referendum campaign was heating up: Referendum 25, which allowed municipals to join together for joint purchase of private power companies. Defeat of Referendum 25 by a vote of 373,051 to 297,919 was attributed by Grange historian George Melton to the infusion of newcomers to Puget Sound cities and the Tri-Cities area; these inmigrants had not participated in the running battles between the private utilities and public power forces that had dominated many of the political controversies since the turn of the century. McLaughlin laid out his views - also reflecting those of other business leaders - in the company's annual report: "The people have been repeatedly been told by these self-seeking politicians and socialists that the vast water power resources of the area belong to them and that they should not be used for private gain or profit." The Teamsters Union and several AFL unions, including the influential Local 77 of the Electrical Workers Union, also opposed the referendum. The rural vote, where the Grange was strong, favored it. [25]

Public power proponent US Senator Monrad Wallgren was elected governor in 1944. The PUDs and City Light collaborated with Wallgren's staff to test the validity of using a non-profit corporation to acquire PSP&L's electrical properties. Such a test case would have to run through the Superior Court to the state Supreme Court for final decision. The Skagit County PUD commissioners agreed to act as the purchaser. They were to arrange an issue of $135 million worth of revenue bonds for the purchase, providing two-thirds of PSP&L's stockholders voted to sell to the PUD. The suit was not filed until 17 April 1946, but it is appropriate to follow the case through, here, in the context from which it originated.

The court site was the Superior Court in Mt. Vernon. There, a vast array of legal talent from New York and Chicago law firms and banking houses were gathered. They faced PUD officials and spectators. The Weyerhaeuser Timber Company even filed as an intervenor in opposition to the prospective sale. On 27 April Judge W.L. Brickey upheld the PUD's right to make the purchase on its own and in behalf of the fourteen PUDs operating in the company's territory. As ninety days delay were permitted before appeal could go forward Weyerhaeuser attorneys chose to take full advantage, thereby postponing the appeal until the fall sitting of the state Supreme Court. During this interim two subsidiaries of American Power and Light Corporation, the Washington Water Power Company and Pacific Power and Light, joined in an initiative campaign to prevent the sale. Their initiative Number 166 was modeled on the 1940 initiative, Number 139, that voters then had resoundingly rejected. Initiative 166 also met defeat, 367,836 against it to 220,239 for it. Even Frank McLaughlin opposed it for "selling the stockholders down the river."

Composition of the state Supreme Court next became a source of conflict. Justice Walter Beal was appointed a Nuremberg war crime trial judge, leaving a vacancy. Justice Edward Connelly was then defeated in the 1946 election by Matthew Hill. Hill had chaired the committee opposing Referendum 25. He refused to recuse himself, however, despite a clear conflict of interest. The defeated Connelly then announced that in September - before the election - the justices had rendered a 5 to 4 decison favoring the PUD. In January 1947 Chief Justice James A. Mallery announced the most recent court vote, 4 to 4, still upholding the PUD purchase. But Mallery decided upon a rehearing of the case on 2 June. One judge was missing, though, and that meant the deciding vote. Missing was Justice William J. Millard. He had been given ample notice of the rehearing but refused to appear. In September he had been one of the five justices who voted in favor of the PUD. Later in June he switched, allying with Hill in the majority. Not surprising were the rumors circulating that Millard had been bribed, particularly when it was revealed that he had borrowed heavily from pinball operators. To deflect charges against Millard the *P-I*'s Fred Niendorff brazenly accused Grange Master Henry Carstensen of accepting a bribe. Credibility for this accusation withered after Carstensen told of a phone call he had received from a caller, who would not identify himself, but who seemed to be setting Carstensen up for a bribe. Governor Wallgren even considered calling a special legislative session to deal with the court's apparent corruption. No special session was called. The new 5 to 4 decision was allowed to stand, declaring the purchase plan illegal. [26]

## Transformation of Women's Roles

It seems clear that war production on the mammoth scale projected by President Roosevelt would have been impossible without deliberate recruitment of women into the manufacturing workforce. They were successfully mobilized and simultaneously transformed from their traditional relationships, at least for the war's duration. Not only was composition of the workforce radically altered by their entry, but equally dramatic was their function in the home. As women moved into the workforce in unprecedented numbers by mid-1942, their role as unpaid help in the family household was fundamentally changed. Should they be mothers as well, that role too was severely challenged. Newcomers to the area faced difficulties that most residents did not have to deal with, housing first and foremost. Given the already crowded housing scene, house and/or apartment hunting proved daunting. When neither could be found improvisation was essential. Working women sought access to trailer homes, converted basements, attics, garages, or seized whatever other opportunity presented itself. The assumption was that it was only temporary. The Civilian War Commission's Home Registration Bureau, abetted by the War Housing Center, stood ready to assist in locating what was available; but that was not much. Building restrictions were lowered to stimulate conversions, and a "share the home" drive was mounted.

Once employed, how would mothers arrange for day care for the youngest? How to manage preteens and teenagers when school is out? How to maintain a household, given food and gasoline rationing, and get to grocery stores. Often stores faced shortages of rationed items. And, usually the chain stores closed at 6 PM. Imagine the normal day: Getting to work on slow moving crowded buses or by car-pooling, then putting in a repetitiously hard eight- or ten- hour day, before returning home through congested traffic to face yet another chore. Next in the routine came making dinner for the man-of-the-house, should there be one, and children. Would there be energy left to entertain the latter before finally escorting them to bed? How were household tasks divided up? If they were, how did they do it?

The Seattle Housing Authority was the only agency prepared to deal with the housing emergency. Acting under the National Housing Authority, which was created in 1937 by the National Housing Act, the SHA initiated the city's first public housing project, "Yesler Terrace". The Act itself had two major objectives: slum clearance and provision for low cost housing. Families evacuated during the clearance phase (158 structures in the Yesler project area, affecting about 1,000 persons) were given top priority in returning to the new homes once the project was completed. Families whose income exceeded the maximum allowed were not permitted re-entry. This first public housing project planned for 690 units. However, the

Map indicating housing projects of the Seattle Housing Authority. The SHA's orginal mandate to replace slum housing with low cost housing was transformed into a program for defense workers. The SHA built about 6,000 housing units during the war. Most were concentrated in the industrial sector of the city where Harbor Island, Boeing, shipyards, foundries, steel and fabricating plants were located.

national defense emergency forced a departure from the Act's intended goal: "Additional homes for war workers became imperative. Low-rent housing must now wait for the duration." One qualification remained: rents were still to be based on "ability to pay", not upon "the economic rental value of the unit". As to Yesler Terrace 269 families were already in residence, 97 were about to move in. Conforming to SHA's unique non-discriminatory policy 24 of the families were non-white, including 12 African American. [1]

Jumping into the emergency the SHA first accomodated married enlisted personnel working at the Sand Point Naval Air Station. That project, begun in early 1941, was for 150 units. But due to the Navy's own discriminatory racial policy the SHA was unable to adhere to its own non-discriminatory policy. By September "Sand Point Homes" was fully occupied. Other SHA projects were in progress before the end of 1941: a Yesler Addition (178 units), Rainier Vista (500 units), High Point (700 units). These were all "permanent" structures, to which would be added Holly Park (1,250 units). Thirteen "temporary" projects would be built during the war. They would house about 2,500 more family units. Dormitories for single men and women were built during the last year of the war. Early in 1943 Reception Centers were established to temporarily accomodate male and female newcomers to the city. Rents in the Reception Centers were $4.50 per week for double occupancy, $5.60 for single occupancy.

The accompanying map (previous page) shows the bulk of the temporary facilities situated in the southern part of the city where shipyards, Boeing, the Kenworth truck plant, Isaacson's Iron Works, and metal fabricating plants were located. Widmer's Trailer Park on East Marginal Way near the Boeing plant accomodated 90 trailers, housing about 200 residents. Rents for space there ran from $12 to $16 per month, electricty and water included. Washing machines cost 25 cents an hour at Widmer's; at some others slot machines accepted nickels every twelve minutes. Should a tenant not have a refrigerator in his/her trailer - refrigerator production was shut down during the war - the ice man made daily deliveries to fill ice boxes. Milk deliveries were made daily as well. Comparable trailer parks were scattered about the Greater Seattle area, approximating small villages in size and social structure. Inevitably informal cooperative activities became part of these living circumstances, as they did in the housing projects of the SHA. Should there still be vacant space "Victory Gardens" often would be planted by the tenants. As accompaniment to the vegetable gardens the Civilian War Commission set up canning centers in the city to enable families without adequate space or equipment to do their canning; instructors lent "how to" advice. To supplement OPA's food rationing program - for which responsibility devolved primarily upon women - a Victory Garden Committee of the CWC encouraged the city's 50,000 "prospective Victory Gardeners" to register in February 1943 so that the amount of land and locations could be identified and the information conveyed to those wanting

*A trailer camp for accommodating families of migrant war workers. These living conditions contributed to the spread of juvenile deliquency reported by the newspapers during wartime.*

to plant: "Already the committee has obtained space for scores of landless gardeners and has enabled others to find residents willing to permit use of their surplus soil".

Locating housing projects and trailer parks near work provided some relief to the transportation problem. This was particularly helpful to working wives and mothers who had to perform multiple functions. In three projects elementary schools were set up, thus easing the problems of the working mothers. Some projects had day care centers. The 6,000 wartime units built by the SHA provided relief for those relatively few who used the accomodations, but these units did not come close to meeting the housing demand. A shift from the SHA's original prospectus was marked on 1 December 1942 when eligibility of the first group of defense industry employees was approved. [2]

Seattle's female employment between April 1940 and January 1943 increased by 55 percent. An additional 20,000 women were expected by July 1943 according to the Day Care Committee of the Civilian War Commission. Though critical to uninterrupted war production, mothers could not be expected to relegate their children to indifferent care - or none at all - just to join the workforce. Nursery

*Migrant war workers were provided with dormitories as emergency housing by the SHA. Some for men only as shown here, some for women.*

schools and day care facilities were needed should mothers continue to be recruited. Through the cooperation of the State Superintendent of Public Instruction, the Day Care Committee of the CWC, and the Works Progress Administration, which funded the staffing, a beginning was made. Rainier Vista housing project is an example of how a day care center evolved. Responding to the problem of working mothers a temporary day care center was improvised while application for Lanham funds was processed. A Child Service Center was erected within 90 days from a $20,000 grant and readied for occupancy in November 1943. Four teachers and two housekeepers staffed the center which was equipped to handle up to 70 children. While preference went to project residents applications were accepted from working mothers in the adjacent community as well.

Working mothers had to make, perhaps, the most difficult adjustments. In historian Karen Anderson's chapter on child care she concluded, "no proposed [social] service generated more controversy than that to establish child care facilities for children of working mothers." Joined in opposition were newspapers, state and local agencies that resisted even the hiring of mothers, let alone providing them with social services, especially child care. To name but a few opponents is a measure of their formidability: the *Catholic Northwest Progress*, *Seattle Times*, Washington State Defense Council, the State PTA, even US Labor Secretary Frances Perkins. Affected mothers of children under age 14 numbered 22 percent of the approximately 123,000 women employed in the Seattle-Tacoma industrial area by the 1944-1945 peak. Low income women of variable status were among the first to seek employment in 1942. Only ten nurseries operated in Seattle by late 1942: three private ones plus seven operated jointly by the Works Progress Administration and the Seattle Public Schools. These nurseries accomodated only 350 children, while 1,500 applicants awaited openings. For mothers living in trailer camps near the Boeing plant the King County commissioners donated land and four portable buildings for a day care facility. Newcomers assigned to the swing shift inspired some desperate mothers to take their children to work then lock them in the car. Their only other choice was to leave them "home" without supervision, unless a baby sitter could be found whom the mother could afford.[3]

Opportunistically, some unregistered day nurseries sprang up. Being unregulated and largely free from inspection by authorities these nurseries were overcrowded, lacked professional staffing, and threatened public health by their indifference to sanitation standards. Under these conditions, by mid-1942 major employers of women, trade unions, and various community and civic organizations joined to promote public day care facilities. Major opposition came from the *Catholic Northwest Progress*: "this government nursery business has an ugly Communist or Nazi flavor". However, so great was the emergency - so long as working mothers were believed essential to war mobilization - that agencies like the School Board and the state Social Security Department became more directly involved. The latter issued a set of guidelines for establishing private day care centers, which in turn were to be certified by county welfare departments, and to be subject to annual inspections. However, state and local financial resources were so strained in handling other priorities that only the infusion of federal money could deal with such a large scale problem. Fortunately Congress had passed the Lanham Act in early 1942 to deal specifically with communities being most affected by the mobilization effort. Lanham funds were applicable to both nursery schools and day care centers. Local school boards submitted their requests to the State Superintendent of Public Instruction who sent those approved to the local Federal Works Agency office. Once approved the State Superintendant administered the funds. To implement the program regionally city, county, and federal authorities met in October 1942 to coordinate a program for 45 day nurseries, 30 of which were to be in Seattle. Parents were to be charged a nominal amount, beginning with a fee of $.50 per child per day. Included were a lunch and two snacks. Given the start of the school year before the October meeting, the Seattle School Board began their preschool nurseries while their application was being processed. It authorized $10,000 to equip the centers, and the Seattle-King County War Chest underwrote the appropriation. Some existing WPA nurseries provided a core progam around which to build the larger one. A host of organizations volunteered to equip the school nurseries. Involvement of the Church Council, Women's University Club, and school manual training classes suggest the breadth of community commitment. Those in charge had to be certified by a physician, and they underwent a two-week training course. Karen Anderson speculates that many supervisors were probably drawn from the ranks of former teachers who, upon marrying, had lost their jobs. The UW responded to this need for child care by opening a course on child guidance and development in fall 1942. Concurrently the Seattle Public Schools offered a vocational school program on Family Life, which had graduated 70 students by January 1943. Training in home nursing classes was provided by the Junior Red Cross. [4]

At Boeing a Committee for Promotion of Nursery Schools was formed by various shop locals in December 1942 to work out a program with the State for Boeing's employed mothers. In January a legislative bill was prepared to provide supplementary funding for nurseries. At that time the Superintendent of Public Instruction had $850,000 worth of Lanham applications before it. Applications had already been approved for 40 nursery schools and 40 before—and after—school care in Seattle, along with two of each kind for Kirkland, near the Lake Washington Shipyard. [5]

The Seattle Public Schools launched an unsuccessful after-school program in fall 1942. Some free programs sprang up in various public housing projects and in local churches, where there were numerous working mothers. When Lanham funds finally reached the city in April 1943 the Seattle Schools began planning once again for a before- and after- school program, plus one for the summer. By June 1943 24 nursery schools were operating. More were planned. The summer program enlisted 500 children. From all these initiatives a solid foundation had been laid for child care in the city. Though falling short of the overall need of working mothers, nevertheless they were allegedly far better than those in comparable war industrial areas in the nation. [6]

But it was not smooth sailing. In August 1943 the Federal Works Agency rejected ths School Board's application for Lanham funds because the board could raise only 28 percent instead of the required 50 percent matching funds. To raise the fees would discourage mothers from working, thereby further reducing the already short labor supply. City councilman David Levine attempted to get major employers of working mothers to make up the difference but this failed, perhaps because of the 1,500 parents using the centers only 258 worked for Boeing, and 140 in the shipyards. Boeing, however, was eligible to apply for such funding on behalf of its own employees but apparently it did not. Its refusal contrasted with the initiative taken instead by its shop locals. Just when the School Board announced a rate increase in November the FWA reversed itself, agreeing to meet all costs not covered by the former $.50 daily fee. [7]

Children under age two were not effectively covered by the above programs. Private homes were an option, but they had to be licensed, thus a bureaucratic entanglement. Also ongoing inspections to enforce standards made that option prohibitively expensive. Group homes were another option, but the Federal Works Agency rejected them. This remained an unmet need. Consequently mothers of infants usually chose to stay home. Day care for swing shift mothers, despite the serious need, was another emergency not met. Also lacking was a program for convalescing children and a broad-based summer program for vacationing children. In general a program for extended day care to cover areas of greatest need never materialized, despite the promising foundation that had been established by fall 1943. Anderson concludes: "[B]y the last year of the war, Seattle officials were able to provide satisfactory nursery facilities in all areas of the city except the housing projects, where some pre-elementary schools remained crowded and poorly equipped." Her judgment however seems a bit harsh in light of the SHA's statistics: In the projects were 10 child day centers, 6 extended ones for ages 5-12, and 5 tenant-sponsored cooperative play groups, all operated under the Public Schools. [8]

However, as confidence in the existing programs grew, more use was made of them in 1944-1945. The Seattle Park Board provided summer recreation programs in its 26 centers, enlisting 714 children in 1944, 1,200 in June 1945. With the School Board, the Parks Department also initiated before- after- school programs during that period: 1,000 children by summer 1945. Lanham funds underwrote these programs. The US Women's Bureau estimated, nationally, that only 19 percent of the working mothers with children age 14 and under placed them in a public care center. When unable to place them elsewhere perhaps as much as 25 percent were left to their own devices. Complementing these public programs were formal and informal ones, programs provided by the YWCA, the PTAs, and neighborhood cooperatives improvised by working mothers. For non-working mothers the Public Schools offered guidance through its Family Life courses, which served partially as a funnel leading some toward volunteer work in the formal nursery schools. All told, public day care programs were succeeding by war's end. Nevertheless, Anderson points to the irony: Public day care centers did not survive into the postwar period, while the Family Life Program did, although it had proven of little help for working mothers during the war. The 1943 state legislature rejected bills drafted by Representatives Julia Butler Hansen and George Hurley to provide state funded child care programs. Most legislators agreed that home is where mothers belonged. Not until the 1970s would a movement be mounted for day care centers, public and private, in response to the growing proportion of working mothers in the workforce. To these working mothers were then added college level student mothers. [9]

## What Impelled Women to Seek Unconventional Work, Apart From Answering to the War Emergency?

The war factory woman was, in the main, a woman with a family and household responsibilties. She tried to maintain and increase her standard of performance in the factory and still maintain her standards for home and family. Faced with major difficulties in marketing for food and in securing any paid household help, she limited her hours of performance in the plant to permit her partially to fulfill her personal and household duties regardless of the factory's scheduled hours. (US Women's Bureau, *Bulletin 208*, "Women's Wartime Hours of Work", p. 3.)

During the early 20th century the proportion of women in the nation's workforce had been increasing as the nation became more urbanized and bureaucratized. This trend slackened during the Great Depression due to the scarcity of jobs and resulting competition with male job holders and expectant unemployed males who lined up to fill any job vacancies. This job competition militated against employment of women, particularly in those lines traditionally held by men: in heavy industry, in those commanding physical strength, in skilled and semi-skilled crafts (which were also union bastions of resistance to women and racial minorities), in the private business bureaucracies, to name a few. An underlying assumption about women was that their place was in the home attending to domestic chores, waiting upon husband and rearing the children. Recruitment of women into substantially all occupations became absolutely essential in the war economy by early 1942. Initial resistance to their employment in traditionally male jobs was adamant. As noted above Local 104 of the Boilermakers union was perhaps the most obstinate, but the Boilermakers were not alone. Historian Karen Anderson indicated even the reputedly radical/egalitarian longshoremen of the International Longshoremen's and Warehousmen's Union opposed their hiring. The Teamster-controlled taxi drivers resisted, as did the Municipal Transit Authority and drivers. Gradually these barriers were worn down as their employment, and that of Blacks, became recognized as indispensable. Most men gradually adapted to their presence, and employers became reconciled to trying out women. Many learned women could actually do it, sometimes better than men. Once female employment in "male" jobs was recognized as "only for the duration" did their employment become peacefully conceded. After the war women were expected to gracefully return to the home, to normality. Also seniority rules practically guaranteed this result. Of course women were not meaningfully asked their opinions. Most surveyed by the Women's Bureau declared their intention to hang on to their jobs as long as possible, or at least find the next best one available. Of these in Seattle, 57 percent of them had been employed before Pearl Harbor.[10]

The War Manpower Commission and Office of War Information stressed patriotism in their recruitment propaganda, but the main appeal to women seeking work was pay, particularly for working mothers. Mothers were 40.5 percent of the nation's female workforce in 1940; by 1944 their proportion was 45.8 percent of the female workforce. For those working mothers in the second youngest age group (age 24 to 29) their husbands probably were in the armed forces. These mothers probably had children age 10 or younger, and they received a minimum of $50 per month ($20 from the government, $22 deducted from their husband's paycheck). Mothers in this age group joined the workforce proportionately in fewer numbers than those in older age groups. Wives of servicemen without children, while better off than the mothers, could not lead halfway decent lives without a paying job. Also was the unrelieved boredom of staying home, particularly for newcomers to the area who probably would have found, at best, an improvised living arrangement. This was enough to drive mothers and childless wives out of the house. Where else but to a job, where there was companionship, novelty, even challenges in addition to a paycheck to make ends meet? [11]

Some comments women made in the "Aero Woman's Page" indicate a range of reasons for joining the workforce. Phyllis Proffer (Miss Boeing, 1942) reported she "always liked men's work better because it doesn't seem so trivial and sissified". Margery Lindberg: "This is my first job, and I really like it quite well". Burnetta Wheeler: "I used to be a housewife before, and the only machine I ran was a washing machine. This is fine for a change and I like the paychecks." Jean Kinkusich: "My job at Boeing is better than my last one in a cookie factory." Louise Lavelle: "I used to be an office worker, so this work is a nice change." [12]

## Discrimination of the Job

Once the novelty of encountering women on the shop floor wore off, the initial sexist displays of whistling at women passing by, sexual innuendos, obnoxious attempts at flirting, all such behavior aimed at keeping women in their place diminished over time. A wide repertoire for work dicrimination was open to men, however. Seniority for White men and their typically superior position in the chain of authority provided abundant opportunities for reinforcing the lower status of women who aspired to upward mobility in the workforce.

Women who wanted to move up in the authority chain - itself an indication they wanted a career, not merely a job - experienced resistance to their aspirations. Recommendations for promotion usually had to begin with a foreman's action. The foreman typically was one who had come up from the skilled and semiskilled ranks, was an old-fashioned trade unionist who, with his trade union brothers, historically had opposed entry of women and racial minorities to their unions. The likelihood that a favorable recommendation would come from such a source was highly improbable. As evidence Karen Anderson indicates that of the 14,435 women employed at Boeing in May 1943 only 3,062 were in semiskilled positions, and 109 were in the skilled roster. That younger, often more attractive, women were promoted should not be surprising. It was a complaint that the Aero Mechanics union chose not to take seriously. She noted that such discrimination was more flagrant in the shipyards. Local 104 of the Boilermakers had accepted women to membership as temporary mechanics only, thereby blocking their ascent to higher job classifications. Intervention by the Women's Bureau failed when the Metal Trades Council (dominated by the Boilermakers) rejected the idea. At Todd's Seattle-Tacoma Shipbuilding yard no women were elevated above the unskilled ranks. [13]

Insufficient pre-employment training for women also operated against their promotion. Although public schools offered "Free Education For Boeing Employees" publicly funded training courses could not accomodate the huge increase in applicants by late 1942. In mid-July 250 women were reported in training, but 1,000 women were needed to take the training for local defense jobs. In-house courses offered by Boeing and other large scale employers shortchanged enrollees by the brevity of their offerings, the effect of which tended to lock women into lower paying unskilled jobs. Not entirely: the Army Quartermaster Corps had an agreement with Edison Vocational School to train women in operation of power machines, contingent upon their agreeing to work in one of the nineteen textile factories under contract with the Corps. Another federal contract for training men and women in air depot operations at Paine and McChord airfields offered a path upward. The UW and public schools offered advanced courses for developing secretarial skills. Night course offerings inhibited attendance, however, when transportation proved too formidable at the end of a hard day's work. And, while the unions could insist on "equal pay for equal work", seniority and job-ratings that subtly distinguished between male and female categories militated against advancement of women. Also, when women tended to do as well or better than men in formerly "male" jobs, such as welding, drafting, and tedious/repetitious machine operations that work was typically stigmatized for being analogous to what women already had be doing at home.[14]

Just as women were entering employment at Boeing in significant numbers the editor of *Aero Mechanic* (11 May 1942) put the newcomers on guard to protect union achievments: "Women defense workers should never forget the fact that the armed forces of the United States are filled with men recruited from the ranks of organized labor...Perhaps the very job they are filling was formerly held by a union man...They have an obligation to those men who will come back...to go back to work at a decent wage, under decent conditions...[which should not] have been lost by disinterested women." The *Aero Mechanic* carried a regular "Aero Woman's Page" which ran a mixture of articles. Some praised women for their job performance, some for their feminity, even providing guidance toward it should they have lost their way. Beauty hints ran in most issues, such as "Permanent Wave Lifts

Tired Spirits"..."Instructions Go To Wallflowers". Recipies were offered to ease them through the stresses imposed by food rationing. One column was a "Production Girl's Diary". Another column: "What They Say", which quoted women about their work; most seemed positive. By September, when women had settled in more comfortably, the "What They Say" column quoted several women on the equal pay issue. All agreed there should be equal pay for equal work, maintaining the union scale. Complaints were frequent about their inability to keep up with the rising cost of living. Transportation costs and difficulties found voice.

An editorial of 5 November reminded women who objected to joining the union that all the benefits and present wage scales came to them free, the result of struggles of their union predecessors to whom they should pay their respects by becoming loyal, active unionists.[15]

As to the productivity of women at Boeing, Karen Anderson points to the monthly output of B-17s, which increased fourfold between 1942 and 1944, while unit cost decreased. This, while the company's labor force remained the same size and there was an incredible labor turnover in the skilled and semi-skilled ranks where men were concentrated. Women were a major proportion of the workforce during that time.[16]

## Militarization of the Economy

### The Volunteerism Phase

Based on prior US experience mobilization of the economy for national defense and then for war seemed predestined to pass from a voluntary to a regulatory phase. Such a cycle evolved during the Great Depression. It began with the National Industrial Recovery Act, conceived as a program for self-regulation of business through setting up of codes for individual product lines and types of trade. Trade associations, then, had been the administrative vehicle for code development and implementation. Large corporations dominated the trade associations and reflected their corporate ambitions. In 1940-1941 neither popular opinion nor the business community shared President Roosevelt's sense of national peril as the German military machine swarmed over Europe. That being the case a period of volunteerism had to be endured before the attack on Pearl Harbor made clear that volunteerism was not up to the task of mobilizing the nation for war.

Limitations to volunteerism became evident early in the defense mobilization period, before Pearl Harbor. In his January 1941 inaugural address President Roosevelt dramatized what was needed by way of production as the nation mobilized for its role as the "arsenal of democracy". One aim was to achieve the capacity to manufacture 50,000 aircraft annually. Aluminum, so essential to airplane construction, was critical in meeting this goal. The Aluminum Company of America (ALCOA) monopolized its production. The Office of Production Management contracted with ALCOA to build five plants, but left it up to ALCOA to determine when to build the plants. ALCOA chose to restrict supply in order to maintain its price structure and thus was in no hurry to fulfill its contract. Edward Stettinius, on loan from United States Steel Corporation and then commissioner for industrial materials, assured the administration there was an abundance of aluminum for defense. However, in the face of severe aluminum shortages, as reported by airplane companies, Senator Harry Truman's investigating committee urged the formation of new aluminum companies not comparably inhibited. This, the administration promptly proceeded to do. At the same time the administration mounted a nationwide scrap aluminum drive. Reynolds Metal Company thus got into the business with a loan from the Reconstruction Finance Corporation. The first price ceiling for the metal was imposed in March 1941, followed by two amendments. ALCOA was then warned on 1 October of a forthcoming price reduction, effective 1 November. Production then moved into gear. On the Columbia River, this applied to ALCOA's Vancouver plant and the start of a Reynolds plant at Longview. *1*

Automobile production proved equally difficult to mobilize. Its leaders insisted on producing cars and trucks at the rate of four to five million a year. Should their wishes be carried out 80 percent of all the nation's rubber would be consumed, 49 percent of its strip steel, 44 percent of its sheet steel, and other vital military resources. With the signing of the Lend-Lease Act in March 1941, to supply Britain and, soon, the Soviets, further stress had been laid on essential supplies. Leon Henderson, head of the Office of Price Administration and Civilian Supply, established 11 April 1941, found this intolerable. Henderson insisted on a 50 percent cut in car production. His Office of Production Management chief, William Knutsen, who was on loan from General Motors, balked at this suggestion, and counter-offered a 20 percent cutback. Cars continued, unstinted, to run off the assembly lines until shortly after Pearl Harbor. On 2 January 1942 a freeze order was placed on the sale of cars and light trucks. On 2 February rationing of cars began, with lend-lease customers first in line. FDR quickly replaced the Office of Production Management with the War Production Board, under Donald Nelson, a former Sears Roebuck executive. Military production finally won first place in the scale of national priorities, although its meaning took months to register. The president followed this up on 30 January by signing an Emergency Price Control Bill to stanch the rampant inflation of 1940-1941. Henderson was put in charge. Finding the steel industry reaching capacity, its production costs declining, and profits rising, Henderson imposed a price ceiling on all iron and steel products. As accompaniment he ordered a wage increase to be drawn from the higher profit margins while denying the industry a corresponding price increase. The OPACS proclaimed it "the most important single action taken by the Office during the entire year". [2]

The fall of France in June 1940 provided the rationale for passage of the Selective Service Act in September 1940, but by a slim margin of one vote in the House of Representatives. The German invasion of the Soviet Union in June 1941 made even more acute the need for a more comprehensive effort at defense mobilization. Yet, it took Pearl Harbor to force an end to the business community's voluntary commitment to full scale mobilization. With war no longer remote, "Win the War" became the dominant theme. A balance between the two competing sectors, deflected through a prism of producer-consumer pressures, continued to be sought throughout the war period.

The Office of Price Administration and Civilian Supply chose, initially, to establish price schedules selectively for what were identified as the most critical products and materials. This required endless conferences for each affected industry, beginning with mere "suggestions and warnings" and voluntary agreements. By August about one-quarter of the wholesale price structure was reported under control. Yet a disturbing 2 percent price rise had occurred during this period. Contributing to this rise were the monthly defense expenditures, a mere $200 million in April, but ten months later they reached $1 billion and were still climbing. Mounting consumer income and expenditures inevitably contributed to the inflation rate as well: from an annual rate of $65 billion in May 1940 to an "all-time high" of $75 billion in August 1941. Another factor was the proportion of private investment in plant and equipment during this period - 50 percent above the pre-defense period of investment. Fortunately, an increase in supply relieved some of the pressure on prices. Production was brought "to a level that was barely short of twice the average level prevailing between 1930 and 1939". While price control seemed "manageable" by the OPA (Civilian Supply had been separated in August), control was highly uneven. Bottlenecks resulted that stymied critical production. It became apparent that broad statutory authority was required to control inflation. The president presented a bill on 30 July authorizing the establishment of ceilings for prices and rents, and regulating the supply of essential materials. After extensive hearings - with submarines destroying supply ships in the north Atlantic as backdrop - Congress finally passed an Emergency Price Control Bill 28 November, just nine days before Pearl Harbor. By 1 December, however, "nearly" 40 percent of the wholesale price structure had been brought under control. Uncontrolled prices continued to rise, thereby putting upward pressure on the controlled prices. Most disturbing to the OPA was the "sharp upward movement in retail prices and the cost of living". Records indicate a price rise between February and December of 15 percent. [3]

After the attack on Pearl Harbor the Japanese advanced into southeast Asia and began cutting off vital supplies of rubber, tin, copra, kapok, tea, spices, vegetable oils, and other relatively unique but vital commodities. Rubber supply – 90 percent coming from southeast Asia - proved most serious. Consequently, the OPA "froze" the sale of automobile tires on 26 December, and directed they be rationed. So, the OPA was inevitably brought back to controlling at least some civilian supply. The OPA considered rationing to be essential for effective price control and soon gained it.

Soon came FDR's "blueprint for victory", delivered to Congress on 6 January 1942. To achieve military production goals of 60,000 planes, 20,000 anti-aircraft guns, 45,000 tanks, and 8,000,000 tons of shipping for 1942 alone the president insisted we must "devote at least one-half of our national production to the war effort". At this time about one-fifth of production was for the military. Obviously civilian consumption would have to be cut back. This meant rationing of civilian goods and regulating their prices to check market driven inflationary tendencies. Consequently, special emphasis would hereafter have to be placed on retail price control. [4]

Driving home the president's meaning for the populace sale of cars and light trucks were frozen 2 January 1942. During January only two retail price ceilings had been set. Due to the loss of Philippine sugar, the reduction of shipping from Hawaii and withdrawal of shipping from Cuba, sugar rationing was begun. Finally the OPA was given statutory control of prices and rents when FDR signed the Emergency Price Control Act on 30 January. Agricultural commodities were excluded from control until such time as they reached 110 percent of parity (they were then at 70 percent of parity), or the highest price obtainable at certain other specified dates. No farm prices could be fixed without approval of the Secretary of Agriculture. Under the Emergency Control Act maximum rent ceilings were to be established in "defense-rental areas". By 11 February 1942 21 additional price schedules had been issued, and about 120 voluntary agreements had been consumated. [5]

## Implementation of OPA's Statutory Authority

Thus far price scheduling had been on a piecemeal basis. Discouraged at the prospect of negotiating thousands more individual price actions in the wholesale sector, while hardly touching the retail sector, the OPA leadership reappraised their strategy. Immediate action seemed critical. "Inflationary pressures were spreading from one commodity to another - from local segments of the economy to the entire business structure". In but one year prices of food, clothing, and household furnishings had together risen 18 percent, and within these categories some commodities had climbed to 30, 40 percent and higher. Too much money was chasing commodities in short supply as curtailment orders forced production cutbacks of refrigerators, washing machines, and a host of other items whose manufacture included materials which competed with the military. While still appraising its strategy the OPA continued to issue emergency ceiling orders. A rent ceiling issued 2 March 1942 affected 20 defense-rental areas. In them 9,000,000 people were housed. Ceilings were placed on some food items. A gasoline rationing order on 18 March climaxed this phase. In the face of these uncontrollable inflationary pressures the president sent a seven-point anti-inflationary message to Congress. He asked for heavy taxation, overall price ceilings, rent control, wage stabilization, farm prices to be set at 110 percent of parity, an expanded War Savings program, rationing of essential and scarce commodities, and discouragement of installment buying. On the following day (28 April 1942) the OPA issued its General Maximum Price Regulation (GMPR), setting the highest price charged in March as an "absolute ceiling over virtually everything that Americans eat, wear, and use." Supplementary orders followed. At the retail level all retailers were required to publicly display the ceiling prices for "cost-of-living commodities" on or after 18 May. [6]

Allocation of control over supplies proved essential to the OPA's price administration. Consumer prices and rationing depended on supply, and supply varied. This meant that OPA had to negotiate with supply representatives in order to set prices. During late 1942 some supply sectors were structured into separate agencies. On 17 September an office of Rubber Director was established within the War Production Board with authority over the rubber program. On 2 December petroleum was placed under the Interior Department as the Petroleum Administration for War, but subject to authority of the WPB. The PAW was empowered to control the distribution of fuel oil and gasoline down to the retail level. On 5 December the Secretary of Agriculture received authority over food production and distribution. This was followed up on 23 March 1943 by assigning this authority to a War Food Administration, within the Agriculture Department. An Office of Civilian Requirements operated within the War Production Board to handle other supply rationing. Victor Thompson, in his study of rationing, concluded: "the original functional approach to civilian war organization soon gave way to commodity or industrial type of organization in many fields." The result was the installation of "commodity czars" for each industrial division. Each was staffed by industry representatives, leading to "self-determination by industry". The OPA, alone, constituted the consumer representative. What remained was some overarching authority to bring control over these contending agencies. Ostensibly this authority would fall to the recently established (4 October) Office of Economic Stabilization, under James F. Byrnes, former US Senator and Supreme Court justice. [7]

Between May 1942 and November 1943 food prices had risen by 15.9 percent thereby raising the cost of living without compensating wage increases. Acting quickly under the new authority ceilings were placed by the Office of Economic Stabilization on 90 percent of food items at the retail level, thereby making it possible to stabilize salaries and wages, and production materials costs. Rent controls reportedly were more successfully handled. In some cases rents were reduced, although that did not appear to be the case in Seattle, as shown below. Tenant tenure became made more secure from a national perspective. Once gasoline rationing was put on a mileage basis both gasoline and tires were better conserved. More food items were rationed. And the successful British program of "point rationing" for commodities in short supply would displace coupon rationing in March 1943. Before point rationing the US had coupon rationing, wherein a single coupon entitled a consumer to a specific amount of a single commodity, 3 pounds of sugar for example. Under point rationing a whole group of commodities were covered, enabling the consumer to choose their ration freely from among a variety of foods. Individual food items were assigned ration points, ranging from one to eight points. The consumer then drew upon these points when purchasing items by using new ration books. The new ration book had four pages of blue stamps and four red pages, each color applying to a different group of commodities.[8]

By the end of October the OPA felt that the new price/rent control program was becoming effective. Rationing, however, was more complex, was constantly improved as they gained more experience. Those items that had subsequently been brought into control by the GMPR (which had become effective in May 1942) had continued their upward pace, however, climbing to 18 percent before May 1942. Subsequent OPA actions dropped the inflation rate to one-tenth of one percent per month as more commodities were brought under control. One critical commodity, cotton, remained outside OPA jurisdiction throughout the war, and would contribute to the postwar inflation.[9]

## Implementation of Rationing, Price and Rent Controls in Seattle Area

### *Introduction*

Full scale mobilization, first for defense and then for war, required the recruitment of volunteers from the civilian population to meet emerging problems. The growing scarcity of goods and services, shortages in the workforce, the improvizational character of dealing with the unfamiliar and unexpected meant a continuous demand for capable people who could spare time and effort from their primary responsibilities, providing they were not dependent upon a paycheck for survival or maintaining accustomed living standards. The multitude of committees formed were typically chaired by prominent business leaders and people drawn from the social elite. Examples are Mrs. A. Scott Bullitt manager of the Stimson family properties to chair the Volunteers Committee, realtor Henry Elliott to head the Fair Rents Committee, Mrs. Neal Tourtelotte to head the Women's Victory Corps, and jeweler Leo Weisfield to chair the Salvage Committee for conducting the neverending salvage drives for tin, newspapers, scrap metals, and fats.

The Mayor's Civilian War Commission, established in 1942, recruited volunteers to help carry out the committee's various support programs. Without heavy reliance on volunteers the OPA, for example, could not have implemented its mandates and stayed within its budget. The Civilian War Commission grew out of agencies established for defense purposes. After the fall of France in June 1940 defense preparations seemed more necessary than ever before. Seattle shifted into gear in December 1940 when a Welfare Council Defense Committee was established. It soon became apparent that special subcommittees to deal with housing, recreation, hospitality, health services, civilian protection, consumer interests, public information, volunteer recruitment and related matters would have to be formed. One of the most pressing emergencies throughout the period was housing for the thousands of workers migrating to jobs in the city's rapidly expanding industries and in its burgeoning private and governmental bureaucracies. Mayor Millikin responded by appointing a Defense Housing Committee in March 1941 to investigate, tally, and register the available housing. To bring the skyrocketing rents under some control he established a Fair Rents Committee. Air Raid wardens and the Women's Victory Corps conducted successive housing surveys for the CWC. The Victory Corps recruited city-wide block leaders, who could be tapped on short notice to meet emergencies. More than 15,000 men and women became well organized air raid wardens. The wardens conducted the city's first blackout test 6 March 1941. Once at war the wardens staged their first review 7 January 1942 for which 13,850 wardens, of a total 16,000, turned out.

Sensing the need to draw all these committees under a single administrative body the City Council passed an ordinance (number 71346) establishing the Seattle Municipal Defense Commission 17 October 1941, only a few weeks before Pearl Harbor. Its first meeting took place five days after the surprise attack, 12 December 1941. Before the end of 1942 Mayor Devin assembled all the volunteer activities under his Civilian War Commission. One major area where volunteers were regularly needed for registration and associated work was in the various offices of the OPA.[1]

Henry B. Owen directed the state OPA office from the White-Henry-Stuart Building in Seattle. Owen had been vice president of Frederick and Nelsons department store in charge of personnel. So impressed was Mrs. A. Scott Bullitt with Owen's administration at Frederick and Nelson and at OPA that she made him manager of her KING radio station after the war. Future UW law professor Alfred E. Harsch directed rent control under Owen. The Region VIII office was in San Francisco, under administration Harry F. Camp, though not for long. In July 1942 the Manufacturers' Association of Washington joined with forty other state trade associations advocating state/local authority. The association requested "the installation here of a competent authority with full power to make necessary adjustments in keeping with local conditions...You can readily understand that [S.F.] has little if any knowledge of the intimate problems confronting the Pacific Northwest." Congressman Magnuson's local political confidant Howard MacGowan wrote him July 1942 from the Office of Emergency Management in San Francisco. Given the regional office's location there he contended: "They will place all contracts and service all contracts. They will allocate our electric power to plants of their own choosing, they will be developing more and more of our resources and dictating who will have charge of them. They control transportation. In fact between OPA and WPB everything is controlled." The Seattle Chamber of Commerce pitched in, alleging in February 1943 that within the past two weeks Northwest shipyards had lost in negotiations for a $1,120,000 contract for small boats simply because the San Francisco War Manpower Commission had designated the area as one of critical labor supply, meaning that with Seattle's labor shortage its yards implicitly could not do the job. The chamber contended the work would not have required hiring of additional men. The WMC soon established a regional office in Seattle, as would the War Labor Board in early 1943. Seattle, also, became the regional OPA office for the Pacific Northwest and Alaska. The Army Transport Service underwent the same kind of decentralization due to the inability of the Bay regional office to handle the mounting work load efficiently and without favoritism. [2]

Critical to implementing the rationing program was reliable and systematic registration of those applying for ration books. The solution was simple and cost next to nothing. With the facilities and bureaucracy of public schools already in place in substantially every neighborhood, nationwide, teachers and staff needed only to be volunteered through their patriotic school boards. The boards did not refuse. In Seattle, when Ration Book Two was issued in March 1943, teachers registered 397,063 Seattleites, issued 330,965 ration books, and handled 70,000 applications for fuel oil. The work was spread over five days. After the initial registration volunteers handled the issuance of supplementary food coupons, fuel oil coupons, gasoline and other non-food commodities as well. [3]

As noted in the introductory section, the retail sector received relatively scant attention initially, while the OPA tried first to bring wholesale prices under control. The OPA headquarters was keenly aware of this neglect and was then conducting a survey of retail prices. Illustrative, while the survey was in progress, I.W. Ringer of the Retail Grocers and Meat Dealers Association of Washington sent a copy of its 16 July 1942 resolution to Congressman Magnuson complaining that dealers cannot absorb the increases in wholesale prices because there is no ceiling on beef and labor costs. Until all costs that affected commodity prices were brought under control no fair prices could be set. With this objective in mind the association advocated "a mandatory national price policy under which the imposition of any and all ceilings at the retail level shall be accompanied by effective controls over all major items of costs at all levels..." This was precisely what OPA was trying to accomplish over endless objections from the business community. A black market in meats quickly developed, proving to be a chronic condition throughout the war. Preparations for the new point rationing system began in early 1943. J.S. Hoffman, president of the Washington Federation of Butchers, claimed that about 10 percent of the meat supply was finding its way to the black market because slaughtering and butchering lacked supervision and restaurants and hotels in the big cities were willing to pay above the OPA ceiling prices. Many of the city's butchers were not even posting the March 1942 price schedules as required, and they were overcharging whenever they believed they could get away with it. When the OPA completed its statewide investigations in early February it found only 27 markets in full compliance out of the 459 markets investigated. Seattle's more compliant butchers accounted for 26 of the 27 (127 shops were investigated in Seattle). OPA offices sent warnings statewide to 52 offenders that regulations would be enforced. To this Ringer retorted either butchers get higher ceiling prices or "we close shop". Ringer threatened a showdown unless the March 1942 ceiling prices were revised: "we are under ceilings a year old and we can't take it". Orders soon came from federal headquarters that the state OPA must crack down on violators. To this threat meat dealers claimed shortages would become even more acute. However the warning letters had the desired effect; most dealers lowered their prices and complied more fully in general. By the end of the month the federal grand jury issued indictments to only three of Seattle's meat markets and one packing plant. However so many violation reports kept pouring into the OPA office that the state OPA office pulled its investigators off other assignments to concentrate on meat violators, focusing on Seattle, Olympia, Centralia, Chehalis, Bellingham, Everett, Renton, and Yakima, moving from one city to the next in turn. Soon OPA investigators discovered that one major channel for the black market was the diversion of meat to frozen food storage lockers. Some consumers were going directly to the farmers, buying meat, and then putting it into their home freezers or in rented lockers. Washington's locker owners allegedly led the nation on a per capita basis: "we have more individual food lockers than any other state in the union". With pressure mounting against OPA to adjust meat price ceilings OPA announced overall meat rationing would go into effect 1 April 1943. At that time the red coupons in Ration Book 2 would entitle each holder to 16 points to cover purchase of an equivalent of one week of meats, hard cheeses, butter, margerine, shortening, edible oils and fish and meats in tin cans or glass containers. Breaking away from the original OPA requirement that applicants declare their home inventories of these commodities, consumers were relieved of that painful, though honorable task. [4]

    Sugar rationing highlighted another aspect of OPA's problems. Its supply was unpredictable, because of submarine sinkings of merchant ships, the supplying of the Soviets whose sugar beet lands lay under Nazi occupation, and the use of sugar in making industrial alcohol. City newspapers paraded an endless series of recipes using sugar substitutes: honey, molasses, and corn syrup for example. Arguing for more sugar for farm families and fruit growers Washington State Grange Master Henry P. Carstensen pointed to warehouses full of last year's beet sugar, helping create an illusion of a permanent predictable supply. Carstensen contended "The present sugar rationing program is working a disproportionate hardship on farm families, who [compared to urban families] depend so heavily upon home-canned and home baked foods [for which they need more sugar than do city folks]." [5]

Gasoline rationing, tied to rubber conservation, proved more complicated. Early in the program a nationwide rubber salvage drive began the last two weeks of June 1942. Contributors were paid one cent per pound for the rubber they turned in, whatever its shape or type. City service stations in the city provided the primary collecting points. Tire stockpiles were transferred to trucks for moving to a central depository. By taking in chronological sequence the following reactions will illustrate some political factors entering into the evolution of gasoline rationing. In September 1942 C.F. Hughbanks, owner and operator of "one of Seattle's largest independent service stations" complained to Ickes, Henderson, Magnuson, and Senator Bone about "fly-by-night" service stations that bite into allotments of established stations unfairly. Robert MacFarlane wrote to Magnuson in October on Seattle Yacht Club letterhead stationery, that since the Navy and Coast Guard have been urging small boat owners to have their boats available some "special provision" should be made about gas. And since saving rubber is not a factor and oil and gas stocks locally are higher than ever "all needs could be met". He asked "Warren" to look into the matter. On 7 November Henderson resolved the issue in his response to Magnuson: "The nation-wide Mileage Rationing Program will place no restriction upon the amount of gasoline that may be needed for the operation of motor boats in the Puget Sound area."

An OPA press release in early November 1942 announced that effective 1 December no passenger car owner will be able to drive more than 2880 miles per year unless he can prove occupational need. To implement the program "The rationing plan will require periodic tire inspections, and driving under 35 miles per hour [is required]." Speeders would even be reported to the OPA, which would then deprive offenders of gas ration stamps. Integrated into the rubber conservation program was the requirement that all tires in surplus of five tires per car were to be turned over to the local Railway Express Agency. Tire recapping was promoted in synchrony with gas rationing: McKales, a service station chain in the city, advertised a 24-hour tire recap service, "Preference Given Boeing Employees". No gasoline was permitted for anyone who was found in violation. As part of the certification process individuals were to apply, between 9 and 11 November 1942, for an "A" gasoline ration book which had coupons sufficient for 4 gallons per week. "B" or "C" books would be issued to those who qualified for more. In an OPA advance release it was reported in Panglossian style: "Seattle, Washington, authorities say conditions there are 'pretty good and improving 'and drivers in the wide-open spaces of the Rocky Mountains are responding cheerfully."

Resistance to gas rationing stiffened as the December starting date neared. Warren Hardy and others with offices in the prestigious Northern Life Tower, telegraphed "Warren" on 18 November 1942: "tens of thousands of people here believe gas rationing will complicate housing problem, disrupt industry and impede war effort". That same day Mary Kennett telegraphed Magnuson: "Seattle will be seriously handicapped with such strict gas rationing as planned...The transit system cannot possibly handle war workers to say nothing of people in non-war work".

The permanent gasoline ration program was installed 1 December 1942. Consumers were issued ration coupons, which they presented to the dealer upon purchase. The dealer, in turn, presented his accumulated coupons to the supplier for resupplying his stock. All dealers were required to register with the local OPA office, at which time each provided an inventory and other pertinent data. Eight different kinds of coupon books were issued. All having A-1 coupons had to use them within a specified period. Seven supplementary coupons could be issued, depending upon the consumer's eligibility. Ride sharing was also promoted by supplying dealers with blank forms to be filled out by those choosing to cooperate in the program to conserve gasoline. Buttressing these conservation efforts an "Organized Transportation Plan" was required for all plants employing 100 or more persons. Reflecting implementation of this plan the *Aero Mechanic* regularly carried a special column - "To And From the Job: Rides—Passengers Wanted" - announcing those who wanted rides and those who could supply rides. Labor unions in the larger plants promoted ride sharing. Community clubs throughout the city and its southern fringe set up ride sharing "depots"; by mid-November 1942 16 depots were operating and planning for more was in the process. A ride sharing drive, to be directed by the Women's Victory Corps, Seattle's block organizer, began in mid-January 1943. This was actually synchronized by Kenneth B. Colman, chair of the War Production Transport Commission. Colman called upon 187 plant transportation committees, the chairmen of the city's rationing boards, and the local OPA office to encourage them to join in the effort. Critical to implementation were the plant transportation committees, which certified applications for supplementary gas and tires for their fellow workers. The Victory Corps, in its survey of 2,500 homes reported 33 percent of the city's workers were ride sharing; 27 percent were car owners who wanted passengers; and 15 percent were using the public transit system. [6]

Gas rationing implementation proved tricky. The original tire inspection deadline of 31 January 1943 was moved to 31 March for "A" gasoline book holders and 28 February for "B" and "C" holders because inspection stations could not handle the volume. Also time between inspections was lengthened to six months instead of four, partly due to the decrease in gasoline consumption. A gasoline shortage was rumored in October 1943, but was quickly denied by OPA offices up and down the coast. The rumor proved true, however, because drivers in late December presented coupons for refills but got no gas; about 60 percent of the dealers had run out of it by noon that day. The state OPA blamed the black market, while independent dealers blamed the military and the OPA. Consequently, members of the Washington Gasoline Dealers Association developed their own preferential rationing program by giving their regular customers preference. Gasoline customers who were not so favored protested loudly to the OPA until the agency mediated on their behalf. That month the OPA enforcers suddenly appeared in downtown parking lots demanding presentation of gasoline ration books. The enforcers confiscated 57 of the 175 books inspected. The OPA set up a permanent force at the Longacres racetrack at the opening of its season and ostensibly at other "non-essential gatherings" to record licence numbers. These license numbers were then forwarded to the local ration board for followup. The names of 3,400 motorists convicted of speeding in May 1944, were turned over to the ration boards. They proceeded to conduct hearings and mete out penalties. And so it went over the course of the war. [7]

As to the role of the city's transit system its general manager Lloyd Graber expressed confidence once a shakedown period for gas rationing had passed. Graber boasted the transit system could handle the anticipated volume, though overcrowding would be unavoidable. Almost three million passengers a week were accomodated, a 10 to 12 percent increase over peacetime volumes. [8]

## *Rent Control and Housing*

By November 1941, rents zoomed out of control, well beyond the means of war workers. The OPA's western director, J.A. Bohn, requested local authorities to appoint a commission of inquiry. Mayor Millikin and Walter Williams, chair of the State Defense Council, named 24 prominent leaders for the commission, under chairmanship of realtor, Henry Elliott, Jr.. Millikin promised that other committees also would be probably appointed as need arose. While awaiting passage of the federal price control bill the commission gave first priority to finding accomodations to evictees because they could not afford the current rent increases. As a guideline Bohn suggested the committee look no further back than 1 April 1940 for a base date from which subsequent rent rises would be judged "fair and equitable". Meanwhile landlords were asked to postpone rent increases . A tentative date of 1 January 1941 was suggested at one hearing, but the Seattle Real Estate Board's representative strenuously objected. When the committee's report came out the first week of January 1942, "profiteering" was noted to be concentrated in the "low rent housekeeping room and small apartment field". Landlords tried to recoup losses during the lean years with high rents now were considered a "deplorable" lot. Nonetheless the committee backed off from the uncompromising landlord protest and deferred action until later. [9]

Rent control brought intense opposition from both big and small Seattle apartment house owners. The OPA selected 1 April 1941 as the freeze date for rents, effective 1 June 1942. Responding to a flood of questions directed to the OPA office, regional rent director Alfred Harsch issued a news release on 6 June which attempted to answer "five of the most common queries from landlords and tenants". A *Seattle Star* editorial of 15 June noted that all cities on the Pacific Coast had accepted the freeze order, but the "greatest confusion and protest is in Seattle". On 16 June the *P-I*'s front page column head conveyed a sense of the opposition: "Rent Freeze Order Rapped As Unfair". Arthur VanderSys, president of the Seattle Landlords Association and chair of the Seattle Homes Registration Bureau of the Civilian War Commission, claimed that of the 1,002 apartment buildings surveyed three-fourths were individually owned and operated. He noted this was "unusual in large cities". With such a large constituency it is not surprising that opposition could be effectively mounted. According to the *P-I*'s Douglass Welch Harsch's office was the scene of a veritable "free for all", all talking and no one listening, while the staff took notes. [10]

Magnuson's office, too, was flooded with protests. which his staff referred to Harsch's office. By mid-June landlords and apartment house owners formed their Civic Housing Association, under management of Floyd Oles, manager of the Washington Taxpayers Association. To accomodate the overflow from the organization meeting at the Chamber of Commerce auditorium a second meeting was held at Eagles Auditorium, where 700 met to hear VanderSys urge a freeze date of 1 March 1942. Harsch's office reminded the protesters that a registration of landlords was in progress and that it was possible for them to claim a higher maximum rent if "major improvements, as defined by law, have been made on rental properties." [11]

Union opposition to escalating rents developed. The 7 May 1942 issue of the *Aero Mechanic* complained of rent profiteering by some unscrupulous landlords who were taking advantage of "over-crowded conditions by boosting rents clear out of reason. Permanent tenants of years passed [sic] have been forced out..."The *Aero Mechanic* noted in its 4 June issue an ominous landlord response to OPA's 1 June rent edict, when one apartment house owner ordered his tenants out and simply closed his bulding. Many of these tenants were Boeing employees. Other apartment house owners, reportedly, contemplated similar action as their organized opposition was taking shape. In late June the AFL, CIO, and Railroad Brotherhoods formed a joint policy board expressing confidence in OPA's chief Leon Henderson and in Harsch to safeguard labor's interests. Harold Gibson, business agent for the Aero Mechanics Local 751, protested against attempts of the "real estate interests" to obstruct efforts to "have the maximum rent date in this area moved forward" inasmuch as rents had risen significantly even before 1 April 1941. A.E. Harding, executive secretary of the Seattle Industrial Union Council (CIO) wrote to Magnuson that landlords are "raising a large slush fund" to lobby against rent control policy. *12*

Floyd Oles joined the fray on behalf of the Civic Housing Association, whose president was VanderSys and future head of the Civilian War Commission's War Housing Center. Oles singled out Henderson for criticism and complained about the OPA's "90,000 men as professional snoopers". He insisted the CHA "will give 100% compliance with the rental freeze order whenever it is put on a fair and equitable basis as provided by law", which would prove to be only the CHA's selected date.

On 13 August the OPA rental division ruled that rents "shall not exceed the total rentals of the units within the building as they existed on April 1, 1941". Representing independent apartment house owners and operators, Harry Williams, secretary of the Apartment Operators Association complained to Deputy OPA Administrator Paul Porter. Although Williams agreed with the need for rent controls, he charged this ruling amounted to "preferential treatment [given to] life insurance companies and large property owning corporations who have vast holdings in multiple housing structures". Responding to these multiple pressures the Seattle rent division announced 29 September: "Government No Longer Fixes Rent On Dwelling Accomodations For First Time" on condition that the rate set by the landlord is not more than that charged for "comparable quarters on March 1, 1942". This was clearly an unmistakeable victory for the landlords who functioned as unit which could be mobilized quickly. Rents had to be registered within 30 days of rental. There was further loosening of OPA control: "Under the amendment the landlord now can set first rent without consulting federal authorities". *13*

Not content with this landlord victory Floyd Oles protested to Magnuson that the new regulation prohibited "sale of any property now being rented...It prevents war workers from investing a part of their savings in the purchase of a home...[This has resulted in a] bottleneck in the housing situation...One is led to wonder if there is not a 'fifth column' in government itself..." When James F. Byrnes was appointed head of the Economic Stabilization Office in early October with authority over OPA and other sectors affecting mobilization, Oles congratulated Byrnes on his appointment and ridiculed the OPA for its "stupidity". *14*

Oles's tactic, not yet widespread in the Northwest, was but a variant that was catching on nationwide. The *Aero Mechanic* reported a study by an AFL economist about landlords who forced tenants to buy their rented homes or be evicted. By contracting to buy the house, with or without a down payment, while agreeing to pay a rent above the rent ceiling, but without a real prospect of buying, the landlord would easily foreclose once the emergency ended. OPA headquarters recognized this tactic and issued an edict to prevent its spread effective 20 October. A down payment of one-third the purchase price was required. Also, eviction could not be executed until three months after an eviction certificate had been filed with the rent control office. Leon Henderson justified this edict as essential to maintaining wartime and worker morale. Prentiss Brown replaced Henderson, who was forced to resign, in January 1943. [15]

When the War Manpower Commission indicated in 1943 that it would cease recruiting war workers for the Seattle area unless more housing became available the City officials and Chamber of Commerce were spurred to action. The City Council had already loosened building restrictions in June 1942 to stimulate remodeling. Restrictions were lowered even more under the War Manpower Commission threat. With 4,882 families still looking for places to live the War Housing Center announced it would handle applications for conversions of houses with spare space into housekeeping units. Also eligible for conversion were vacant stores and other buildings. The federal government agreed to take care of taxes, assessments, mortgage payments, insurance, maintenance and repairs during the length of the lease under this conversion program. Center director VanderSys indicated special concern was for the older immigrants coming to the city with their families and crowded into hotel rooms. The Women's Victory Corps, in this tightening housing situation, foraged for living spaces, conducted a door-to-door canvass to learn and list sleeping rooms, board and room, kitchen privileges, and housekeeping setups. Newspapers cooperated by publicizing their effort. The *Times*'s 15 August Sunday edition, featured the CWC's "Share the Room" campaign in its rotogravure section. Because of a notable increase in the listing of rooms in private homes and family facilities the Homes Registration office moved to more capacious quarters occupied by the War Housing Center in the Douglas building. By the end of 1943 construction permits for 10,000 new homes had been issued and 3,000 conversions had been made. Family listings numbered 6,988, though applications totaled more than twice that number. Single room applications, on the other hand, outran listings 12,469 to 8,403. [16]

While conflicts over rent control ran their course more public housing was becoming available early in 1943. The Seattle Housing Authority, as the largest rental agency in the city, opened a project in January for temporary housing in White Center to accomodate Boeing workers. Applicants had to demonstrate need and their occupational classification had to be accepted. Close on the heels of this project opening came jubilant news from the National Housing Agency that 22,171 additional housing units were to be available between January and July to house an estimated 55,427 war workers and their families. The Lanham Act covered funding of all but 4,000 units of the 22,171. The 4,000 other units were to be privately financed. All units were of the 'temporary' category, mainly prefabricated structures capable of being assembled within 45 days. Twelve hundred units were in the

The Wartime Economy—Militarization of Economy/OPA     95

"Victory Gardens 101". Here two instructors are showing how it's done. Victory Gardens were urged upon households as a means of extending food supplies beyond what was rationed. Neighborhoods with empty lots were ideal. Cooperation among the family farmers was essential and contributed to neighborhood esprit. Five community canning centers complemented the gardening and rationing programs.

Georgetown area, another 400 just north of Sick's baseball stadium, and another 400 in West Seattle. [17]

The contest between the OPA rent control office and the real estate board and the apartment house owners continued throughout the war. Only the latter two groups remained under some control a year after V-J Day, when OPA was finally phased out. This contest is treated below.

### *Food Price Control and Rationing*

Ration Book Two was issued 1 March 1943 to implement the new point rationing program. In conjunction with this issuance, and to supplement the limited supply of fresh vegetables, the Agriculture Department and the the War Production Board encouraged families to plant "Victory Gardens". A special Victory Garden fertilizer was soon made available to those who were interested. The OPA announced to consumers that there would be price raises in February for a number of canned goods. Not all foods were under price ceilings, and some foods being

## The Wartime Economy

Rationing registration was done nationwide through the public school system as illustrated in this school auditorium. Teachers, school clerks, and custodians were "volunteered" for the task—a bureaucracy already in place. In Seattle, when Ration Book Two was issued March 1943 teachers registered 397,063 Seattleites, issued 330,965 ration books and handled more than 70,000 applications for fuel oil, over a five-day period.

produced used ingredients not yet covered by a ceiling price. The combination of uncontrolled commodities combined in a final product with those under control made price control even more complicated. In addition to OPA's efforts the *Aero Mechanic* and the "women's" sections of daily newspapers were full of advice on how to use ration books wisely, how to prepare foods economically, how to substitute one item in relative abundance for one that was not, how to maintain household appliances which were no longer being manufactured, how to maintain clothing, and answers to a variety of other consumer problems. Further complicating ceiling pricing was the fluctuating status of food supply. How wages and cost of living were tied together and affected aircraft productivity are best illustrated in the case of Boeing workers.

Supplementing OPA's efforts the Aero Mechanics union joined with other AFL and CIO unions to form the Labor Consumers' League to serve as the union watchdog and consumer advocate. The Aero Mechanics, being the largest Seattle union, led the protest through its newspaper which was read even by those not

# Betty Crocker
## Explains What You Want to Know About
# Point Rationing*

COMPILED FROM GOVERNMENT SOURCES BY THE HOME SERVICE STAFF OF GENERAL MILLS, INC.

*Let's call it "Food Sharing"... for that's what it is!

### WHY FOOD IS BEING RATIONED

To save the lives of American soldiers. Our young men, fighting on battle fronts all over the world, must be well-fed and strong. To give them the food they need as vitally as ammunition... to help supply our fighting allies... we in America must go without some of the food we used to buy freely. But *everyone*, through point rationing, will be able to get his fair share of the food that is available.

### WHAT FOODS ARE AFFECTED NOW

Beginning March 1, in addition to coffee and sugar, commercially canned and bottled fruits, vegetables, soups and juices; frozen fruits and vegetables, and dried fruits will be rationed. Other foods may be added at any time, so keep an eye on your local paper. You may apply for "War Ration Book Two" sometime this week. Watch your local newspaper for time and place.

### WHO IS ENTITLED TO WAR RATION BOOK TWO

Every adult and child in your family who has War Ration Book One (the sugar book). One member of your family may apply for *all* your new books. He must bring with him two things: (1) a declaration of the extra canned foods your family has on hand... *not counting home preserved foods*, (2) the sugar ration books now being used by your family (you cannot get Book Two without Book One).

### HOW TO DECLARE YOUR CANNED FOODS

You are entitled to have on hand for every member of your family 5 cans, bottles or jars, *eight ounces or over*, of commercially packed fruits, vegetables, juices, soups, chili sauce, ketchup, on February 21. If you have more, it's nothing to be ashamed of... *if you declare them to your ration board*. You also declare the coffee you had on November 28, 1942 over one pound for every person 15 years or older.

### HOW TO USE POINT STAMPS

In this first ration period, March 1 to April 1, use *blue* stamps lettered A, B, C. *Numbers* on stamps are their *point value*. Every person is allowed 48 points for this period. Each rationed food has a specific point value... which may change from period to period. You will give your grocer stamps (torn out in his presence) equal to the exact point value of what you buy, plus your money.

*Your grocer can't give you change in stamps, so don't waste your low point stamps on high point purchases.*

### WHAT NON-RATIONED FOODS ARE MOST PLENTIFUL

Grain products, such as enriched bread, cereals and flour, and locally grown fresh fruits and vegetables are still plentiful in America. Learn their nutritional values... how they can be substituted for other foods that are scarce. With wise planning you can still give your family varied, interesting and nutritious meals. Home Service Departments of food companies, utilities and newspapers can help you.

## How to Use Your Ration Book to Best Advantage

**MAKE OUT MENUS FOR ENTIRE WEEK.** List all the food you have to buy, and see how much rationed food you'll need. Then...

**COUNT YOUR POINTS.** If you haven't enough to buy the rationed foods you'd like, change some of the high point items on your list for low point items, or substitute non-rationed foods. Point values will be given in the newspaper and posted in your grocery store.

**LEARN ABOUT POINT STRETCHERS.** Cereals, enriched bread, fresh fruits and vegetables and many other foods are not rationed. Use them as often as possible to give your family nutritionally balanced meals every day. Use rationed food only when you can't plan your meal without it.

**AVOID WASTE.** Learn to use all edible parts of food. Plan to use leftovers appetizingly.

Write to General Mills, Inc., Minneapolis, Minn., for two new free booklets, "POINT RATIONING BULLETIN" and "POINT STRETCHERS", ways to use non-rationed foods and feed your family well.

### 5 Important FOOD SHARING  BROADCASTS

*Claude R. Wickard, Prentiss Brown*
*Major General E. B. Gregory*
*Milton S. Eisenhower*

PRESENTED BY BETTY CROCKER, FEBRUARY 22 TO 26

LISTEN TO **KOMO** AT 11:45 A. M.

**Your Grocer Is Doing All He Can to Help**
Your grocer is also rationed. He has to turn in points he gets from his customers to replenish stock. He is doing his best to supply you with good foods. Help him—shop once a week, *early* in the week, and *before* noon.

 **GENERAL MILLS**
*Makers of Flours, Cereals, Vitamin Products, Commercial Foods and Naval Ordnance*

Copyright 1943, General Mills, Inc.

When the British system of Point Rationing was introduced March 1943, the newspapers ran this simplified explanation by Betty Crocker of how it works.

employed at Boeing. Local 751 also broadcast on Radio Station KRSC each Monday and Friday at 6 PM, "Voice of the Aircraft Builders". Local 751 was becoming the liberal voice of labor. Recognizing that many consumers hesitate to report price violations of their grocer or meat market for fear of reprisal the 25 March 1943 issue of the *Aero Mechanic* announced a "mass meeting" for 8 April for all those interested in price control problems. "Five or six hundred" people attended the meeting at the Senators Ballroom to consider, among related matters, the mass picketing of price violators. The Little Steel Formula came under attack for holding down wages while prices were still rising. In May the Labor Consumers' League complained of rent "chiseling" by some hotels, which treated vacated rooms as permanent and then charged the higher day rates instead of the weekly rates. In early June the LCL, after congratulating the local OPA office for some recent price rollbacks, returned to its attack on the Little Steel Formula, hoping to catch the attention of FDR and Congress. The LCL began picketing meat packing plants in June when the National Meat Packers Association contested a ten percent rollback in meat prices. Packing plant owners in Seattle were charged by pickets as wholly opposed to the government's price control program, its price roll backs and subsidies. Swift's local plant was first to be picketed, soon followed by informational picketing outside the Public Market and the Security Market. The LCL contended the meat packers' resistance was but one step of big business to eliminate price controls altogether. Small meat packers and dealers in the area, represented by the Puget Sound Meat Packers Association, and the Seattle Retail Meat Dealers Association expressed interest in meeting with the LCL to deal with the alleged present meat "famine". When OPA labor office chief, Robert Brooks, visited Seattle during a nationwide tour, he congratulated the LCL for its work, urging local unions to join in helping the OPA control prices. Following this advice the LCL decided to flood the courts with violation cases and began instituting suits in the Superior courts. In August charges were brought against two alleged price violators, one for violating rent ceilings, the other for overcharging on a shoe repair. In December the LCL took credit for keeping Seattle's cost of living lower than the national average during the period from 15 September to 15 October 1943. And so it went.[18]

Rationing was essential for rationally and fairly allocating scarce commodities among producers and consumers while mobilizing the nation for war. To hold down the cost of living price and rent controls had to be imposed. Should they get out of hand labor unions would insist that wages be increased to match rising living costs. Should labor be denied justifiable wage boosts strikes might well follow with or without labor leader authorization. Strikes and their repression would not only impair the war effort, but domestic unrest would probably spread under banners alleging war profiteering whether that accusation was reasonable or not. Labor conscription might seem a justifiable alternative should production disruptions become common, but in a war to preserve democratic institutions this would be intolerable for a significant number citizens and civic leaders. The risks were too great should that alternative be chosen. However, in acting as the consumer protector and advocate in the federal administration, OPA administrators might seem to the present conservative-leaning Congress as potentially too protective should OPA be given authority over wages as well. Recognizing this possibility Congress granted wage controls to the War Manpower Commission under which a Wage Stabilization Board would operate. How the dynamics and interplay of these forces evolved locally can be illustrated in the efforts of Boeing management to stanch the incredible turnover of its workforce and of the Aero Mechanics Union to gain wage scales comparable to those allowed shipyard workers.

### Boeing and Local 751 vs. WPB

To make price controls and rationing succeed OPA and War Production Board authorities insisted labor costs had to be brought under control. Disparities, however, existed across sectors of the economy. Also, wages for the same job varied from region to region. Shipyard wage scales were significantly higher than those in the aircraft industry, so much so that skilled and semi-skilled aircraft workers were leaving for the shipyards "in droves" and to other higher paying jobs. Differences in pay scales were attributable largely to the relative strength of trade unions. Shipyards tended to be unionized historically by the metal trades unions, of which the Boilermakers were the backbone. Aircraft production was a comparatively new industry and as such was in the process of being organized. The aircraft industry in Southern California, recognized as the Pacific Coast bastion of the open shop, successfully resisted unionization. When Boeing won a contract for thirteen B-17s it chose to recognize its Aero Mechanics Union, Local 751 in 1936. Boeing wanted to stabilize its workforce for the long run by accepting a wage scale that was highest in the industry. For its part Local 751 promised not to strike and Local 751's parent, the International Association of Machinists, promised to mount an organizing drive in Southern California to take wages out of competition. By July 1942 unionization of the industry in the south was still thirteen months away.

A nationwide wage stabilization package for shipyards had been agreed, effective on the West Coast, 6 July 1942. The War Production Board stated it "intended to follow the pattern laid down in the shipbuilding stabilization conference". Its "intention" proved fanciful, even deceptive, as we shall see. The intransigence of eight Southern California airframe builders made the difference.[19]

On the heels of the successful shipbuilding conference the WPB announced a series of conferences for the aircraft industry to be held in Los Angeles beginning 6 July 1942. Representatives of the nine Pacific Coast aircraft manufacturers and the AFL's IAM and the CIO's United Automobile, Aircraft and Agricultural Implement Workers attended. Other representatives came from the War, Navy, and Labor departments, the War Manpower Commission, and the OPA. Paul Porter, chief of the newly established Wage Stabilization Branch of the WPB, would preside. Spokesman for the WPB stated the conference aims: develop a stable labor force, stabilize wages at a level designed to check inflationary tendencies, "maintain present sound labor relations in the industry" - this in the face of alarming workforce turnover and longstanding protest of the Aero Mechanics Union. All parties promised their "fullest cooperation". [20]

The *Aero Mechanic* compared average shipyard wage scales with Boeing's: $56 per week in the former, and about $40 at Boeing. That Boeing's average was $8 less than the Labor Department's "Health and Decency" standard drove home the point that in fairness a significant upward revision was justified. To do nothing meant Boeing would continue to hemorrhage its workers. War Manpower Commissioner Paul McNutt estimated Boeing's labor turnover at 130 percent: to maintain a workforce of 30,000 the company had to hire 150,000 workers over a one-year period. Entry level hourly pay was pegged at 62.5 cents, cumulating to a whopping $100 per month. Top pay was $1.23 an hour. Illustrating the monthly budget of an "average" Boeing employee ($.93/hour rate) the 17 December 1942 *Aero Mechanic* showed the following:

| | | | |
|---|---:|---|---:|
| Rent | $33.75 | Stamps | $ 1.00 |
| Groceries | 60.00 | Bonds | 18.75 |
| Milk | 4.85 | Gifts-donations | 3.00 |
| Heat | 8.00 | Union dues | 1.50 |
| Insurance | 6.00 | Phone | 3.15 |
| Gas-Oil | 5.00 | Cleaner | 2.00 |
| Rides to work | 4.80 | Shoes | 2.00 |
| Car Payments | 25.00 | Hair cuts | 1.50 |
| Medicine | 3.50 | Wife's Vanity/Hair | 2.00 |
| Dentist | 3.00 | Entertainment | 3.00 |
| Paper | 1.15 | Furniture | 10.00 |
| Magazines | 1.00 | | |
| | | | $203.95 |

That Seattle's cost of living exceeded that of any other West Coast city underscored the unfairness since the Southern California Aircraft Industry (SCAI) paid the lowest scale on the West Coast. Its wage scale became a magnet used by Paul Porter of the Wage Stabilization Board. Ominously, for the aircraft workers, on 16 July 1942 the National War Labor Board announced its Little Steel Formula, "to end the tragic race between wages and prices". The formula allowed a 15 percent increase above what the cost of living was 1 January 1941; however the War Labor Board limited that increase during 1942 to less than 3.5 percent despite an inflation rate in excess of 12 percent during 1941-1942. [21]

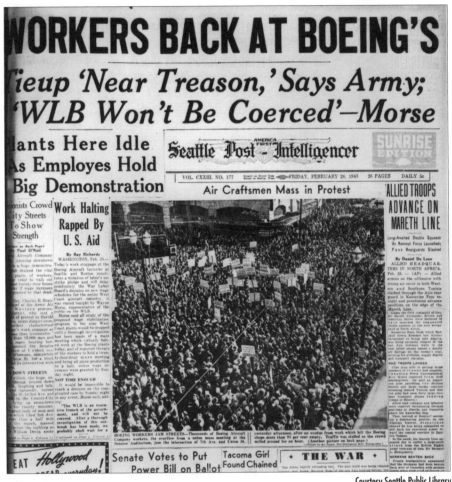

This protest crowd of Boeing workers was provoked by the measly hourly wage raise of 4.5 cents granted Boeing workers after eight months of tedious negotiations with the War Production Board to bring aircraft wage scales more in line with those of shipyard workers, whose base pay was at least 20 cents more per hour. Boeing labor turnover hovered around 100%. How critical this protest was in forcing re-examination of the issue is attested by the upward revision finally granted in August 1943.

The conference was quickly recessed on 16 July from the original Hollywood location and reconvened in Washington D.C. 22 July, where it stalled. Washington Congressman John Coffee brought the issue and puzzling delays to Congress's attention on 20 August pointing out that since 21 July IAM representatives had been in Washington D.C. awaiting the conference's reconvening. Federal representatives hesitated to act without authorization, and no one seemed to know who might provide it. An OPA representative, "Mr. Gilbert", alienated the labor delegation by denouncing collective bargaining itself. In announcing a succession of reconvening dates, he added insult by arrogantly bypassing the labor representatives. When President Roosevelt paid a surprise visit to the Boeing plant, 22 September, employees wondered if he had gotten Coffee's message. It seemed so, for in the 24 September issue of the *Aero Mechanic* was news that Paul Porter and a Bureau of Labor Statistics agent were to depart for Southern California to study the wage issues. The newspaper speculated that Boeing would be treated separately. [22]

The slowness seemed measured. When it was announced 28 September that Porter would be taking over for the War Labor Board as head of the Wage Stabilization Board the new date for the hearings in Los Angeles was set for 13 October. Then the hearings began anew. Local 751 representatives insisted on their original wage proposal of a $.90 to $1.60 hourly wage range (to be based on a new and more objective job evaluations/classifications formula). They coupled this demand with a retroactive clause and acceptance by industry to maintenance of membership agreements. To this Porter piously cautioned union representatives that wage scales could be allowed only "to correct inequalities or substandard living conditions". [23]

Faced with a steady migration of its male workforce to higher paying jobs, Boeing asked the WLB to consider a wage scale range of $.95 to $1.50. The company explained its labor turnover was 94.8 percent during the past nine months: 20 percent among the semiskilled, 19 percent among the skilled, and 43 percent among "beginners". To maintain its present force Boeing was ready to hire an additional 4,000 males. As an editor of the *Aero Mechanic* put it: "Boeings can no longer hire any other labor *but women*..." The company and Local 751 were in basic agreement at this time on job classifications. However, the Southern California Aircraft Industry classifications bore little commonality with Boeing. Their IAM locals supported Local 751's package. SCAI's disagreement would prolong the negotiations. At a mass meeting in the Civic Auditorium 9 December those in attendance were told: "according to our information [Paul Porter] is determined to recommend...the program submitted by the SCAI..." Five months of waiting had been consumed for an honest response to the obvious pay inequities. Porter postponed any decision, allegedly due to the illness of his statistician. The cause of the high labor turnover was clear, yet the federal authorities seemed catatonic in response to the emergency. Local 751, finally, was able to persuade the WLB to hold hearings on its proposal 8 January 1943. Senator Mon Wallgren informed Local 751 leaders of his support and of the fact that Truman's committee, of which he was a member, would soon be coming to the West Coast for hearings on the dispute.[24]

At the 8 January meeting in Washington the CIO locals and IAM presented a common front. While awaiting the WLB's final verdict an attempt to get support from the state Senate failed by a vote of 23 to 20. The House had previously voted unanimously for a resolution backing Local 751. Weeks passed until finally the WLB issued its decision: 4.5 cents increase for Boeing employees and 7.5 cents for "a large number" of the Southern California workers. On hearing the news an estimated 97 percent of Boeing employees staged a demonstration walkout, though not a strike. The *Aero Mechanic* reprinted a Portland *Oregonian* editorial of 27 February that protested the WLB's decision. Wayne Morse of the WLB sharply criticized the work stoppage, insisting the WLB would first investigate how it came about before continuing the WLB's ongoing study of the wage structure in the industry. Morse seemed to consider Porter's decision tentative. Gibson then called for a membership meeting at Eagles Auditorium for 25 February to decide what action to take next. Members voted for a 7 March mass protest meeting at the Civic Auditorium where Senator Wallgren would be the featured speaker. A delegation then left to persuade Mayor Devin to speak to the crowd that had marched to the County-City building. When Devin emerged he admitted little knowledge of the wage issue, which was up to the WLB, rather than him, and he expressed gratification that the workers were to return to work and continuing their notably patriotic contribution to building the Flying Fortresses. The 7 March meeting drew a full house. Except for drawing national attention to their plight and that of the aircraft industry, all this proved unavailing until the "shipyards scandal" broke in August.[25]

Before then negotiations had been taking place with the WLB's Joe Keenan, Boeing executives, and Local 751's leaders to somehow sustain B-17 production at scheduled levels. Boeing's Philip Johnson recommended two ten-hour shifts in place of the three eight-hour shifts as a means of dealing with the labor shortage. That did not carry far. Concurrently the Chamber of Commerce was staging its Flying Fortress labor recruitment campaign, pleading with area employers to free up as many workers as they could spare. After months of Local 751's negotiations the company also instituted a hot lunches program, and was about to build a cafeteria for plant 2. Responding to employee complaints, Boeing initiated a ten-minute rest period. Meanwhile the War Manpower Commission was pressuring the WLB to correct its past ruling and raise the Boeing scale. Coinciding with these promising developments was the current shipyard investigations (covered above in "The Wartime Economy–Introduction"), resulting in a at least a 10 percent cutback in shipyard employment.[26]

Finally in late August the WLB gave in. Boeing was allowed to raise its wage scale to an 82 cents entry level, topped at $1.60 per hour, with eight steps in between. The pay was retroactive to 3 March. Twelve vacation days per year were won as well as other union gains. Recruitment gathered steam after this attractive settlement. Between 26 September and 23 October the union reported clearing 2,348 "Flying Fortress builders" through the union hall, a result of the combined efforts of Boeing, the union, and the Chamber of Commerce's Flying Fortress committee's recruitment drive. Sealing this outcome the Chamber's committee, with War Department approval, staged an Army combat show at the UW football stadium attended by Air Force commander General "Hap' Arnold, Bob Hope and his entourage, plus British Field Marshall Sir John Greer Dill. A downtown parade preceded the show with General Arnold standing in review. Nailing down this result the War Manpower Commission issued orders designed to channel an anticipated 14,000 steel shipyard workers mainly to Boeing but to other higher priority operations as well. Just to be sure the WMC ordered "all nonessential businesses and manufacturing firms" in Seattle, Bremerton, Everett, and Tacoma to restrict their employment to 31 August 1943 levels. Boeing then prepared to welcome the 2,650 persons recruited from the Midwest by assigning personnel to greet the newcomers and their families at the railroad station where arrangements were also set in motion for transporting the new workers, to tide them over with loans, to arrange for housing, and to counsel them. [27]

With wages finally stabilized Boeing was now ready to start building B-29s at the Renton plant. Morale had been given an incalculable boost both for management and for employees. The company and union had waged this battle together. In 1948 they would split over contract negotiations and Local 751 would strike. The Teamsters were brought in as the company's preferred alternative to the Aero Mechanics Union. In the end Local 751 was restored as bargaining agent. This postwar series of events will be covered below in the chapter "1948: Liberalism in Disarray". [28]

## Salvage Drives

Salvage drives were essential to an economy unaccustomed to recycling materials once their primary use had been satisfied. Rubber tires, as has been seen, were collected first under a form of compulsion. No gas could be sold until one was certified to have given up all tires in excess of five. The CWC's Salvage Committee, under jeweler Leo Weisfield's direction, organized these drives which depended largely on volunteers. A fourth tin can drive was mounted in January 1943, attesting to the ongoing character of them in general. No sooner was one drive completed than a fresh one was started for the commodity. Newspapers even provided graphics for flattening tin cans. Scrap metals, newspapers, clothing, even hosiery for parachute manufacture were sought. School grounds, playfields, and empty lots often served as the initial collection points, from there to depots, then to the processors. Perishable cooking fats, were taken to the local butcher who granted usually two extra food stamps in exchange for the fat.

When one year's accumulation of scrap metals was collected in July 1943 from a depot at Second Avenue and Wall Street, the commanding general at the Port of Embarkation furnished the trucks and manpower: five trucks and drivers plus ten "Negro" soldiers. Bailing the scrap had caused a bottleneck leading to the huge accumulation. Once the Northwest Steel Rolling Mill in Ballard volunteered to use its compressing equipment for bailing the work moved ahead. The captain in charge avowed "the army needs the metal and we want to be sure they get it". Not only that but he promised more trucks and manpower should they be needed.

Quantities collected were impressive: tin cans were piled into 56 freight cars in October 1943. A fifth tin can drive started up January 1944; by August shipments were reported "up"; by November "More Tin Cans Needed" according to the *Times*. "Negro" soldiers from a First Avenue cantonment usually loaded the tin and scrap

Scrap aluminum is being unloaded at one of the collection depots. Jeweler Leo Weisfield chaired the CWC's Salvage Committee. For some commodities drives were repeated in quick succession throughout the war.

*Becuase 90% of the nation's rubber came from Southeast Asia, the OPA "froze" all tire sales 26 December 1941. In November 1942 to conserve rubber supplies, all car owners with more than five tires per car were required to turn in their surplus. Retreading of tire casings was introduced as a further conservation measure.*

metals onto Army trucks for delivery. Newspaper drives were mounted as competitions among schools. Occasionally there were drives for furniture and equipment destined for Army bases and USOs when such requests were received. After June 1944, when the Allied armies advanced over France, the Lowlands, and Germany, clothing drives were mounted to clothe the refugees left behind. *29*

Typically the various drives originated at Victory Square, the especially wide street between Fourth and Fifth avenues and University Street, amid fanfare accompanied by much newspaper and radio publicity, including neighborhood newspapers. OPA's programs benefited psychologically from these drives because they emphasied the shortage of everything that civilians were accustomed to having providing they had sufficient money for purchasing. Deprivations suffered during the Great Depression, however, must have prepared many for their wartime shortages as well.

## The 1944 Elections, City and General... Livelier?

Indifference to city elections continued downward, judging from voter participation in the 1943 primary. Only 16 percent voted, followed by a measly 24 percent in the March runoff. That the mayoral seat was not at issue undoubtedly was a factor, although turnout for the mayoral election of 1942 was not impressive either. That a war was going on and most vital decisions affecting the city were made elsewhere must be factored in. How many newcomers registered and voted is unknown, although their proportion to those who voted was probably less than for those who were established residents in the city. City politicians concentrated on the peripheral such as vice, police corruption, and traffic congestion. Federal policies and programs are what really activated the city's life, distinguishing that which was different from what had been. Political campaigning focused on matters that might lay within the power of city politicians to affect - those three items just noted. Incumbents rode the wave of prosperity, attributing prosperity to themselves as much as they reasonably could. Few incumbents lost their seats; nor did William F. Devin once he overwhelmed Earl Millikin in the 1942 mayoral race.

City politics became serious business in 1944, however. It was a presidential election year preceded by the winter mayoral race. The left-wing Washington Commonwealth Federation, which shunned the 1942 and 1943 elections, paid attention to the 1944 election by running *New Dealer* editor Terry Pettus for the city council and Florence Bean James for the school board. City councilman James Scavotto earned the WCF endorsement for mayor as did state Representative Jeanette Testu for a council seat, whether they wanted it or not. The WCF intended to make a comeback from near extinction by joining a revived New Deal coalition to re-elect President Roosevelt. Not to be dismissed as a factor was the Soviet Union, now an ally, other than the ultimate enemy. The Soviet Union was impressively rolling back the Nazis on the Eastern front day after day, all to the relief of the nation at large. In this context Red-baiting proved less successful than it had been. Although Devin employed this tactic his linking Dave Beck with the opposition probably was more decisive. Beck's overriding power and influence was ever-present and was widely resented, whereas the communist "threat" seemed much less real. [1]

The 1942 national election had brought sufficient numbers of conservatives to Congress that President Roosevelt's veto of the Smith-Connally Anti-Strike bill in 1943 was overridden. By this override and the nation's conservative drift away from New Deal social reform programs prospects for the Democrats in 1944 seemed dim. Fearing a repeat of the successful open shop movement that followed the Great War, CIO president Phillip Murray met with Sidney Hillman in July 1943 to persuade Hillman to lead a drive to re-elect FDR in 1944. Having been eased off the War Production Board as a result of business pressure on FDR, a depressed Hillman sparked to life at the suggestion. Together they won enthusiastic approval from the CIO's executive board. The CIO Political Action Committee was born.

Hillman quickly mounted a nationwide sweep to assess the strengths and weaknesses among the old New Deal constituencies. In labor this meant drawing in as many of the AFL locals as possible, attracting Blacks aspiring for inclusion, renewing diverse union ties, even appealing to the pro-Communist minority in the labor movement. It meant accomodating professional party machine leaders, farmers, progressive Republicans, known liberals, and church groups. While Hillman acted as the catalyst the CIO provided the organizational backbone of the drive as well as its financial support. Realizing that the Democratic party had lost much of its popular base Hillman staged a nationwide voter registration drive, working through CIO fourteen regional offices, spreading downward to states and cities and doorbelling in wards and precincts. During his visit to Seattle in September 1943 Hillman set up the CIO-PAC's northwest regional office, naming Roy Atkinson regional director and Jerry O'Connell, who had been CIO's Montana director, assistant director. The City Council cooperated by setting aside the week of 25 September as voter registration week. So successful was the drive nationwide that Congressman Martin Dies, chair of the House Un-American Activities Committee, sought access to the PAC's bank records. Hillman rejected this request, but invited Attorney General Francis Biddle to have the FBI examine them to learn if CIO-PAC had violated the Smith-Connally Act. When the FBI cleared the PAC Dies charged the PAC with being in league with the Communists. But so successful was the registration drive in Dies's own district that Dies withdrew from the Texas primaries. These successes captured FDR's attention and an invitation to consult with the president on the matter of a vice presidential running mate, one that at least the PAC would not oppose. [2]

While the political context for 1944 was being set nationally Seattle staged its primary election in February. Devin led runnerup James Scavotto by more than 15,000 votes. The *P-I*'s veteran city hall reporter, Carl Cooper, predicted that sheriff W.B. Severyns's third place votes would fall mainly to Scavotto and Frank MaCaffrey's fourth place votes would go largely to Devin. The huge winning margins piled up by council incumbents Mrs. F.F. (Mildred) Powell and John Carroll assured their victories in the finals. As between Jeanette Testu and Alfred Rochester for the third council position, it could go either way. Pettus and James lost in the primary. Complicating predictions was expectation that in the finals 30,000 more votes would be cast than had been cast in the primaries.

The mayoral finalists began with Devin Red-baiting Scavotto in a "sensational" radio broadcast for having sought and got support from the Washington Commonwealth Federation, "He has climbed onto their band-wagon and become close friends with their editor, Terry Pettus, and Howard Costigan and Hugh DeLacy". In questioning the WCF's Americanism he implied the same for Scavotto. Scavotto promised a clean city, "Vice and venereal disease must be kept to the lowest possible minimum". He accused Devin of being a do-nothing mayor, to which DeLacy supplied detail. But when the campaign heated up on Wednesday the 8th, Scavotto claimed nothing more than having support of ordinary working people, while Devin beamed accomplishments made during his administration in meeting wartime demands for more housing, improving the transit system, requiring police crackdown on gambling and prostitution, and establishing a leading civilian defense program. As in 1942 Devin again received the backing of the AFL's Leo Flynn. Scavotto attributed to Devin the loss of shipbuilding contracts to Oregon and California by reason of conditions exposed in the recent local shipyard investigations. Finally the Teamsters came out of hiding on the Saturday the 11th, attacking Devin, predicting the mayor's re-election would be the "first step in a reactionary program planned for the city and the state..." Scavotto boasted "Seattle can and should be the New York of the Pacific Coast", implying that Devin was at fault for it not happening. Once the Teamsters entered the campaign Devin repeated his 1942 attacks on Dave Beck: "The forces of the Washington Commonwealth Federation and Dave Beck have taken over my opponent's campaign..." Judging from the newspaper coverage it is apparent that Scavotto never moved beyond generalities while claiming nevertheless that he had a program. The election results showed the effect of a lackluster campaign. Devin won re-election by a majority of almost 17,000 votes (57,672 to 40,738). Mildred Powell and John Carroll each got more than 65,000 votes, and third place on the council went to Alfred Rochester, with 39,219 votes. [3]


Warmup for the 1944 general election was occurring just as Allied armies were opening up the Second Front in Normandy. To avoid violating the Smith-Connally Act's prohibition on union political contributions the CIO Political Action Committee became the National Citizens PAC. Its aim was to restore the decaying New Deal coalition. To minimize the influence of the Red-tainted WCF the King County Democratic Central Committee banned the precinct caucuses, where the WCF had been particularly effective in mobilizing its forces. District caucuses were substituted for the banned precinct caucases. Gas rationing provided justification for the change. The Democratic Party platform endorsed FDR for a fourth term and Henry Wallace for his running mate. The party at the state level backed Referendum 25. Referendum 25 would permit Public Utility Districts to join together for joint purchase of private utilities. At issue specifically was Puget Sound Power and Light's city properties and those in most western Washington counties. In addition the pension union's Initiative 157, to extend benefits, won a place on the ballot and it had Democratic Party support. Clarence Colman of Everett was elected chairman of the state party by defeating WCF-backed Ed Carroll, who had held the party chairmanship since 1936. Among the eighteen delegates to the national convention were some WCF members as alternates, Tom Rabbitt and Charles Savage. Delegates-at-large were two labor unionists, the PAC regional director Roy Atkinson, and Jess Fletcher of the AFL Building Service Employees Union. [4]

When Senator Homer T. Bone resigned to take a judgeship on the Ninth Circuit Court of Appeals, Congressman Magnuson chose to run for the US Senate. Magnuson had earlier flirted with the WCF and cultivated a close association with Dave Beck. Beck despised the WCF for its linkage with the ILWU and the fact that the Teamsters were contesting the ILWU for control of warehouse workers. The Teamsters had withdrawn from the State Federation of Labor as a step of Beck's for gaining control of it. Beck also was instrumental, along with Mayor Millikin, in turning back the CIO attempt to gain control of the Aero Mechanics Union in 1941. As noted above Millikin had opposed WCF influence in the local Democratic party and was dependent upon Beck's support. Hugh DeLacy filed for Magnuson's vacated seat in the First Congressional district but found himself challenged by two former WCF officers, Tom Smith and Howard Costigan. DeLacy drew support from three AFL unions, two of which were left-wing, the Building Service Employees Union and the Ship Scalers and Dry Dock Workers. Local 79 of the Machinists' Union also joined in support. The *P-I*'s Fred Niendorff reported interest had reached a "crescendo" in the Democratic Party, "where it is feared a split of the vote among the regular Democratic candidates might result in the nomination of a left-winger." Implied were the candidacies of DeLacy and Charles Savage in the Third Congressional district. As it turned out, DeLacy was better able to mobilize the WCF's old precinct apparatus than either of his two major opponents, and he won with 11,202 votes. Costigan finished 2,100 votes behind DeLacy. Despite the indifference of the *Times* and *P-I*, interest had fairly surged in the 11 July statewide primary contest. Of the 796,302 registered voters 369,293 actually voted, a dramatic upswing in participation. Unsurprisingly, Magnuson won the senatorial nomination. Senator Mon Wallgren, who had chosen to run for governor, also won nomination to run against incumbent Arthur B. Langlie. Wallgren's prospects did not look good and he received 100,000 fewer votes than the governor. WCF-backed Charles Savage won the nomination to run against against Fred Norman in the Third Congressional district. [5]

Since 1944 was a presidential election year the City Council opened the public schools for registration during the week of 25 September, perhaps prompted by Sidney Hillman's visit. This was all to the good, but then there was the campaign. Red-baiting surfaced when veteran City Councilman and former labor leader and interim mayor (1931-32) Robert Harlin won the Republican nomination to run against DeLacy. From his record DeLacy was admittedly vulnerable to such an attack, and Harlin lost no time in doing so, claiming DeLacy represented an "alien and destructive group which seeks to seize power and sovietize the United States". John Coffee, running for re-election from the Sixth Congressional district that included southern King County and Pierce County, had the traditional backing of the WCF. Coffee was also Red-baited, as was Charles Savage in the Third district race. Charles Lindeman replaced Boettiger at Hearst's *P-I*. After the Boettigers departed, John to active duty, Anna to the White House, the *P-I* resumed its opposition to the New Dealers, and supported Harlin, Savage's opponent Fred Norman, and Coffee's opponent. The *Times*, wanting a harmonious congress to support the expected Republican administration, promoted Republican candidates. [6]

Several Seattle businesses made special concessions to their workers to encourage them to get out and vote. Downtown and University District stores remained closed until 11:00 AM for morning voters. Todd Shipyards denied overtime work that day. Boeing released 3,000 employees from its engineering department, a more conservative element than members of Local 751, at 4:30 PM instead of 6:00 PM. The 7 November turnout in the state was overwhelming: 84.5 percent of those who registered in the state voted; 82.7 percent voted in King County, while in Pierce, Snohomish and Kitsap counties about 87 percent voted. Roosevelt's margin over Dewey was 125,000 votes. Wallgren rebounded from his poor showing in the primary and defeated Governor Langlie by 28,830 votes. Magnuson won the Senate seat for the first time, defeating former Tacoma mayor Harry Cain, who was still on active duty in Europe, by 452,013 votes to 364,356. DeLacy defeated Harlin for Congress by more than 15,000 votes. Henry Jackson overwhelmed Payson Peterson in the Second district by 74,676 to 48,974 votes and Savage edged Norman by a slight 4,439 votes. John Coffee defeated Thor Tollefson by a margin of 28,960 votes. Two Republicans won congressional seats: Walt Horan in the Fifth district and Hal Holmes in the Fourth. Russell Fluent, a WCF member, became secretary of state. WCF-backed candidates won impressive victories overall, an indication of a temporary decline in the effectiveness of Red-baiting as a campaign tactic. Two years later Red-baiting proved its efficacy as the key to anti-New Deal victories.

Historian Albert Acena points out the unevenness of the voting. Seattle voters abstained from voting for congressional candidates in significant numbers. For example 18,000 Seattleites who voted for Magnuson for the senate abstained from voting for the congressional candidate. 12,000 Seattleites who voted for Mon Wallgren in the gubernatorial race abstained from casting a congressional vote. The relative disinterest in the congressional races in Seattle made possible a DeLacy victory. WCF-backed candidate Charles Savage won his Third District congressional seat, which included Kitsap County and part of Seattle. The latter's opponent, Fred Norman attributed his loss to recent migration of shipyard workers to Kitsap County. Also, DeLacy led Harlin by 9,124 votes in Kitsap County and by slightly more than 6,000 votes in Seattle.

Referendum 25 lost by 75,000 votes, which was probably due to the influx of newcomers to the state. Newcomers as a voting element were unfamiliar with the issues involved in the forty-years-long struggle for public power. Supporting this interpretation, Referendum 25 lost by a 50,000 vote margin in King County, where newcomers were most heavily concentrated. Seattle City Light, in King County, had provided the leadership in the public power movement for forty years. The WCF's offspring, the Washington Pension Union fared differently in the voting. The pension union's Initiative 157 lost in the state by almost 215,000 votes. In King County, where the strength of the Washington Pension Union was concentrated, Initiative 157 lost by almost 49,000 votes. This decline of voter support for the WPU initiatves in King County is carried over to 1948. In 1948 its Initiative 172 passed statewide because of the rural vote, but it lost in Seattle. [7]

What did the WCF do in the post-election euphoria? With its president Hugh DeLacy elected to Congress, its executive secretary Tom Rabbitt called a Ninth Annual convention for 18 March 1945 to write its epitaph. Rabbitt viewed the WCF as having fulfilled its historical role as an anti-Fascist organization and that it no longer had a useful role to play. Acena writes:

> "Its demise unintentially marked an end to the popular front era which was almost co-extensive with the New Deal and second World War eras. The WCF dissolved in the interest of preserving unity in the Democratic Party."

That the Washington Pension Union had really displaced the WCF as the left wing organization with a mass base, and that the WCF had degenerated into a whispy "paper" organization by 1942, must be taken into account as well. The Washington Pension Union carried on the work of the dissolved WCF, with much the same leadership. Its effective demise, along with the "Old Left", was postponed until 1950, partially marking the end of an era. [8]

## 1946 City Election

Having served as mayor for almost the entire wartime period and at the height of a reinvigorated economy, William F. Devin was generally conceded victory in the 27 February primary. Who would contest him in the 12 March runoff became the focus of what the *P-I* declared to be the "hottest primary mayoral election in recent years". Eighty thousand voters were expected to vote in this first postwar city election. Who should file once again but Lieutenant Governor Victor A. Meyers. Meyers had made a joke of his run against Arthur B. Langlie in the farcical 1938 mayoral race. Would the electorate take his bid seriously this time? A former band leader and perennial lieutenant governor, Meyers was probably the most colorful politician in the state. But then voters might have considered the number two spot among the state's elective offices not to be taken seriously either. Meyers, not Devin, became the target of the six other primary contestants. One, councilman Frank McCaffrey, charged Meyers with drawing "left wing support". A fellow Democrat and war veteran, Joseph P. Adams, was expected to give Meyers the strongest challenge. True to expectations Meyers won the opportunity, trailing Devin by about 10,000 votes. Adams ran a poor third, McCaffrey a worse fourth. In the council race the three incumbents led handily: James Scavotto, W.L. Norton, and Bob Jones. Three others would run in the finals against them: Rev. F. Benjamin Davis, Frances Davis, and Terry Pettus, editor of the *New World*. For the unexpired two-year term Robert Harlin led, and then was to be challenged by Charles Carroll in the finals. [1]

Nominally city electoral offices were non-partisan. People usually knew the party alignment of most candidates, and especially that of mayoral candidates. Devin attracted traditional Republican support, business and professionals, and church goers. Whenever this coalition was dispersed public power, City Light vs. Puget Sound Power and Light, became the paramount issue. Public power had always drawn substantial support from the business community and from social reformers associated with the Church Council. Many influential persons in the latter group were alienated from the Democratic leadership and the Teamsters at this time because of their racist stance against the Japanese during the evacuation and later upon their return. The Church Council leaders lent a comforting shoulder to these victims, when not directly intervening on their behalf, as in the case of Arthur Barnett and Mary Farquharson. Since the City Council refused in 1943 to renew PSP&L's franchise after its 1952 expiration, the coalition held together. Meyers had always run for state office on the Democratic ticket. He openly declared as much for this mayoral race and was then regularly in conference with state party leader Jerry O'Connell, who had promoted the party's concern for the 1946 city election. To make Meyers look like a "machine" politician, Devin assumed the pose of a "non-partisan" mayor. When the Teamsters union declared its neutrality in this election Devin found no need to repeat the strategy employed in his previous two races, when he linked his rival with a "Dave Beck-Gottstein-police/vice/corruption" coalition. Also Devin drew approval from sixteen state AFL leaders who followed Leo Flynn's traditional declaration for the mayor. However, Meyers earned support from the huge Aero Mechanics Union. [2]

Non-partisanship disappeared when both the Republican party and Pro-

America threw their support to Devin. Devin's newspaper advertisement of the 9th listed an impressive wartime record of municipal improvements made under his regime. He took full credit for the improvements, and Devin pointed to the splendid volunteer work of the Civilian War Commission, which operated under the mayor's jurisdiction. The advertisement contrasted sharply with the lack of any comparable record from his rival, let alone any concrete program Meyers might envision. The race became strictly partisan: "conservative" as defined by the city's Republican party vs. "liberal" as defined by the state Democratic party. Results in the runoff offered few surprises: Devin defeated Meyers 70,542 to 54,249 and all council incumbents were re-elected. All bond issues passed, and most importantly a new city charter won overwhelming approval. [3]

The 1911 city charter had been amended over the years. The last time a complete overhaul had been attempted was in 1926. The 1946 charter still holds today. The fifteen freeholders came up with a version that had the backing of the Municipal League, the Central Labor Council, community clubs, the League of Women Voters and other women's groups. Draft copies were widely circulated to invite citizen input, unlike the previous 1926 version. Terms of office for elected officials were set including most critically that of mayor. The mayor's office would be for a four-year term, begun in 1948. Instead of a 1947 municipal election, the next one would be when six council seats would become open in spring 1948, four of them for a four-year term, while the two lowest vote-getters in the 1948 election held office for two years until 1950. Beginning in 1952 the offices of mayor, four city council positions, and that of corporation counsel were for four year terms. [4]

# PART 2

# THE SEATTLE CIVIC UNITY COMMITTEE

### INTRODUCTION

Racial tensions that developed during World War I, and that carried over to the early postwar period, were about to be repeated in the 1940s. The greatest inmigration in US history, up to that time, occurred from about 1915 to 1920. African Americans moved out of the South to jobs and prospects of freedom in the industrial cities of the midwestern and northeastern states. Southern Whites also migrated for industrial work, but they carried their Negrophobia with them. They competed for jobs, and the whole panoply of opportunities spun off that economic base. Racial incidents were common; some escalated into riots, of which eighteen were recorded from 1915 to 1919. The most serious one occurred in East St. Louis 2 July 1917 and resulted in great loss of life. Chicago's riot of 1919 resulted in deaths of 15 Whites, 23 Blacks. The same pattern of inmigration emerged in 1940, and with it the repetition of racial tensions. This time, however, African American leadership took on a more determined stance than it did during the Great War. [1]

Employment opportunities for African Americans provided the key to better housing, education, and cultural amenities. Their access to the range of prospective social and economic benefits during the buildup to a war economy from 1939 to early 1941 had proved disappointing. The crux of the problem problem lay in the combination of employer resistance to their hiring and to labor union restrictions against nonwhite membership. Richard Polenberg contrasts the behavior of Black leadership during World War I with that during the second war. Polenberg observed that demonstrations of loyalty and conciliating behavior had gained Blacks nothing during the first war, nor the period between the two wars; this time most Black leaders determined to fight toward racial equality immediately. Jobs on the massive scale required meant that significant numbers of Blacks ultimately would have to be hired, knowing from past experience they would be "last hired". Germany, which had made race central to its policies since the mid-1930s, provided a ready-made argument. Black leaders pointed to the hypocrisy of one of the nation's avowed war aims, expressed in the "Four Freedoms". Implicit in each of the four freedoms was racial justice. White liberals and the radical left joined with Black leadership against the racial injustices they witnessed. If the wartime opportunity was not seized, Black leadership knew nothing of lasting value would be won. [2]

The racial discrimination practiced by defense contractors, labor unions, and by the armed services led A. Philip Randolph of the Brotherhood of Sleeping Car Porters to promote the March on Washington Movement for 1 July 1941. Randolph intended to "shake up white America". This kind of direct action in which Blacks of all classes, and from both North and South would participate, excluded Whites. The federal administration faced a serious threat to defense production should the march take place. Was it possible to keep a lid on racial unrest while quieting the anxieties of Northern and Southern racists? This seemed an intractable problem. Failing to dissuade Randolph to call off the march, President Roosevelt and his advisors met with a Black delegation on 18 June, and out of this meeting came a draft of Executive Order 8802. One week later the order was signed after Randolph agreed to its modest provisions. A Fair Employment Practices Committee was established to investigate complaints of discrimination, though it lacked power to enforce decisions reached from its investigations. Also, as jobs gradually opened up for Blacks – about one million during the war, two-thirds to Black women – most of the militancy was siphoned off by then. Polenberg concluded: "most substantive gains seem to have occurred as a result of manpower shortages rather than FEPC action". Polenberg's conclusion about the nation as a whole is equally applicable to the Seattle-Tacoma industrial area during the war. [3]

Framed in this context: a mass migration of Whites and Blacks out of the South to defense jobs in the industrial midwestern and northeastern states, and to the Pacific Coast, crammed into inadequate, aged housing where that existed, competing for access to limited public accomodations, to existing public schools and sharing cultural amenities - all provided flashpoints to which racism might apply the torch. Race riots did explode in 1943. Early in June sailors attacked Mexican Americans in their Los Angeles ghetto over a period of four days in the so-called "zoot suit riots". Elsewhere Blacks were the victims, first in Detroit on 23 June; a second a month later in Harlem, though not involving Whites directly. There, it was a spontaneous mass protest against continued Black exclusion from the rest of American society. That one did not occur in Chicago was due to Black leadership prevailing upon the mayor to take early preventive measures. In Chicago, Blacks also had been steadily absorbed there between the wars, though not contentedly. Not so in Detroit, where defense jobs attracted a sudden influx of Southern Whites. The Detroit riot lasted two days amid such intense violence that Federal troops were called in to gain control. For several days troops patrolled the streets. Before it was over twenty-five Blacks and nine Whites were killed. One important byproduct of the Detroit race riots was formation of the Civic Unity Committee Movement. Civic leaders recognized that racial tensions were bound to persist and war production would be disrupted in the process. Typically CUC's lacked authority. They were heavily dependent upon volunteer staff and leadership, and woefully lacked adequate funding. Little could be accomplished under the circumstances. In addition, an unspoken policy to minimize publicity about "racial incidents" and evidences of racial discrimination minimized reporting about them. The Seattle CUC shared these limitations, but it was the only CUC that continued into the the 1960s. Its first notable achievement lay in paving the way for the peaceful return of the Japanese evacuees. Then the Seattle Civic Unity Committee turned to the problems of integrating African Americans into the city's cultural life. [4]

On 5 February 1944 Faber Stevenson, executive secretary of the Council of Social Agencies wrote Mayor William F. Devin, urging "the creation of a committee to prevent the development of interracial tensions, and to foster tolerance toward minority groups". As the city's African American population was tripling Mayor Devin had become aware of the mounting evidence of discrimination. Added to difficulties encountered in entering the job market was the appearance of "Whites Only" signs in cafes and restaurants, taverns, theaters, motels and hotels, and at public recreational facilities. And where such signs did not appear other indignities were projected upon African Americans. Responding in part to the above suggestion Devin manifested his genuine concern at the first meeting of the Civic Unity Committee later that month: "The problem of racial tensions is one which is frought with a great deal of dynamite because it deals with long established fears that have brought about racial prejudice...It is going to affect us as a city not only during the war, but also after the war. Now, it is our duty as citizens to face the problem together; if we do not, we shall not exist as a civilized city or nation very long". Notably, neither the *Times* nor *P-I* carried the mayor's announcement of the CUC's formation. The African American *Northwest Enterprise* did. For Howard Droker, historian of Seattle's CUC, this demonstrated the CUC's low-key approach: "The Committee preferred not to be known". That the CUC accomplished substantially all that it set out to do, might well be attributed to that kind of approach, at least in the 1940s. Most people, then, had yet to be convinced racism existed in their fair city. [5]

About the only relief from discrimination was found in the Seattle Housing Authority's (SHA) public housing projects. Administrator Jesse Epstein initiated on his own authority a policy of racially integrated housing, beginning with the Yesler Terrace Project in 1940. Other Authority wartime projects were in all-White sections of the city, where they were implemented over the protests of the surrounding population. Boeing and Todd Shipyard had their own housing divisions to accomodate their recruits. They complained to the federal authorities against continued integration of SHA dormitories built for single defense workers. Along with other business firms Boeing and Todd Shipyards argued it was no time for "social experimentation". When the dormitories did open Boeing and Todd asked for and got police assigned at their opening, but Epstein just as quickly got them called off. No significant racial incidents occurred in the projects during the war. Although the projects accommodated proportionately more Blacks than Epstein would have preferred, this was due in part to the general shortage of private housing and to the racially restrictive covenants enforced by city realtors. In responding to the CUC request in April 1944 for information on private housing in the city Epstein indicated that even in 1940 "the incidence of substandardness in negro [sic] housing was more than two-times the average for the city as a whole". Overcrowding was typical. With such limited housing options, applications by Blacks for public housing more than doubled in 1943, (from 15.5 applications per month in the first half of the year to 39.3 during the second half), and they were increasing. The SHA housed 217 Black families at the time of his report. At war's end the same area in the city that had housed the original Black population, then housed three times that number, about 10,000 more people in housing that already was largely substandard in the beginning. [6]

There were many indications of racial discrimination in Seattle. The Parks Department had originally reserved one day each week for Blacks at the Colman Pool on the shore of West Seattle's Lincoln Park. Fearing the spread of venereal disease, the pool was cleaned after use by Blacks. When four Black UW students were denied admittance to the pool in July 1941 Bernard Squires of the Seattle Urban League protested to Mayor Earl Millikin. Although the mayor promised an end to the segregation policy he took no action to enforce it, and protests were renewed in 1944. P-I columnist Douglass Welch reported denial of hotel accomodations to the famous Black tenor Roland Hayes in March 1942. Helen Harris, head of the Minorities Committee of the International League for Peace and Freedom, responded in April 1942 to complaints from nursing aspirants that the Red Cross and Harborview Hospital rejected Black applicants. The hospital superintendent informed Harris that, "We advise young colored women wanting nursing training to go to one of the several schools in the country where they train only colored nurses." So disturbed by the the growing number of cases of discrimination, and of police harassment the Christian Friends for Racial Equality was founded by Black and White clubwomen. In May 1943 a White employee at Pacific Car and Foundry, who objected to "skilled Negro workers receiving higher wages than many whites" won approval of a Captain Strecher of the Thirteenth Naval District to segregate the restrooms. Neither company officials nor union leaders accepted blame. Neither took action to reverse the policy when a fellow employee, Marjorie Pitter, protested on behalf of the Black men. Pitter's group persisted and eventually won, and Captain Strecher was transferred out of the district. Many such incidents were patiently recorded by the *Northwest Enterprise*, but rarely by the three major dailies. Although there were occasional incidents of police harassment and even brutality, Chief Kimsey seems to have earned the confidence of the Black leadership, in the view of historian Howard Droker. However, Kimsey announced in September 1943, that: "We are preparing for anything that might result from a crowded, *mixed*, and excited wartime population". (italics added). [7]

Simmering also was the African American resentment at the humiliations dealt Black soldiers at the nearby Army bases, located at Fort Lawton at the edge of Seattle's upper middle class Magnolia district and at Fort Lewis just south of Tacoma. A Black cantonment also was stationed on First Avenue in downtown Seattle. When Black soldiers took leave in the city, police and other authorities feared a racial explosion might erupt from any random racial incident that might be ignited by some daily confrontations. Indicative of the Army's discriminatory policies, Fort Lewis Blacks were assigned snow shoveling duty on the city's streets in February 1943. Relegation of Black soldiers to a segregated PX added more insult. Their accumulating anger finally burst 14 August 1944, when Black soldiers raided the barracks of the "Italian service unit". After the brief attack one Italian was found hanging from a tree. From the resulting court-martial of forty-one Black soldiers, twenty-eight were convicted and thirteen were acquitted. The guilty were given jail terms ranging from 4 to 25 years. [8]

An anxious Mayor Devin sought information on interracial committees from the Conference of Mayors. Although the executive secretary of the Conference of Mayors reported only Detroit and Baltimore had such a committee, Seattle was apparently the third city to form one. From this start a national information network among social agencies took shape. Included were the American Council on Race Relations, the Southern Regional Council, the various local chapters of the NAACP and Urban League, as well as their national offices, and the President's FEPC. [9]

When the National Urban League's executive secretary Lester Granger surveyed fifty-five CUCs in 1945 he found a high degree of uniformity in their makeup. Although typically interracial in composition, professionals were over-represented, left wingers were absent, and business leaders were highly visible. He concluded: "membership is eminently respectable, but not remarkable for qualities of dynamic leadership." Mayor Devin pointedly chose as members those known to him for their "racial tolerance", who also commanded respect in the community. Seattle's CUC was chaired by a bank president, George Greenwood, who had openly opposed the Japanese evacuation. He proved an effective leader, given the chosen low profile of the CUC. Arthur Barnett, also had opposed the evacuation and was the attorney for Gordon Hirabayashi, whose curfew violation case reached the US Supreme Court. Dr. Felix Cooper of the Urban League, Rev. F. Benjamin Davis of the Mt. Zion Baptist Church, and Lew G. Kay of the Goon Dip Company all lent an interracial feature to the CUC (when sociology professor of the UW, S. Frank Miyamoto, returned from the evacuation he was appointed). Business leaders included Mrs. A. Scott Bullitt of the Stimson Realty Company, iron works executive Henry Isaacson, the Northern Pacific's Robert MacFarlane, and clothier Alfred Shemanski, who was also president of the UW's board of regents. The CIO regional director Roy Atkinson and A.E. Martin of the AFL's Electrical Workers Union represented labor. Attorney Paul Bangasser was known for his civic concerns. Educators were represented by political scientist Linden Mander of the UW, and Mrs. Henry B. Owen of the Seattle School Board. In sum the Seattle CUC seemed to be a cut above Granger's national profile. It proved considerably more activist, particularly in the 1940s. Also, the CUC collaboration with both the NAACP and Urban League in dealing with individual cases and issues probably contributed to the exponential expansion of their memberships during this period. The Seattle NAACP started with 85 members and claimed 1,550 by 1945. The Urban League "tripled" during the 1940s, requiring a staff expansion in 1947. Both organizations, in turn, worked with the American Civil Liberties Union, the Anti-Defamation League, the Christian Friends for Racial Equality, the Council of Churches, and the American Friends Service Committee, an altogether an impressive local network. [10]

A July 1944 letter of president Greenwood to Ray Haight, Relocation Officer of the War Relocation Authority, provides a situation profile of Seattle and a projection of what the CUC intended to do in the future. Haight was clearly testing Seattle as the prospect for resettlement of the Japanese evacuees loomed. Greenwood indicated the two "fields of racial tensions" that seemed the most evident were the Negro and the Jewish populations. The former seemed clearly the more important to him, with the CUC devoting "practically all of our time to a study of it..." While contending that Seattle has been a "tolerant community" the city has "experienced a great increase in population, and many of our new people, both white and negro, [sic] have come from the south, [thereby complicating] our problem".

A sub-committee examined the most likely flashpoints: housing, transportation, recreation, employment discrimination, and "police attitudes". While "relieving congestion in negro [sic] housing...conditions are still bad", although housing authorities "have been very helpful". "Little discrimination" was found in the recreational field, although there is "occasional discrimination in restaurants and roller rinks, but our best public dancehall [the Trianon Ballroom] admits negroes [sic] and whites without discrimination."

In transportation, he continued, there are "serious difficulties", particularly when there is overcrowding, "with fault on both sides". However, transit authorities are aware and "doing all in their power to alleviate it." As to police attitudes there have been complaints of "excessively severe" treatment of "negroes *[sic]* under arrest". In conference with police authorities they deny any discrimination. And although sure that discrimination exists in employment practices among industrial employers and unions "we are not yet ready to form any conclusion".

In general, Greenwood continues: "We have avoided all publicity thus far, preferring to work quietly until we felt that we were in a position to make a statement that could be backed up with authoritative information." In this connection the CUC was collaborating with "an institute of government sponsored by the University of Washington", with the CUC presenting four sessions, one an evening session downtown. He concluded, recognizing that the CUC would have to deal with the "anti-Japanese feeling, but until the Japanese return to Seattle, we do not expect that this will be a serious matter." [11]

### Return of the Evacuees - Not Easy

From the time a Japanese "combat team" was recruited in February 1943 to prove their "patriotism", it nonetheless took little time for shaping opposition to the return of the evacuees. A shortage of farm labor led the Seattle Chamber of Commerce to endorse Congressman Henry Jackson's resolution "to investigate all activities of the Japs in the U.S. and see if there is a conflict between the WRA and Army in handling evacuated Japanese". Two issues were entwined here. One was the farm labor shortage, to which the captive labor pool in the relocation centers afforded a prospective solution. The other was the suspicion among western state Japanophobes and their congressional delegations that the WRA was coddling the internees. The *P-I* headline of 23 April 1943 caught this ambiguity: "Return Of Japs Here Opposed By Chamber". In late July acting director of the WRA, Leland Burrows complained to Congressman Magnuson, who had been an ally of Beck since at least the 1930s, that he saw no justification for Dave Beck's Teamsters Union's "widespread attempt to drive these people from employment in the produce business". Filling the paranoic air, the *P-I*'s 23 September edition reported "Revelations" by Oregon Congressman Lowell Stockman of land purchases being made in Oregon (Ontario, Nyssa, and Vale): "Infiltration of East Ore. *(sic)* By Japs Hit" . Picking up on information supplied by Magnuson, the *P-I*'s 25 September edition ran a headline, "Japs Reported Buying in Wash." *(sic)*. Continuing: if true a "tri-state alliance" will be formed to abolish the WRA. Also expressing alarm were

Washington congressmen Hal Holmes and Wenatchee apple orchardist Walt Horan.

Disturbed by Magnuson's public statements attacking the domestic Japanese, Anna Roosevelt Boettiger wrote him in October: "We already have in our country an alarming growth of racial antagonisms, and it seems to me that you and others are merely aiding and abetting this growth". Undeterred, Magnuson complained to Colonel Moffett of the Western Defense Command about the release of those of "mixed marriages" to "prohibited areas". Magnuson telegraphed: "Vast majority Coast residents violently opposed...To the contrary it is stronger than ever..." Throughout 1944 Magnuson's secretary Claire Atwood assured the many constituents who wrote him: "I am sure he will continue to advocate the point of view [that they should not be permitted to return] and exert every effort to keep them from doing so." [12]

Following announcement of the Army's "Permanent Exemption Plan" the *Times* and *P-I* reported the return of some evacuees in their 20 September 1944 editions. First to return appeared to be Kaoru Ichihara. She had been sent to Minidoka originally but was released in March 1943 to Spokane, where she worked for the Church Council. Gertrude Apel, general secretary of the Seattle Church Council, convinced authorities to permit Ichihara's transfer to Seattle, where she arrived 15 September to assume her former position with the Church Council. In this first group also were wives of Nisei servicemen. Uneasiness about their return was indicated when some applied for re-employment at Firlands Sanitarium. Dr. Kenneth Olson, superintendent of the sanitarium, was blocked by the city health commissioner, Dr. Ragnar Westman, from employing the fifteen applicants. Westman allegedly feared for their safety and the community's reaction. Mayor Devin told the *P-I* he "was opposed to use of the Japanese-Americans as nurses at the sanitarium at this time", and that: "The city government can't be the first to accept them". As to police protection against prospective violence Sheriff Harlan Callahan insisted he be presented authoritative documentation before conceding to it.

Brothers Takhashi and Fukashi Hori were observed sorting through items they had stored in the basement of their Panama Hotel. To Kent the Yamagawa family had returned to bid on farm property they had previously leased. Kent mayor Grant Dunbar warned that although the intensity of anti-Japanese feeling had subsided: "A lot of people have made up their minds not to stand for it." Fulfilling his prediction farm groups in the valley formed the "Remember Pearl Harbor League" to "keep the Japs from resettling in the valley." [13]

The Supreme Court ruled in December that "Loyal Nisei Can't Be Held In Camps" as reported in the *Times*, 18 December 1944. The *P-I* gave fullest coverage, which was notable for its objectivity. Included was a large photographic spread:

"Jap 'Ghost Town' to Live Again?", picturing boarded up buildings and store fronts. Outgoing-Governor Arthur Langlie, still unable to distinguish American Japanese from the enemy, Japan, charged the ruling was "premature"..."It is one which should be arrived at when the problem could be appoached without the emotional tendencies which naturally are present while the nation is at war with Japan". Mayor Devin, countered that they were entitled to protection, now that "the war department has satisfied itself that those American Japanese who are permitted to return...are not dangerous to the war effort". That same day the *Star* gave front page emphasis in a long article about opposition forming by the Remember Pearl Harbor League. Its president, dairyman Ben Smith, announced the league is "definitely opposed to return of the Japanese", continuing: "No member of the league will do any violence to any Japanese, but we gravely fear that irresponsible persons may do them some harm". Smith claimed pledges from 500 persons in the valley "not to lease, sell or rent to Japs". The American Legion's state commander promised a thorough examination of the Japanese problem at its next executive board meeting.

The *P-I* continued its objective coverage on the 19th, emphasizing the process will be "gradual" and "selective", as it reported the WRA had already relocated 32,000 evacuees to the Midwest and eastern states. This left 61,000 in the relocation centers, plus 18,700 in the Tule Lake segregation center. Reporter William C. Schulze found UW president Lee Paul Sieg and Seattle School Board officials "extremely optimistic about prospects for fitting Japanese youngsters into present classes". The UW's director of student affairs, Dean Newhouse, reminded Schulze that "Before the war we had nearly 400 Japanese students" and that their relations with other students was "always a pleasant and untroubled one". He added, the UW will go out of its way to welcome them back. Acting school superintendent Samuel Fleming saw "no reason why Japanese youngsters will not fit beautifully into our schools here." The *Star* continued its emphasis upon the opposition being formed, this time by the American Legion. On the 20th it returned to the agenda of the Remember Pearl Harbor League, listing its "seven points" against return of the evacuees.

The *Times* ran an editorial on the 20th: "Loyal Citizens Should Be Received on Their Merits", repeating the War Department's statement that "mass exclusion is no longer a matter of military necessity." Unmoved, and warming to the occasion in January 1945, newly elected Governor Monrad Wallgren (who had chaired the hostile Pacific Coast congressional delegation in 1941-1942), with "out-thrust jaw...declared emphatically" his opposition to their return. Most of the letters in Senator Magnuson's "Japanese" file contain the "We don't want them back" theme. Art Ritchie, writing on Japanese Exclusion League stationery, reported, "anti-Jap organizations are springing up everywhere. Many are vicious. Some want to boycott Japs and others want to ride them out of town on a rail..." Hoping to get an amendment to the constitution to prevent "ANY MORE" Japanese from becoming citizens, he invited Magnuson to join the JEL. [14]

With valley farmers, produce merchants, veterans groups, the Teamsters union, Seattle Central Labor Council, and "patriotic" groups coalescing against resettlement of the evacuees Mayor Devin brought his Civic Unity Committee into play. Heartened by a visit from "a high ranking general" to deal with the anticipated trouble, Devin acted. Assured by the general that little opposition to the Army's orders was expected from the "Jap-haters" Devin had the CUC call a meeting of leaders of these groups to inform them of the Army's determination to resettle the evacuees with as little friction as possible, and to urge their cooperation. American Legion and Veterans of Foreign Wars representatives said they'd go along with the Army. Charles Doyle of the SCLC insisted "we won't be responsible for how many are hanging from lamp posts". Ten produce dealers on "produce row" refused to remove their "no-Japs" signs. Mayor Devin later recounted the Teamsters offer of a statue or picture of General McArthur as "number one Jap-hater" to be mailed out to known anti-Japanese. Devin wired McArthur, who denounced the proposal. Opposition steadily evaporated. Arthur Barnett of the Church Council and attorney for Gordon Hirabayashi, credited the education program of the CUC with playing a major role, along with the University of Washington, and special police training for the "handling of minorities". From my reading, perhaps the single most critical factor in defusing the opposition were the performance and sacrifice of the 442nd Regimental Combat Team and the 100th Battalion. As the most decorated army units, which bore a disproportionate number of casualties, their record seemed decisively to disarm the "patriotic" opposition. [15]

A survey of the Seattle Nisei was completed by the Council of Churches 31 December 1945. Most of the Church Council's work on behalf of the Nisei was done by its Nisei Steering Committee. Various social agencies, public schools (only the principal at Roosevelt High refused cooperation), and church groups cooperated in the Steering Committee survey. Estimates show between 3,500 and 4,000 Nisei returned to the city. "Impressions" gained from the survey were many. The job situation was "very negative", due in large part to traditional union discrimination. The most frequent types of employment available were housework, stenographic, and office work. The US Employment Service found it difficult to place them in job openings as soon as the prospective employer learned they were Nisei. Dispersion impeded social interaction, and the young had no place to "get together". Discrimination from "their colleagues" in the floral and vegetable businesses made it difficult to get re-established in those lines, although some were "doing very well". The Christian Friends for Racial Equality handled many of the discrimination cases. At the public schools the Nisei "were barely tolerated, rather than welcomed". Nevertheless their reception "has been much better than expected". Complicating re-integration efforts was the hesitancy of the returnees "to make contacts or go out in public for fear of negative reactions...[their] uncertain and bewildered state of mind...They need encouragement." Leadership drawn from the Nisei had still not come forward. A concluding remark brings home their predicament: Where there was no "prejudice" before the war, now there is. [16]

The Church Council had played a key role in the Japanese community before the war, but now sought a different relationship. In anticipation of the return of the evacuees its Joint Conference on the Future of Japanese Church Work saw the "opportunity of working out a new religious pattern in race relations because the old racial denominational churches have very largely gone out of existence." It looked forward to "integrating Japanese-Americans into Caucasian life completely". Commenting specifically on the Baptists, "our policy is to refrain from opening new segregated churches under any conditions [excepting] the only [segregated] one which might be reopened is the only one in Seattle, where we have property and a group of people who have stayed together during the evacuation." Executive secretary Gertrude Apel accused Baptist minister Emery Andrews of doing "everything in his power to discredit and undermine any united program." Sally Kazama recalls that at that time the wiser solution would have been to establish a community church because none of the congregations was large enough to support separate ones. Today segregated churches prevail. [17]

While these internal conflicts within the Church Council were running their course the council effectively pursued its social service program. Two hostels had been set up to deal with the transition of evacuees to civilian life. One was at 1236 Washington Street, the other at 1610 King Street. While being able (by April 1946) to accomodate almost a thousand adults and children, lodging was provided for 526 people for one to fourteen nights from 1 July to 22 October 1945. In a report of 3 April 1946 the hostels noted that 360 servicemen and 211 Hawaiian and Alaskan Japanese had checked in for lodging and help. The hostels became an effective social center and a place for establishing business and employment contacts. Although employment was not their focus the hostels found jobs for 402 people, an impressive accomplishment when opportunities were so limited. [18]

After West Coast restrictions against return of the Nisei had been lifted in January 1945 the War Relocation Authority established field offices in West Coast cities, where about 80,000 evacuees were expected to return. The WRA included Issei in their program. From his earlier work, while an inmate at Fort Missoula and later at Minidoka, Iwao Matsushita was assigned Special Relocation Officer in Seattle. Ironically, he remained a parolee of the Justice Department, having to report regularly to the local Immigration and Naturalization Service, while concurrently on the federal payroll until termination of the WRA program nine months later. In this position he and his co-workers performed much the same kind of work undertaken by the Church Council. However, the WRA had more resources and was better able to penetrate the federal bureaucracy.

Housing was partially provided by those Issei who had previously operated hotels. Many returned to resume their former roles. The WRA, Church Council, and the JACL made referrals as hotel space became available. The former Japanese language school was converted into an emergency housing facility. Some evacuees who had sufficient savings leased or purchased multi-family dwellings and rented to their fellow victims. Complicating the housing allocations was the existence of restrictive housing covenants directed against racial minorities and ethnic groups in many upscale sections of the city. These tended to confine the search for living facilities.

In seeking employment for the returnees these three agencies encountered the long standing opposition of trade unions (excepting the building services union, which had admitted Japanese before the war). The Teamsters union went so far as to prevent the shipment of Japanese grown produce from reaching markets in the spring and summer of 1945, until the Justice Department threatened an anti-trust suit. Employers exhibited considerable ambivalence, as well as outright resistance in hiring. The Maryknoll Catholics were more fortunate, inasmuch as it found jobs in its own enterprises. Illustrative of the depth of trade union opposition and that of real estate agents, is the experience of Shiro Kashino, a veteran of the 442nd Regimental Combat Team, who had earned six Purple Hearts, a Silver Star, and a Bronze Star for Gallantry. When looking for a home he was told homes were being reserved for returning veterans; the implication seemed to be that even as a veteran his Japaneseness somehow excluded him from qualification. After completing a course in air conditioning, unions refused him admittance, thereby forcing him to look elsewhere for work. Eventually he caught on as a successful automobile salesman. [19]

When the WRA was succeeded in 1946 by the War Agency Liquidation Unit the latter conducted a survey, *People in Motion: The Postwar Adjustment of the Evacuated Japanese Americans.* The period covered might be considered the "settling in" phase of their "adjustment". What follows is a summary of some observations of its two special investigators, sociology professors S. Frank Miyamoto and Robert O'Brien.

> Acute hardships were being experienced by the Issei without Nisei children to whom they might turn for support (p. 116). However, since the "capital wealth...remains largely concentrated in the hands of the Issei...the Nisei are thus

economically subordinated" (p. 118). In effect, this tended to restore some degree of Issei authority lost by them during the evacuation period.

Occupationally, there was an "unusually high percentage of the Japanese American workers who are engaged as service workers (except domestic and protective), proprietors and managers, and clerical or kindred workers...Chief among the establishments which now hire the Japanese...are some of the best hotels in the city and the hospitals, chiefly the Columbus and Providence, which are Catholic institutions, particularly of the Maryknoll group...[P]ositions at the downtown hotels, as well as in the building services union, is said to be the product of the WRA effort." A far more impressive number of store and stock clerks, typists, stenographers, and comparable activities are, however, "employed by various Civil Service Agencies, [of which] the Veterans Administration is perhaps the heaviest employer...especially of those with veterans status...Nisei are now increasingly looking to federal agencies for white-collar jobs." Of industrial employment the garment industry was the main source, while the Olympic foundry's employment of "some 40 Nisei" was most in such industrial lines, although small numbers found work in the shipyards and in some boiler works, presumably non-union shops. (pp. 118-21).

In terms of business enterprises, "The majority of businesses which have reappeared...today represent the type which are principally dependent upon the Japanese community and the multi-racial population of the Jackson Street district...It has been variously estimated that between 180 and 200 hotels are now operated by Japanese Americans...The larger proportion [of which] are third-class hotels located in the marginal areas of the business district." (pp. 128-29). [20]

## The CUC and African Americans

As to employment discrimination, the CUC joined with other groups in seeking legislation for a state Fair Employment Practices Commission. Leading toward this legislation was a disturbing report from a survey on the status of minority races conducted in early 1946. Employment statistics on non-white employment showed the following:

| Year | Month | Employed Non-whites | Percentage of workforce |
|------|-------|---------------------|--------------------------|
| 1943 | July  | 3,288               | 2.2%                     |
|      | Nov.  | 4,405               | 2.6%                     |
| 1944 | Jan.  | 4,412               | 3.0%                     |
|      | Nov.  | 6,957               | 5.0%                     |
| 1945 | Jan.  | 7,521               | 5.2%                     |
|      | June  | 6,606               | 4.9%                     |
|      | Dec.  | 3,069               | 4.1%                     |
| 1946 | Jan.  | 2,863               | 3.6%                     |

Just after the Japanese surrender Greenwood, in anticipation of extensive layoffs, wrote to fifteen of the area's largest employers to do it "proportionately [to minimize] charges of undue or unjust discrimination". In discussion with Dean Hart, executive secretary of the Urban League the CUC learned that employers are "generally antagonistic [now that] they are no longer under the stress of a labor shortage...The [United States] Employment Service was alleged to have knuckled under to employers." Furthermore, Hart continued, the AFL resists, except for the Ship Scalers and the Building Service Workers Union. And although the CIO unions are more "liberal" they are secondary to AFL unions in the industrial sector. In May 1946 Hart complained to the United States Employment Service headquarters of the rude treatment accorded Black applicants at the USES's city office, and asked for a survey of its practices. When Greenwood discovered in February 1945 that the Seattle Blood Bank was segregating Negro blood from that of Whites he asked Director Dr. Robert Mullarky to discontinue the practice. The nation and city were clearly drifting back to prewar race relations patterns. How far the drift remained to be seen. [20]

Reviewing the employment situation in 1947: an Army veteran, Thomas J. Allen, became the first Black driver hired by the Seattle Transit System. A second had also been hired and three more were in the training program. The Seattle Public Schools hired Thelma Dewitty and Marita Johnson as its first Black teachers in 1947, also the year when the School Board finally allowed married women to teach. In fall of 1944 the Seattle Charter Revision Committee asked Greenwood about including a clause in the new charter outlawing employment discrimination. Greenwood cautioned against it, while advocating enforcement by the Civil Service Commission of anti-discrimination policies already in existence against City department heads who were known for their discriminatory practices. When a House-passed FEPC bill was awaiting state Senate action in 1945 Greenwood sent out "URGENT CALL" letters to "Dear Friends" urging them to press their senators to approve it. After its failure Greenwood recommended an "education program" to secure passage of such an employment bill in the next session. While working with other groups in the 1947 session CUC's new chairman Henry Elliott congratulated traffic judge Roy DeGrief for hiring the first Black bailiff, Robert Marshall. The Christian Friends wrote the CUC in March 1945 that Negro hospital patients were being segregated into private rooms at Columbus, Providence, and Seattle General hospitals. Swedish Hospital would not even admit Blacks. Upon confirming this information, Greenwood wrote Dr. Walter Hiltner, president of the King County Medical Society asking him to "correct this situation". Corrective action was soon taken to discontinue these hospital practices, and also with respect to nursing schools operated by the hospitals. With the cooperation of the Washington State Nurses Association the CUC conducted a statewide survey of these nursing schools. The very questionnaire set in motion the termination of current practice, which had denied Blacks admission. [22]

As a demonstration project, the original institute of government - which featured an address by Dr. Robert Weaver, a leading scholar on race relations - turned into a formal, Annual Institute on Race Relations the CUC co-sponsored with the UW. Weaver spoke to an overflow audience at the UW's Guggenheim Hall. Weaver's speech was well covered by the newspapers and radio stations. President Raymond Allen was so impressed with Weaver that he reportedly had offered him a faculty position. Taking advantage of its growing reputation the CUC sought membership from the general public. Joiners were soon found as speakers on CUC's behalf. Some served as workshop leaders. Working closely with the UW's sociology department the CUC co-sponsored its original census survey of the non-white population. Also produced with that department's faculty was a cemetery study indicating the general observance of restrictive covenants among cemetery operators, and a hesitant start towards the abolition of those covenants. The UW's Institute of Labor Economics produced a basic study on job opportunities for racial minorities. Not only did the CUC conduct its nursing school survey, but it also surveyed one on the medical profession. When the US Supreme Court ruled against restrictive covenants in 1948 (Shelley vs. Kramer) the CUC met with the Seattle Real Estate Board to discuss its ramifications. This proved the last such meeting with the Board. Seattle realtors continued this practice by other strategems. [23]

Clearly activist, now, the CUC pursued the Veterans Administration for allegedly discriminating against Black employees and job applicants. It supported an investigation by Lewis Watts in February 1947. Watts was a graduate student in the UW's School of Social Work and later became executive secretary of the Seattle Urban League. Indicative of VA attitudes was one case among Watts's reports in which a supervisor told one Black who had been in an "unassigned capacity" for "quite a long while", that the VA never promotes "Negroes" higher than grade 4. When Watts himself applied for a "social work" position for which he had been certified, the VA told him it would "antagonize" others in the VA and in the "community" should he be appointed. Shortly thereafter the VA wrote CUC Henry Elliott that steps were being taken to "correct" these practices. [24]

Gradually more positive results came from the CUC's conscience-raising efforts. In June 1948 CUC Irene Miller reported, "The majority of our leading hotels have an excellent policy of non-discrimination. However, some smaller hotels continue to discriminate." When Watts became the Urban League executive secretary he got an agreement with the League that all hotel matters would be referred to the CUC, which, through its contacts within the business community, they could best end discriminatory hotel practices. Miller reported in October 1949, "All Seattle schools of nursing now accept nurses without discrimination with respect to race, creed, or color". As to many cemetaries, however, discrimination continued on racial grounds. Miller did not mention passage of a State FEPC bill in 1949, in the course of which the CUC had gathered support from many professionals and business leaders, as well as key legislators. Miller concluded that private housing remains "our major problem". [25]

Some detail related to passage of the State FEPC bill is merited. As noted above, during the 1945 legislative session a state fair employment bill passed the House of Representatives, but it was bottled up in the Senate committee. After the session Dean Hart and Rev. F. Benjamin Davis of the Urban League convened a group of those who had been its foremost advocates, including three CUC board members and Irene Miller. Miller, in the strategy review, alleged the prominence of the left-wing group turned off some conservative senators who had been approached by the left-wingers during the bill's promotion. One of the left-wingers, attorney John Caughlan, volunteered they would agree to stay in the background next time, should that strategy be agreed to. Two subsequent meetings were held in June that included more CUC representatives. At the second meeting Arthur Barnett was elected temporary chair of a fair employment practices committee. But after several subsequent meetings disagreements between those wanting "more immediate action" and the more staid committee members led to an informal agreement that the two organizations would work for fair employment legislation by their own means. Subsequent meetings broadened participation of the more conservative group, which elected Frank Bayley, Jr. its chairman. He, with Barnett and judge James Hodson were to draft a bill. They began operating in August 1946 from a spare room at the CUC office in the Second and Cherry Building. The 1946 election, however, led to an overwhelming victory of Republican legislators, who resisted the notion that employment discrimination existed. House Bill 26 emerged, but it was so emasculated with amendments that it died in the Senate Rules Committee. To correct the impression that discrimination in employment was significant the CUC persuaded the UW labor economics department in 1948 to produce the job opportunities study referred to above. This study reported disproportionately widespread unemployment among minority groups since the war's end: 16.8 percent among Blacks and 4.11 percent among other minorities, which contrasted with a slight 3.11 percent unemployment for Whites. The study helped convince the more liberal 1949 legislature that employment discrimination existed on wide enough scale to justify legislative action. A new committee was formed to push a bill through. Leadership went to Republican Senator Alfred Westberg of Seattle. CUC historian Howard Droker outlines the conflict over campaign strategy: the Urban League wanting a statewide educational campaign to awaken the public's awareness, and the CUC "elitist" approach by which minority groups would keep a low profile while singling out "respectable and influential" sympathetic public figures in and out of the legislature to take the lead. The CUC strategy prevailed.

This left a residue of bitterness among those in the Urban League camp. The latter played only a minor role in the campaign according to Droker. The new bill was passed at the 1949 session and signed into law by Governor Arthur Langlie. The board's composition and non-activist functioning would soon become a source of controversy. [26]

From the CUC record covered above it seems clear that its deliberative approach to the general problems of race relations in the late 1940s did much to alert the general public to the fact that race discrimination, particularly that against African Americans, was widespread. Its careful promotion of factual surveys lent credibility to its claims and to its social agency cohorts. Howard Droker considers the CUC's role in paving the way for the peaceful resettlement of the Japanese evacuees, considers its "greatest wartime success". In sum, the CUC's work proved indispensable to whatever advances were achieved by civic activists in the 1950s and 1960s.

# Recreation and Entertainment Scene of the 1940s

## General Entertainment

Recreation was provided for both the civilian population and service men and women. While they shared most recreation in common such as movie theaters, dance halls, roller rinks, bowling alleys, and the like special facilities were supplied for service men and women stationed in or near the city as well as those in transit. The *Seattle Star*'s Friday issue throughout 1943 carried on its front page a "Service Men's Week-End Where to Go List". This list included places to dance, sport facilities and events, places where refreshments and entertainment were scheduled, religious services/activities, and where overnight accomodations might be found.

A general Service Men's Club at 1322 Second Avenue was available for Whites only with dancing from 8:30 to 11 PM. A "Victory Canteen" also was maintained at the Union Station, keyed to receiving fresh arrivals off the trains. Service women intermingled at the YWCA and the Army's operation at Jefferson Park there being practically no facility specifically for them. "Negroes" went to the Colman Club at 23rd Avenue and East Olive Street, a YMCA facility in the heart of the African American district. The *Star* noted "Negro" parenthetically until November 1943 when the qualifier was dropped, though not to signify the end of segregation. Over the objection of the local NAACP, which opposed such segregated facilities, the City Council contributed $10,000 toward adapting this YMCA facility in spring of 1942 for a 1 September opening. In one large room fifty double decker bunks were set up for sleeping. This facility by January 1943 provided recreation for more than 2,000 soldiers and sailors besides sleeping 875 men. Sam Groff wrote a series of articles in the *Times* concerning Seattle's service hospitality problems. On the

Colman Club Groff referred to the club's "midget dance floor" where 300 "Negro" soldiers were having a "wonderful time dancing in relays", spilling out to the porch and eventually to the lawn. The hostesses admitted it was "a bit crowded". In writing brief biographical notes of some soldiers he observed, "a good percentage [of them] had been under heavy enemy fire", fighting "shoulder to shoulder with men of other races..." Manager John Copeland explained planning had been for an anticipated 500 Black servicemen in the area, not for the 6,000 to 7,000 who actually arrived. [1]

Claiming to be the "largest" in the nation the US Army's Jefferson Park Recreation Center where "some 100-odd buildings",mainly barracks, were laid out in Army cantonment style, displacing the nine-hole golf course formerly in the area. For those wanting participant sports facilities and equipment were offered for baseball, softball, tennis, badminton, golf, and bicycling chief among them. Swings and a merry-go-round were there in a "carnival setting" should children need a diversion. In the new guest house free overnight facilities were provided for service women and married couples at a cost of 50 cents for the husband or wife. To be near their husbands who were awaiting shipping out, wives worked there at 75 cents an hour which was 12.5 cents more than entry level for Boeing employees. Single servicemen were assigned to the barracks. A huge canteen offered refreshments, reading material and other comforts. In September alone 55,000 service men and women took advantage of the offerings, about 2,000 per day and numbers increased each week. In accordance with service protocol "Negroes" were excluded. The War Chest Fund opened a Servicemens Club in January 1941, and soon supplemented its overnight space by taking over an upper floor of the Armory building. Public transportation to recreation and entertainment locations was either free or paid for at reduced rates. [2]

A new Service Men's Club sponsored by the *Star* and The Washingtonians was opened at 1011 Second Avenue on 30 October 1943. Opening night was reserved for men only, while "all Seattle" was invited for the following day. The King County War Chest had put up $27,000 toward its completion; the USO was to take it over in 1944. Above the first floor central lounge were clubrooms, a gymnasium for exercise, and steam baths for relaxation. [3]

For service men stationed in the city and Puget Sound area athletic leagues were set up each sport season. For basketball a six-team Puget Sound League found teams competing from the Sand Point Naval Air Station, Fort Lewis, Fort Lawton, Paine Field, Whidbey Island Naval Air Station, and the 44th Division. The services even had a football league that included one team from the Quilayute Coast Guard Station on the Olympic peninsula. A civilian complement to the service athletic teams came from various business firms in the greater Seattle area. Boeing's soccer team had improved so much that it was scheduled to meet the league leading

Wickman Pie team in the semi-finals. Faring less well, Boeing's basketball team in February 1944 was running a poor fourth place in the Northwest Basketball League far behind league leading Alpine Dairy. Interleague play seems to have been rare if at all. [4]

Movie theaters probably provided the easiest entertainment. Fifteen theaters downtown were supplemented by a like number of neighborhood houses where second run movies could be seen. Vaudeville survived at the Rivoli located at First Avenue and Madison Street, although vaudeville shared time with a movie. Sometimes the Palomar Theater at Third Avenue and University Street, one block downhill from Victory Square, similarly offered vaudeville. [5]

Dancing took more preparation than movie-going. Public dance halls were downtown, in Renton, in the farming towns of Kent and Auburn, and along Highway 99. On the northeast edge of the city lay the Bothell Way Pavilion where Bert Lindgren's band played for those looking for "old time dance". South on 99 was the popular Spanish Castle midway between Seattle and Tacoma; north on 99 was equally popular Dick Parker's. Downtown the Trianon Ballroom was the only one "open to Negroes", though limited to "Jim Crow" on Monday nights. That the Trianon conceded even this came from its signing the enormously popular African American bands, most notably those of Lionel Hampton and Duke Ellington; in these bands were some Seattle players whose local followers exerted pressure for Black access. Paul de Barros writes, "After the Hamp dance, the Trianon instituted a regular policy of hosting 'Colored Folks' Monday-night dances..." which some in the Black community referred to derisively as "spook nights". [6]

Other dance halls were the Dreamland, the Crescent, the Avalon, the Senator at the Eagles Temple, and the various servicemen's clubs. Swing shift workers could leave work some nights and dance to their heart's content at the Trianon and Crescent. The latter remained open for them on Sunday morning from 1:15 AM to 5:15 AM, offering $25 for the winner of the fox trot contest. Similarly the Spanish Castle remained open for swing shift dancers from 2 to 6 AM.

Should civilians and service men and women be looking for something more exciting there were the numberless after hours clubs that Paul de Barros so colorfully wrote about. Many of the clubs had operated before the war as speakeasies and night clubs under police "protection". Some of these alternately closed and reopened until the economy livened up in 1940 just as swing music was peaking in popularity and big bands were flourishing. More ballrooms and night clubs sprang up downtown, plus more than twenty running roughly along Jackson Street from

Fifth to Twelfth avenues passing by the Chinese Gardens on Sixth Avenue in Chinatown. Best known were the Congo Club in the basement of the Bush Hotel, the Ubangi near Seventh and Jackson, the Elks Club close by, the 411 on Maynard Street, the Black and Tan on Twelfth. Here Black and White clientele and racially mixed couples found easy accceptance. To the north near 23rd Avenue and East Madison Street were the Savoy and the Washington Social Club. Common practice for members of touring Black bands - after they had played at the one of the downtown dancehalls, hotels, at the Civic Auditorium, or the Moore Theater - was to drop in at any of the after hours clubs and jam with their bands. For those couples and groups primarily looking for jazz these became prime destinations. [7]

Norm Bobrow was the jazz impressario equivalent of the Moore Theater's Cecilia Schultz. Bobrow was a New York City transplant. Starting with the promotion of the White Gaylord Jones jazz band on the UW campus, Bobrow moved by stages to off-campus venues, each time responding to overflowing jitterbugging crowds, leading to a Trianon booking lasting from 1938 to 1942. As the biggest ballroom in the Northwest, accomodating up to 5,000 dancers, "More people met their future wives and husbands at the Trianon than anywhere else in Seattle" according to manager Ted Harris. Early in 1940 Bobrow booked the "Gay Jones Orchestra" and the African American Palmer Johnson Sextet into the prestigious Metropolitan Theatre for "Seattle's First Swing Concert". Here was Seattle's own talent showing its talent! Bobrow fanned out, renting the Moore for some of the famous travelling jazz bands as well as Palmer Johnson and Gay Jones. When Fats Waller was booked for the Moore in July 1941 the president of the Black Musicians Union, Local 493 (the White Local 76 banned Blacks from membership) asked Bobrow to help the union pay to have Waller also play for their dancers at the Senators ballroom. No problem. All through the 1940s and into the 1950s Bobrow brought Black and White jazz bands to the city. Touring Black musicians reportedly found Seattle a haven relative to cities in the rest of the country. [8]

## Classical Music and Fine Arts Scene During 1940s

Robert Willis wrote in the May 1945 *Argus* that "Seattle is now actively supporting a season of music and entertainment [that] would have been an impossibility five years ago". "Little theatre" was represented in four places, two on the UW campus, Glenn Hughes's Penthouse and Showboat theaters, and two off campus were the Jameses' Seattle Repertory Playhouse, and the Tryout for "experimental" plays. The Ladies Musical Club continued throughout the period with its annual series, locking in at the Metropolitan Theater for its offerings. The Seattle Symphony's short seasons were performed mainly at the Music Hall. By far most active was Cecilia Schultz's various series at the Moore Theater that extended over the entire year. All through the 1930s Schultz had been bringing classical artists, groups, and opera companies to the city. In 1934 she staged five concerts at the Civic Auditorium, each performance attracting 5,000 people, itself attesting to the broad popular appeal of this brand of mass entertainment. Based on this success the Moore Theater, in need of comparable audiences, signed Schultz - now recognized as the "only woman manager west of Chicago" - to a long term contract. On the UW campus the Associated Women Students sponsored a short annual series. A musical series, also on campus, kept classical music alive during the summer interlude. [1]

Seattle attracted world class artists in the "classical" repertoire as can be seen from the following sample drawn from the *Argus* for February and March 1941, also later issues through 1944. While the Seattle Symphony played at the Music Hall on the UW campus Vladimir Horowitz's piano recital of 3 February 1941 was followed the next week by the Budapest String Quartet, judged by many as the world's finest. Violinist Zino Francescotti was featured in March as was Metropolitan Opera's Lawrence Tibbett. The Ladies Musical Club offered the celebrated soprano Dorothy Maynor in February, followed by pianists Sergei Rachmaninoff and Artur Rubenstein in March. Widely acclaimed Marian Anderson was featured at the Moore, annually. Indeed Schultz not only signed up African Americans Maynor and Anderson, but almost as often Paul Robeson, Roland Hayes, and only less frequently a young baritone Todd Duncan, whom Gershwin chose to sing Porgy. Hayes sang at the Moore in February 1943 followed by a special recital for Black soldiers at the Port of Embarkation. That same month Marian Anderson sang for "a censored number" of Black soldiers at the First Avenue Cantonment. All consistently captured rave reviews in the *Argus*. All artists just mentioned appeared almost annually under Schultz's sponsorship, or by the Ladies Musical Club or the Associated Women Students. Among the many other artists were pianists Robert Casadesus, Claudio Arrau, Josef Hoffman, Egon Petri, Artur Schnabel; violinists Jascha Heifitz, Erica Morini, Nathan Milstein, Yehudi Menuhin, Bronislaw Hubermann. Some of the artists were young and promising, some neared the end of their careers, while others were at their very peak. Among the many singers were Ezio Pinza, Helen Traubel, Laritz Melchior, Grace Moore, Spokane's Patrice Munsel, the youngest ever to join the Metropolitan Opera, France's melifluous baritone Martial Singher, Brazilian soprano Bidu Sayao, James Melton, and John Charles Thomas. Most singers came from the Metropolitan Opera. Often, when either the Ladies Musical Club or the Associated Women Students scheduled a pianist or violinist, that artist would also perform for the Symphony, thereby doubling the incentive for booking agencies. [2]

Inasmuch as a city's musical taste and level of sophistication is symbolized by its symphony orchestra a look at Seattle's is merited. Its weak financial underpinnings led necessarily to short seasons and limited rehearsal time. Also, because of its financial frailty Seattle Symphony management rarely was able to sign conductors to long-term contracts. Some left on their own, most notably Karl Kruger, who migrated to Detroit where he soon established one of the nation's foremost symphonies. As Nikolai Sokoloff was rounding out his third year, the 1940-1941 season, he tendered his resignation, and the new president of the symphony board, Paul C. Harper, launched a fund raising campaign and audaciously signed up the world renown, erascible Sir Thomas Beecham of the London Philharmonic for the 1941-1942 season. Weary of London bombings Sir Thomas looked forward to combining Seattle's short season with one he could also command in Vancouver, B.C. By this stroke Harper's campaign proved a rousing success. So was Beecham's first season, which opened at the Music Hall, where the symphony joined with the San Francisco Opera Company in three opera performances just two weeks before the symphony's season-opening concert. The operas were "Manon", "Rigoletto", and "Tannhauser", each starring world famous singers Tito Schipa, John Brownlee, Lawrence Tibbett, Bidu Sayao, Jussi Bjoerling, and Lauritz Melchior. Such distinguished casting seemed typical during the 1940s. Beecham stayed for two seasons, entertaining Seattleites with antics on and off the podium, acidly embarassing some errant musicians during rehearsal, wildly gesticulating from the podium, sometimes "crooning", "hissing", but to sellout performances often capped by thunderous applause. At his first performance he earned the permanent enmity of the *P-I* when he halted midway through a Delius piece at the sudden flash of light from its staff photographer Art French, shouting: "You, out!. This is an insult to the audience". Through it all he reportedly brought the orchestra to a new level, although Hans Lehmann characterized his programming: "Sir Thomas only schedules the music of three composers, Mozart, Delius, and Sibelius". Lehman exaggerated. Beecham also did Beethoven, Brahms, Hadyn, and Dvorak, but he was a traditionalist who shunned the Baroque and most adventuresome of 20th century composers like Schoenberg, Bartok, Hindemith, Shostakovich, and Stravinsky. Post-romantics like Gustav Mahler were bypassed completely, although this was true of musical fare elsewhere as well in the 1940s. Their time would come in the 1950s. The *P-I*'s Suzanne Martin showed no respect for the distinguished conductor, harassing Sir Thomas in her columns regularly, inspiring fellow columnist Joe Miller to credit her with responsibility for Beecham's unexpectedly early exit: "She and 'Cissy' Schultz have put more gumption into our local music in the last six years than it ever had before in its entire history." [3]

For the 1943-1944 season the symphony board scrambled to find a new conductor, a "permanent" or long-term one if possible. Shifting away from reliance on "guest star" conductors, the Symphony board chose a relative unknown, Carl

Bricken. The board was impressed with Bricken's academic career at the University of Chicago and University of Wisconsin, where he organized music departments and orchestras. Bricken also found the necessity of short seasons and abbreviated rehearsal time a handicap. Few donors were drawn into the fund raising net to the despair of one board member, who wrote "Certainly we cannot have a real symphony orchestra supported by only 450 people." The orchestra limped along during the war years, then launched a "Development Fund" campaign in May 1945, aiming at $100,000, toward which a large proportion had been pledged by the time the season opened. Widespread publicity encouraged Bricken to plan for eight concerts on Monday and Tuesday nights. Thrown in were some "popular" concerts and four for school children. By October all eight Monday concerts scheduled at the Moore had been sold out. The season was a huge success, so much so that ticket sales for the 1945-46 season broke all records. The membership drive was impressively widening sponsorship. Trouble came in 1946-47. A summer series at the UW football stadium was expected to draw 35,000 to 40,000 spectators, from which the board expected to raise $60,000. Unseasonal rain storms, however, dashed all those expectations. The regular season performances were transferred to the Civic Auditorium, where they were graded mediocre. Lowering their sights somewhat the board's annual sustaining fund drive set a goal of $60,000 but failed that. Then symphony members revolted against Bricken's leadership. With one year left under his contract Bricken was kept on despite the protest. The problem remained as to how to face this season of discontent? [4]

Out of the blue came a joint announcement from the Seattle Symphony Orchestra and the Tacoma Philharmonic that they would coordinate their respective concerts under a common management. Tacoma's Eugene Linden and Seattle's Bricken would share conducting. Linden was then age 36 and had been the Tacoma Orchestra's conductor for the past fifteen years. Other Northwest cities were invited to join in, thereby inspiring the name Pacific Northwest Symphony Orchestra. Bricken conducted the first concert in November and brought a "near-tumultuous reception". Linden conducted the two following concerts and received similar rousing receptions. The second set of concerts were less well received, and Bricken tendered his resignation, effective in April 1948. Linden conducted the last two concerts, which were so well received that Linden was named the new leader. Linden proved popular with both the orchestra members and audiences alike. [5]

The orchestra members set up their own Washington Symphony Society to drum up statewide support. A committee of the Musicians Association met with the Seattle Symphony Board to iron out differences, but no resolution resulted. The Board decided to cancel the symphony's 1948-49 season since it was unable to sign up other musicians. The Musicians Association wanted to choose its own conductor and orchestra members, to determine the season's length, and the music to be played. The Association preferred Linden. Cecilia Schultz lent her considerable influence to the musicians by joining them. Together they gave sixteen concerts with Linden conducting at the Moore during the 1948 season, "playing better and to a fuller house each succeeding concert". The same musicians also played in Tacoma and Olympia. *Argus* columnist David Pennell concluded the group "has a new efficiency and morale that are winning a new audience." Such turmoil attracted biting criticism in *Time* magazine, for having two rival orchestras (Seattle Symphony and Seattle Orchestra). *Time* reported the upstart musicians marched into the elitist Rainier Club unannounced, where the board was meeting. They offered to run the symphony themselves. Signs were not good for the 1948-49 season at this point because there were no resources with which to sign up a permanent conductor. And the board and musicians could not agree on who should run the operation. Boycotts of the respective orchestras were threatened, which forced a rapprochment. The two groups bonded as the Seattle Symphony Orchestra, Inc.. Schultz continued to manage it for the season, while the Seattle Symphony Board canceled its program. Out of this intramural fracus came a compromise that averted a repetition of the last season, and Manuel Rosenthal signed as musical director and conductor for the 1949-1950 season. Linden agreed to serve as "resident" conductor. The French conductor Rosenthal emerged as a candidate because of his current proximity in Tacoma where he was composer in residence at the College of Puget Sound. The UW's new Music School director Stanley Chapple agreed to conduct the Children's Concerts. All looked promising for the future. Not known about Rosenthal was the status of the woman he lived with. But that is a later story.[6]

Cecilia Schultz provided the backbone of Seattle's musical entertainment in the 1940s. She had signed a ten-year contract with the Moore Theater management in 1935. Because of her success her contract was renewed in 1945. It's easy to see why. At the Moore hardly a day went by without an engagement. Sometimes a matinee preceeded an evening concert. To keep the theater bustling Schultz promoted a number of series, each of a different character and audience appeal such as "Cecilia Schultz Attractions" and "Greater Artist Series". In some years she promoted a "Saturday Night Concert Series" or "Sunday Matinee Series". In 1945 she introduced the "De Luxe Theatre" in addition to the regular series. The De Luxe Theater included jazz artist Hazel Scott, folk singer Josh White, the Foxhole Ballet, Gracie Fields, and Bill "Bojangles" Robinson, and the dancer-harmonica team of Draper and Adler. By the end of the winter season Schultz would usually have signed up one of the touring symphonies such as the Philadelphia, the Minneapolis, or the San Francisco. In the fall, just before the opening of the Seattle Symphony season she would often invite the San Francisco Ballet or San Francisco Opera Company to the city for a series. The Seattle Symphony collaborated in these pre-season affairs, giving its members additional income and a warmup opportunity, often as not, the opportunity to get better acquainted with a new conductor.

Schultz lived at the Moore Hotel, an adjunct to the theater. That she was able to sign up the same artists year after year indicates a warm and friendly relationship with them. Her spacious apartment quarters afforded a comfortable facility for casual as well as formal socials with the guest artists. Almost all performers came with established and distinguished reputations and were considered "famous". Their coming provided good newspaper copy and abundant photo opportunities. Of course all this helped pack the house consistently. Some artists whom she regularly signed up were noted in the introduction. Some from another category should be added for overall perspective on Schultz's operation: the Ballet Russe de Monte Carlo, the Don Cossacks Chorus and Military Dancers, the Katherine Dunham Dancers, ballet dancers Alicia Markova and Anton Dolin, the Trapp Family Singers, the Westminster Chorus. Without Cecilia Schultz Seattle would have, indeed, have been the cultural "dustbin" that Sir Thomas Beecham is alleged to have characterized Seattle. [7]

The Moore management terminated Schultz's contract abruptly in 1949, when it turned the theater over to the Seattle Revival Center. Schultz continued by transferring her programs to the Metropolitan Theatre and Civic Auditorium. And, as noted above, she joined forces with the dissident musicians of the Seattle Symphony as its manager for the 1949-1950 season.

The Ladies Musical Club, formed in 1891, was Seattle's pioneer classical music organization. The LMC continued its policy of introducing at least one young and promising American artist along with those with established reputations. Usually four or five concerts were offered per season, but not always. Sometimes an "Extra Attraction" was offered such as Roland Hayes in 1947 and Artur Schnabel in 1948. A sense of LMC's programming is suggested from the following sample. For the 1941-1942 season Dorothy Maynor opened its series, followed by the widely acclaimed American violinist Albert Spalding, Artur Rubinstein and French pianist Robert Casadesus, then world famous violinist Nathan Milstein. Included in 1942-1943 were America's "greatest woman violinist" Carroll Glenn, then the Metropolitan Opera's young mezzo-soprano Blanche Thebom, pianist Vladimir Horowitz and closing with tenor Roland Hayes. When Horowitz canceled none other than Artur Schnabel was substituted. Schnabel brought with him an uncompromising program that began with a Bach, followed by Beethoven's Opus 78 sonata, a Mozart, and ended with Beethoven's last piano sonata Opus 111. This con-

## Recreation and Entertainment Scene of the 1940s   145

trasted so markedly with the modest programs of the period, that it bears mentioning. It seemed Beethoven's impassioned Appassionata sonata was played by most pianists, while ignoring Beethoven's deeply complex last sonatas entirely. Only Rudolf Serkin's equally rare concerts were comparably as challenging, exposing audiences to seldom heard sonatas of Franz Schubert. Serkin and Schnabel were among the few pianists who added Schubert's great piano music to the concert repertoire.

The 1943-1944 program returned Carroll Glenn plus two young American sopranos, Florence Kirk and Anne Brown. They were followed by the young and already "eminent" Chilean pianist Claudio Arrau and tenor John Charles Thomas. The 1944-1945 series saw the return of Arrau, the introduction of the Metropolitan's Martial Singher and Bidu Sayao, topped with the "world's greatest woman violinist" Erica Morini. The LMC moved to the Civic Auditorium for a Horowitz concert. The LMC's gesture toward American talent was the American Ballad Singers, a sextet conducted by musical folklorist Elie Seigmeister. Among the American artists introduced in the later 1940s were pianist William Kapell and violinist Isaac Stern. The LMC continued its tradition of presenting public concerts throughout the year from its skilled amateur and professional members. [8]


The Associated Women Students of the University of Washington offered an annual concert series. The AWS sometimes took its cue from the LMC's previous series and from Schultz's stable of performers. The quality and range of the the AWS series is indicated in the1944-1945 series which started with Robert Casadesus, followed by the Metropolitan's Rose Bampton, then violinist Zino Francescotti. Adolph Busch, of the famous Busch String Quartet, brought his Little Symphony to the Meany. The series concluded with Metropolitan tenor James Melton. Variety in their programming showed with their first concert of the 1945-1946 season, the Spanish dance group of Rosario and Antonio. The widely popular Paul Robeson came next and was followed by the Puerto Rican pianist Jesus Maria Sanroma playing some Gershwin. Sanroma was especially famous for playing both Gershwin and classical compositions. Yehudi Menuhin arrived from his armed forces tour, and was followed by Swedish soprano Karin Branzell. Not until the music department livened the 1947 summer interlude was a fresh element introduced. Alexander Schneider from the Budapest String Quartet and the UW's piano division head, Berthe Poncy Jacobson teamed up for concerts at the Meany. The charismatic Schneider also developed a chamber orchestra from among his students, affording them the opportunity to show their talents. Stanley Chapple arrived in 1947 to chair the Music School, and he too brought novelty. Chapple staged summer concerts of contemporary American composers that summer and the next. The UW's Gerald Kechley's Prelude and Allegro for orchestra found an appreciative audience. The Music School also joined the Extension Division in sponsoring concerts occasionally at the Women's Century Club. They introduced the newly formed Paganini String Quartet to Seattle audiences. Not only that. The Paganini played a string quartet of Bela Bartok, a city first. [9]

Nellie Cornish's school struggled for survival after she retired in 1938. A new director, Mrs. Sarah McClain Sherman, took over in January 1940. Sherman conducted a survey for the benefit the Board of Trustees where she judged the faculty "excellent" and took heart from the projected plans of the department heads. However enrollment at that time was a slight 585. Sherman cancelled some faculty contracts in March including ballet instructor Bonnie Bird [Gundlach], avant garde composer John Cage, and "Madam" Camerlynck. Within three months Sherman's optimism had withered, "we were wrong in trying to run the school on contributions..." She recommended reorganization and refinancing by "trying to get substantial business men to renew their interest". Aunt Nellie had found Seattle's "substantial business men" too tight fisted even during the prosperous 1920s. In early 1940 the city was uncertainly pulling itself from the Great Depression. Discouraged in her attempt Mrs. Sherman resigned in May. Unwilling to conduct a search for a replacement, the Board then accepted a faculty plan for governing the school. Not surprisingly enrollment full time dropped from the 585 at the start of the year to 528 by January 1941. Yet, even half-hearted discussion about finding a new director did not take place until October 1941. The half-hearted effort quickly faded from further Board discussion. Instead, the trustees put the financial burden on the students. The Board agreed in December that in the future students would have to furnish their own costumes for all public performances. This was not an auspicious prospect just as the city was hesitantly adapting to the wartime imperatives. [10]

Service inductions decimated the faculty in 1942. Some faculty were tempted away by better paying jobs in defense industries. So dispirited was the Board in meeting faculty payroll by May 1942 it even considered closing the school. In futility, the Board desperately asked the UW to take over the school. Meanwhile the brain drain continued. Yet war-induced prosperity brought increased enrollment, which was 944 for the 1942-43 session. Three new faculty were hired in the art department: painters Guy Anderson and the UW's Jacob Elshin, and architect Lawrence McDonald. But the latter was soon lost to the draft. With promise ahead three more staff were hired. Stephen Balogh, one of the new faculty, served in effect as an acting director for the war's duration. Funding was found in 1944 for a master class in dance offered by the renowned Anthony Tudor. With the economy picking up the Board's spirits also lifted. Fresh donations finally dribbled in from those "substantial" business men and women. Donations were bountiful, ranging from $500 by Mrs. A. Scott (Dorothy) Bullitt, to $1500 by Mrs. Harry Treat. [11]

The Board resumed its search for a new director when the war was over. It also began a long period of catching up on postponed maintenance, buying supplies and equipment, repairing pianos, and adding staff. In this flare of optimism the Board approved the faculty's granting scholarships to promising students who needed financial assistance. They geared up for more recitals, theater and dance productions in this postwar euphoria. When J. Byron Nichols accepted the directorship in September 1946 on condition that unless endowment funds could be found he would resign. Nichols went to New York to contact various foundations, beginning with the Ford Foundation. He approached the Carnegie Corporation, the Field Foundation, the Guggenheim, Whitney, and Rockefeller only to learn that they had other commitments or required matching funds, which the Cornish Board could not raise.[12]

> As the war approached and the depression decade drew to a close, the early phase of Seattle's art seemed to end, and a period of transition intervened with the dissolution of certain patterns and a regrouping of individuals and interests. (Martha Kingsbury, *Northwest Traditions*, p. 11)

When *Life* magazine featured four Northwest artists in its 28 September 1953 issue it attracted the most prominent nationwide attention thus far to some of the region's distinctive artists. Titled, "Mystic Painters of the Northwest" it emphasized a common thread of Asian mysticism that seemed to bind them together, Zen Buddhism specifically. Yet, the four – Mark Tobey, Morris Graves, Guy Anderson, and Kenneth Callahan – painted in quite different styles, each choosing key symbols that had little or no commmonality. Their respective styles of the 1940s seemed to bear little relation to their paintings of the 1930s, when each was reaching toward his unique personal expressions that found outlet during the 1940s. Clustered around the "four" and interacting with them were other artists sharing a common aspiration in their works, integrating earth, even the cosmos, and humankind/life forms, a "Northwest School".[13]

When *Some Work of the Group of Twelve* was published in 1937, of the "four" only Callahan and Graves were included. Three of the painters were Issei who were studying European painting styles hoping to incorporate some elements into their accomplished Japanese modes. One among them would attach to the Northwest School, Kenjiro Nomura. Not included among the twelve was Mark Tobey who was still in England. Only Morris Graves seemed to be approaching his mature style, represented in the booklet by his famous "Moor Swan" (1933). Young as Graves was he had already gained national recognition. His paintings were already included in the permanent collection of San Francisco's Palace of the Legion of Honor. He was chosen for representation in the First Annual Exhibition of American Art in 1936. When New York's Marian Willard visited the area in 1939 she was escorted to Graves's La Conner studio and was so taken with what she saw that Willard began showing Graves's paintings to her New York patrons. In 1942 more than thirty of Graves's paintings were included in a New York exhibition "Americans 1942". His works were thenceforth included in the Whitney Art Gallery's annual exhibitions. The Phillips Gallery in Washington, D.C. immediately included his paintings in their three-man show, and would regularly include his paintings in the future. Guy Anderson, though a sustained painting companion of Graves, soon to be in company of Tobey as well, was developing his own distinctive style. He would incorporate elements of Northwest Coast Indian art in his large scale compositions inspired by northwestern Washington's earthforms and heavy skies. Callahan's style of the 1930s, in which the influence of the Mexican muralists is most evident, is displaced by themes fusing earthly life forms with the cosmos in the manner of William Blake. What drew these painters together in the late 30s was in part the Federal Arts Project of the Works Progress Administration (1935-1939). Joining them there was Nomura, William Cumming, and other young artists kept alive by painting and sculpting. As editor of the weekly *Town Crier* Margaret Callahan and her published art critic husband, Kenneth, offered their home and intellectual nourishment, plus food on the table (they were the only ones with jobs) to the other artists. With Tobey, a Baha'ist, Graves a Zen Buddhist, and Anderson immersed in the same literature, all knowledgable and respectful of Asian art, it was inevitable that their styles would be influenced accordingly. [14]

Picking up where the Federal Art Project left off, the National Council for Art Work established "Art Week" in 1940. Its aim was "[T]o secure a means of livelihood for the artists and craftsmen of America. [It] becomes also a practical program for safeguarding the cultural resources of America." Locally the Seattle Art Museum did its all to keep artists alive and well. For artists of Japanese ancestry, however, it could do little to help these uprooted artists. One, woodcraftsman George Nakashima, never returned. He was invited by a former employer to Bucks County, Pennsylvania, where he set up his world famous furniture making and design operation. [15]

Among the younger painters who would be grouped in the Northwest School was George Tsutakawa. Though born in Seattle, from 1917 to 1927 he went to school in Japan. He returned to finish high school in Seattle and entered the UW, where he studied painting under Europeanists Ambrose Patterson and Walter Isaacs, and sculpture under Archipenko and Dudley Pratt. Tsutakawa would travel to the Alaska salmon canneries every summer, netting as much as $150 each season, which he used to pay for tuition at the UW and lunches and carfare. Toward the end of his formal education he encountered Tobey, Graves, Anderson, Callahan, and the budding painter twenty-year old William Cumming. Cumming's formal training consisted of classes at Cornish and acceptance into the Federal Art Project and its extraordinary milieu. Tobey had wanted to learn from Kamekichi Tokita and Nomura, who, until Tsutakawa's entry into the constellation were too timid to respond. Tsutakawa became the go-between, often at his family's store that George managed upon graduation. He became a "Sunday painter" due to the family obligations. Pearl Harbor cut short this social/intellectual percolation when it had barely begun. The Tsutakawa Company was treated by the Alien Property Custodian as an alien business and was confiscated, leaving the family destitute. His uncles and their families were transferred to Minidoka; his sister's family to Tule Lake. Nomura and Tokita were evacuated. Nomura had already gained a wide reputation for his Seattle street scenes, and he was the first person of Japanese ancestry to be exhibited by the Museum of Modern Art. Evacuated to Minidoka, he painted its dreary life and accomodations. Like other evacuees they lost practically everything. Oddly, Tsutakawa was inducted into the army in 1942, before formation of the 442d Battalion. Transferred to Camp Robertson, Arkansas then to Camp Fannin, Texas he became the camp commander's "pet artist", giving him the opportunity to pursue his own artistic impulses as a sideline. Upon his return to Seattle he enrolled at the UW and was step by step folded into the Art School faculty in 1947. Anxious to engage the art faculty with the "downtown" artists whom he had known before Pearl Harbor he was "shouted down". [16]

The downtown artists gravitated around Dr. Richard E. Fuller and his Seattle Art Museum. So too, the art patrons of the city. Together they bought the paintings of Graves, Tobey, Anderson, Callahan, and encouraged the promising young ones of their circle. The museum exhibited their works, sometimes giving one man shows. The Callahans wrote about this gathering Northwest School, as did Nancy Wilson Ross. The Northwest Annual Art Exhibitions, the 27th in 1941, exposed the public to works of regional painters, traditionalists and avant garde alike. Some of the latter even won awards beginning with Graves's "Moor Swan" in 1933, Anderson 1944 for "Sharp Sea", Carl Morris 1946 for "Out of the Coulee". 25 paintings from SAM's permanent collection were circulated in 1942 by the Western Association of Art Museums. Included were "Moor Swan", Nomura's "Street", Ray Hill's "Coast Road", Callahan's "Accident", Tobey's "Algerian Landscape". Richard Fuller, SAM director, provided impetus toward recognition of local and regional artists. [17]

The SAM joined the war effort by sponsoring a war poster contest in 1942. Themes reflected patriotism and the strains of wartime, "Back Him Up With Production", "Keep It Under Your Hat", and "Oh Baker, Bake Another Batch". Corporal Irwin Caplan won the first place award with "Full Speed Ahead". Mrs. Paul Foley won a prize for "When Questioned Keep Mum - It's Smart To Play Dumb".[18]

"PEACE!" When the Japanese surrender was announced 14 August 1945, thousands of people, cars and buses flooded the downtown streets, honking horns, aimlessly cheering, crying for joy, randomly hugging and kissing. This scene is at Fourth Avenue and Pike Street.

Courtesy P-I Collection at the Museum of History and Industry

The SAM kept more than busy during the war. Complete gallery changes numbered more than one hundred each year, averaging ten or more changes each month. One-quarter to one-third of the changes reflected its "dedication to our local artists through juried exhibitions and one-man shows". Some were devoted to the war, as noted above. But also there was need to exhibit works that portrayed "good will among nations" which coincided with the movement toward formation of a "united nations". Contributing to this effort three travelling exhbits were shown, one for modern British paintings, plus Museum of Modern Art's "Romantic Paintings" and its "Abstract and Surrealist Art in the United States". When the International Maritime Conference came to the city in 1946 the entire museum was devoted to "Seattle's Own Art of the World". [19]

To pump up a citizenry jarred so suddenly into war the mayor's Civilian War Commission set up "Victory Square" in the city's widest downtown street, University Street between Fourth and Fifth avenues. On 1 May 1942 the city's "war center" celebrated completion of a 75-foot replica of the Washington monument. Throughout the war a noontime event was staged in Victory Square attracting crowds sometimes numbering into the thousands. Every bond drive, salvage drive or any attempt to engage wide popular support for some cause or another usually started in Victory Square. Touring speakers and entertainers promoted the war effort and stirred their audiences forward. Everytime one of armed services awarded an "E" for efficiency to one of the city's industrial plants it was cause for celebration. Major victories were also cause for celebration, like the crucial battle of Midway, a turning point early in the war. [20]

## PEACE!

An unparalleled and an emotional outpouring erupted at 4 o'clock on 14 August 1945 when news of the Japanese surrender was announced. Since the bombing of Nagasaki on 9 August surrender negotiations had been uncertainly, tediously progressing. Would the Japanese fight on to the last man? Would the US have to send invading forces to the islands with serious loss of lives? Anxiety existed everywhere. Thousands of people and cars crowded downtown streets, honking horns, aimless cheering, tears, hugging and kisses randomly given described Seattle. Fourth Avenue and Pike Street seemed the most congested, traffic barely moving. Free of automobile and bus traffic Victory Square was crammed. So taken was Mayor Devin that he declared an official one-day holiday. Devin soon caught the spirit and stretched the holiday to two days. Governor Wallgren followed suit. Since there were no guards parks and beaches were shut down. Liquor stores were shut down, but were under police protection. The city had experienced nothing like this before, not even the celebration on the Great War's armistice day. [21]

# EDUCATION
## THE UNIVERSITY OF WASHINGTON: INDISPENSABLE TO CITY'S ADAPTATION TO MODERNITY

The UW stepped up its Army and Navy ROTC programs in the nation's war mobilization effort. These programs soon became basic training programs that led directly to active service. The Navy College Training, the "V-12" program, began enrolling students in July 1943 under a quota set at 1,130. About 900 students enlisted in the Army program. Living space was provided in the women's dormitory for 600 males once the 300 women were evicted. Negotiations with various fraternity houses provided more housing. The "Commons" in the Home Economics building basement was adapted to serve as the mess for military trainees. Civilian student enrollment fell by more than 3,500. More than one hundred faculty took leaves of absence for active military service, employment in a vital war industry, or in government service. Several departments directly engaged in war-related research. The UW had been supplying Boeing with engineers and top executives for years and would continue in that role. The university's first special contract research agency, the Applied Physics Laboratory, was established in summer 1943. It was funded by the Navy, specifically for developing a fuse for detecting submarines.[1]

If not inspired by the war, long-range planning was certainly accelerated by that experience. Opportunities for funding education in general seemed more promising than ever before. While the necessity had always been there, the depression years had blocked serious efforts toward addressing education needs, including higher education. Given those years when simple survival was a top priority, neither the money nor public leadership was there for education. Even the prosperous 1920s was marked by niggardliness in funding public education as the business community strove mightily to impose a 40 mill limit on real property taxes while fighting the imposition of taxes on intangible property, and a graduated income tax. The 40 mill tax limitation finally won in 1932, at which time taxes on intangible property was resisted. The graduated income tax also was defeated when the state Supreme Court declared the recently enacted income tax act unconstitutional in 1933. Higher education and the public schools suffered from such parsimony. The fact that the governor during 1925-1932 was hostile to public education in general, opposed protections against child labor, and had imposed special hardships upon the UW did not help the situation. [2]

In the altered wartime/postwar climate, the most promising opportunity for the university was the establishment of a medical school. The first attempt in 1884 was aborted when the Territorial legislature approved establishment of a medical school but neglected to fund it. To care for the indigent sick King County established in 1894 a hospital in Georgetown, then on the southern fringe of the city. A private hospital, the Seattle General, was built in 1895. The Oregon-Washington Medical Association in 1903 discouraged the regents from seriously entertaining the idea. Instead the regents modestly resolved to create a department of medicine whenever it was deemed appropriate. The City set aside the upper three floors of the Public Safety Building to deal with acute care in response to the city's astounding population spurt, when Seattle's population more than doubled during the century's first decade. Two more private hospitals began operations in quick succession, the Swedish in 1910 and Providence in 1911. A 1927 survey of public hospitals in the city and county indicated deplorable conditions. The King County Medical Society urged the county commissioners and city council to authorize a $2.75 million bond issue for a new county hospital to be located on First Hill overlooking Elliott Bay and appropriately named "Harborview". Occupied in 1931, Harborview held 425 beds, had outpatient facilities, and residence for two hundred nurses and students. As Clement Finch notes in his school history, Harborview became the intellectual center of the local medical profession, but not a teaching and research hospital. The King County Medical Society managed the hospital for all practical purposes and its doctors provided free medical service to the indigent. King County was the only county in the state where doctors provided free services. When the old age pension bill, Initiative 141, was approved by the voters in 1940 free service was extended to qualified pensioners as well. However, because the Society decided the initiative's sponsor, the Washington Pension Union, was a political organization it resolved in October 1942 to abolish free service to those applying under Initiative 141. [3]

Lacking at Harborview was a teaching and research program. For that a full blown academic program was essential and on a scale that only a university could provide. This proposition was so expensive for everyone concerned that hardly a serious thought was accorded it. However, during the wartime period and its accompanying prosperity, all this changed. For one thing thousands of veterans, funded by the G.I. Bill of Rights, would be returning to colleges and universities to continue their often interrupted higher education or to start it from scratch. Of these many would enter medical schools. Also many older medical doctors would soon be retiring and would need to be replaced. Inspired by the advances in medicine during the war future medical education would have to embody basic research in all health sciences fields. Few established schools were then up-to-date. It was expected that better doctors would emerge out of these medical schools abreast of current scientific knowledge and anxious to apply it. Washington state was one of ten states without a medical school. In the postwar years Seattle had a population base to justify the establishment of a medical school and wartime prosperity also suggested a medical school could be adequately funded. What seemed particularly true for Washington and Seattle, held true for the rest of the nation as well to judge from a memorandum issued by the American College of Surgeons and the American Medical Association 10 May 1944: "It is therefore felt that the medical profession should take the leadership toward establishment of a graduate and post-graduate medical school under the auspices of the University of Washington...[and that the legislature should appropriate funding for it during its 1945 session]." The board of trustees of the Washington State Medical Association met on 14 May 1944 to discuss the proposition presented by Dr. David Matheny of the State Board of Medical Examiners and A.J. Hockett superintendent of the King County Hospital System for establishing such a school at the UW. The board agreed to appoint a committee composed of a doctor from each congressional district plus Dr. David Hall of the UW's Health Center as an ex officio member. A subcommittee was quickly formed to discuss the proposition with UW president Lee Paul Sieg, meeting with the UW president on 18 May. Although initially distrustful of the committee's authority Sieg warmed up when he read the Washington State Medical Association's minutes. Sieg made his acceptance contingent upon including a dental school. This found easy acceptance and was soon followed by one on the 18th with the UW Regents, who were easily brought into the fold. It was decided to have a bill drawn up for presentation to the Legislature at its 1945 session. [4]

Meanwhile Dr. A.J. Hockett, superintendent of Harborview, was asked to draw up a postgraduate education plan. In it he argued for the university's centrality. To broaden support for the proposed medical school the Seattle Chamber of Commerce lent its imprimatur, soon joined by the left wing Washington Pension Union, the CIO, the Washington State Labor Federation, Federation of Women's Clubs, and others. Strength was added to the UW's position by the existence of a School of Nursing under Dean Elizabeth Soule. Soule sought to upgrade the nursing program in tandem with establishment of a medical school. To further help impress legislators the UW Library was actively building its health sciences collection. With all their forces and programs in line the medical school committee next met with Governor Langlie 22 July, where it encountered some resistance. Hesitant to express his own opinion Governor Langlie announced it was his constituents who would be unwilling to fund such an expensive proposition. He expressed some skepticism about the estimated annual operating budget of only $450,000. The governor was not alone in his dissent. Senior faculty and deans feared the medical school funding would divert funds from other deserving departments. Assuming most resistance came from Republicans inside and outside the legislature, the committee turned to the Democratic party floor leader in the senate for strategy, Albert Rosellini. Uniquely qualified politically, Rosellini was the cousin of Dr. Leo Rosselini, an attending surgeon at Harborview and a strong ally of the prospective medical school and was also Chairman Pro-tem of Harborview's Board of Trustees. Rosellini insisted on a bill that would win bipartisan support and wrote the enabling bill with that in mind. What emerged was a capital budget of $3.75 million and an operating budget of $450,000. The bill passed 6 February 1945 with only one dissenting vote. Newly elected governor Mon Wallgren signed the bill 15 March 1945. [5]

The search committee selected Dr. Edward Turner as the Dean of the Medical School. Turner graduated from the University of Chicago's masters program, earned his M.D. from the University of Pennsylvania, and completed his internship at the Billings Hospital of the University of Chicago. Most recently he had completed eight years administering the medical school program at Meharry University. Turner accepted the offer because he was impressed by the initiating role of the medical associations, and he was convinced there was minimal town-gown tension. Turner rallied his supporters to the cause in his first annual report: "[Due to rapid] advances in the diagnosis and treatment of human ailments...they necessitate marked changes of certain phases in the training of the physicians of today and actually render obsolete the methods of a generation ago." He proceeded to list those changes, stressing the critical function of basic research, upon which effective clinical practice must depend. In his words: a medical school must provide "thorough sound basic education in medicine and an intelligent productive program of investigation". By pointing the UW medical school toward a broad scale scientific research mission in the health fields the entire university became more oriented comparably in other departments as well. Some of those departments already were producing research of immediate value. The UW, in step with universities elsewhere, was adapting to modernity, with the medical school leading the way. [6]

Until the Health Sciences building could be built those relevent departments already existing on campus had to remain where they were and accomodate the new faculty recruits, known as "star boarders". A Board of Health Sciences recommended that the medical and dental schools be started in fall of 1946 and that every possible effort be made to have clinical facilities available for dentistry by fall of 1948, otherwise funding might be jeopardized. Of the three hundred candidates who applied for admission to the medical school fifty were selected by the admissions committee, which "endeavored to avoid anything in the nature of quotas involving race, creed, or sex." In fact quotas, consciously or not were set, and they guided admissions practices until required to adapt to federal affirmative action guidelines in the 1970s. Judging from photographs of graduating classes, the number of women admitted seemed to be four, until the 1970s, regardless of class size. Nonwhites also appeared to be comparably limited until the 1970s. [7]

Convinced that a teaching and research hospital was essential to the fulfillment of a medical school's mission, Turner assigned that his top priority. Wedded to this was employment of a full-time clinical faculty, a clear break with the past that the American Medical Association was urging nationwide. With such a hospital and faculty in place the entire medical school curriculum, here and elsewhere, would be reconstructed, and accompanied in Turner's view, "[with the breaking down] of departmental barriers". A teaching and research hospital facility was predictably a few years off, however. Affiliation agreements with various area hospitals had to suffice. Harborview Hospital was central to implementation of this interim program. Dean Turner explained to President Allen that he and Dr. Edwin Bennett, general superintendent of the King County Hospital System, had agreed to having two major hospital divisions - Medicine and Surgery - each under direction of those same division heads at the UW. A second affiliation agreement was made with Children's Orthopedic Hospital, effective fall of 1948, for the departments of pediatrics, orthopedics, and preventive medicine. Another affiliation was forged with Firlands Sanitarium where tubercular victims were treated. A fourth affiliation, this with the US Marine Hospital, rounded out the first stage, thereby facilitating the planned teaching and research program. The problem with this plan was that none of these facilities was prepared to implement it. [8]


That the university's new president Raymond Allen was a physician helped Dean Soule in her ambitions for the nursing school. Soule's cause was strengthened by the fact that there was a nationwide shortage of nurses and declining enrollment in nursing schools. This "nursing crisis" inspired special funding from private and government agencies for studies in nursing education and service. At the UW President Allen began by approving sabbatical leaves for doctoral study for the medical school faculty. Allen's public statements made clear his holistic view of the health sciences. Allen also advocated raising nursing to the "level of other professions". Indeed, to neglect raising nursing standards would have left a vacuum in the health professions that would, necessarily, have to be dealt with later. Allen became more directly involved by naming himself chair of the Advisory Committee to the Washington Nursing Study. This nationwide assessment of nursing was prompted in part by recognition of the more professional functions that nurses performed during the war: administration of intravenous fluid, prescribing and applying new and proven antibiotics, developing methods of physical therapy to speed patient recovery, and providing psychiatric assistance. Indicative of the fresh attention given this traditionally undervalued profession, the American Cancer Society's support of the nursing school's application for a program in cancer detection and control led to addition of cancer detection to the curriculum in 1947. The State Medical Association lent its influential voice in support of advanced education for nurses. Apprentice programs were added for high school graduates that would qualify them for advanced training in nursing schools. With this momentum the six national nursing organizations joined together in 1948 to establish the first consolidated accreditation for nurses. Nursing was now aligned with other health professions in the drive to lengthen lives and mediate pain along the way. [9]

Not all was smooth sailing for the UW in relation to the King County Medical Society. Dean Turner had been regularly meeting with the society concerning the teaching program at Harborview. Several society members were dissatisfied with the way things were going. Addressing the society in 1948 Turner spoke his hope: "that the Society would not permit a few individuals to sow so much discord within the medical profession itself that it would prevent the school from developing into the institution that it could become." He continued by suggesting that "some of our physician members needed to take this to heart and that we should cease standing in our own way…so that we can make the progress that we should as a medical group."[10]

The Society played defense against group practice and what they called "contract medicine". Dean Turner and a growing number in the medical field, on the other hand, found solo practice and fee for service obsolete. First to feel Society's bite was Group Health Cooperative. As a consumer controlled organization Group Health members prepaid for service, the medical staff engaged in group practice, and the cooperative established a program of preventive medicine. Membership could be on an individual/family basis or by group. The latter included labor unions, granges, business firms, and other corporate bodies: "contract medicine". Should such an organization succeed it menaced traditional medical practice. Consequently the Society worked to sabotage this threat. It denied membership to Group Health Coopertive doctors, hospitals denied them hospital privileges and would not admit Group Health patients. Only the relatively new Virginia Mason Clinic accepted Group Health patients, although it too was having problems with the Society. Failing to come to some agreement with the Society Group Health Cooperative filed a law suit November 1949, charging the Society with conspiracy in restraint of trade. Although GHC lost in superior court it won on appeal in the state Supreme Court in November 1951. [11]

*1949 was a momentous year for the UW. Its Health Sciences Building was completed in June; it won accreditation from the Association of Medical Schools in October. In basic health sciences research the Medical School was on its way to national leadership, a testimony to Dean Edward Turner's faculty recruitment program. The photograph is of the Health Sciences Building, June 1949. the pedestrian bridge crosses Pacific Avenue.*

The 1948 general election not only astounded political pundits when President Truman won re-election, but it also resulted in passage of a new state pension initiative that affected the medical school. The Washington Pension Union sponsored Initiative 172 to undo legislation passed by the 1947 state legislature that emasculated WPU's 1940 initiative, Number 141. The WPU returned in 1948 with Initiative 172. It not only set a pension floor of $60 per month for senior citizens and the blind, eliminated the 1947 lien law, but it also gave pensioners free choice of their doctors and dentists. Its passage presented the medical and dental schools with difficult problems related to clinical teaching and the affiliation agreements. Previously the medical school had treated patients at Harborview without charge, but with passage of 172 fees would be paid to those doctors selected by patients. Turner worried that standards of practice would be impossible to enforce since the school would no longer be in authority. The UW also would be placed in competition with private doctors, potentially fueling town-gown tensions. Also, for Harborview to maintain solvency the dean insisted it "must have from 175 to 200 patients at all times covered by Public Welfare and under the care of the private physician of their choice." In summary, the dean saw 172 as a threat to the teaching and research program before the UW obtained its own hospital. Funding of the latter, in fact, had been sidetracked by outgoing governor, Mon Wallgren, who eliminated it from the 1949 budget. Complications all around, and that was not everything.

Anxiety about accreditation was pending in fall 1949, when the medical school was to be surveyed by the AMA and the Association of Medical Colleges. Fortunately, friendly key legislators approached the UW about hospital funding, Republican Senator Clinton Harley, chair of the Senate appropriations committee, and Democrat Ed Riley, chair of the House appropriations committee. Each promised to do all in his power to appropriate the money. Heartening too was completion of three units of the Health Sciences building and their occupancy in January. Affiliations with the surgery departments at Swedish and Providence hospitals were also in place. [12]

Anxiety about the effects of Initiative 172 were soon allayed. Turner credited "a large share of the profession [for recognizing] our problems and [they] cooperated to make it possible to carry on the basic teaching program." Relief at this coincided with clearance of the school's first hurdle: accreditation. On 22 October 1949 accreditation was won and with it came admission into the Association of Medical Colleges. The medical school's first graduates entered the profession, 10 June 1950. In the medical school's Fourth Annual Report, 1949-1950, the dean conceded that the consequences of Initiative 172 had been less severe than anticipated: "[It] was possible to salvage the clinical teaching program to the point where effective and basically satisfactory training for undergraduate medical students has been possible". The Harborview staff had been reorganized and a large number of physicians were added "to guarantee adequate income from recipients of public welfare". However, in the 1950 election Initiative 172 was replaced by Initiative 178 and Harborview's budget was cut. Since there was no funding for the painfully sought teaching and research hospital, resort to Referendum 9 was tried in the 1950 election. Referendum 9 needed only a majority favorable vote but it lost by one-third of one percent. An embittered Turner acidly commented to President Allen that if only the UW Alumni Association had mobilized its vote for Referendum 9, rather than its opposition to it the outcome could have reversed. The UW would not get its hospital until 1959, six years after Turner's retirement. [13]

While establishment of the medical and dental schools most clearly marked the transition of the University of Washington to modernity it reflected the national movement toward systematic attention to health management, recognizing that clinical practice must be based on science and scientific research. Fruition of this movement was made possible by the economic prosperity of the time. Funding on a national scale was possible for the first time. In less dramatic ways the UW was brought forward, as faculty and departments supported work of the Seattle Civic Unity Committee. Responding to the region's demographic transformation the Sociology Department produced the first data on nonwhite population groups in the area. Inspired by the nationwide rash of strikes in early 1946 the university established an Institute of Industrial Relations in April 1946 under Dr. William Hopkins (renamed Institute of Labor Economics) to deal with the general "breakdown" in labor-management relations. One of its first contributions to Civic Unity Committee work came after failure of the legislature to pass a fair employment practices act in 1947; its staff produced a study of job opportunities open to nonwhites in the Seattle area. The publication documented widespread employment discrimination, paving the way for passage of an FEPC act in 1949. To awaken the public's awareness of racial minorities in their presence the university joined with the CUC in sponsoring a demonstration project on race relations in April 1948; its success led to the Annual Northwest Institute on Race Relations. [14]

While the university's leadership failed to protect academic freedom in 1948-1949 it nonetheless should be credited for its nationally significant role in the wave of Cold War hysteria that began to grip the nation - this too, a transition toward modernity. President Allen redeemed himself in the eyes of civil libertarians, however, by facing down the professional patriotic groups in 1949 like the American Legion, Pro-America, and Daughters of the American Revolution, editorialist Ross Cunningham of the *Times* among others, over the hiring of controversial Malcom Cowley as a Walker-Ames lecturer for 1950. Cowley, a former editor of the *New Republic* and a respected literary critic was invited by newly appointed English Department chair, Robert Heilman. The Board of Regents had to act on his recommendation, which President Allen accepted and defended before the board on 13 May. This was just four months after the regents had fired three professors and placed three others on probation as a result of the tenure committee hearings in fall 1948. With the exception of regent George Stuntz, Allen convinced the board to authorize Cowley's appointment. How exceptional was this recent action? For this the reader can find some coverage in the "Postscript". [15]

# Seattle's Public Schools: A Vital Cog in Mobilization, Turn to Future

Seattle Public Schools as an integral component in the region's war mobilization efforts has been described in the chapter on the wartime economy. Its leaders and teachers adapted a curriculum and facilities to better meet the manpower needs of industry, those of the burgeoning bureaucracies in government and private business, and to ease the transition of high school graduates into the armed services. The facilities and staff volunteered to register the civilian population in the nation's rationing programs. The schools joined with volunteer organizations to support nursery schools and day care centers, many of which operated under school auspices. Family Life courses were offered to prepare its graduates for working in nursery schools, making it possible for mothers to take jobs in war industries and the bureaucracies. Day-care nursery schools remained open in the postwar years. Although the State Education Department reduced its contribution toward the upkeep of nursery schools and would no longer underwrite deficits as in the past, Superintendent Samuel Fleming found from a parental survey that they were willing to pay $1.50 per day per child. On that basis nine of the current eleven nursery schools remained open, most in the city's public housing projects. However, with reduction of state aid play centers for older children were closed. [1]

School building construction had been minimally addressed during the 1930s due to the depression, and to the 40-mill property tax limitation that business leaders won in 1932. The War Production Board banned construction of permanent school structures. By war's end there was no mistaking the existence of a huge backlog of postponed construction and maintenance work.

Working for the school system was its mostly positive high visibility during wartime. It effectively created a dependable constituency of its own. When the

School Board submitted a $10 million school construction bond issue in March 1946 all the newspapers, the Municipal League, five radio stations, labor unions, the League of Women Voters, the PTA, and the Federation of Women's Clubs joined forces in support. Voters approved it "by the highest number of votes accorded on any issue or candidate on the ballot". The vote in favor was 90,000 with only 14,000 voting "No". [2]

Indicative of the transitional character of the system in the immediate postwar period was the mushrooming of evening school enrollment. In 1940 there were 9,421 students, dropping in 1944 to 6,268, then climbing to 8,297 in 1945 and 12,221 in 1946. Feeling its way, and unaware of the constitutional issues raised by religious education in the schools, the Board authorized the Council of Churches to conduct an experimental program for 150 boys and girls of Green Lake school in 1946. In May 1947 the Church Council requested released time for religious education, arousing so much community opposition that the Board decided to discontinue it for the time being. Still insensitive to church-state issues, the Board, in February 1948, authorized use of the new Memorial Stadium, without charge, by Youth for Christ for the conduct of its Easter services. In time the Church Council recognized the constitutional issues at stake and opposed religious instruction or display in public schools. Before long the US Supreme Court would rule such practices and policies unconstitutional. [3]

Also transitional was teacher hiring. No African American teachers had ever been employed by Seattle's schools. Rachmiel Forschmiedt volunteered to secure signatures of parents favoring the hiring of teachers regardless of their race, color, or creed. On motion of Board member James Duncan, who as an officer in the International Association of Machinists who had opposed their admission to that union, requested Superintendent Worth McClure to reply that hiring of teachers had always been on the basis of best qualified, and that the Board did not intend to change that policy. The following year the new school superintendent Samuel Fleming pointed to "quite satisfactory" results in other school systems that employed "Negro" teachers. Fleming asked the Board to reconsider the issue and authorize their hiring, providing their qualifications were "equal to or above the qualifications presented by other applicants". After some discussion the Board instructed Fleming to proceed accordingly. When Thelma Dewitty and Marita Johnson were hired in fall 1947 the National Conference of Christians and Jews congratulated the Board. To this the Board replied, "This is not a new policy or program...but merely the carrying out of a long established policy to employ those with the highest qualifications for the position." As a category, African Americans were not alone in receiving attention. Women teachers had been forced to resign in the past, upon marrying. Part of the rationale had been opposition to their continued employment should their spouse be employed. During the depression this had appeared justified, but it fell short of reasonableness in more prosperous times. Postwar prosperity brought the issue forward, particularly in light of married women being hired regularly under an "Emergency Service Classification". As of 27 June 1947 there were 329 Emergency Service teachers in the corps. In presenting the report to the Board Fleming recommended adoption of a new policy allowing employment of married women teachers beginning fall 1948. The Board agreed.

Slowly the Board was adapting to the changed demographics brought by the great migration to the Pacific Coast states, and increased employment of married women in general. That racism was widespread over the entire nation and that the war had consciously been fought in part against racial, ethnic, and religious stereotyping that rationalized discrimination...all this must have influenced the Board. However, unlike the Board's discussion of its married teachers policy no detail is supplied regarding racial discrimination. [4]

Vocational training classes had proved their relevance during the war. The Board had answered the need for them by converting some older school facilities to training war workers and renting space elsewhere as needed. Expansion of Edison Vocational School was clearly essential if the Board was to continue this program into the postwar period. Returning veterans, particularly needed to be accomodated. In September 1946 Edison's abutting neighbor, Broadway High School, was closed. To appease Broadway alumni Edison was renamed Broadway-Edison Technical School. It had five departments - English, Social Studies, Science, Mathematics, and Commercial - which provided evening as well as daytime classes. Garfield High absorbed Broadway's high school students. [5]

Friction with the Municipal League peaked in spring 1947 with the League assuming a markedly imperious tone. When the League polled its members in 1944 it found them dissatisfied with students' spelling and reading proficiency. Following discussion among its members, the League in May 1945 recommended that the Board authorize an "educational audit" by a "recognized expert". The Board neglected to act on this recommendation. In summer 1946 the League resubmitted its proposal, contending that it must be satisfied that citizens receive the "greatest possible return" on their investment of $12 million. While the League found many things in the system to be "proud of", it believed "there is room for improvement". The cost of the audit would by a slight $50,000 or less, a "wise" expenditure. Fleming firmly rejected their proposal, contending the system was conducting an audit on an ongoing basis and it had its own experts for the purpose: "we test as we teach". [6]

When the School's administration saw its construction budget whittled away by rampant postwar inflation it called for help. For a special meeting of 6 August

1948 the Board gathered together its predictable ally, the PTA, and surprisingly its formidable watchdog critic, the Municipal League. Representing the PTA was its executive committee, the League was represented by attorney Richard Thorgrimson. In 1946 the School's building construction budget totaled $12,771,052. Two school levies (1942 and 1944) had netted about $2.25 million. The 1946 bond issue added another $10 million, while the State authorized expenditure of $506,623 from its coffers. The last new building was constructed in 1940, when an ancient T.T. Minor was replaced at a cost of $5.35 per square foot. Marking the rate of inflation was the Loyal Heights addition, costing $9.72 per square foot; the 1948 addition to E.C. Hughes was contracted at $15.46 per square foot. Obviously inflation was impeding implementation of any long range building plans. The Board figured their plans had to be cut back more than 50 percent. Given the "rapidly rising elementary school enrollments" it was necessary to defer many other projects while assigning high priority to those schools. To cut expenses along the way federal surplus structures were acquired to serve temporarily as classrooms and nursery schools. Forty classrooms had been added to two junior high schools and construction of three more junior highs was progressing at sites recently acquired, though their completion was "three or four years" away. When completed they would ease the pressure on elementary schools by absorbing grades seven and eight; however $6 million was needed for that purpose. Elementary school projects in progress required another $1 million plus. To pay for them either an 18-mill special levy was a possibility, or another bond issue would do it. If the levy route was preferred (to avoid bond interest charges) it was thought best to offer it one amount at a time, 18-mills too forbidding a request. Awaiting construction was a new School District administrative building. Whether to place a 5-mill levy on the 1950 ballot or to follow Board member Dietrich Schmitz's advice and have the PTA "make one drive, as required for a bond issue" preoccupied the Board. It voted for the bond issue. Meanwhile a Referendum Number 7, asked voters to approve a $40 million bond issue for public schools in the upcoming fall election. Voters approved the bonds 395,417 votes to 248,200; in King County the measure won overwhelmingly 116,841 to 73,277. If only inflation could be held in check these funds would serve their intended purpose. That was a big "if" as the nation marched into the Korean conflict. [7]

# PART 3

# THE POSTWAR ECONOMY

### INTRODUCTION

Expectations were widespread that a return to prewar conditions was in store once wartime production ceased. There was genuine fear that unemployment would recur as industry cut back its employment rolls. A ripple effect would dry up consumer demand. Helplessly, the nation would revert to the days of the Great Depression. Absent in this conception was any role the federal government might play in preventing this gloomy outcome. Cancellation of wartime contracts, it was widely believed, would cancel a federal role. Yet, it should have been clear that as long as it was under federal compulsion that plants were converted from producing consumer goods for a peacetime market to those needed for war, that this necessarily placed responsibility for reconversion upon the federal government as well. Indeed, to prevent a recurrence of the rampant inflation, depression, and violent strikes that followed World War I, federal administrators took the lead for postwar planning early in 1944. The planning process included state and municipal governments as well. Industry leaders and their trade associations, in any case, would never have allowed the federal government to escape responsibility to play a positive role in reconversion. Industry leaders dominated the various federal agencies during the war in implementing wartime mobilization and they would largely remain in bureaucratic places or in key influential positions to sustain many of the advantages industry had gained during the war. In general, though, they favored policies promoting inflationary measures, rapid lifting of wartime controls. These were precisely the policies the President resisted to prevent a rampant inflation that would destabilize the economy, creating unmanageable social and political unrest. Anti-inflationary programs like the OPA were still in place. How much longer the

OPA would remain was uncertain, given the pressures from the business community to eliminate the agency. Also, they fully expected to continue keeping organized labor in the strait jacket that its own wartime "no strike" pledge and the Smith-Connally Anti-Strike Act had placed it in. Failing that, their congressional allies could be relied upon to pass appropriate legislation...and Congress did, following the largely successful strikes of early 1946. This mixture of contending forces and policies is dealt with in the sections to follow.[1]

An undercurrent of optimism lay just below this pervasive feeling of uncertainty about the future. Reflecting the transformation of the Western states during the war and the ambitions of some industry leaders, C.T. Bakeman, director of development for Puget Sound Power and Light, found in his Eastern visits, "the door is always open to the 'man from Seattle'." He saw low cost electrical power as an attractant to Eastern capital, particularly for aluminum. But he acknowledged cheap energy itself was not a sufficient draw. Bakeman pointed to the western markets that had opened up by population growth alone: "two to four times the buying power it had from only four years ago". He indicated "flourishing local enterprise", improvements in transportation, abundance of raw materials as factors and optimistically concluded "labor strife" is no longer a problem. At the Western States Council conference in September 1945, anxiety surfaced about maintaining the momentum of Western industrialization. Time was short for outlining "a pattern for placing government-owned plants in the West in private operation after the war [so] vital to the maintenance and development of the West's industrial economy." Government-owned aluminum, steel, and aircraft plants were among the candidates. At the conference Boeing's H.O. West spoke for the one industry which war had brought so spectacularly to life after a long gestation period. That it was so heavily concentrated on the West Coast gave it special prominence at the conference. In telling "What the Aircraft Industry Wants", West, curiously, made no reference to any role for the federal government. Was such a role subsumed? Perhaps. Representing the Bonneville Power Administration, a federal corporation, Ivan Bloch spoke of its potential, already demonstrated during the war, in support of industrial development. BPA's function in promoting agricultural development of the Columbia River basin was drawing near as well. [2]

In mid-July Seattle was holding its own relative to the rest of the country insamuch as a substantial proportion of war contracts were still current, not yet cancelled. The Chamber of Commerce alerted local businesses to the prospect of acquiring government surpluses during the conversion period; the surpluses ranged from whole plants, office equipment, to armed services supplies. As to the latter, army and navy surpluses provided cheap startup clothing and equipment supplies for "G.I Joes", "Chubby and Tubbys" (still in existence) and outlets on First and Second avenues such as Warshal's sporting goods store on First Avenue and Madison which replenished its stock with these surpluses. Since the early postwar textile industry concentrated on producing more expensive clothing lines these surplus stores helped supply the demand for cheaper, durable lines especially those for work and outdoor recreation clothing.

Also the Chamber conducted a statewide survey of postwar jobs. Nationwide unemployment was expected to reach 5,000,000 in three months and 8,000,000 by spring, according to federal reconversion director John Snyder. The Chamber's survey showed unemployment in the immediate weeks would be somewhere between 10,000 and 37,000 in King County. It expected manufacturing industry to lose about half its wartime labor force, dropping down from the wartime peak of about 100,000. But it expected their absorption elsewhere in the local economy. One area of high expectations was the housing market, in which 20,000 workers were surely going to be kept busy for the next three to five years, building perhaps 3,000 homes annually, as soon as building supplies were forthcoming. Hotels needed modernization, hospitals needed renovation and new ones needed to be built; the UW was about to embark on a building program of its own. By the end of August the number of posted job openings had fallen to only 5,000 just as extensive layoffs had finally set in. Governor Wallgren's advisory committee on development began identifying potential public works projects to deal with the growing problem. Senator Magnuson's office came into the job picture and was confident federal funds could be mustered. Mayor Devin was also responding, identifying deferred maintenance projects totalling $5 million that could be put in place. By November the State allocated $3,421,600 to Seattle from the $20 million authorized by the state legislature. All of these measures stood in sharp contrast with the period following World War I. [3]

An optimistic note was sounded also by Nathanael Engle, UW director of its Business Research Bureau. Writing in December 1945 Engle projected a picture of substantially full employment in western Washington once the process of reconversion was accomplished. Boeing, for one, was still filling its government contracts and expected to employ at least 50 percent more workers than before the war, and the company denied rumors that it was closing its Renton plant. Shipbuilding shifted largely to repair and reconstruction; but still the industry anticipated sustaining employment at about 23 percent above prewar levels. Shipbuilding had ceased hiring through the Boilermakers Union, and Puget Sound Bridge and Drydock announced it was laying off 700 of its 4,000 employees. On the brighter side, the backlog of housing and other construction demand was expected to keep the forest products industries well above prewar levels. Engle foresaw infusion of new, small scale business, stimulated by government-insured loans to veterans choosing to start a business under the G.I Bill. J.E. Louttit, manager of the Industrial

Department of the Seattle Chamber of Commerce, noted the introduction of these new small businesses and commented: "In some cases we find inefficient plants [being replaced by new ones and] many plant owners have taken advantage of surplus war real property." Loutitt found that 109 new industries had been started between March and December 1947, representing a capital investment of $9,822,300. [4]

Indexes of Business Activity, published in *Pacific Northwest Industry*, indicate economic trends and effects of the war and levels of activity for the Seattle-Tacoma area. Electric energy consumption between 1939 and 1950 moved upward without interruption. Using 1935-39 as the base the index for 1939 was 111.8, 183.1 for 1942, 261.7 for 1945, 276.1 for 1947, 347.0 for 1950. Electricity sales in Seattle for November 1946 broke the record for monthly sales, and December sales exceeded November's. The Pacific Northwest power shortage of 1948/1949 registered only a slight increase between 1948 and 1949 for the Seattle-Tacoma area: 324.6 for 1948 and 325.2 for 1949. Indicative of the vitality of Seattle's economy just after the war: March 1946 retail sales, as measured by department store sales, outran increases in general business activity. July department store sales set a new record indexing at 367 while August's remained high at 364. Logs and forest products car loads for December 1946 through January 1947 increased from 138 to 157 despite car shortages throughout the region. Lumber production remained relatively low, indexing at 108 in November and rising to only 111 in December 1946. Complaints filled the air though because faster rail service was needed, as were more steamship lines and air services. The Port of Seattle drew criticism for lack of initiative, although it was in the process of directing the construction of the Sea-Tac airport. Turning to Seattle's cost of living, the consumer price index registered steady increases starting with an index reading of 101.1 in 1939. The consumer price index climbed without interruption: 121.1 for 1942, 129.2 for 1944, 132.2 for 1945, 142.4 for 1946, 160.8 for 1947, 172.9 for 1948. The index dropped slightly to 169.1 in 1949, when the economy was floundering, but it resumed its upward movement to 180.8 by November 1950. [5]

The resiliency of the economy was registered by Puget Sound Power and Light in its annual report for 1948. Despite the five-month strike at Boeing, followed by a long waterfront strike which restricted shipping, 1948 was considered a "good year". The report claimed the state ranked sixth in per capita building construction: "some 32,000 families in the Seattle area plan to buy or build a house within the next three years." The state also ranked second nationally in retail sales per capita. [6]

Non-farm employment in King County showed a downward trend in 1948, some of which the state Employment Security Department attributed to Boeing sub-contracting out of the area during its prolonged strike. The department noted in its February 1949 report a near 6 percent drop in non-farm employment in King County. Boeing registered the only increase. The UW's Nathanael Engle, reviewed "area problems" that surfaced in 1949. Engle noted a "modest" upturn in unemployment, a decline in farm prices, restraints imposed on business by the power shortage, an increase of freight rates, and the relatively higher steel prices imposed by the industry's basing point pricing system. Business failures in 1949 were three times those in 1947, and there was worry about federal spending policies, "on which much of the area's prosperity rests". Yet Engle and his *PNI* colleagues concluded the 1950 would be "another good year for business." Would the Korean War lead to another war mobilization effort on the scale of World War II? That takes us beyond the scope of this volume. Bear in mind, however, President Eisenhower's admonition in his farewell address, about the growing "military-industrial complex" as a critical feature of the nation's political economy. What had begun in World War II hardly missed a beat thereafter. [7]

### The Postwar Labor Force: Where Did the Women Go?

The Seattle Chamber of Commerce assessed the postwar labor market in 1944 and concluded there would be a demand for of 314,000 workers. How did its analyst, Nathanael Engel, arrive at this figure? He started with the 108,000 new jobs created by the war. He deducted 12,000 postwar out-migrants and 11,000 women who would be leaving war work. To this he added 37,000 returning veterans, plus an expected 122,000 peacetime jobs, plus the 192,000 jobs that existed in 1939. From the survey sample he estimated 21 percent of the newcomers would leave the city and 30 percent of the women "will withdraw from the labor force". With this survey as context we can turn to the dynamics of the postwar labor market expecting full well the wartime labor force would be reconstituted. Would the critical role that women played in wartime serve as a catalyst for its longer term recomposition? [8]

Government contract cancellations at Boeing, the shipyards, and by government offices inevitably carried sharp reductions in employment. From the large scale employers a multiplier effect was transmitted down the line. Women and African Americans, being the last hired, were the most vulnerable workers. Neither group had much seniority and this became a handicap for them. When the federal government cancelled Boeing's contracts, the company was unprepared. So, too, was the Aero Mechanics Union. The latter advised those with less than four years of seniority to begin looking elsewhere for jobs. The company hoped its women employees would simply submit and return home, thanking them on their way out the door. Historian Karen Anderson has noted that most women lost their shipyard jobs within two weeks of V-J Day. To guarantee this result the Boilermakers Local 104 had ruled earlier that women would not be allowed to accumulate seniority. In its *104 Reporter*, the Local 104's business agent congratulated the women for work well done, but, "Now we are faced with cutbacks in shipbuilding, and you are being taken off the production team". Also working against Blacks and women, too, was the general practice of awarding war veterans seniority equal to their time in the service if they returned to work for the same employer. Veterans also added to the growing labor surplus. Granting veterans priority in hiring complicated the chances for reemployment elsewhere for those women and Blacks who were laid off. Unlike women workers at Boeing, African Americans had not been granted full union membership by Local 751; consequently, they accumulated no seniority rights. [9]

When retail sales boomed as workers began spending their wartime savings some job opportunities opened up during the months after V-J Day. A small proportion of those laid off workers were absorbed, but at lower wages. As job prospects dried up during the transition, some returned to their former homes, though fewer did so than anticipated. Single women workers had no choice but to remain in the labor force. They tended to take any job available and receive unemployment compensation while looking for work. However, to qualify for compensation the Washington State Employment Security agency required that they had been involuntarily dismissed and were actively seeking "suitable" employment. The agency's normal interpretation of "suitable" was found to be that of a job category equivalent to that from which he/she had been terminated. The agency, however, had subdivided jobs into "male" and "female" categories. To find jobs for women who had been employed in manufacturing proved practically impossible when the pool of qualified men was dramatically increasing. Also the seniority factor came into play by unions and employers. Most married women workers, but particularly older married women, resisted returning to their prewar domestic chores. While Karen Anderson credits Local 79 of the Machinists Union with banning sexual discrimination of the sort noted above Local 79 nevertheless obstructed employment of women in the machinist field because seniority rules prevailed, and women had accumulated practically none. Cumulatively, by 1946 men were replacing women workers throughout the state, according to the USES. [10]

Karen Anderson, in her study of women in the wartime labor force, concluded: "Thus, the exodus of women from the labor force after the war was to a great extent accounted for by younger women, indicating that household responsibilities, especially those connected with childrearing, still acted as a strong deterrent to the employment of women". It would take the civil rights movement of the 1960s and 1970s, along with the cumulative increase of women in the nation's labor force to seriously challenge sex as a primary determinant of job qualification. [11]

# Return to a Civilian Economy – Role of OPA

The Office of Price Administration operated during the war to prevent the potentially devastating effects of runaway inflation. Consumer protection inevitably accompanied the OPA operations. Indeed, OPA offered the only direct federal protection to consumers. Before introduction of such controls, however, resistance to full scale mobilization for war production from the business community had to be met. Reflecting that resistance in Seattle was the Civic Housing Association, as described in the chapter on the militarization of the economy. This resistance was partially overcome after President Roosevelt's "blueprint for victory" speech in early January 1942, which was followed by Congressional enactment of the second Emergency Price Control Act on 30 January. The OPA issued the General Maximum Price Regulation on 28 April 1942. There was no historical precedent to guide OPA administrators; consequently they learned in the course of developing the regulations. Necessity required that the process be gradual, educating the public and cajoling the business community with concessions when its lobbyists applied inescapable pressure. Business leaders, for example, applauded the appointment of James F. Byrnes as director of the Economic Stabilization Office, which FDR established in October 1942, a result of mounting opposition to OPA and its director Leon Henderson. Overarching authority over the economy was given to Director Byrnes. Henderson was considered too protective of consumers, too sympathetic to labor unions, and he was forced to resign in January 1943. Labor unions were the only effective consumer lobby, which, in Seattle, was the Labor Consumers League, as described in the chapter on militarization of the economy.

During wartime, despite these pressures for raising prices and rents, and to lift controls over rationed commodities, OPA held retail price increases to slightly more than 3 percent from May 1943 to August 1945, and wholesale prices to less than 2 percent - an incomparable achievement. The destabilizing effects of inflation were thereby successfully resisted. With stable prices came steady growth of income for all sectors of the economy. Soon after V-J Day came the question: How much longer would these controls remain in effect? And what should be done to avoid the catastrophic inflation and economic dislocations that followed World War I?

The OPA was faced with both the "pent-up demand for consumer goods" and its corollary, the business confidence in boom-level consumer spending. Reinforcing domestic demand were expenditures expected from the unique foreign market as Europe rebuilt, in many cases from scratch. The OPA had conceded by V-J Day that, where market conditions for particular commodities allowed for decontrol, this would be allowed on condition that decontrolling would not contribute to inflation. Should a specific decontrolled commodity lead to inflation it would be returned to control, as in the case of citrus fruits. The OPA decided, for example: "neither price ceilings nor rent ceilings were [to be] actually removed in advance of market developments..." This policy was also applied to gasoline, fuel oil, and all other rationed commodities except sugar.

OPA administrator Chester Bowles removed controls immediately on gasoline and fuel oil and all blue point foods, plus such minor items as toys, some jewelry, notions, and cigarette lighters. Rationing of meats, fats and oils, butter, sugar, shoes, and tires remained on the ration list. "Dismayed" at the alarming numbers of evictions on "flimsy pretexts" Bowles emphasized that rent controls would continue and would be removed one area at a time. The War Production Board gave the go-ahead to automobile manufacturers to reconvert their plants and announced it would remove from its rationing lists all but 40 commodities on Monday 20 August. The OPA listed specifically for anxious homebodies: mechanical refrigerators, washing and sewing machines. The War Production Board director Julius Krug warned controls would remain on commodities "in danger of hoarding, pre-emptive buying and stockpiling", and on critical materials in short supply such as tin, crude rubber, and lumber. Most exciting in Seattle seemed to be the end of gasoline rationing, although most stations remained closed while victory celebrations preoccupied the citizenry. "Fill 'er up" signalled war's end as much as anything when cars lined up at the gas stations.

To stimulate employment at the production level in nonwar industries, local WPB director Joseph E. Gandy announced its field offices had been allowed to authorize industrial construction up to $1 million, while adding that restrictions on residential construction were to remain in place. Given this stimulus four new business firms planned expenditures totalling $3,500,000. Of these four the Ford

Motor Company was putting a parts supply facility near Fourth and Spokane Street; Kaiser, a sand and gravel plant; Monsanto Chemical options on two pieces of property; and Reichhold Chemical Company a basic chemical plant. From Senator Magnuson's office came news that a large proportion of Navy contracts would go to Puget Sound yards. Short staffed during the war, many retail stores and automotive repair shops were bidding for labor, just as an exodus of wartime workers was observed heading east over Snoqualmie Pass. The Chamber of Commerce reported being contacted by some some forty big companies about prospects. Several large local firms: Isaacson Iron, Kenworth Trucks, Pacific Car and Foundry, the Doran Company, Western Gear Works, Webster-Brinkley Company, Stetson-Ross Machinery, and Bethlehem Steel already were in the midst of reconverting their operations. [2]

While cautioning labor and industry to exercise restraint President Truman removed the Little Steel Formula from wage control. Collective bargaining gained authorization to proceed in its prewar channels, should that actually be possible. CIO president Phillip Murray indicated that 70 to 80 percent of his unions were prepared to open contract negotiations. Wage increases were expected to be keyed to sustaining the take-home pay levels achieved during wartime when overtime pay was common. At the same time the 40-hour week was reestablished nationwide. By this measure and a general maintenance of employment, industrial production had turned "upward" by November. Retail sales had reached all-time highs, thereby encouraging new investment in business expansions in the months to come. The genuine fear of a return to Great Depression years dissipated. [3]

Removal of the excess profits tax effective 1 January 1946, allowed physical reconversion costs to be charged against the higher tax of 1945. This allowed plant reconversions to occur much faster than anticipated. Also, federal expenditures surpassed expectations. In overall effect employment and income were kept at wartime levels. By December consumer prices were a mere 0.5 percent above August levels, wholesale prices up by 1.3 percent, and farm prices up by 1.8 percent. Nonetheless the OPA fretted about growing speculation, which was occurring outside its jurisdictional compass. Those sectors were securities, real estate, and some commodities that had never been under control such as rye and cotton. The OPA judged: "[P]eople were betting on inflation", and were hoarding some commodities and holding back production of others in anticipation of higher prices. OPA reported "The consequences were felt not only in the markets where speculation was registered on the trading boards but in wage negotiations as well." The rub here was that wage contract negotiations were being conducted on the basis of existing, non-inflationary premises. Should inflation occur subsequently those wage scales would quickly be thrown out of whack. This is what happened. Manufacturers, responding to their factory shutdowns during the spectacular strike wave of early 1946, pressed for removal of all price controls. OPA administrators were certain that management intended to pass wage increases on to consumers, probably inflating prices more than justified by the wage package. In the consumer goods sector textile and apparel commodities proved the most difficult to control. This caused "an inflationary pressure of unprecedented magnitude", according to the OPA. A black market even developed for those commodities. Faced with these trends President Truman asked Congress, in his January 1946 State of the Union address, to renew the stabilization statutes. [4]

Automobile production symbolized reconversion for the nation as no other industry did. The OPA set average factory prices in early 1946 for all makes at approximately 3.5 percent above the 1942 level, unless changes in design specifications might justify a price hike. Ceiling prices for Ford, Mercury, and Studebaker were established for spring 1946. Dealers were required to absorb all or part of the price increases, since their margins still were higher than their prewar average of about 12 percent. [5]

In the food sector price adjustments were made for meat products to increase supply. Price controls remained for poultry. Measures were taken to conserve flour consumption, partly to meet obligations to the United Nations Reconstruction and Relief Administration. Continuation of federal subsidy programs for meat, flour, and dairy products kept price increases below their potentially lower free market level. However, wage increases of about 16 cents an hour in meat packing houses - a result of recent strikes - forced a price adjustment upward for meat. [6]

Textiles, according to the OPA, were marked by a continuation of strong inflationary pressures that carried over from wartime. Demand was transferred from the armed forces to the civilian sector, which had been penned up during wartime. Manufacturers keyed postwar fabric production toward more expensive garments, choosing that retail sector with its higher markups, instead of low priced ones. That market was left for the future, while Army-Navy surplus stores took care of some of that demand. Contributing to the short supply were the low wages paid in the Southern textile mills, which slowed the movement of workers into those mills until better job opportunities in other lines dried up. [7]

The increased cost of steel, resulting from the steel strike settlement in February 1946, forced the OPA to make concessions to steel producers in order to speed up the plant-reconversion process for industries dependent upon steel. Carbon and alloy steel products were allowed an average increase of $5 per ton, pig iron upward by 75 cents per gross ton, steel castings up by 4 percent. Automobile production was the first to be affected, forcing an additional price rise onto the wage hikes and benefits package won by the United Automobile Workers in its strikes against the industry. [8]

To accelerate building construction the OPA attacked the problem on several fronts: masonry materials, lumber, steel reinforcing bars, electrical and plumbing products, hardware, and durable consumer goods. The OPA worked with the US Employment Service in labor recruitment. The agency resorted to area/regional pricing and distribution, with an emphasis on residential construction. Douglas fir and western hemlock prices were raised by an average of 3 percent to meet the huge demand for residential construction. West coast log ceilings were raised an average of $1.25 per thousand feet to reflect the recent wage increases. Comparable price increases were allowed for other lumber products, varying from region to region. Complicating housing construction was the desire on the part of OPA officials to satisfy the need of veterans for low cost housing. (The GI Bill guaranteed loans to veterans of $2,000 toward home purchases.) On a June 1946 visit to Seattle an OPA official contended a large quantity of lumber was diverted to the black market. Consequently, the Civilian Production Administration witheld 15 percent of its construction authorizations for low cost housing for veterans. But there were too few OPA agents available to break up the black market. In addition seven lumber mills, two of which were in Seattle, had been fudging on lumber widths. While admitting to selling non-standard size lumber (1/4 inch thinner) and selling to dealers as though it met the standard width, the lumber mills contended the buyer "had his choice to take it or leave it". The OPA fined the mills to the tune of $1,625,000. [9]

Rent control in early 1946 was extended to 23 new areas to curb "inflationary rent movements" when evictions in those areas experienced housing shortages for the first time. During the first quarter of 1946 215,110 housing registrations nationally were recorded, bringing the total since V-J Day to 15,360,558. Of the 1,340,955 landlord petitions for rent increases, filed since the beginning of rent control, 763,193 had been granted. Most "alarming" to the OPA office was the acceleration in the number of evictions, one-half of which were due to "no overt act or fault of the tenant". The eviction rate was attributed to the "recent purchase of dwelling units for self-occupancy". Allegedly, landlords often used evasive sales contracts - a wartime practice referred to previously. The tenant agreed in this contract to "purchase" the dwelling then pay a monthly rent, the mortgage payment, that is above the posted ceiling, whether or not the "purchase" was genuine. Evictions during the quarter were 67.7 percent higher in 1946 than for the same quarter in 1945. Returning veterans seemed most affected. [10]

*Life of Office of Price Administration was extended three weeks after President Truman vetoed a weak Congressional extension bill. The flurry of inflationary price and rent rises during the interim prompted passage of a new bill much like the vetoed one.*

# The Seattle Sunday Times

SEATTLE, WASHINGTON, SUNDAY, JULY 21, 1946.

## CONFEREES COMPROMISE ON O.P.A. EXTENSION; RENT CONTROLS STAND

### RISING COST OF LIVING JOLTS MARRIED VETS ATTENDING UNIVERSITY

### HEAT WAVE TOPS 100 IN OTHER AREAS

### 2 Boys Drown, Third Saved By Firemen's Quick Action

### ARMY, NAVY BLAMED FOR PEARL BLOW

### LAKE BRIDGE OPENS TOO OFTEN FOR U.S. CRAFT, SAY DRIVERS

### NEW BOARD WOULD RULE ON CEILINGS

*Courtesy Seattle Public Library*

## The Phasing Out of OPA

By June 1946 OPA administrators fretted that their anti-inflationary measures might come to naught should the agency be dismantled. They saw prices rising to inflationary levels if not checked. Textile prices offered an example of what might occur generally should OPA be terminated. Because OPA had no control over textile prices, textile prices increased by 12 percent during the first quarter of 1946 and cumulatively to 38 percent since V-J Day. In other markets considered "sensitive" prices had increased by 4.4 percent in the first three months of 1946. [11]

OPA's dilemma was to speed up production in the direction of full capacity, allow benefits to industries undergoing reconversion, and yet minimize inflationary effects in the process. Production and reconversion had been proceeding apace in both the nondurable and durable goods sectors. However, signs were emerging that consumer demand was weakening, thereby convincing OPA administrators that higher wages were essential to sustaining consumer demand. This view was not widely shared in the business community. President Truman had caved in to the latter when he recommended justifiable wage increases, but allowed affected businesses to compensate for the higher labor costs incurred. Yet, as of June 1946, the OPA observed average wages in manufacturing had actually declined by 8.7 percent from the wartime levels, despite the recent nominal wage hikes: "in real terms [wages] thus declined 13.0 percent between January 1945 and June 1946." By way of contrast corporations expect their "most profitable of all peacetime years and after taxes to surpass even the wartime profit peaks." Despite these alarming disparities price control was temporarily terminated 30 June 1946. [12]

For six weeks before that 30 June deadline a Price Control Extension was bitterly contested in Congress. Organized labor and consumer groups wanted a year's extension for OPA, while the National Association of Manufacturers and the National Retail Dry Goods Association pressed for its termination. The latter two drew reinforcements from individual industry/business field advocates asking individually for their own exceptions from control. Four members of the Senate Banking Committee, including its chairman Robert Wagner, New York Democrat, and Hugh B. Mitchell of Washington submitted a minority report, charging it would be the "death sentence for effective price, wage and rent stabilization". Senator Mitchell appeared on the American Forum of the Air to debate "What Should We Do About the OPA?". He argued, that it was a gamble to abandon price controls and that "runaway" inflation would follow, thereby throwing production "entirely out of gear". Chief among the bill's provisions were transferring controls over food and agricultural commodities to the Secretary of Agriculture; giving control over nonagricultural commodities to a three-man board; decontrolling all "non-essential" commodities by the end of 1946; ending controls on meat, poultry, and dairy products on 30 June; granting cotton products more special concessions, removing thereby any obligations of manufacturers to produce more low cost clothing than they chose to. Finally, the agency's putative life would be extended one more year, to 30 June 1947. This bill emerged the last week of June, and was met with scathing denunciation. Senator Moore, Oklahoma Republican, for example, linked OPA extension with the CIO-Political Action Committee as a measure intended to "destroy our capitalistic system". Moore was not alone. Yet Senate Democratic leader, Kentucky's Alben Barkley and House Speaker Sam Rayburn told President Truman he should sign the bill because it was the best they could get. Nevertheless Truman vetoed the bill on the 29th, and justified his action the next day in a nationwide radio broadcast, urging "every business man, every producer and every landlord to adhere to existing regulations, even though for a short period they might not have the effect of law." Truman contended "the bill continues the Government's responsibility to stabilize the economy and at the same time it destroys the Government's power to do so." Labor leaders praised the President. The National Chamber of Commerce cautioned "unrelenting self-restraint" in holding the line on prices. The head of the National Institute of Real Estate Brokers suggested that rent increases should be limited to 15 or 20 percent, considered slight from its viewpoint. From its national survey the institute seemed to favor the lower figure. Democratic leadership in Congress was embittered at the veto. Its life not extended, OPA was dead.[13]

During the period 30 June to 25 July, while all controls were removed, prices shot up in every market. The Bureau of Labor Statistics reported that between 30 June and 16 July the index to daily spot market prices on 28 basic commodities had risen by 25 percent. In Seattle butter prices jumped by 12 percent. The OPA sent shoppers out in the city. The shoppers reported huge price increases for meat and fish amounting to 25 to 30 percent just one week after decontrol. Beer brewer Emil Sick assured drinkers he was holding the line, having just been allowed a price increase on 25 June. Some Seattle landlords could not restrain themselves. Exuberant, they posted rent increases immediately. Reputedly landlords were the most recalcitrant group to restrain during the war. Their recent actions inspired acting mayor Mike Mitchell to recommend to Mayor Devin the creation of a "fair rent" committee when the mayor returned from vacation. Already in place was the mayor's emergency housing committee. Worried that OPA opponents might jump the gun by raising prices unconcionably, the Master Builders Association advised local business groups to "hold the line" for fear of OPA revival. The Commerce Department commented "Perhaps the most striking aspect of this recent behavior is that the large increases occurred despite the prospect of reimposition of O.P.A. controls and a roll back to June 30 levels". It added that without this expectation prices would have increased even more. With this alarming evidence Congress was forced to act, which it did by passing a Price Control Extension Act on 25 July. This extended the life of OPA to 30 June 1947, though it was in an emasculated form, bearing essentially the same elements as the vetoed bill. Truman conceded it was the best Congress seemed capable of, "better" than the previous one, "price increases far fewer...far smaller". [14]

The Extension Act singled out some commodities for decontrol. Authority over agricultural commodities was transferred to the Secretary of Agriculture. Appeals from decisions of the OPA and Secretary of Agriculture could be made to an independent Price Decontrol Board whose decisions were final. As to nonagricultural commodities, all controls were to be removed by the end of 1946 if they were judged not important to business or living costs. "Importance" was determined when supply and demand were in or near balance. Industry advisory committees were enabled to petition the Price Administrator for commodity decontrol and to register their appeals to the Decontrol Board. With this machinery in place the OPA authority was steadily eroded in the year ahead, although ceiling prices and rents were rolled back to 30 June levels. By 30 September consumer and wholesale prices had climbed by 10 percent since 30 June, spot market prices by 22 percent. Real wages for factory workers declined by 4.2 percent, even though they received a nominal average wage increase of 4.8 percent. [15]

As to rent controls during the five-week interval of decontrol, these were minor compared to evictions, which were "widespread". Unlike rent increases made during the interval, evictions were irreversible. Due primarily to insuring some rental housing for veterans, eight new areas were brought under rent control, Seattle included. The OPA also assisted veterans in their housing needs under authority of the Veterans' Emergency Housing Act of 27 August 1946. Just how much "protection" was given veterans from landlords and realtors, the waiting period before a veteran could be legally evicted was shortened to 4 months from 6 months, and from 3 months, where that had been the norm, to 2 months! [16]

Under direction from Congress the OPA was directed to move with dispatch to eliminate all controls by 1 January 1947. OPA administrator Paul Porter, who had stubbornly delayed the aircraft workers wage inequity adjustment, 1942-1943, when he was in charge of wage stabilization, quickly removed controls on all livestock prices 15 October. The *Times* observed that Seattle housewives still would not find meat at the "corner butcher shop". The Seattle Retail Grocers and Meat Dealers Association's I.W. Ringer advised "patience"...[insofar as] "it would take 60 to 130 days before any large quantities of first-class meat reaches retailers..." That very day prices of low grade meats "Jumped 50 cents" per hundred weight. The 16 October *Times* reported some shops already were charging as much as three times the OPA prices. Accompanying the OPA removal of all controls on flour and coffee on the 17th came the warning that the OPA had set 1 November as the date for terminating the remaining controls, local offices must close on 4 November. The *Times* reported on the 21st: "MORE BEEF FOR SEATTLE SOON", as "cattle began to pour into Seattle's Union Stockyards"...600 head by count, equal to one week's supply before decontrol. On the 23rd the *Times* reported "Controls Off All But 3 Foods": sugar, rice and syrups, as the OPA "virtually ended wartime price controls over food and beverages today." Not quite: On 9 November Truman announced the end of wage controls and lifted price ceilings on all commodities except sugar and rice. For good reason Truman insisted on retaining control over rents and evictions. [17]

## SEATTLE HOUSING IN EARLY POSTWAR PERIOD

The regional economist of the Federal Housing Authority and future UW professor of business administration, Bayard Wheeler, observed in August 1947, "The current housing shortage arises from 3 main causes: population increase, increase in the rate of family formation, and an inadequate volume of new construction." Current vacancy rates in Seattle were at 1.6 percent, compared to the prewar average of "some" 5 percent. Wheeler judged the vacant units were themselves substandard, and that "war enriched families" already with homes, were looking forward to upgrading what they had and were ready to pay for them, thus contributing to the demand. The new homes purchased by those in this upwardly mobile group, $8,000 plus category, provided the market. Such prices were not affordable to most families, particularly to freshly discharged veterans, most of whom have "moved in with relatives or into the 'hand me down' units left by higher income families." Despite the two year lapse no long range planning was underway to meet the housing needs of low and middle income families.

When the War Production Board removed the restrictions on allocations of construction materials, contractors could choose who they would build for. Construction of stores, factories, and amusement places were most profitable, while residential construction was low on their lists, except for the more expensive homes. To deal with this problem the federal Office of Housing Expeditor was established in January 1946, headed by Wilson Wyatt. Under it local emergency housing committees were created through which the local housing expeditor worked. Mayor Devin established one for Seattle. A goal of 2,700,000 low and moderate cost homes was established for the nation. Preference was accorded to veterans for either renting or purchase. Given the shortage of trained skilled workers an apprenticeship-like program was implemented. Wyatt promoted prefabricated homes in whole or in parts, to lower construction costs. The agency provided mortgage insurance for up to 90 percent of costs at 4 percent interest. These "Wyatt funds" were also used to build access roads to timbered areas in the Northwest. To expedite logging the Agriculture Department was authorized to permit logging above sustained levels, as though this had not been standard Forest Service practice. Under the Wyatt program, by December 1946 948,900 homes had been started, of which 584,300 were completed, nationally. "Temporary" federally-funded housing units, built during the war, were dismantled and made available to "distressed colleges and cities", of which Seattle and the UW were beneficiaries. According to Wheeler the apparent "success" of the Wyatt program led to its dilution and to Wyatt's resignation 4 December 1946. The private construction industry was unable and/or unwilling to address the obvious need of lower income families until it had satisfied the more profitable markets first and joined the AFL building trades unions in opposition to the Wyatt homes. The industry regarded the federal government as an interloper which stepped in to fill the void. No significant expansion of residential construction took place during those first ten months of 1946. On the contrary, during the first quarter of 1947 housing starts decreased compared to the same period in 1946 by about 26,000 nationally. Wheeler attributed this slump to high construction costs - mainly for building materials, which had risen by 12.5 percent between November 1946, when OPA was effectively terminated, and March 1947. His own study of Seattle family income found that although it had increased by 79 percent since 1940, construction costs had "outstripped" that rise by 100 percent. Extrapolating from these estimates Wheeler found new housing of average quality in Seattle ranged from $4,000 to $5,000, placing 25 to 30 percent of families outside that market and those "will continue to wait." [18]

Turning more specifically to Seattle the National Housing Authority authorized quotas in 1943 for the construction of Title VI permanent private housing. By October 1945 of 11,161 units in the Seattle area were substantially completed. This program was then terminated. A working group for housing was formed, consisting of the Housing Committee of the Chamber of Commerce, the Mayor's Veterans Housing Committee, the Joint Veterans Housing Committee, and the Governor's Housing Advisory Committee. This group observed that in the absence of controls between 15 October 1945 and 15 January 1946, "a mad scramble began to obtain materials...Unrestricted construction started". This group recommended construction of 25,460 housing units between 1 January 1946 and 31 December 1947. Complications abounded, however. Building materials were in short supply. So was the supply of skilled labor. According to the Chamber's housing committee the remaining restrictive federal regulations and controls were hampering "rapid completion of construction". Adding to the shortage of lumber was the larger profit margin local lumber producers extracted by shipping lumber out of the area. Consequently, local distributors and builders were having difficulties getting their "just share", which the Chamber estimated to be twice the actual supply they were receiving. Given this problem the group recommended *more* governmental authority and autonomy for the Seattle district's remnant OPA office. Share, they added, should be based on relative population growth, which would rank the region higher for its proportionate share. Washington state ranked second nationally in the relative increase of its civilian population, in absolute numbers 221,000 between April 1940 and July 1945. The group argued: Because private housing could not be expected to outbid commercial or government projects the Federal Housing Authority should be prohibited from paying for overtime and granting bonuses for building trades labor. As to the latter, it advocated expansion of apprenticeship training programs to increase the skilled labor supply. Not forgotten was rental housing. This group urged alteration of OPA rental policies to provide incentives for construction of new rental units. [19]

During the war most new construction was done by the Seattle Housing Authority. In contrast to new construction built under private auspices the SHA's housing accomodated non-whites. Among non-whites African Americans represented 15 percent of SHA residents, in number 813 Black families at war's end. For Blacks housing would prove an unending problem outside the federal housing projects, due to the resistance of realtors and existence of restrictive covenants in all-white neighborhoods. As noted above the acute shortage of housing persisted all through the war period. With some 40,000 veterans expected to return by spring 1946 this situation could only get much worse. It did. When Mayor Devin appointed his emergency housing committee in January 1946 he expected it to come up with answers. It didn't or couldn't. With lumber being diverted to higher price markets elsewhere, and a two-month's long lumber strike just ended, resupplying local dealers would take time. Other building materials also were hard to come by. A Seattle Housing Center was set up to handle applications. Its "open up your homes to veterans" campaign was proving fruitless. And most veterans could not afford current rents anyway. A veterans housing survey was conducted in late 1946, revealing 20 percent of married veterans doubling up in trailers and rented rooms. Taking advantage of Congress's passage of the "Mead Resolution", in September 1946 the SHA leased five sites to veterans: its "Quinsite Homes" project. Among the sites were former reception centers at Michigan Street and Blanchard Street, which the SHA leased to the UW for its veteran students. By year's end 7,055 veterans occupied the five sites. When it appeared the housing shortage was proving a deterrent to recruitment of new faculty for the UW's new medical school and other departments, it acquired temporary war surplus housing. The UW built new prefabricated duplex housing in Union Bay Village on the western edge of the upper middle class Laurelhurst district. In its annual report for 1946 the SHA observed: "many veterans were able to solve their own housing problems by building their own homes; others were able to buy or rent". It should be added, an untold number of veterans moved in under their parent's roof during their transition to civilian life. The SHA took up some "slack". Testifying in Seattle before a congressional housing committee in December 1949, SHA director Charles Ross, recommended a figure of $3,489 as the cutoff for family income in the city's housing projects. Those with more than that income would be evicted. However, he expressed caution with respect to minority groups, who comprised 28 percent of the projects' population. They were having trouble finding housing outside due to restrictive covenants. As to "temporary" units under SHA jurisdiction he advised disposing of them as "rapidly and expeditiously as possible". [20]

Housing for low income families, particularly non-whites, would prove insoluble in the face of realtors' stubborn opposition throughout the next two decades. In 1963, when the City Council refused to enact an open housing measure on its own authority, that courageous body instead prepared an open housing ordinance for the 1964 city election. Voters rejected it by a two to one margin. As a result the Seattle Civic Unity Committee closed itself down. [22]

## Labor in Early Postwar Period

On a scale not matched since 1919, nationwide strikes in early 1946 were mounted to bring wages more in line with inflation that had run far ahead of wage increases since 1939. Most strikes brought wage increases, though by no means did wages catch up with the rising costs of living. Yet, President Truman was pressured by business associations to authorize compensatory price increases. On 14 February Truman instituted a new wage-price policy permitting employers to recover through price adjustments any wage increases that had been contracted. A number of industrywide price increases in March was permitted in the manufacturing sector, in part to stimulate production. Settlement of the steel strike, for example, brought wage increases that, when passed along as price increases, affected all manufacture dependent upon steel. In March alone there were 2,726 price adjustments compared to a monthly average of 1,744 since V-J Day. [1]

Wages during the war never caught up with the rate of inflation. The no-strike pledge, coupled with President Roosevelt's threat of a "labor draft", for which he was practically assured congressional support, given the anti-union cast of Congress, also restrained labor activism directed to correct apparent inequities. The Wage Stabilization Board, acting with the OPA to counter inflationary pressures, was always fearful of setting off a wage-price spiral. Consequently the WSB kept wages in line by its constrained interpretation of the Little Steel Formula. Besides, it was easier to control wages than profits, in part because "Labor" lent itself to hostile propaganda: "unpatriotic", "slackers", "draft dodgers" among the basket of possible epithets to hurl at the public in whipping up opposition. As it turned out anti-labor bills passed anyway, most notably the Smith-Connally Anti-Strike Act in 1943, on the heels of the nationwide coal strike and the looming specter of United Mine Workers president John L. Lewis. Soon after V-J Day this would all change. To begin catching up with wartime inflation unions nationwide sought wage adjustments and they struck when necessary. [2]

Elimination of the Little Steel Formula hardly a week after V-J Day, and resumption of collective bargaining opened the door to long suppressed labor contract negotiations. With inflation running fast ahead of real wages this was as inevitable as it was justifiable. The result, as noted, was the "greatest" strike wave in US history. The nationwide steel strike had been in progress since 19 January. A settlement recommendation by President Truman was accepted by the United Steel Workers but was rejected by Benjamin Fairless of US Steel, who exclaimed he never knew what a "fair" profit was. Next, the United Automobile Workers struck against General Motors. The UAW strike was followed by a strike against the nation's meatpackers involving 300,000 workers. The electrical workers union failed in their negotiations, thus resulting in a nationwide strike of 180,000 electrical workers. Locally some calming effect transpired when 46 steel fabricating plants in the Seattle area settled their differences with the International Association of Machinists, Local 79. Comforting news also came from Seattle's telephone workers when they agreed not to raise the pay issue until June. But the real trouble lay ahead.

The nationwide coal strike began 1 April in which 2,000 Washington state coal miners participated. President Truman placed the mines under federal control and followed this action by filing a federal injunction to prevent the union from striking when the mines were returned to private ownership. On 23 May began a dramatic railroad strike, "dramatic" for its widespread economic impact. The night of 24 May Truman went on a national radio hookup to announce that he would bring in the Army to run the roads should the workers not return to work the next day. Failing to end the strike with this threat the president addressed Congress, asking for a temporary measure allowing him to draft strikers into the Army, subjecting them to his authority. As he was speaking word came that the strike was called off. [3]

When the federal government lifted restrictions on home and industry construction, effective 1 October 1945, the first major postwar strike in the Pacific Northwest region started in the last week of September in the lumber industry. The lumber unions had barely been held in check for more than a year while arbitration was attempted. When that recourse failed to earn workers a 20 cents an hour pay raise more than 60,000 AFL workers walked off their jobs. The International Woodworkers Association of America (CIO) was about to conduct its strike vote, and when they did their 40,000 IWA members joined in effect with the AFL strikers, posing a formidable adversary to the employers. Lumber inventories for home construction practically dried up, making the housing shortage even more acute. The strike lasted until early December, when the operators settled with the Tacoma workers for a 15 cents an hour raise. Other unions followed suit. [4]

Soon after the lumber strike started maritime workers along the entire Pacific Coast went on strike 1 October. It had been long brewing. At the instigation of Labor Secretary Lewis Schwellenbach a strike had been postponed in April 1945 while a federal fact finding committee was appointed to study the issues. Concurrently the AFL decided to challenge the CIO maritime unions by forming their own maritime federation, which included the Teamsters, Sailors Union of the Pacific, Seafarers International Union (SIU), and the Masters Mates and Pilots Union. Meanhile the CIO unions scheduled a strike vote for 15 June 1945. Federal authorities then threatened to man the ships with Naval personnel causing the SIU to withdraw its members nationwide from the ships, forty in Seattle. The ILWU president Harry Bridges then softened the CIO position by agreeing to accept the fact finding committee's recommendations, which the CIO unions grudgingly accepted. That proved not to be the end of the matter, however.

The CIO seamens' unions won a monthly wage increase of $17.50 from the Wage Stabilization Board, but the Seafarers International Union won a larger increase from the shipowners which the WSB then denied. When the SIU struck it was in reality against the WSB, not the shipowners; the federal government thus became the target. Volatility was soon added, when the Committee of Maritime Unity (CIO) reopened negotiations with the Waterfront Employer's Association. On 1 October 1946 the CMU struck the entire coast when WEA's president Frank Foisie stalled negotiations. In Seattle's harbor upwards of 70 deep sea ships stood idle. Idled also were about 2,000 of Seattle's longshoremen plus another 1,500 around the Sound. To their numbers should be added another 600 to 700 marine engineers in the Sound's ports. Alaska Steamship Company's supply ship for Alaska also remained at anchor, while Alaska residents anxiously waited while their food supplies dwindled. The local press focused on Alaskan distress. AFL maritime unions also carried on their own battle with their employers, thereby complicating termination of the shutdowns. Inconclusively the strikes ended 19 November 1946 with the CIO unions winning a 15 cents an hour pay raise and appointment of a federal fact finding commiittee to study safety conditions; size of sling loads was a chief concern. Resolution of these issues did not occur until settlement of the 1948 maritime strike, to be covered below. [5]

Postwar strike activity also affected the three Seattle daily newspapers. Local 202 of the International Typographical Union struck the three Seattle dailies in mid-November 1945. The strike was to be a long one. The three dailies operated improvisionally until 18 November. Local 202 twice rejected agreements worked out by its international and local officers and the dailies. The newspapers finally shut down. Mayor Devin's fact finding committee worked out another contract which the rank and file once again rejected. After 56 days a fourth attempt finally succeeded on the eve of the nationwide steel strike in January 1946. The printers won pay raises of $2.65 and $2.90 per day, retroactive to 1 September.

When the nationwide steel strike began in January 1946 about 750 steel workers walked off the job Seattle at the Bethlehem Steel plant, the Seattle Rolling Mill, and at 44 other fabricating plants. Most affected were plumbing and heating suppliers. In anticipation of a steel strike shipyards and Boeing accumulated large steel inventories as buffer. Attesting to the volatility of labor unrest, a four-days transit workers strike ended after they won an 11 cents per hour pay raise for drivers, coupled with a quarterly bonus of $100. Transit shopmen also won pay increases. Accompanying these developments was the reorganization of the State Federation of Labor, ending a years-long rift during which the federation lost affiliates and effectiveness. Evan (Ed) Weston of the Boilermakers union won the presidency, ousting James Taylor. Already a reaffiliation movement was in full swing and the powerful Teamsters planned to rejoin. [6]

It would not be long until a host of anti-labor bills would pass through Congress. Congressman Henry Jackson wrote WSFL president Ed Weston on 17 January 1947 "As you know, anti-labor proposals have poured into the Congressional hoppers at an unprecdented rate during these first days of the session...They are mainly intended to destroy the whole organized labor movement and the process of collective bargaining..." The stage was set for debate over the Taft-Hartley bill. In the eyes of organized labor President Truman had to redeem himself for his actions during the 1946 strike wave. Though a longshot Taft-Hartley might be just the vehicle. [7]

# BOEING AND THE POSTWAR ECONOMY

At war's end people were generally aware that only the war had pulled the nation out of the Great Depression. Most of Seattle's population anticipated severe cutbacks in shipyard employment that depended on government contracts. Aircraft production also might be sharply reduced, there being no immediate demand from the armed services. However, the commercial market looked promising because it had been undeveloped before the war. Long distance air travel was certain to increase dramatically and construction of SeaTac Airport, nearing completion, played to that commercial market. Trans-Pacific and trans-Atlantic routes required development and when linked with transnational routes the result promised a vast international air travel network. Toward this end the Seattle Chamber of Commerce joined other Pacific Northwest cities to "fight for a direct Oriental airline across the North Pacific through the Seattle-Tacoma gateway".

The Seattle Chamber of Commerce sounded an optimistic tone on the labor supply. The Chamber predicted that 70 percent of those who migrated to the city would remain and that Boeing's payroll would probably double. The Chamber also found shipyard employment holding surprisingly steady, and the acute housing shortage promised to help the lumber industry. Puget Sound Power and Light (PSP&L) euphorically contracted with the Electrical Workers Union for a 15 percent wage increase. PSP&L proclaimed in its 1946 annual report that 1946 was "bigger and busier than any previous year in the [state's] peacetime history". Continuing this rosy outlook into 1947 PSP&L reported housing demand to be "acute"; that 167 new industries had been established in metropolitan Seattle; that Boeing's landing of contracts for 215 B-50s promised additions to its present 17,000 workforce; and the state's farm production had attained an all-time high value.

Complementing this prospective transportation network for the postwar economy was a land route to Alaska that had been punched forward during the war. [1]

Unlike shipbuilding the aircraft industry had a future in the US. Perhaps it might even be the future or at least a vital part of it. Taking the thesis developed by Roger Lotchin of the "metropolitan-military complex", and Richard Kirkendall's expansion of it - "the military-metropolitan-industrial complex" - and applying it to Boeing and Seattle, a pattern of complementary relationships emerged. Convinced of the effectiveness of strategic bombing, the Army Air Corps wanted an air force of 70 groups. To get this large a force the Air Force leaders had to compete with the Army and Navy for funding at a time when cutbacks were the order of the day. Also, the federal administration sought a balance among the military and naval components. The aircraft industry had to be kept alive and well if the Air Corps was to have its planes. The third complementary element was for states and their metropolitan regions to escape the anticipated effects of the economic downturn during reconversion. To do this a foundation had to be laid for their future....upon an industry that potentially seemed to hold the future. [2]

The area-wide mobilization generated on behalf of Boeing by the Chamber of Commerce, civic, and political leaders during the war was sustained and broadened after the conflict. A semblance of panic set in as the Renton and Wichita plants were shut down and the Seattle core operation's workforce was sharply cut back. Auguring the future, however, the Army lost control of its air force component. The United States Air Force was established in 1947 in recognition of its critical role during the war, thus freeing the Air Force from Army subordination. Henceforth its leaders could directly lobby political leaders and propagandize their mission. They gave top priority to sustaining the aircraft industry for both commercial and military objectives.

The US obviously dominated the industry worldwide at war's end. The industry was in a position to expand upon that superiority if political leaders could be appropriately swayed. In seeking measures to build up commercial aviation Senator Hugh B. Mitchell proposed creation of an air policy board. President Truman appointed such a board in 1946 to propose a national policy for the industry. Boeing's president William Allen argued before the Air Policy Commission in fall 1947 that the industry needed both commercial and military production if it were to be sustained and advance technologically. When the commission proposed that air power be the base on which to build national defense Secretary of the Air Force Stuart Symington appealed to the Republican controlled Congress for support. He was relying on their isolationist propensity and the concomitant appeal that air power had to its leadership - commitment of ground forces was anathema to them.

Congress voted much that was requested by appropriating funds for a 70 group air force, thereby joining the demand for both commercial and military aircraft.[3]

Responding to the emerging antagonisms with the Soviet Union the federal government allocated modest increases for purchasing bomber and transport planes, thus boosting Boeing's workforce from 14,000 in 1947 to 18,400 by spring 1948. An improved version of the B-29 (the B-50) entered the market, along with the Stratocruiser, a passenger plane with freight versions. The Renton and Wichita plants reopened. The five-months-long strike of the Aero Mechanics Local 751 in 1948, which is to be covered below, barely dented Boeing's output.[4]

With 16,800 of its workforce employed on Air Force contracts Boeing's total payroll topped 25,000 by summer 1949. However, the current contracts would be filled at the end of the year. The Stratocruiser market was shrinking and there was little prospect of more commercial contracts sufficient to sustain its workforce. When plans surfaced to build the B-47 jet bomber at Wichita instead of Seattle, fear mounted locally that the Wichita decision indicated an incipient policy to decentralize the industry and to move it from the "vulnerable" coastal states. Washington's congressional delegation galvanized into action.

Air Force Secretary Stuart Symington evaded the decentralization issue and chose to console now-Congressman Hugh Mitchell in May 1949:

> "[He foresees] no serious curtailment of production activities [at Boeing] at the present time...Before the cancellation of the B-54 contract the amount of business placed with Boeing necessitated a large percentage of subcontracting. Boeing ranked No. 1 of all airframe prime contractors, having 37% of the dollar value of the business. After the cancellation of the B-54's, Boeing still ranks No. 1...with 29% of the airframe business...Present production plans...will enable Boeing to continue operating at approximately the same relative level."

Symington's reassurance proved unconvincing to many key people and organizations. Although Allen still refused, after the 1948 strike, to recognize the International Association of Machinists (parent of Local 751) as the Boeing bargaining agent Allen unblushingly persuaded IAM president A.J. Hayes to write Symington, 4 August. Hayes wrote about "reports current in the community concerning the possibility of substantial curtailment of operations in the Seattle plant...if present directives of the Air Force Officers who specify the type of military aircraft work which may or may not be performed in the Boeing Seattle plant are permitted to stand." Copies were sent to Mitchell and Allen, with whom he also met directly. Allen told Hayes it was his original plan to keep the B-47 work in Seattle. [5]

Senator Magnuson persuaded Air Force Secretary Stuart Symington to visit Seattle. Governor Arthur Langlie called in his fellow Republican governors from Oregon and California to join in accusing the Air Force "of wrecking the regional economy, [and opening] up opportunities for Communists on the West Coast..." As it had during the war, the Seattle Chamber of Commerce similarly formed a Save Boeing Committee, 16 August 1949. The committee proceeded to form a veritable national network aimed at transferring B-47 work to Seattle. It seemed every conceivable organization in the city and state was mobilized in the effort, along with groups selected elsewhere along the coast. Mitchell wrote President Truman 24 August: "The people of the Seattle area are alarmed over the threatened disruption of the great Boeing Aircraft organization...on the theory that Seattle is a 'vulnerable' area." Mitchell commented that this was contrary to the assurances Symington gave him "last May". Continuing, "As you well know, Seattle and the Pacific Northwest generally have been hardest hit by unemployment and the loss of Boeing jobs would only intensify this condition." He concluded that Seattleites would be dismayed to learn Seattle was an "expendable area".

Truman probably discussed Mitchell's letter with Symington, for Symington wrote Mitchell on 31 August: "The Air Force has never indicated the necessity for moving the Boeing Company from Seattle. We foresee the use of the Seattle facility for the production of the C-97, the B-50, certain sub-assemblies for the B-47, the construction of the B-52 work-up to develop and produce certain guided missiles, and other research projects. There is no reason why Boeing should not retain its management and engineering offices in Seattle." At the end of this lengthy letter Symington claimed Boeing "agreed with the Air Force position [to shift B-47 work to Wichita] because of Seattle's 'relative strategic vulnerability'." If this reply was reassuring in long range terms, it was not. The Air Force seemed adamant by insisting the West Coast was vulnerable to Soviet attack. In an interview Shelby Scates conducted with Mitchell on 11 January 1994, the former congressman and senator insisted that it was Senator Magnuson's personal contact with the President that turned Truman away from accepting the Air Force argument. Whether or not Magnuson played such a critical role, as alleged, that factor must be seen in the context of all the united pressures being exerted upon Symington from the West Coast aircraft industry, their governors, chambers of commerce, affected labor unions, and an aroused public. All doubt was removed by the end of October when *American Aviation Daily* reported: "Air Force Disclaims Policy of Strategic Relocation of Aircraft Plants". [6]

When the US entered the Korean War on behalf of the United Nations in summer of 1950 the proposal that the National Security Council had submitted earlier in the year was implemented. The NSC obtained the $50 billion military budget it had recommended. The projected budget was so large that dividing it among the rival services was relatively easy. Boeing got its share, bringing its workforce up to 28,000 by summer 1951 once the Air Force allocated the B-52 contract to the Seattle plant. Given this huge contract Boeing was now put in financial position to move ahead in commercial aircraft development. The company proceeded to invest this capital into what became the 707. Boeing gained a one-year advantage over Douglas and its DC-8 in developing a commercial jet and "single-handedly had ended the Douglas domination of the world's commercial airplane market." President Allen, although resenting this dependence upon government, declared "the only thing worse than government is no government business". Experience gained in building B-52s proved invaluable in developing the 707; the 707 could also be adapted for military cargo use. [7]

# 1948: LIBERALISM IN DISARRAY

### PRELUDE

The year 1946 saw the Democratic party split apart as most New Dealers were forced out of the Truman administration. Some resigned from dissatisfaction at its apparent conservative drift. Interior Secretary Harold Ickes resigned in February over Truman's appointment of California oil man Ed Pauley to administer the naval oil reserves. While having promised his full backing to OPA administrator Chester Bowles, Bowles resigned after losing faith in Truman's dedication to OPA. Although Truman did veto passage by Congress of the OPA extension bill he eventually signed essentially the same kind of bill three weeks later. By the end of November little remained of OPA except rent controls. Commerce Secretary Henry Wallace soon followed Ickes and Bowles. But Truman fired Wallace for attacking US foreign policy, 12 September, in a speech at Madison Square Garden. Co-sponsors of the Madison Square Garden speech were the National Citizens Political Action Committee (NCPAC) and the Independent Citizens Committee of the Arts, Sciences and the Professions (ICCASP). Although Truman required little urging it was Secretary of State James F. Byrnes who supplied the push.

During the heated 1946 congressional elections Truman played no effective role. Instead, Wallace attracted the most intensive scrutiny due to his insistence that the US should seek understanding with the Soviets, by recognizing spheres of influence. His criticism of US foreign policy left the impression that he was pro-Soviet/pro-communist. As the foremost New Dealer still in the Democratic party, Wallace's prominence added fuel for the anti-New Deal forces.

The 1946 congressional election proved how effective the anti-communist/anti-Soviet rhetoric could be. In the Seattle area left-wing Congressman Hugh Delacy lost his seat to Homer Jones by a margin of 49,000 votes after winning a bitter fight in the Democratic primary. As president of the notoriously pro-Soviet Washington Commonwealth Federation DeLacy defeated the former executive director of the WCF, Howard Costigan by nearly 6,000 votes. Jones compiled a mere 21,289 votes in the primary as compared to the 22,744 votes for Costigan; there seemed little prospect for a Jones victory in the November runoff, least of all an overwhelming one. Nonetheless Jones compiled 113,289 votes to DeLacy's 64,155. Costigan's red-baiting of DeLacy was continued by Jones, though with a decisively different outcome. He must have picked up substantially all of Costigan's anti-communist votes and benefited from the huge turnout for the finals. Voter turnout for the election finals was more than double that of the First District primaries, about 170,000 compared to about 73,000 votes. In 1944, when the Soviet Union had attained uncommonly favorable popularity in the United States, in the Seattle area it was more emphatic. Hugh DeLacy's 1944 victory was undoubtedly due to the Soviet-US alliance and the USSR's startling victories on the eastern front against the Germans. Neither was a factor by fall of 1946. By then fissures in the wartime alliance had become quite apparent as the Soviets asserted control over Bulgaria and Romania and had signalled its expanionist ambitions to George Kennan, who was in charge of the US embassy in Moscow. Kennan analyzed Soviet behavior and urged a containment policy in February. In March Winston Churchill lent dramatic force to these premonitions with his "Iron Curtain" speech at Fulton, Missouri. Trouble spots were accumulating almost daily.

Factoring into the local election process during the week of the November election was a waterfront strike. Led by the Northwest Committee on Maritime Unity (CIO), it was into its thirtieth day. Public patience was wearing thin. That DeLacy had the backing of the NCMU could not have helped him. Nor could the feud running its course within the Democratic party. Jerry O'Connell was executive director of the Democratic State Central Committee, but also he was assistant regional director of the NCPAC (National Citizens-PAC, originally the CIO-PAC). Governor Monrad Wallgren was closely allied with Dave Beck and the Teamsters union, bitter enemies of the CIO's waterfront unions. Annoyed by O'Connell's presence Wallgren forced him temporarily out of Olympia upon order to the party's chair, Harry Huse. However, pressure mounted by the NCPAC forced the governor to recall O'Connell to the state capital, thereby conceding the party's control to the executive secretary, patronage along with it. O'Connell would soon follow the Wallace Democrats into the fledgling Progressive Party, when he became its state chairman.[1]

DeLacy's candidacy was no help to Senator Hugh B. Mitchell. Mitchell had been Senator Wallgren's secretary for 13 years and was appointed US Senator by

Wallgren when the latter was elected governor in 1944. Mitchell was an ardent New Dealer and a favorite of the Washington, D.C. press corps. Given Mitchell's popularity, DeLacy chose to bundle his campaign with Mitchell's by urging voters to "Vote for the Two Hugh's". Whether Mitchell had agreed to this tactic is unknown, but he ran against former Tacoma mayor Harry P. Cain, who ran a strong senatorial race in absentia against Warren Magnuson in 1944 while he was on active military duty. Cain opposed "big government", though he believed wartime restrictions were being removed too hastily, particularly rent controls. Mitchell lost by 60,000 votes. The anti-New Deal mood of the electorate spread: Tacoma's veteran New Dealer Congressman John Coffee lost to Thor Tollefson; losers in the state legislative contests were other WCF leaders, Tom Rabbitt and William Pennock president of the Washington Pension Union, who were accompanied by leftists George Hurley and Richard Murphy. Conservative, anti-New Deal Democrats fared well in their re-election bids. Pertinent here is that in 1948, when DeLacy was active in the Progressive Party campaign, the national PP office transferred him to Ohio for campaign work, thereby removing a prominent red-baiting target from Washington state. Voters in the First District returned Mitchell as its Congressman in 1948. [2]

Turning to the national scene, while Wallace became a lightning rod for Republicans most New Deal Democrats gathered around him temporarily as the hope of the party. Failing that, there was expectation among some that a new party might be built upon his candidacy, unless Truman re-asserted the New Deal agenda. However, the New Deal liberals were deeply divided between the remnant of Popular Front liberals and those who were anticommunist/anti-Soviet. At this stage most Popular Front liberals were either in or associated with the vital CIO component of the old New Deal coalition. Concurrently within the CIO, an intense battle was in process, the purge of Communists and left-wingers from leadership positions. Critical in the CIO at this juncture was election of the anticommunist Walter Reuther to the presidency of the powerful United Automobile Workers in early 1946. The UAW became a raider of left-wing unions when each of them split along Popular Front/anticommunist lines after 1948. At this time CIO president Philip Murray, though anticommunist, and sympathetic to the purge, wanted to avoid splitting the CIO itself. An attempt by the NCPAC and the ICCASP to revive the Popular Front in late September 1947 was boycotted by the liberal Union for Democratic Action. Inasmuch as the election was a disaster for New Dealers this defeat was sufficient to cause a breakup of NCPAC and ICCASP on the communist issue, and the coalescence of anticommunist liberals in a new organization, Americans for Democratic Action (ADA).

Popular Front liberals had already forged the Progressive Citizens of America (PCA). The ADA absorbed several CIO leaders, though not yet president Philip Murray; he remained a vice president in the PCA. To which group the CIO would align as a unit was essential to the success of either. The PCA was attracted to Wallace for his foreign policy advocacy. The New Dealers gathered around the ADA in opposition to Wallace's views on the Soviet Union and the ADA did not tolerate communists. The difficulty among liberals lay in founding a noncommunist liberalism. Historically, the difficulty was the Communist Party's infiltration of every liberal organization that succeeded in developing a mass base. In Washington state this had been the fate, successively, of the Unemployed Citizens' League, the Washington Commonwealth Builders, the Washington Commonwealth Federation, and the Washington Pension Union. [3]

Starting from their disillusionment with the Truman administration, the ADA New Dealers found the organization drifting inevitably toward support of the administration. The Truman doctrine for military aid to Greece and Turkey gained support from many in the ADA. Also the Republican-dominated congress was proving so reactionary that Truman was driven toward adopting more liberal policies. A small knot of liberals remaining in the administration, among whom Truman advisor Clark Clifford was the most influential, were meanwhile developing strategies to oppose Republican initiatives. Truman's veto of a tax-cut bill won ADA support, but most dramatic and crucial was the President's veto of the Taft-Hartley Bill 20 June 1947. Although his veto was overriden it did realign the organized labor movement with the administration. Coming but two weeks after Secretary of State George Marshall's Harvard speech outlining his plan for the economic recovery of Europe the ADA abandoned its neutrality and thenceforth backed Truman. Further cementing the ADA's growing support for Truman was his calling a special session of Congress in November 1947 to implement the Marshall Plan, the European Recovery Plan. Truman also laid out an anti-inflationary program. Both encountered bitter Republican opposition, and set the tone for the coming general election in 1948. But the defining element in Truman's fresh policies, insofar as the liberals were concerned, was the Marshall Plan. The PCA and Wallace opposed it while the ADA embraced it. Although invited in, the Soviets treated it as a threat to their strategy, then in process, for extending their control over eastern Europe. That the European Recovery Plan became limited to recovery of western Europe proved inevitable under these circumstances, deepening the rift between the two regions and solidifying the lines of opposition in what was fast becoming the Cold War. In the course of his European tour Wallace became convinced that the Marshall Plan was a mere extension of the Truman Plan and was inspired by Wall Street and the military. Wallace viewed the Marshall Plan as irreconcilably dividing Europe. [4]

Preceding formulation of the Marshall Plan another step had been taken toward Cold War conditions. Under pressure from his Attorney General Tom Clark, FBI Director J. Edgar Hoover, and egged on by the Republican congressional leadership, from which a more extreme internal security package was expected, President Truman promulgated Executive Order 9835, 22 March 1947. The order was to test the loyalty of all federal employees. In the Executive Order "disloyalty" was not defined, nor was "subversion", nor were "reasonable grounds" laid out as the basis for dismissal. Due process for appeal was ignored. The attorney general issued an ever-expanding "blacklist" of suspected subversive organizations; its first list was issued in December 1947. The House Committee on Un-American Activities was revived in October 1947 and began with an investigation of Hollywood screen writers and film stars; some would later achieve notoriety as the "Hollywood Ten." They and others were blacklisted and driven from their careers. Next in line for investigation were the radio business and the nascent television industry. This reactionary drift induced the executive board of the Progressive Citizens of America to consider forming a third party built upon Wallace's popularity. Wallace drew large audiences during an autumn speaking tour. Was there a chance to win the presidency and counter the Truman policies? Who could be sure at this stage? [5]

President Truman followed with a New Dealish state of the union speech, written by that knot of remnant liberals who remained in his administration. They submitted a strong civil rights draft proposal aimed at protecting African Americans from violence and discrimination, promising them greater opportunity. But threat of a Southern congressional revolt caused Truman to withdraw the proposal. While Truman was thus vascillating the PCA was moving decidedly toward formalizing a third party organization by establishing a National Wallace for President Committee. The ADA claimed it was Communist inspired. The CIO's Philip Murray then came out unequivocally against Wallace and the PCA. He purged the CIO's national office of known communists and those he considered their followers. The shared fear among liberal critics of the third party was that it would split the Democratic vote and guarantee a reactionary Republican victory. Damaging to Wallace, however, was the Communist overthrow of the Masaryk government in Czechoslovakia in late February 1948. This action convinced many wavering liberals of the Soviet intent to rule eastern Europe. Troubling to them was Truman's apparent inefficacy, not the man to lead the party to victory in 1948. General Eisenhower seemed an appealing alternative; so too did Supreme Court justice William O. Douglas. [6]

Within this broad context we can turn to the local/regional scene as events unfolded in 1948.

## Seattle, the Nation in Microcosm?

In Washington state the November 1946 election brought not only a Republican majority to the US House of Representatives, but to the lower House of Representatives of the state legislature as well: 71 Republicans and but 28 Democrats. The state Senate was evenly divided at 23 for each party; however, the Spokane area Democrats could usually be counted upon to vote with the Republicans. Of central importance here was the election of Albert F. Canwell to represent Spokane's Fifth District in the House of Representatives.

During the 1947 legislative session one of the major bills passed was one that eliminated the $50 minimum for old age pensions. The bill also tightened eligibility requirements, it gave the state a lien on the estates of the pension recipients, and it deprived pensioners of their choice of doctors when they applied for medical aid. Medical aid to pensioners also suffered budget cuts. By these provisions the pension law was converted to a relief measure. The Washington Pension Union opened a campaign for raising the minimum pension to $60 and eliminating those strictures enacted by the 1947 legislature. Also the WPU promised to work for more public schools funding, and to enact a fair employment practices bill. The House countered two days later, 4 March, by passing Albert Canwell's resolution establishing a joint un-American activities investigating committee, the drafting of which was attributed to Fred Niendorff, legislative correspondent for the *Post-Intelligencer*. Niendorff's front page story on 13 December 1946 pointed the direction toward which the legislature was moving. A coalition of Republicans and Democrats reportedly had caucused to deal with communist infiltration of the UW campus, labor unions, political organizations, and the public schools. Niendorff wrote: "Efforts are now being made to break the Communist grip on the Democratic Party in the State of Washington and honest Democrats are working with the Republican Senate majority to extend this housecleaning to all our state institutions and to non-political groups in which they have seized control." Niendorff's contention was a gross exaggeration. The Communists never achieved such control, though at least some among them undoubtedly sought it. They tried mightily to convince their followers that they actually had gained control when the state Democratic party accepted the platform written by the Washington Commonwealth Federation at the 1936 party convention. Ironically, this illusion was cultivated on one hand by conservatives to exaggerate the power of the New Deal/Popular Front liberals by painting them "Reds." These liberals contributed to this illusion by exaggerating their successes to attract a following. [7]

President Truman's loyalty order of March 1947 and revival of the House Un-American Activities in October lent credibility to formation of the Canwell Committee and to its future conduct. In Seattle, Jess Fletcher, a vice president of the Building Services Employees' International Union, asked in January 1947 for an audit of its Local 6 books. Fletcher accused the local's president William Dobbins a well-known Communist, and fellow officers Ward Coley and Merwin Cole of radicalizing the local. Its affairs were thrown into disarray. Internal hearings by the Canwell Committee started on 30 September and newspaper reports began appearing 9 October, continuing into November in both the *P-I* and *Times*. Advance accounts of Fletcher's public testimony were supplied by the Canwell investigators and FBI, all of which pointed to the local's takeover by Dobbins, Coley, and Cole for the CP. Later, when public hearings on the University of Washington got underway, the committee hearings coincided with the Soviet Union's blockading of Berlin in June 1948. In this warlike atmosphere, twelve leaders of the CPUSA were indicted by the Justice Department, charging them with conspiring to violently overthrow the US government. The Cold War's effects were clearly cutting deeply into domestic politics, wherein political dissent of any kind would be alleged to be part of the "Communist conspiracy". [8]

> The first set of putative "fact finding" investigations of the Canwell Committee began 27 January 1948 and concluded on 5 February. Their focus was on the Washington Pension Union, which had inherited the role of the former Washington Commonwealth Federation. The second set of hearings, concentrated on the University of Washington and the Seattle Repertory Playhouse; they were transacted between 19 and 23 July. Between the two Canwell hearings was a City election and the start of a momentus strike against Boeing that would last until early September, by which time a critical maritime strike was underway. That strike would not be settled until after the dramatic general election of 1948, by which time the UW's Faculty Committee on Tenure had begun its hearings on those faculty members charged by the Canwell Committee with guilt either of Communist Party membership or of its "Fronts".

Vern Countryman, in his study of Un-American activities investigations in Washington state, notes that Canwell had imbibed his anticommunist views by witnessing the 1934 Seattle waterfront strike. He later drew sustenance from observing strikes in the automotive industry. Claiming to have worked closely with members of the US House Un-American Actvities Committee and the FBI, he accumulated files on persons and organizations suspected of Communist and Communist front activities. These, he considered subversive, conspiratorial, traitorous. Liberals who supported reforms and policies which the CP advocated were mere dupes. In a campaign speech Canwell proclaimed: "If someone insists there is discrimination against Negroes in this country, or that there is inequality of wealth, there is every reason to believe that person is a Communist." He would later include President Eisenhower and John Foster Dulles on his dupe list. As he had

Anti-Canwell Committee protesters picketed the hearings on the Washington Pension Union, January 1948. Hearings on the UW faculty and the Seattle Repertory Playhouse were conducted 19-23 July. In the wake of these hearings the UW conducted its own version at which the civil rights of the accused were observed.

served also as deputy sheriff in charge of Spokane County's identification bureau, Canwell's fellow committee members endorsed his convictions, most notably Senator Thomas Bienz a Spokane Democrat, who had introduced the companion measure in the Senate. [9]

Rules established by Canwell for the legislative committee's fact-finding investigation placed the proceedings outside normal constitutional protections. The right of the accused to cross examine hostile witnesses, the right to due process, the right against self incrimination were denied. A defendant's lawyer was prohibited the opportunity to object to testimony as to its veracity or prejudicial character. A lawyer was allowed only to give his client advice. Repeatedly Canwell insisted to the defense that no information was to be admitted that was not "pertinent" to the investigation. In contrast informants and "expert" witnesses were permitted to submit pages of irrelevant testimony without objection or challenge. Among the most flagrant examples were testimony of Howard Rushmore (see especially incoherent paragraphs from pp. 190-98 in transcript of second report), and that of George Hewitt (pp. 248-59 in second report).

So much for "fact-finding". The person accused of Communist or Communist front activities, or who had been a Popular Front liberal, was presumed guilty of unspecified subversion until proven innocent. However, no procedure was allowed to prove one's innocence. Canwell made clear at the outset that constitutional protections would not be adhered to: "We are not going to debate any of the issues regarding the constitutionality of this committee, or its method of procedure." From these investigations, which denied suspects their constitutional rights, some relevant legislation was supposed to be enacted. Instead of the presumption of innocence, which the court system is intended to respect, the committee's procedures stood the judicial system on its head.

As will be covered in the account of Canwell's hearings on the UW in July, in the striking case of Professor Melvin Rader, Canwell never acknowledged Rader's innocence even after hostile testimony was later proven to be perjured. The perjurer, George Hewitt, was never extradited nor prosecuted. The committee's chief investigator William Houston even had Hewitt spirited out of the state before he could face perjury charges. Hewitt continued to perform as an "expert" witness whenever called by other such investigating committees and despite the FBI's full knowledge of his perjury. So obsessed was Canwell that during the John Goldmark libel trial in 1963-1964 he would once again confront Rader as if they had never covered essentially the same ground fifteen years before. Canwell, incidentally, was not reelected in 1948 and was defeated for every other public office for which he subsequently he enlisted. When he ran for the Senate in 1948 he made certain to his audience that "Those who attack the committee are either ignorant or subversive". He continued as a private investigator, published in 1958 the *Vigilante* (two issues only) and later the *American Intelligence Service*, which figured prominently in the Goldmark trial. That his handling of the earlier hearings played a part in his rejection seems credible.[10]

The setting for the committee's hearings seemed particularly apt, considering its objectives. There it sat, the formidable looking Armory of the 146th Field Artillery, squat and intimidating across from the high school football stadium near the southern base of Queen Anne hill. Standing at the ready were uniformed officers of the state patrol. An overflow audience attended the hearings, requiring the installation of sound equipment to carry the proceedings out of the hearing room. Sign-carrying pickets marched on the streets outside the Armory, often shouting their protests. Local and national news services were well represented, including radio stations. Hearings devoted to the Washington Pension Union started auspiciously. On the first day WPU president William Pennock was ejected from the hearing room when he started reading from a prepared statement. Former state Representative Edward Pettus, father of *New Dealer* editor Terry Pettus, shortly followed

Pennock for creating a "disturbance". Expert witness Louis F. Budenz, a former managing editor of the *Daily Worker*, was then called to the stand to describe in detail (pp. 1-60 of first report) the overall operations of the Communist Party. The upshot of his testimony was that the CPUSA was under Soviet control, conspiratorial in nature, and aimed at the violent overthrow of the US government.[11]

That the Washington Pension Union was singled out must be attributed in part to its leadership in the successful 1940 campaign for Initiative 141, the pension initiative. Voters approved it by a majority of almost 100,000 votes. Newly elected governor Arthur B. Langlie, acted to impede its implementation and successfully led opposition to another pension initiative, Number 151, in 1944. When he won reelection in November 1948 (Mon Wallgren served as governor, 1945-1948) he faced another successful pension Initiative, Number 172, which he believed was a Communist conspiracy to bankrupt the state.

James T. Sullivan, first president of the Washington Old Age Pension Union, who also was known to be free of Communist taint, was next called to the stand to give a brief history of the Washington Old Age Pension Union (its name was changed in 1944 to Washingon Pension Union). Sullivan was elected in 1936 to the House of Representatives "to clear up the mess in Social Security and to help the aged people" affected by the policies of state social securities administrator Charles F. Ernst. During the 1937 legislative session Ernst had repeatedly urged liberals like Sullivan to "withold any legislation we had in mind" and he "would do the right thing for the old people of this state". Disheartened that nothing was done, Sullivan conferred after the session with WCF executive secretary and radio speaker Howard Costigan and others. Together they conceived the idea of a pension union. Articles of incorporation were filed April 1937. Then, according to Sullivan, he and other volunteers fanned out over the state, returning to Seattle for a meeting every Saturday at the Moose Hall. What began as a "loose organization" grew like "wildfire", inspiring its first statewide convention in October. Meeting at Broadway High School auditorium, Sullivan was elected president. Within one year thirty thousand people were enrolled. Elected to the state Senate in 1938, Sullivan returned to the 1939 legislative session determined to get satisfactory pension legislation enacted over the opposition of Ernst, whom he accused of attempting "to starve the old people, rather than feed them". Sullivan claimed to have led the fight from the Senate floor trying to defeat Ernst's "infamous poverty, pauper acts".

Sullivan and pension union secretary Homer Huson gathered copies of social security acts from substantially all the states, selected what they considered their best features and compiled them into an initiative, Initiative 141. All the time spent by them in their pension union work was volunteered time. When projects of the Works Progress Administration were cut back in 1938 and 1939 the WPA workers union, the Workers Alliance, "folded up". The alliance, like the Washington Commonwealth Federation, had come under Communist domination. The WCF, itself, had lost substantially all effectiveness by this time.

The 30,000 membership of the WOAPU appeared to have the largest mass base of any reform organization. Its membership was spread over the entire state, unlike the WCF with its concentration in King, Pierce, and Snohomish counties. Jess Fletcher, president of the Building Service Employees Union, Local 6, and himself a Communist until 1944, testified that he attended the CP meeting in 1937 when it was decided that the CP should take over the WOAPU. At that meeting were Hugh DeLacy, Howard Costigan, Tom Rabbitt, and William Pennock. Costigan testified that initially the CP leadership opposed the WOAPU as they tried to sustain the Workers Alliance and the WCF. But, while treading water, they charged Costigan with the job of establishing a "dual union": the WOAPU. Six months passed before the CP leaders gave up on the Alliance and, allegedly, decided to take over the pension union.

Costigan, as executive secretary of the WCF, and like Sullivan a founder of the WOAPU, sought a position for his then-WCF secretary William Pennock. This move was intended to build him up, "politically" according to Sullivan. But it also entailed replacing Huson with Pennock. Huson, according to Sullivan, had been handling "fifteen to twenty thousand" grievance cases voluntarily. Pennock went on the WOAPU payroll, apparently its first paid employee. It was not long before four liberal lawyers (Paul Coughlin, Ed Henry, Mark Litchman, and Henry Kyle) who had been handling grievance cases for free, were displaced by John Caughlan. Dues were introduced. Members of the Workers Alliance steadily drifted into the pension union, few among them were of pension age. Resolutions were regularly passed authorizing contribution to various allegedly Communist front organizations. At the 1940 pension union convention in Seattle, at which Sullivan noted relatively few old people in attendance, Sullivan tendered his resignation. In resigning Sullivan claimed the union no longer served the aged people of the state, but had become preoccupied with foreign policy in support of the Soviet Union. N.P. Atkinson was named his successor. [12]

The testimony of key informants above - Sullivan, Huson, Costigan, Fletcher, plus that of Nat Honig - outlines the origins of the Washington Old Age Pension Union and its career down to 1940. About a dozen other people also testified. Some had been Communists, some not. All named names, including those of a few University of Washington faculty members. All would be called before the committee in the second set of hearings in July. [13]

## The 1948 City Election

Just two weeks after the first tumultuous Canwell hearings concluded the city staged its primary election. The hearings might just as well taken place a thousand miles away for their miniscule influence upon the campaigns. No candidate seemed affected by them; they never emerged as an issue worthy of attention although the *P-I* attempted to do so in an editorial banner stretched atop its front page of 2 March. The editorial implied that Devin's opponent Allan Pomeroy once had the backing of Jerry O'Connell, who was presently state chair of the Progressive Party. Neither did the gathering storm over the fate of the Seattle Transit System command attention, nor that of the Puget Sound ferries, so vital a transportation link of the city with its cross-Sound neighbors. The Streetcar Men's Union contract was about to expire and the Transit Commission refused to negotiate a new contract; the commision offered a 3 cents an hour wage increase, take it or leave it. The commissioners contended to grant more would mean they could not apply the system's profits toward discharging its bonded debt, and that the expected deficit would cause the commission to raise fares. A strike loomed as a possibility. As to the ferries, the Puget Sound Navigation Company refused to operate its Black Ball ferries unless it was permitted to raise fares by 30 percent. Meanwhile ferries were operating on an emergency schedule. Governor Wallgren was exploring buying out the line and entertaining condemnation proceedings. Neither issue emerged as a topic worth discussion. [14]

William F. Devin had been mayor for six years and was running for reelection again. He had ridden the wave of federal wartime financing of the economy and claimed credit for the prosperity it brought. Vice and police department corruption had been fought over in his 1942 and 1944 campaigns. Devin spiced those campaigns with attacks on Dave Beck, linking him with police corruption and charging Beck with seeking control over the city's entire labor movement. In the February primaries Allan Pomeroy ran only about 3,000 votes behind Devin. He linked Devin with "a small clique of downtown business men, who want to keep new business, new industry and new payrolls out of Seattle", and he accused the mayor of stagnating the city's growth, making it a "one-horse town", as contrasted with its rival cities, Portland, Vancouver, B.C., and San Francisco. Devin dodged this issue, while urging voters to pass the $4 million bond issue for better street lighting to reduce the number of nightime traffic fatalities. [15]

Like the pull of gravity, gambling and vice soon took center stage. Rev. Newton Moats, chair of the Church Council's Civic Rights Committee, announced the Council's support of Devin, accusing the slot machine and gambling interests of putting up $150,000 toward the mayor's defeat. In this vein the "gold braid" among the police department were linked with opposition to the mayor. (Policemen in this group competed for appointments to areas where gambling and vice flourished under police protection.) Pomeroy deflected this allegation by accusing Devin of allowing the wholesale operation of pinball games near schools while banning them in private clubs: highschoolers spending their lunch money on pinballs! Pomeroy could not resist lambasting Devin for having appointed George Eastman police chief in August 1946 despite Eastman's third place rating among the candidates. Eastman estimated the slot machine business was worth 15 to 16 million dollars annually should they be authorized to operate, and that decision lay with the mayoral office, not with the police department. Eastman blamed by Pomeroy, who was a member of the US Attorney's staff, for the putative rise in crime, and he threatened to resign if Pomeroy won. When Devin claimed credit for running a closed town Pomeroy reminded voters that it was the armed forces officers who forced him close Seattle down to the extent it was. [16]

Ed Fussell conducted a timely police department survey for the *Times* by comparing Portland and Tacoma with Seattle. Fussell found Seattle the "best" of the three. But, in all three "vice" was the biggest "headache", while Seattle's ban of slot machines showed it to be strictest; and all three tolerated small stakes gambling. As to the supposedly "non-partisan" character of the city's elections, the *Times*'s Ross Cunningham found Pomeroy's support coming from Democrats who lost their King County jobs when Commissioner Archie Phelps was defeated in the 1946 election. Pro-America, an organization of Republican women, once again lined up behind Devin and all city council incumbents running for reelection. [17]

As in previous elections the AFL's Leo Flynn brought sixteen AFL locals into line behind Devin: "He has recognized and upheld the principles of free trade unionism, free collective bargaining and the right to strike." Also, the Municipal League endorsed Devin. The City Council's biggest vote getter, Mildred Powell, also endorsed Devin: "there have been fewer broken homes, and fewer children without food since the present city administration began its persistent war against gambling." Powell claimed not to have had a single complaint "against either a gambling house or or a house of prostitution" for the past 12 months. But, despite these strong declarations for Devin it was expected to be the closest mayoral race in years, "unpredictable". [18]

Before the absentee vote count Devin led by a mere 705 votes, but Devin's supporters had worked hard among the prospective absentees and it paid off. The final tally was Devin 67,179, Pomeroy 64,880. Both bond issues won overwhelmingly, one for street lighting, the other for upgrading the parks, playgrounds, and the zoo. All council incumbents won reelection, Powell led the pack again with over 80,000 votes. [19]

## The Great Boeing Strike of 1948

The Aero Mechanics, Local 751 was the city's largest union during the war. Through its *Aero Mechanic* the union also became organized labor's liberal voice, indeed that for the city as well. Local 751 had experienced a serious internal leadership struggle during 1940-1941, as described above in the "Wartime Economy" chapter. The CIO's attempt to organize Boeing workers at that time was defeated in large part by the resistance organized by Dave Beck and the City administration: Mayor Millikin and Police Chief William Sears. As the dominant figure in Seattle's organized labor movement, Beck had established warm working relationships with the city's employer associations in the 1930s by helping them to eliminate "cut-throat competition" and to prevent strikes. Beck became an outspoken defender of the the company. Boeing management undoubtedly looked favorably upon Beck and his Teamsters union, given its alternative of dealing endlessly with a comparatively miltant Local 751. Leadership of the Aero Mechanics was distinctly responsive to rank and file pressures from the shop floor upward to the union officers. Unlike most AFL and Teamster unions it was uniquely democratic in operation. Boeing's new president, William Allen made clear before long that he intended to break Local 751. Should he be able to force Local 751 into a strike that might be viewed as breaking its contract, Allen might then choose to recognize another bargaining agent, with approval of the National Labor Relations Board, the Teamsters for example. This is the strategy that unfolded.

According to the Aero Mechanics Union, "after five full months of fruitless attempts to negotiate a new contract with Boeing" Local 751 called for membership meeting on 24 May 1947 to conduct a strike vote. By secret ballot 3,817 union members voted in favor of striking, 237 opposed. Negotiations between Boeing and Local 751 continued inconclusively from June through December 1947. The company rejected arbitration of unresolved issues by insisting that it have veto power over any recommendation made by an arbitration board. In early March 1948 both the President's Air Policy Board and the Congressional Aviation Policy Board had recommended large funding increases for military aircraft and for traffic aids to commercial airlines. Also during this first week of March 1948, the Aero Mechanics filed a petition with the National Labor Relations Board asking the Board to authorize an election on the issue of the union shop. The petition contained more than 10,000 signatures, far more than required for such an election. The NLRB agreed to hold the election during 22 to 26 March. Local 751 stressed the importance of a heavy turnout because the Taft-Hartley law required that a majority of those "ELIGIBLE" must vote in union shop elections. At Boeing 13,324 workers were eligible to vote. Members were reminded that job security/seniority could not be protected without the union shop. Of the 12,824 who voted 12,324

"THE STRIKE AT BOEING" as depicted by the *Aero Mechanic*, 13 May 1948.

voted for retaining the union shop. Negotiations again were set in motion but got nowhere, although the company - which had not increased wages for two years, while inflation was running its course after the demise of OPA - offered a wage increase of 15 cents an hour. This was but half that Local 751 aimed for. Local 751's next offer to arbitrate was rejected. The District Council then met with 350 shop committeemen who voted to strike effective 22 April should Boeing refuse its final offer of 20 April.

The strike began without approval of the Grand Lodge of the Machinists Union. When Boeing president William Allen wired the International Association of Machinists' about the strike, International Association of Machinists president Harvey Brown assured Allen the strike had not been approved. To this Allen wrote Brown that Local 751 was out of compliance with Section 8D of the revised National Labor Relations Act, and therefore Local 751 was not legally representative of the Boeing workers. Boeing indicated its willingness to deal with officials of the IAM, but it rejected inclusion of anyone from Local 751. Allen was willing only to discuss what the IAM intended to do with those in Local 751 who had called the strike, and to negotiate the cost of damages incurred by the company as a result of the strike. Since the IAM demurred and Allen remained adamant the prospective conference was called off. Under these circumstances the IAM Grand Lodge finally authorized the strike, effective 28 April. [20]

Coincidentally, Boeing was informed on 18 April that it would be awarded new defense contracts. It was predicted that the Renton plant would reopen in about three weeks. Housing authorities were surveying the housing situation with that in mind. Its Wichita plant had already been reactivated.

> "Thunder on the left". On the same 18 April 1948 the Progressive Party of Washington held its founding meeting at the Civic Auditorium with about 2,000 in attendance. All speakers attacked the Democratic Party. Chief among them was Jerry O'Connell, expelled executive secretary of the state Democratic Party. Now, he was executive secretary of the state PP. Elmer Benson, chair of the Wallace for President Committee and former Minnesota governor also was on the podium. Wallace was scheduled to speak in Seattle 21 May, Spokane on the 22nd. In parallel action, at Eagleson Hall across the street from the UW campus, the PP formed a Young Progressives of Washington. The PP promised a "peace parade" on 1 May. The left-wing weekly *New World* (successor to *New Dealer*) would cover the state PP throughout the year, and would run a steady commentary on the Boeing strike, waterfront strike preparations, the International Woodworkers of America's internal conflict within the CIO, progress of the Initiative 172 campaign, and the Canwell hearings. Covered were peripheral aspects about Canwell committee members that the dailies ignored. [21]

The 1948 Boeing strike was the most critical of any against the company, 21 April to 13 September. The strikers returned to work still without a contract. President William Allen refused to recognize the Local 751 while continuing to contest the NLRB ruling that the strike was legal. Boeing eventually won in court 31 May 1949, when the District of Columbia Appeals Court overruled the NLRB. During the strike Allen had collaborated with Dave Beck in undermining the Local 751's jurisdiction; consequently the NLRB agreed to stage a representation election on 1 November 1949. Local 751 won with 8,107 votes to the Teamsters 4,127.

By mid-May the Boeing strike was reaching an early climax. Mayor Devin responded weakly by appointing a "study" advisory committee composed of Rev. Stephen Bayne, business leader Nat Rogers, and attorney Philip McBride. Could they reasonably be expected to understand or empathize with the union's side of the dispute? Meeting the propaganda challenge Local 751 began reporting on the strike twice a week on radio station KING. In June Boeing countered with its own radio "drama": two wives talking about the "WONDERFUL" jobs opening at Boeing. Marking the early collaboration of William Allen and Dave Beck, the latter ordered truck drivers to drive through the picket lines if necessary to make their deliveries. Strikers also were setting up along the railroad tracks to obstruct deliveries from that sector. Local AFL leaders pleaded with the company to "reach an understanding in the American way and spirit." Meanwhile Boeing was advertising for 1,000 new workers for its Wichita plant, where Boeing had increased its payroll from 1,515 as of 25 March, to about 4,000 by 20 May. The company hoped to hire 6,000 to 7,000 new employees by 1 August according to the *Times*. The *P-I*'s front page of 21 May carried an editorial, accompanied by a photograph of a Boeing-Wichita employment advertisement. The editorial: "Killing the Goose," commented: "the only Boeing advertisements in Seattle papers relate to the strike which has brought the production of planes to a virtual standstill...But the effects are being felt in every walk of life...Already the city has lost millions of dollars in work in sub-contracts which have been sent to Wichita, to Portland and to California...It's time for both sides to give a little ground." The *New World* urged readers to donate food to the strikers, to write their senators, to get their own unions to support Local 751.

That same day presidential candidates Henry Wallace and Thomas E. Dewey spoke in Seattle. Wallace spoke before an estimated 5,500 to 7,000 people who paid $1 for admission. About 3,000 filled the Eagles Auditorium to hear Dewey. He praised the Canwell committee, tore into "American communists", and spoke glowingly of the promise of the West. The *Times* featured a front page photograph of Wallace being interviewed by the erstwhile liberal Mrs. Adele Parker, along with an account of Wallace's speeches, in which he flailed the Canwell committee. On the front page of its second section a photograph showed Wallace addressing, according to the P-I, a "cheering, jeering crowd" of about 3,000 next to the UW campus. [22]

By the end of May it seemed clear that a maritime strike was unavoidable. Contracts of five maritime unions were to run out 15 June, including the International Longshoremen's and Warehousemen's Union (ILWU), Marine Engineers Beneficial Association, Marine Cooks and Stewards, and the National Maritime Union. At stake was control of the hiring halls. The ILWU won that control in the bitter maritime strike of 1934. It was not about to give it back to the Waterfront Employers Association, who had abused their power over hiring during the 1920s and early 1930s. As in the past the maritime unions agreed not to settle separately with the employers should strike action be necessary. A temporary injunction had just been issued and the unions were ordered to appear in court 21 June to show cause why it should not be made permanent. Worry was that under Taft-Hartley the court might agree with the employers that the union hiring hall was illegal, since it resembled the outlawed closed shop. In Seattle the Northwest Joint Action Committee failed to get an audience with President Truman when he spoke at the high school stadium. Concurrently, the Washington Pension Union's Initiative 172 signature campaign gained steam when the Congress awarded the state $300,000 for its pensioners and aid to dependent children, but due to restraints imposed by the 1947 state Legislature the funds could not be spent. Governor Wallgren was not expected to call a special session to address this issue. [23]

Dave Beck set the tone for labor relations that summer in addressing the annual Teamsters Union meeting in early July. Beck promised to break the Aero Mechanics Union, to raid log haulers from both the AFL's Lumber and Sawmill Workers Union and the CIO's IWA, to challenge the ILWU for control of the latter's warehousemen, and he praised the Canwell Committee for its work. Governor Wallgren was guest of honor, after he appointed Beck a UW regent and chosen a Teamster, Paul Rovelle, as state director of the Transportation Department. From that position Rovelle was accused by the CIO of collaborating with the Teamsters in the log hauler raids. Along with the Teamsters' plans to upset organized labor came federal judge George B. Harris's ruling, under Taft-Hartley, requiring a 60-days cooling off period for the maritime workers. The new strike date was set for 2 September. At the annual meeting of the State Federation of Labor the delegates issued a resolution condemning Beck's disruptive tactics. Timidly, it issued a mild censure of Boeing for resorting to Taft-Hartley. [24]

To reaffirm the membership's commitment to carrying on the strike Local 751 called a special membership meeting for 23 June. About 8,000 members turned out at the Civic Auditorium, declaring their unmistakeable enthusiasm for continuing it. At Boeing the Teamsters had formed the Aeronautical and Warehousemen Union, sending organizers through Local 751's picket lines to sign up Local 751 members. A Teamster attorney, Samuel Bassett, recalls that Allen came to Beck's office to request assistance in breaking Local 751. Boeing sweetened the offer to strikebreakers by increasing the hourly pay rate by 15 cents. Affected were about 1,000 strikebreakers, but Boeing extended the pay increase to any returning workers. Also a back-to-work movement was in full swing. *Aviation Week* reported that a total of 3,650 hourly employees and 926 other workers returned as of 28 June. Rather dispirited, the Aero Mechanics chose a more optimistc view, by indicating that fewer than 3,000 members had returned to work by mid-July. However the NLRB added to Local 751's woes by awarding voting rights to new hires, thereby threatening a favorable vote for Local 751 in any future bargaining representation election. The NLRB continued to insist Local 751 was the legal bargaining agent, and the board extended its hearings. On 20 July the NLRB ruled Boeing was engaged in an unfair labor practice. The NLRB ruled that Local 751 had complied with the 60-day notice provision; therefore the strike was legal. The *Aero Mechanic*'s 29 July issue jubilantly proclaimed: "UNION IS WINNING STRIKE", followed with a two-column head: "Strikebreakers Rush From Plant". Local 751 officers then applied for the return of its members to work. Paralleling these developments was Local 751's steady gathering of wider public support from other unions, businessmen, and the general public through its twice-weekly radio programs, advertisements, and far-flung distribution of its *Aero Mechanic*. Flagrant use of Beck's Teamsters also contributed to defeat of Boeing's back-to-work movement. Businessmen in general had felt intimidated by Beck, but often had to accept his terms just to stay in business. Much of the general public considered him a "labor racketeer". Boeing was not helped when the *Times* refused to carry its regular Victor Riesel column recounting Beck's raiding record, "all in the name of a crusade against Communism". In the context of the steady reporting of strike's progress and widespread sympathy with the strikers red-baiting rang hollow. The *Aero Mechanic* carried Riesel's critique of Beck and the Teamsters, that the *Times* had rejected, on 19 August. [25]

While the Boeing strike was at fever pitch the second set of Canwell committee hearings got underway 19 July. They were directed, as noted above, against alleged Communist infiltration of the University of Washington, and against the Seattle Repertory Playhouse on suspicion that it was a recruiting agency for the CP. These hearings will be covered below, following coverage of the maritime strike, which began on 2 September.

Boeing's Allen remained adamant. He would not accept the NLRB's ruling and insisted the strike was illegal. He refused to negotiate and would not reinstate strikers. On 27 August the Aero Mechanics staged another membership meeting at the Civic Auditorium open to the general public. There, a resolution was voted to urge that Boeing bargain in good faith with the union. Meanwhile penalties accumulated against Boeing for refusing to abide NLRB examiner's ruling. Each day cost Boeing $172,000. Also B-50 bomber production was slowing down, thereby bringing pressure from the Pentagon, according to *Business Week* of 17 September. Allen finally decided to call off the strike on 13 September. It was hardly a victory for 751, however, because they returned without a contract. Hearings and litigation continued. Boeing appealed the NLRB's ruling that the strike was legal on 22 November. The company finally emerged victorious on 31 May 1949, when the Circuit Court of Appeals of the District of Columbia overruled the NLRB. Local 751 later, on 31 July 1949, petitioned the NLRB for a representation election to contest the Teamsters for bargaining agent status. At last, an election date was set for 1 November. The results showed: Local 751 with 8,107 votes, the Teamsters with 4,127 votes and 401 votes for no Union at all.

During the interim period Teamster organizers, reportedly, were allowed by Allen to "do whatever they wish and are now going in each shop asking members of 751 to join and when they refuse they call them abusive names, prod them in the ribs and do everything to cause the men to talk back. If they do the Teamster organizers report them to the management and they are fired." [26]

When a contract was finally negotiated in 1950 Local 751 lost the union shop, which the union won in 1937, and it lost the seniority system established during the war years. Boeing was given full power to promote, demote, and lay off workers on the basis of the company's judgment of their "competency, performance, and availability". Seniority would apply where there is "substantial" equality when considering the above factors. "Performance Analysis" became the measure of a worker's performance, evaluating performance by a "point" system. Local 751 was left, in effect, with having to rebuild the union practically from scratch. [27]

Ironically the Aero Mechanics Union had become the liberal voice of labor despite its purge of the local's left wing leadership in 1941. Recall, at that time

*Sept. 13, 1948, picketing on the last day of strike.*

Local 751 had fought off a CIO organization drive while the state CIO was conducting its own purges. Recall also that the dispute within Local 751 was ignited when African Americans were admitted to membership, an act that was quickly overuled by the parent Machinists union. That abortive action was consistent with CIO philosophy of racial integration. Without that left wing leadership Local 751 remained a racist union. The CIO's early defeat made it possible. Nevertheless Local 751 became the liberal voice of labor in the greater Seattle region by concentrating on bread and butter issues, consumerism as reflected in its leadership of the Labor Consumers' League and the frustrating efforts to bring wages in line with inflation. Had the CIO won control of the Aero Mechanics local there was a high probabilty that Blacks would have gained more jobs at Boeing than the mere 1,600 who did. And they certainly would have accrued seniority rights which Local 751 denied them until 1948. Probably workplace integration at Boeing would have opened avenues of social integration in tandem.

As the Boeing strike was drawing to a close another protracted strike got underway on the waterfront, with opposite results. The strike began on 2 September, at the end of the 60-days cooling off period that began in June.

## Waterfront Strike: Victory for ILWU After Failure of Employers' Anti-Communism Strategy

The Waterfront Employers Association was still guided by the unrelenting Frank Foisie and Gregory Harrison. They were determined to break the ILWU and destroy Harry Bridges by continuing their anticommunist strategy. Labor historian Charles Larrowe observed that Taft-Hartley was tailored to Foisie and Harrison's specifications. Each year every union officer had to file an affidavit with the NLRB swearing he was not a Communist, nor a member of any organization that advocates the overthrow of the US government. Failure to sign while remaining a union officer, constituted criminal behavior and brought penalties of $10,000 or ten years imprisonment, or fine and imprisonment. Since T-H banned the closed shop this implicitly affected the union-controlled hiring halls. Already on the East Coast and Great Lakes regions NLRB examiners had ruled the union hiring halls discriminated against non-union workers. Foisie and Harrison were sure they could at last "get" Bridges and have the NLRB rule the union hiring halls illegal on the West Coast as well. When a board of inquiry was appointed by President Truman in June it ruled that should a strike occur it would represent a national emergency. As such, federal intervention would be required. Shortly before the NLRB conducted a poll among the ILWU members, concerning the WEA's last offer, Foisie and Harrison mailed to each longshoreman a summary of the dispute. The summary concluded: "Under its present leadership, the ILWU has been guided strictly by the Communist Party Line." This Red-baiting had been going on since the 1934 strike and was consistently ignored by ILWU members, who had become even more loyal to Bridges as a result of two failed attempts by the FBI and Immigration authorities to deport him. The coastwide poll showed unanimous rejection of the WEA's offer: 26,695 to zero.[28]

From its start the WEA refused to negotiate with a union whose leaders refused to sign the non-Communist affidavits. When Bridges had the members vote whether he should sign the affidavit they voted "no" by a ten to one ratio up and down the coast. (Bridges did sign such an affidavit in 1949, when the Teamsters were raiding ILWU's warehousemen.) Larrowe factors into the WEA's strategy their expectation of a Dewey victory in November, which they were certain would bring the ILWU to its knees. In the Puget Sound and Gray's Harbor ports more than 2,500 longshoremen walked out. In Seattle 23 ships were affected. The only Washington ports not affected were those in Tacoma, Port Angeles, and Anacortes, which remained in the International Longshoremen's Association since the 1934 strike. Three Seattle stevedoring firms, who were not WEA members, signed contracts with the ILWU. Barge service to Alaska was disrupted as well as Army transport ships operating from the Port of Embarkation. In Seattle the ILWU's Bill Gettings allowed the few ships still arriving to unload perishables, mail, baggage and personal belongings. The Marine Cooks and Stewards members left their ships that afternoon. On 3 September the *P-I* declared Seattle a "Ghost Port" as 15 to 20 deep sea ships "scurried out of the harbor before the deadline". Picket lines were quickly established. The Marine Firemen's union joined the strike after their negotiations failed. The Marine Engineers Beneficial Association (MEBA) had a "tentative" agreement with the WEA, but it was contingent upon all unions signing on. In contrast with the *Times* the *P-I* made no reference to the hiring hall issue, referring primarily to the wage dispute instead. The ILWU demanded a 18 cents an hour increase for straight time and 27 cents for overtime. The WEA offered 10 and 15 cents respectively. On the 3rd the Port of Seattle's warehousemen joined the strike. For its part the WEA decided not to break the strike and shut down operations, confident Taft-Hartley would suffice.[29]

When Bridges arrived in Seattle on 7 September to discuss strategy the policy concerning military cargo was altered to allow the private stevedoring companies that had signed contracts with the ILWU to handle cargo at the new pay scale. The Army also would not be hampered should it choose to handle its cargo, providing they not use "military work battalions" as it had threatened to do during the war. This understanding proved tentative, however. In mid-September the Army attempted to hire off the docks in Seattle and San Francisco instead of hiring through the union hiring halls. Mass picketing of Army docks forced the Army to discontinue its attempt. Thenceforth only Army cargo moved along the coast. Meanwhile the WEA and the Pacific American Shipowners Association continued to resist negotiations until the signing of non-Communist affidavits by the ILWU and Marine Cooks and Stewards officers. Heartening to the strikers was the decision by the Seattle Central Labor Council to make no attempt to break the strike. However, a pledge by the Tacoma International Longshoremens Association local that it would not work diverted cargo, was reversed in early October. The Sailors Union of the Pacific, a bitter opponent of the ILWU, pressured the Washington State Council of the Maritime Trades Department (AFL) to oppose the ILWU. The SUP sealed its ILWU rivalry and signed an open shop contract with the shipowners.[30]

The course of the strike was proving so worrisome to CIO president Philip Murray that he decided to intervene on behalf of the strikers in late October. Although he was bitterly opposed to Bridges, he now called for all CIO affiliates to lend their support. Murray stated:

> The direct challenge by those employers of the right of the workers to select negotiating committees of their own choosing is a threat to every labor union in the country; it represents an attempt to establish a new pattern of company

"Dockers Will Handle Army Cargo..." The postponed maritime strike began 2 September 1948, one week before the Boeing strike ended. The Waterfront Employers Association expected a Dewey victory and one of their own, but President Truman's surprise victory brought the WEA to the bargaining table instead.

unionism...Acting for the National CIO I am extending every possible help to the unions to achieve this objective...[T]he differences over specific issues in dispute can be specially negotiated away once collective bargaining is resumed.

I have urged the U.S. Maritime Commission and other appropriate agencies of the government to lend their good offices..."

Murray then approached the employers, offering: "We'll guarantee that the longshoremen will live up to a contract you will agree on if you will drop your insistence that Bridges and the other officers sign the non-Communist affidavits." At this point - 44 days from the strike's start - Bridges offered to step aside and have the union elect a new negotiating committee. The WEA bluntly said this was not the issue: "The problem...is the future administration and observances of any contract between ourselves and the ILWU, under its present leadership." Just after Truman's reelection in November the growing opposition to following the Foisie-Harrison line, led by officers of the Matson Lines within the WEA, forced them out of the negotiating process. [31]

With the employers losing enormous amounts of money, and Bridges remaining as popular as ever among the rank and file, it seemed pointless to continue what had become a lockout, not a strike. The WEA's new leadership decided once and for all to "get along with Bridges". Negotiations finally got underway 4 November, with the National CIO guaranteeing contract compliance, and having one of its executive officers sitting in on the negotiations. The strike/lockout lasted ninety-five days, into the first week of December and they resulted in a great victory for the ILWU and the affiliated maritime unions. They retained control of the all-important hiring halls, and got a satisfactory wage settlement. [32]

The contrasting results of these two major strikes - defeat of Local 751 and victory for the ILWU - may be attributed primarily to Truman's unexpected re-election. Had Dewey won the WEA probably would have persisted in its employment of Taft-Hartley to declare illegal the ILWU's control of the hiring halls. This had been the strategy of Foisie and Harrison. Their continued failure since 1934 to get Bridges deported and fruitless Red-baiting by Foisie proved too disruptive. Also Bridges was respected for enforcing their contracts. A parallel for this strike was the 1936 strike against the *Post-Intelligencer*: when FDR was re-elected Hearst caved in soon after the election, knowing the NLRB would force a collective bargaining election which the *P-I* was sure to lose.

In the middle of these prolonged and critical labor disputes the Canwell Committee hearings resumed on 19 July. In foreign affairs tensions were approaching a climax. Following the takeover of Czechoslavakia the USSR blockaded all land routes leading to Berlin on 24 June. The Western powers responded by installing an airlift into the city; it would last for 321 days. Throughout the period outbreak of war seemed a real possibility.

## Canwell Hearings on the University of Washington and the Seattle Repertory Playhouse

Carey McWilliams writes:"Throughout the hearings, the professors were browbeaten and incessantly rebuked by the chairman and by counsel 'for making speeches,' although the longest answers any of them gave were mere fragments by comparison with pages given over to outpourings of [Howard] Rushmore [a former CPer and then a Hearst newspaper columnist], who regaled the committee with 'inside' stories about the assassination of Leon Trotsky and similar items. In this fog of delusion, the professors spoke vaguely of 'a right of silence' and then again of 'a right of free speech'. The truth is that neither the defense nor the prosecution had the most remote notion of what subject was really under investigation. A more chaotic and jumbled record it would be difficult to imagine." [33]

Prior to the hearings Canwell investigators appeared on campus to meet with all faculty who were to be subpoenaed. They advised the faculty members to go to the committee's offices and disclose all their subversive activities and affiliations. Carey McWilliams reports about one person with a commission in the Navy reserve, who was told they had definite proof of his CP membership. The person insisted he never had been a member. He was then told that unless he cooperated with the committee by admitting party membership and naming names, he would lose his job. Authoritatively he was informed a person could be a party member without knowing it, and that he was a "dupe". Under this coloration the hearings proceeded. McWilliams suggests that it was heresy the committee was ferreting out, and that the UW administration pursued this same path in conducting its own subsequent hearings. Dr. Raymond B. Allen assumed the university presidency September 1946. His deanship of the University of Illinois medical school was a large factor in choosing him inasmuch as the UW was setting up a medical school. Significantly, in his inaugural address Allen sounded the theme of his predecessor, Lee Paul Sieg: a faculty member should never stray in public statements from the area of his professional competence. In other words, faculty should not presume they were entitled to free speech and opinion like the rest of the citizenry. In the context of the forthcoming Canwell hearings this attitude would contribute to the outcome for the university. [34]

During the pension union hearings, as noted above, several UW faculty were identified as Communists. Committee secretary Senator Thomas Bienz (Democrat, Spokane) insisted there were "not less than 150 Communists or Communist sympathizers on the faculty". Fred Niendorff of the *P-I* and Ross Cunningham of the *Times* had been arguing persuasively, all through 1946 and 1947, that the UW should be investigated for harboring Communists and fellow travelers. When Regent Joseph Drumheller of Spokane was a state senator, he urged an investigation of subversion at the UW as early as 1939. Drumheller cautioned fellow Democrat Bienz that it was probably no worse at the UW than on other campuses. Drumheller concurred with Bienz that suspected faculty should be ousted. Regents George Stuntz and Dave Beck similarly sought an investigation. Allen, while initially soft pedalling the Communist threat, met with bitter criticism from other newspapers about the state for expressing his reservations. Whatever was his predisposition Allen soon developed a complete rationale for the subsequent actions of the regents, then he would in turn propagate them nationwide.[35]

During the first set of hearings on the Washington Pension Union the following faculty were alleged by witnesses to be CP members: Harold Eby, Melville Jacobs, Joseph Butterworth, Maude Beal, Sophus Winther, Angelo Pellegrini, Ralph Gundlach, Melvin Rader, Joseph Cohen, Herbert Phillips, and Garland Ethel. Each was interrogated by Canwell and his investigative staff before the public hearings began. Canwell remained certain before, during, and after the hearings that Rader and Cohen were Communists, although the published hearings seem convincingly to refute him. As to Eby, Ethel, Jacobs, Beal, and Pellegrini, they admitted to past membership but refused to name names. Winther named names, including Joseph Cohen. Butterworth, Phillips, and Gundlach refused answers to question of party membership. When Gundlach was asked by Houston if he believed in the existence of God even Canwell ruled the question out of order.

Outside the Armory sign-carrying pickets marched in protest. One, Jerry O'Connell, executive secretary of the Progressive Party of Washington, was arrested for "creating a disturbance", but he promised to return when released. Inside the hearing room proceedings were tumultuous. Herbert Phillips was teaching at Columbia University that summer and indicated he was willing to submit a deposition in response to the committee's questions, but he was unwilling at his own expense to return to Seattle. President Allen suspended him, an action the Washington Committee for Academic Freedom deemed premature. Under these circumstances Phillips returned at his own expense. At the hearing Phillips was ordered removed from the witness stand for refusing three times to answer whether or not he was now or ever a member of the Communist Party. His attorney John Caughlan was also ejected when he attempted to question the committee about his client's dismissal.

Shortly the Seattle Repertory Playhouse was alleged to be a communist front.

## 1948: Liberalism in Disarray      229

Its co-director Florence James jumped to her feet when her attorney was denied reading a letter about recalling witnesses, shouting: "We demand those witnesses be put on the stand". She was ejected. Ethel was cited for contempt. To this drift in the hearing procedures assistant professor Arthur Smullyan was invited by the *Times* to comment on the hearing procedures. Smullyan taught at Williams College before joining the UW Philosophy Department two years previously. He asked: "In view of the systematic suppression of the traditional instruments of self-defense, may we continue to speak of this as a fact-finding investigation?"

On the 21 July six students, a veterans counsellor, and two attorneys were ejected from the hearing room. Professor Melville Jacobs was ordered to leave the witness stand when he refused to name names. Maude Beal also refused to name names and was similarly dismissed, thus was created a raucus circus that passed for civility, a consequence of setting aside constitutional protections. [36]

The harshest line of questioning seemed reserved for Cohen and Rader. Winther and Nat Honig identified Cohen as a party member. Also committee investigator Aaron Colemen had accused him of party membership before the public hearings began. Coleman accused Cohen of having made speeches in Geneva, Switzerland, to which allegation Cohen protested he had never been to Geneva and that "Joseph Cohen" is a popular name, hinting there was mistaken identity. When Houston asked Cohen if he had been a party member Cohen answered:

> When I was called in by Mr. Colemen, I took the initiative in calling to Mr. Coleman's attention -
>
> *Mr. Houston*: I'm speaking of your Federal service, now.
>
> *Mr. Cohen:* Yes, I was commenting on that question.
>
> *Mr. Houston:* Well, it's a different Coleman from the Coleman of the Committee, isn't it?
>
> *Mr. Cohen:* I'm now referring to a conversation I had with Mr. Coleman of your Committee. And Mr. Coleman called me in to confront me with certain accusations of having been a member.
>
> The allegations that he made were that I had made speeches in certain parts of the world where I had never been. I tried to get completely from him any basis there might be for such charges and my attorney advised me at that time to turn over to him the transcript of the conversation between - or an interview between my self and members of the F.B.I., and since you've referred to it I'd like to comment on that....
>
> My case was investigated, a complete report was made and I was completely exonerated....
>
> *Mr. Houston*: Were you ever interviewed by any F.B.I agent?
>
> *Mr. Cohen*: None other than the - for the occasion of this interview, the copy of

which - a transcribed copy of which I turned over to this Committee on my own initiative.

*Mr. Houston*: You have a copy of an interview that you've had with the F.B.I., then.

*Mr. Cohen:* And so do you in your records have a copy of the same interview.

*Mr. Houston:* That you -

*Mr. Cohen*: Which I turned over to you...

*Chairman Canwell*: Well, Mr. Cohen, so that we understand each other, Mr. Coleman of our Committee approached you, telling you we had in our files -

*Cohen* : Yes, sir.

*Chairman Canwell*: Have you any objection to that having been done in advance of the hearing?

*Cohen:* No. I stated to Mr. Coleman that I was quite ready to speak with him...and I hoped that he would let me know what information he had so that it could be corroborated in advance of these hearings. Apparently I got some but not all the information.

*Chairman Canwell:* That is all. You may be excused. Thank you for appearing.

That the Committee had all this information correcting Coleman's information about Professor Cohen and continued the kind of harassing public interrogation as excerpted above calls into question the committee's motives and competence as much as any other investigation, except that concerned with Professor Melvin Rader. *37*

## *The Case of Melvin Rader*

In the Committee's recapitulation of their interrogations of UW faculty members listed above professors Cohen and Pellegrini are omitted. That of Professor Rader reads:

> "During the period from 1935 through 1947, as shown herein, Professor Melvin Rader has been associated with as sponsor, member or other capacity at least twelve organizations whose announced platforms and whose activities have closely paralleled the Communist Party Line through its varying phases regardless of whether those policies and activities were in agreement with, or opposition to, the internal or foreign policy of the United States Government. Each of these organizations has been cited as a Communist Front by one or more of the following: Attorney General Tom Clark, Attorney General Biddle, Special Committee on Un-American Activities or the Joint Fact-Finding Committee of California.

> Professor Rader has also been a member, sponsor or officer of two organizations whose policies have perfectly reflected the Communist Party Line.

Investigator Houston led off his interrogation of Professor Rader by asking for yes or no answers to specific times and locations at which Rader was alleged to have spoken before Communist front organizations. To each successive question Rader pleaded there was no way that he could answer precisely without danger of perjurying himself. He answered similarly to questions about his alleged sponsoring of front organizations: one supporting "Loyalist Spain", another the Joint Anti-Fascist Refugee Committee, which was on the US Attorney General's list. When Rader asked to comment on that list Canwell cut him off: "I don't think that is pertinent." When Houston volunteered to break the question into more distinguishable parts to satisfy Canwell Rader responded:

> I would like to remark that it seems to me, the classification or labeling of organizations as subversive is the proper function of the judicial branch of government, where in courts of law there are objective techniques and procedures for determining these matters, and I would say that -
>
> *Mr. Houston:* Mr. Chairman, I don't think this man should criticize an official function of the Attorney General of the United States...

To this Canwell cautioned Rader "about extending remarks into the record here that are not - oh, perhaps too pertinent. Houston then proceeded on the same track, and Rader responded much as he had previously. When Houston complained that "the man has no memory" Canwell told Houston to be less precise about times and places, and be satisfied with approximations instead. Houston then asked: "Well, have you followed the Communist Party line, Doctor?" To this Rader replied: "I have never been and am not now a follower of the Communist Party line."

When asked by Houston about his book, *No Compromise*, Rader explained that for the later British edition he had written a preface declaring his loyalty and sympathy, "not only to American democracy but to the whole concept of democracy internationally and specifically to France and England." Persistent in pursuit, Houston then asked Rader if he had, as reported in the 30 June 1939 *P-I*, been a member of the Harry Bridges Defense Committee, which objected to procedures seeking Bridges's deportation. In answering he could not be certain, Rader was then countered with Houston's declaration, as reported in the *P-I*, that the committee was on the Attorney General's list. Rader countered that the *P-I* was not a reliable source for such information.

Rader was next asked to respond to the testimony given the previous day by George Hewitt in which Rader was alleged to have been in New York in the summer of 1938 or 1939, attending a Communist Party school. Rader simply answered, "No." When Rader proceeded to read from notes he had prepared for this question Houston insisted that he had "a right to know what he is reading, you know", and when Rader had prepared them. When Rader explained that he wanted to be as accurate as possible, since he had to account for a large block of time, Houston rose to the occasion:

> That's why I want you to tell us now and not need a prepared statement before you knew what questions I'd ask. Had you made these notes in - years ago I think they'd be very admissible in evidence, but I certainly don't think notes that were made, not under oath, and only a few hours ago are admissible.

After Canwell indicated the notes were not being submitted in evidence Houston continued in hot pursuit: "Where were you in 1938 in the summer?" Rader objected to the question, explaining that he taught at the UW until the termination of the regular term in mid-June, and that he had taught summer school "until about August 1st" after which he went with his family to Canyon Creek Lodge near Granite Falls for about "a month and a half." The questioning dragged on, during which time Canwell asked Rader not to use his notes. A frustrated Houston concluded by asking if Rader would be "willing to work with our investigators...in definitely and positively ascertaining with evidence, of documentary evidence, where you were in 1938 and '39, which you don't remember." To this Rader announced that he "would be glad to work with the Prosecuting Attorney of King County, or any of his deputies, or governmental officials of the State of Washington, that my counsel would approve."

Undeterred by Rader's retort Canwell proceeded: "We will lend our entire facilities to getting that information, if Mr. Rader will cooperate with us. That is as fair as we can offer." Houston objected to Rader's performance at this time: "we attempted to cooperate with Mr. Rader during the course of the investigation; he refused. We subpoenaed him to the office; he refused to talk. Yesterday we asked him, prior to the testimony of [Hewitt] to sit down with the witness and confront the witness, the witness talk with him; he refused." [38]

We now know from the investigative reporting of Edwin Guthman of the *Seattle Times*, and from Rader's own book, *False Witness*, and from my own introduction to this account of the Canwell hearings, how all this turned out. However, the author is struck by the great tenacity with which the committee pursued professors Cohen and Rader, Cohen from mistaken identity, apparently; Rader because he seemed to faithfully follow the party line, whether or not he was a party member. The committee seemed more obsessed with running down "fellow travelers" than actual party, or ex-party members, while always pursuing ever more names to be dropped in its hopper. That the committee took special pains to follow the lead that Rader gave them, by mentioning his family's vacationing at Canyon Creek Lodge, that its investigators traveled there, took the lodge's register which contained the Rader entry, and sat on this evidence until confronted with Guthman's report - all this speaks to the point that they were out to get Rader, perhaps above all others. [39]

Focusing on Rader's exoneration by Guthman, historian Lorraine McConaghy portrays the *Times*'s predicament. Its Ross Cunningham and the *P-I*'s Fred Niendorff had been lent a free hand in exposing alleged communist infiltration of the UW. Indeed, the Hearst newspapers had been crusading about communism in the public schools, colleges and universities nationwide since the early 1930s. Due to Cunningham's zealotry the *Times*'s managing editor Russell McGrath replaced him with the young Guthman, expecting and getting objective coverage of the hearings. Disturbed by the treatment of Rader by the committee and the cloud of suspicion that he saw suspended over him the *Times* publisher Elmer Todd assigned Guthman to investigate the Rader story in May 1949. Todd claimed "This is wrong. You just don't treat people this way." Guthman completed his investigation in July, but the *Times* postponed publishing it until 21 October out of fear of public reaction, then in the context of Cold War anxieties abuilding. When capping its front page with: "Red Charges of Canwell False...Clearing Rader" it balanced that with a subhead under its logo: "10 U.S. Reds Get 5 Years..." McConaghy concludes the committee was "almost entirely a creature of the press" and that despite its correction of a terrible injustice the *Times*, in this case, nonetheless felt the need to conform to its sense of the public mood, and moved with considered caution before exposing itself to accusations that it might be "soft on communism". [40]

The Seattle Repertory Playhouse and its directors, Burton and Florence Bean James, were the third target of the Canwell investigators. Ever since Florence James returned from a visit to the Soviet Union in 1934 and spoke glowingly about the USSR, the Jameses came under suspicion. Their 1936 production of Cifford Odets's *Waiting for Lefty*, convinced many conservatives of Jameses' leftish political leaning. When they staged the *San Juan Story* in 1946, with its "one world" and pacifist theme, the *P-I* found fourteen subversive incidents in the play. Ronald West, a recent historian of the SRP, writes: "SJS damaged the Playhouse more than the previous decade's *Waiting for Lefty* and [O'Neill's] *Hairy Ape*..." The Jameses formerly were instructors in the Drama division of the English Department in the 1930s, while they concurrently directed the SRP, a civic theater they established in 1928. Burton James was quietly dismissed in 1937; Florence, in 1938, but amidst wide public controversy and in violation of the university's own due process policy. Location of the SRP one block off campus, on University Way, led to continued close ties with the university community, faculty, and students. These intimate associations endured after the Jameses' dismissals. A bitter rivalry flourished between Glenn Hughes, then division head and later director of the UW's Drama School and the SRP. This rivalry led ultimately to their firings from the UW. Hughes persisted through the 1930s in tactics that he hoped would lead to his control of the SRP. In this he failed. The Canwell hearings contributed decisively to his success in the aftermath, although no evidence of his direct involvement is documented. [41]

Several witnesses called before the Canwell Committee testified that the SRP was a recruiting center for the CP, that it regularly staged fund raising performances, and that its childrens' program was for indoctrination. When the Jameses were called individually to testify they insisted upon legal representation, and justifiably termed George Hewitt a perjurer for claiming to have seen her in Moscow, from which he left in 1933. Florence James did not go there until 1934. The Jameses were cited for contempt, Florence being photographed as in a stage farce, under the strong arm of a state patrolman: "the first time a policeman ever laid a hand on me." While their trials proceeded upward to the state Supreme Court, which dismissed their appeal in early 1949, attrition of the SRP proceeded. Burton James reported the Canwell Committee's pressure on the "school system" to withdraw the childrens' program from the SRP. Unsurprisingly, the UW's Drama School took the SRP over September 1948. The touring theater also fell to Glenn Hughes. He then announced plans for a civic theater "downtown". Groups that previously purchased blocks of tickets for the SRP plays no longer subscribed. The demise of the SRP was clearly in view. The UW purchased the property from Norman Fitz September 1949. Futilely the Jameses considered first the Madison Street Theatre then Norway Hall as venues for continuing. The curtain wound humiliatingly down on Seattle's first vital civic theater, an early victim of the Cold War. [42]

## Results of the 1948 General Election

How significantly would the Progressive Party cut into Truman's Democratic vote? Given Washington state's radical reputation, would its votes favor a third party?

Washington followed the national trend in casting a majority for President Truman: 476,165 votes for Truman to Dewey's 386,315 votes. As was true in many states where Henry Wallace was expected to bite into Truman's vote, most prospective Wallace voters feared more Republican reactionary legislation and chose Truman. Wallace's 31,692 votes in the state did not affect the outcome. In contrast, Republican Arthur B. Langlie defeated incumbent Governor Mon Wallgren by almost 100,000 votes. Langlie piled up an unexpectedly big margin in Seattle, which pundits thought Wallgren would win. The fact that Initiative 172 - the pension initiative - also lost in Seattle, where the Washington Pension Union was based, suggests that the Canwell hearings on the WPU heavily influenced Seattle voters. All Progressive Party candidates were defeated, most by large margins. No longer having DeLacy hanging onto his coattails former US Senator Hugh B. Mitchell won a congressional seat in the first congressional district by defeating incumbent Homer Jones by a bare 8,000 votes. Henry Jackson won reelection overwhelmingly in the second district against his perennial opponent Payson Peterson. Democrat Charles Savage, a favorite of the Progressive Party, narrowly lost to Russell Mack by less than 5,000 votes. In Congress, nationally, the Democrats regained majorities in both houses, a fact that labor leaders attributed to the anti-labor legislation promoted by the Republican-controlled Congress of 1947-1948. [43]

Albert Canwell and fellow committee member Thomas Bienz, who ran as a Republican, also met defeat. Ironically, the Washington Pension Union's Initiative 172 won by a majority of 58,000 votes. Even more ironical was the margin of its defeat in the Greater Seattle area, where its author and sponsor, the Washington Pension Union, was centered. The WPU had been the first target of the Canwell committee. Its hearings had been in the city, where it lost by almost 30,000 votes. Voters in the hinterland, however, overcame that negative vote. Initiative 172's victory came from the more conservative sections of the state, certainly not from the "liberal" Seattle area. The pension initiative countered the actions of the 1947 legislature, which had wiped out most of the pension measures established by Initiative 141 in 1940. Initiative 172 set a $60 per month floor for senior citizens and the blind; a cost of living adjustment was attached. The 1947 lien law was eliminated. Free choice of doctors and dentists was reinstated. Grants for dependent children, widowed mothers, the unemployed, and physically handicapped were made more generous. WPU President William Pennock fully expected Governor Langlie to shift the financial burden in funding 172 to the general public with an increase in the sales tax, which he had done in 1941 to meet the costs of 141. [44]

## The University of Washington's Tenure and Academic Freedom Committee Hearings

Now we turn to the University of Washington to learn how it dealt with the faculty accused by the Canwell Committee. Proceedings began 27 October 1948, one week before the general election.

President Raymond Allen had been appointed to his position primarily on the strength of his wide experience in graduate education and most recently as dean of the College of Medicine at the University of Illinois. Not only was he was expected to oversee the development of the UW's medical school, but also to lead the UW toward national recognition as a first rate university in general. Barely after one year as president Raymond Allen - now under heavy pressure from the Board of Regents, as well as the *P-I*'s Fred Niendorff and the *Times*'s Ross Cunningham, could not, in the words of historian Jane Sanders, "stave off an investigation, and he turned his attention toward the insurance of internal due process according to rules of tenure that the faculty expected him to follow." The regents, however, had not yet formally accepted the revised Administrative Code that had been drafted in 1941. Wary that the code might impair regental authority the regents prefaced their acceptance of the code by reasserting their authority: the president and faculty served at the pleasure of the regents. [45]

Before the university began its own investigation President Allen felt the need to defend himself and the university against charges of colluding with the Canwell Committee and of abridging academic freedom. If one is to judge from the proceedings against professors Cohen and Rader, as excerpted above, then Allen's sensitivity, if not his judgment, seems highly questionable. Whether he would have acted differently had he not been under such heavy pressure, particularly that of legislators who voted university funding, is unknown. But it was a factor. And, being newly appointed he might have been innocent of the full implications of the Canwell hearings and their potential impact on the UW and the broader issue of academic freedom here and elsewhere. This is not known. However his predisposition against liberals, tainted by condecension, is indicated early during his tenure: "[We hope that] we can sharpen the edge of thinking among our fine liberal-minded friends." In October 1948 he wrote an open letter to "Friends of the University of Washington" defending Canwell against charges, apparently those made by Carey McWilliams in the *New Republic*, of conducting a "witch hunt" and smearing "liberals with a red brush". Writing to Columbia University president Dwight Eisenhower in 1949, Allen defended the Canwell committee's actions: "I am still of the mind that [the hearings] conducted as they are in an atmosphere of some dignity and consideration of individual rights, it is going to be extremely healthy for the university and the State as well as the individuals concerned". Allen made clear before the tenure committee began its hearings that current membership in the CP disqualified any faculty member from further employment, although such a qualification was never specified as a condition of employment. UW historian Charles M. Gates found that Allen's "mind was made up before the hearing began [and] that the deliberations and conclusions of the Tenure Committee did little or nothing to change it." Furthermore, Allen never defined his relationship to the committee, but acted to control its proceedings as much as possible. To three tenure committee members' contention (professors Rex Robinson, John Sholley, and Richard Huber) that CP membership was irrelevant, Allen retorted their's was an "unrealistic point of view". He did make clear that CP membership itself, past or present, was sufficient, in his opinion, for dismissal. The CP's very secrecy cast suspicion upon all former and present party members; in no way could such faculty be trusted in their academic performance, according to Allen. And should any of the defendants prove evasive or equivocating, or not have come previously forward and admit to past or present membership that too might be ground for dismissal. [46]

Procedures for the Faculty Senate's Committee on Tenure and Academic Freedom were at sharp variance from those of the Canwell Committee. Each person charged had the opportunity to be represented by counsel, to receive notice of charges against him, to file an answer, to present evidence in his own behalf, and to cross examine witnesses against him. The discrediting of Joseph Kornfeder's credibility by attorney Ed Henry is an example of what might have been done during the Canwell hearings had court procedures been followed. The Faculty Senate appointed the eleven members to the Committee; President Allen participated in the committee's proceedings. Tracy Griffin, as counsel for the University, stated its position: "that the Communist Party of the United States is not a free agent, that it is a branch of the Comintern and Cominform of Moscow, and that a member of the Party under the theory and philosophy, and particularly under the practices of the Party, cannot be a free agent." Another counsel for the administration, A.R. Hilen, added, "So we make the direct issue that he becomes incompetent by the very fact of remaining a member of the Communist Party and participating in its activities for any length or period of time." Here, it should be noted the party was still a legal entity. [47]

Sanders, Gates, and Countryman provide abundant detail on the tenure committee proceedings which continued until mid-December 1948. Ironically the committee assumed the Administrative Code was a valid operational document. Not until Allen submitted the committee's findings to the Regents did it become known that although Allen had approved the code and it had served as the set of guidelines for the committee's conduct, the Regents had never approved it. The five conditions for dismissal listed in the Administrative Code are: incompetency, neglect of duty, physical or mental incapacity, dishonesty or immorality, and conviction of a felony involving moral turpitude. Notably absent here was any reference to "subversive" activities, what might constitute them, nor that engagement in such alleged activities was a condition of employment. Notably, a majority of the committee declared "that the Tenure Code does not authorize dismissal for any cause not listed in Sec. IV". [48]

The administration filed complaints before the committee against six tenured faculty on 8 September 1948. Current CP membership was the charge against three: Joseph Butterworth of the English department, Ralph Gundlach of the Psychology department, and Herbert J. Phillips of the Philosophy department. The administration alleged that party membership inevitably affected their academic performance, whether or not evidence to the contrary could be presented. Three former party members - Harold Eby and Garland Ethel of the English department, and Melville Jacobs of the Anthropology department - were alleged to be equally as guilty as the others. The eleven committee members were: law professor J. Gordon Gose; assistant director of the School of Journalism Merritt Benson; H.B. Densmore chairman of the Classics department; Zoology professor Melville Hatch; Chemistry professor Rex Robinson; Home Economics School director Jennie Roundtree; J. Richard Huber, chairman of the Economics department; law professor John Sholley; professor Curtis Williams of the School of Education; Geology department chairman George Goodspeed; and Thomas G. Thompson, a professor of chemistry and director of the Oceanography Laboratory.

Upon concluding its hearings the committee unanimously recommended that professors Eby, Ethel, and Jacobs "should not be disturbed [with respect to their continued employment]". Eight members of the committee saw no basis for recommending termination of professors Phillips and Butterworth: "We conclude that in [their cases] the fact of membership in the Communist Party alone furnishes no basis for removal under the Administrative Code, as presently constituted." Five of those committee members recommended that the code be revised to make that a condition of employment; they objected to making such a condition retroactive, however. The other three members recommended dismissal of Phillips and Butterworth. Committee members Robinson, Sholley, and Huber opposed their dismissal because the code made no reference to CP membership as grounds for their firing. It made no difference, anyway, what the code stated since the Regents had never approved it and they were therefore free to pursue their judgment unimpeded. [49]

All eleven members of the committee agreed that refusal to answer questions posed by the Canwell Committee was insufficient ground for dismissal. As to Professor Gundlach seven committee members recommended his dismissal, chiefly for his evasions to questions asked by President Allen outside the committee hearings, to alleged "bias" in his research (which was contradicted by testimony of his peers inside and outside the UW and by several of his students), and to the direct use of his research in the election campaign of Hugh DeLacy. Countryman makes the point that Allen ventured outside the tenure committee recommendations and decided on his own the relevancy of CP membership. And in doing so he violated the Administrative Code. [50]

In presenting his report of 17 January 1949 President Allen interspersed his own commentary. Over the previous months he had pulled together the following rationale. Concerning the cases against Butterworth and Phillips Allen professed some embarassment suffered by the UW and himself, when he had publicly declared earlier that there were no Communists on the faculty. None came forward "to either disabuse the public...or to come to the President to admit the fact." These men "were carrying on activities which were in high disfavor in the University community...[W]hy did they keep their membership secret?" Allen further contended that since his public "statement" disqualifying Communists from teaching had "never been challenged...I therefore regard it as...the policy of the University..." Furthermore, they are "in no way absolved by their tardy admission of membership." He was unmoved by the objections of committee members Rex Robinson and John Sholly, who found, in the absence of any advance notice from the president, there was no "neglect of duty." In conclusion, Allen recommended to the regents that Phillips and Butterworth be dismissed because of their party membership, and that Gundlach be discharged for his evasiveness and deception. He left the decision on Jacobs to the Regents, while recommending retention of Eby and Ethel, admonishing them for "their extremely bad judgment." Allen concluded his report and recommendations, asserting: "Men must be free, of course, but they must also be free, and willing to stand up and profess what they believe so that all may hear. This is important, if not the most important, point of our American heritage of freedom." What Allen is suggesting is that "men" should make public their most private of beliefs and actions, which is what the US Constitution is meant to protect...quite contrary to Allen's concept of the American heritage. A "loyalty oath" is one element that would qualify under his conception, and that was finally declared unconstitutional in the early 1960s. [51]

Two days before the Board of Regents met to consider President Allen's recommendations Fred Niendorff wrote on 20 January, the day on which transcripts of the committee hearings were completed, that at least three Regents would recommend dismissal of all six of the accused faculty. Apparently they chose not to be dissuaded from their predisposition to fire the six, whatever the evidence, which they chose not to read. To be factored in to the Board's quick action two days later was the threat from legislators, Senator Virgil Lee and Representative Grant Sisson, that the UW's budget "will be influenced by steps taken to rid the University of Communists and fellow travelers." Regents Beck, Stuntz, and Drumheller, backed by counsel Tracy Griffin, argued for dismissal of the six men for having the bad sense to ever join the party in the first place. As to Eby, Ethel, and Jacobs, their attorney Ed Henry persuaded a majority of the Board to amend their vote. Niendorff wrote, "A switch of only one vote would have resulted in the dismissal of all six..." The three men were placed on a two-year probation, a sentence that confirmed, in the view of Carey McWilliams, that it was heresy that was being sought and banished, not communism per se. And, in my view, that it was really liberalism which was under siege. That was the heresy. Liberals, by promoting social, political, and economic reforms were often joined in their advocacy by the CP. Sometimes the CP managed, here, to take over liberal organizations such as the Unemployed Citizens League, the Washington Commonwealth Federation and the Washington Pension Union. In this context liberals and liberalism became ever more vulnerable to attack, particularly as the Cold War heated up. By promoting the "guilt by association" line the opportunity to roundly defeat liberalism as represented in its New Deal version proved irresistible. [52]

## National Significance of the University of Washington Investigations

Ellen W. Schrecker, in her *No Ivory Tower: McCarthyism and the Universities*, placed the Canwell Committee investigations and its sequel at the University of Washington in the larger national context of civil liberties repressions of the early postwar period. For one, the Canwell hearings followed the pattern established by the Rapp-Coudert un-American activities investigations in New York state, which became the model applied in other states. Chief among the tactics was use of essentially the same set of "expert" witnesses on the "Communist conspiracy"; disallowing normal courtroom procedures with repect to witness testimony; extracting names from witnesses, then achieving maximum publicity for uncontested allegations of participation in the conspiracy; and use of various "Communist front" lists to prove non-Communists of being guilty by association with these fronts. [53]

Schrecker assigns to the University of Washington the distinction of being the "first important academic freedom case of the Cold War". Its critical importance lay in the rationale given by president Raymond Allen for faculty dismissals: that CP membership by itself provided sufficient ground for faculty dismissal. He wrote extensively pressing this argument, and spoke to audiences nationwide. Although this viewpoint had "become common currency" as a result in large part by the Rapp-Coudert hearings, the UW cases simply "gave them greater saliency".

By drawing upon academic anti-Communists like Sidney Hook, Arthur Lovejoy, and T.V. Smith to illustrate from the writings of Marx, Lenin, and Stalin that overthrow of governments by force and violence was the ultimate objective of the CPUSA the color of scholarly credibilty was given to Allen's position. By ignoring all contrary evidence the rationale proved convincing: "that all Communists followed all of the Party line all the time". Contributing forcefully to public acceptance of this rationale was the part played by the American Association of University Professors. In addressing the Communist issue in its 1947 report the AAUP stated: "So long as the Communist party in the United States is a legal party, affiliation with that party in and of itself should not be regarded as a justifiable reason for exclusion from the academic profession." This rule was never enforced by the AAUP. In the UW cases the AAUP leadership postponed for seven years before taking action, not only on the appeals of the UW faculty seeking redress, but on a host of appeals from victims of other institutions. At that time (1955) the AAUP chose not to censure the present University administration for the actions of the previous one. [54]

Vern Countryman, whose study of the Canwell Committee and the UW tenure committee hearings is the most thorough one available, concludes:

> Neither in the investigations conducted by the legislative Committee on Un-American Activities nor in any investigation resulting from the committee's work has there been any disclosure of "un-American activities" on the part of the persons or organizations investigated. [55]

In closing this section on academic freedom a paragraph written by Robert MacIver, in his *Academic Freedom in Our Time*, is pertinent.

> In sum it is clear that the direct and indirect modes of political control, operating mainly on the state and local level, have, taken together, a powerful impact on education. The more they are utilized the greater the peril to academic freedom. State institutions are particularly exposed to them, but in degree they affect private educational institutions as well. The degree to which these types of political control are employed is an index of the unhealthiness of public opinion. For they are invoked in order to coerce educational authorities and to reduce educators to conformity. All this is done in the name of loyalty or patriotism, as a "protection" against communist inroads. A highly significant aspect of the situation is that it impinges on the local autonomy that has been so important a feature of American educational systems. State prescriptions mean that state officials acquire power of supervision, armed with rights of enforcement and penalization, over local boards. [56]

# 1950: END OF AN ERA?

In many ways the November 1950 off-year election capped the 1940s decade. Certainly this was true of the nearly fifty years-long duel between Seattle City Light and Puget Sound Power and Light for control of the city's electrical power distribution systems. PSP&L's City franchise was to expire in 1952. Voters were to decide whether or not to buy the company's electrical properties in the area over which they had been competing. But even its end was frought with controversy. The initial vote count on Proposition C, authorizing the bond sale for PSP&L's purchase, pointed to a narrow defeat. How this was turned around will be covered below. In this election public schools across the state continued to win voter support; a majority of 147,217 state voters supported the $40 million bond issue for public school building construction. The Seattle Public School Board painstakingly prepared the district's portion of the bond proposal by drawing favor from the board's major critic, the Municipal League and its venerable supporter, the PTA. By contrast, in Seattle its Proposition A for a civic arts center, and Proposition B for a new public library, were defeated. This defeat was attributed to the presentation of too many bond issues being offered at one time. But, also voters tend to veer away from supporting cultural/intellectual propositions except in the best of times and 1949-1950 did not qualify.

Equally less fortunate was the UW's Medical School. Referendum 9 included the UW request for a teaching and research hospital, but its $10 million item was linked with other funding for the state's institutions of higher learning, amounting to $20 million. Because the UW portion represented 50 percent of the total it probably contributed to the bickering among all the specified beneficiaries, and to its defeat by a mere 2,340 votes, or as Dean Edward Turner bitingly observed, but one-third of one percent. Turner blamed this result on failure of the UW Alumni Association to support the bond issue. [1]

At issue too was the Washington Pension Union sponsored Initiative 176. If passed, senior citizens would be paid a $60 minimum monthly pension. Governor Arthur Langlie countered by framing Initiative 178 to set new qualification standards by which thousands of current beneficiaries would be dropped from the rolls, saving the the State an estimated $25 million annually. Since voters overwhelmingly approved the pension union's Initiative 141 in 1940, the WPU and Langlie had fought over its provisions and subsequent attempts of the WPU to increase benefits. The WPU in 1942 tried to raise the minimum and to permit pensioners to work in war industry and agriculture without losing their benefits. Its Initiative 151, lost by a 65,000 vote margin, 160,084 to 225,027; 77,545 voters ignored it altogether. Clearly, the WPU was losing its mass appeal...almost. For the 1948 election the WPU put forward Initiative 172 to counteract severe modifications enacted by the 1947 legislature. This, the year of President Truman's astounding re-election, also favored Initiative 172; Initiative 172 won 420,751 votes to 352,642 despite its loss in Seattle, the home of the WPU. The off-year election of 1950 finally brought the first direct faceoff between the two belligerents. At this time the economy was shaky and the US was at war in Korea, suffering sharp reverses. The WPU's Initiative 176 suffered a resounding defeat, 534,689 against, only 159,400 votes for it. The governor's Initiative 178 won by nearly 100,000 votes, 394,261 to 296,290. For all practical purposes this defeat meant the effective demise of the Washington Pension Union and with it the influence of the "Old Left". It had assumed leadership as its fostering parent, the Washington Commonwealth Federation, wearily expired following the Nazi-Soviet Pact of August 1939. During its career the pension union focused popular attention on the fate of the aged and the dependent population. It seems doubtful that public compassion would have been touched as profoundly if not for the WPU advocacy. This running debate over welfare issues began in its contemporary form during the Great Depression. In the 1990s rising costs for health care broadened the welfare issue in general by drawing attention to the need for universal health care. At heart welfare is a moral issue demanding a political solution, as was true in the antecedent debate. [2]

Turn now to Proposition C, the City's acquisition of PSP&L's electrical properties in Seattle. On 17 November 1943 the City Council voted to notify investors that the City would not renew the company's franchise in 1952. PSP&L's Frank McLaughlin complained bitterly in the company's 1947 annual report, that: "By declaring the Company out of business in 1952 the City had hogtied, hamstrung, and prevented the effective functioning of the Company [inasmuch as the Company cannot attract investment or improve and extend its operations]". Mayor Devin, an alleged PSP&L backer, called a conference in September 1947 between McLaughlin and Bert Heggen, president of the Puget Sound PUD Commissioners Association, to learn whether or not the PUDs would be willing to purchase PSP&L's properties, then sell Seattle's portion to the City. Heggen suggested Devin work it out with the company, but no agreement emerged. However, in 1949 the state Supreme Court ruled in favor of joint purchase. Where Devin stood on the issue is unclear in light of a letter from him to Congressman Hugh Mitchell, when Mitchell was sponsoring legislation for a Columbia Valley Authority. Devin referred Mitchell to a proposal he made to Congressman Henry Jackson, 25 April 1949, that in any CVA legislation states should be allowed to acquire "wholly or partly all facilities including dams and dam sites...at any price which would not exceed either the cost of construction or the cost of allocated power with interest at 3% during the life of such construction." Devin's strategy must be viewed in the context of the time and his close association with the governor and apparently with PSP&L as well. At this time, to protect the private companies from threats posed by the public power forces Governor Langlie proposed creation of a State Power Commission in his annual message for 1951. Its enactment was delayed until 1953. By it the commission could potentially put the State into the power business, and obstruct more acquisitions by the PUDs. This very issue in 1935 split the public power forces. City Light superintendent J.D. Ross was pitted against veteran public power proponent Senator Homer T. Bone. Bone's state legislative liaison, Kenneth Harlan, drafted such a bill. Since 1911 Ross had successively fought off previous attempts at placing publicly owned utilities under an overarching state commission that controlled all electrical utilities, private and public. Ross succeeded in 1935 as well by heading off the proposed legislation.[3]

Seeing the inevitable, Mayor Devin called the parties together 2 June 1950 to settle upon a price for taking over the company's 78,000 customers. PSP&L estimated each customer required an outlay of about $650. City Light superintendent Eugene Hoffman countered with a $288 estimate. The company decided to "split the difference", which amounted to a total $30 million, and financed by 30-year revenue bonds at 2.5 percent interest. This proposal was submitted 23 June to representatives of the City Council, McLaughlin, Hoffman, and Corporation Counsel Van Soelen, with Devin presiding. Based on the report of the accounting firm Ford, Bacon, and Davis the price was set at $25,850,000. Voters would have their chance on 7 November to pass judgment, though no thought was given to the consequences for the company should voters disapprove the transaction.[4]

To everyone's surprise - and the negotiants' dismay - Proposition C lost by a margin of 832 votes. On a recheck of the votes the margin was cut to only 92 votes. In fact, on the 18th the auditor's office "discovered tabulation errors of several hundred votes in its unofficial returns". On 17 November - ten days after the election - fresh developments: County Prosecutor Charles Carroll had persuaded the county commissioners to fund $5,000 toward a recount. The matter was clouded in Carroll's mind by the stock market trading in the company's stock based on information that the measure was then leading, but before any public announcement was made to that effect. Seventy-five precincts were rechecked, resulting in a tentative "Yes" vote. PSP&L's stock rose on the basis of that information. Absentee ballots remained to be tallied. A partial count of the absentees showed a lead of 126 votes. But, in the absence of any proof of fraud County Auditor Robert Morris indicated that no court would order a recount. Carroll contested Morris's announcement on the 19th, claiming there would be an attempt to tamper with the absentee ballots. On this basis Carroll tried to dissuade Morris, but the county auditor refused to budge from his contention that the proposition had failed to pass by the 92 votes noted above. Morris, however, had already been reported as saying that it appeared the measure would pass by 500 to 600 votes, based on the absentee ballots. Meanwhile counting of those ballots continued, reportedly mounting to a 519 "Yes" vote majority as of 20 November. "Finally" the final tally was announced, giving a 681 vote majority...but that still was not the end of it! On 24 January 1951 the vote was "recanvassed" changing the "final" numbers to 65,616 "Yes" votes to 64,892 "No" votes for a "Yes" majority of 724. Signing by the election board quickly followed on 26 January. The agreement was signed 27 February 1951. Included were PSP&L's real estate in the competitive area, its structures and improvements, the obsolete steam plant in Georgetown, substations, transmission lines, its distribution system, general plant accounts, maps and records. Mrs. Alice Ross - widow of James D. Ross the late superintendent of City Light and BPA's first administrator - enjoyed the proceedings, expressing regrets that her late husband was not there to take it all in. [5]

Witness here the atrophying of the public power movement, beginning with the rise of the Bonneville Power Administration and its administration of the Northwest Power Pool, through which the private utilities gained decisive access to the public-generated power that they had ideologically opposed in the past. Contributing to this atrophying process was the massive influx of out-of-state/region people who had no historical ties to the movement.

# Postscript

World War II set in motion irreversible changes for the nation, the region, and the greater Seattle area. Industrialization of the West Coast took root on an astounding scale and with such rapidity as to be inconceivable were the nation at peace, not war. Capital was supplied by the federal government primarily, not private enterprise. What made industrialization irreversible was the kind of investments represented. The aircraft industry became concentrated in two West Coast centers, Southern California and the greater Seattle areas. As a relatively new industry that endured a prolonged period of gestation, its birth would not have occurred so quickly had it not been for the unprecedented demand for aircraft for war. Before 1940 there was no substantial market for airplanes. After the war the problem was how to develop a civilian market. No substantial infrastructure existed for expanding air travel. Putting such an infrastructure in place became a national priority in the postwar period. Somehow the aircraft industry had to be sustained while the civilian sector underwent development. The required capital investment was made possible once the Air Force was freed of Army control and when the independent Air Force received funding for a 70 group air force. This meant government contracts for the industry. For Boeing the money thus earned was invested in the civilian side of its operations. To this sustaining process the Korean War added impetus. Boeing won the contract for B-52s and was able to invest in the civilian 707 passenger craft. With the 707 Boeing ended Douglas's domination of the commercial market and proceeded to establish its own domination of it. This new industry did not have an impact equivalent to that of railroads in the late 19th- early 20th centuries, nor the automobile industry of the 1920s. In the postwar economy the aircraft industry's concentration in Southern California and greater Seattle had a comparable regional effect. The aircraft industry propelled those economies, lending to each region their unique postwar character.

The entry of the Bonneville Power Administration into the Pacific Northwest economy and politics was cemented during the war. Its administration of the Northwest Power Pool made it a key player in the development of the region's energy supply. BPA demonstrated its growing influence when it served as a broker between Puget Sound Power and Light and Seattle's City Light and the PUDs. Its control of the marketing of electrical energy generated by the Columbia River dams placed it centrally for implementing the basin's postwar irrigation projects, supplying electricity below market rates for the Hanford works and the aluminum industry, and cheap electricity for the region's businesses and households. In its 25 July 1947 *BPA Currents* the administration made clear what its values were with respect to electricity and the basin's salmon fisheries: "The [Interior] Department agrees that the interests of the Columbia River fisheries should not be allowed to indefinitely retard full development of the other resources of the river...[D]evelopment of the Snake and Columbia are such that the present salmon run must, if necessary, be sacrificed". Conceived in the context of the Great Depression the Bonneville and Grand Coulee dams were meant to deal with unemployment, resettlement of farmers, and to respond affirmatively to the regional public power movement to which City Light had provided the backbone since the century's first decade. That President Roosevelt was predisposed toward public power and had a close association with City Light's J.D. Ross stretching back to 1931, also contributed toward Columbia basin development. Yet, administrators of the BPA, the Army Corps of Engineers, and the Bureau of Reclamation never were called upon to re-examine those preconceptions, testing their current relevancy. BPA's first administrator was J.D. Ross and he chose to link the power generated by Grand Coulee and Bonneville. To the dismay of Wenatchee's Grand Coulee promoters and the private power companies Ross decided electric rates would be set at the delivery point, "postage stamp" rates, akin to rural free delivery, instead of at the dam sites.

The Bureau and the Corps built substantially all the Columbia's dams. The Bureau managed the irrigation projects and joined with the Army Engineer Corps and the BPA to assign energy production as the primary mission of the dams. The energy generated seemed sufficient for the time being to subsidize the projected Columbia Basin Project, to sustain the aluminum plants (simultaneously breaking ALCOA's aluminum monopoly) by charging less than market rates for energy, and to continue supplying the Hanford works. For the Corps it also had to keep channels open for navigation all the way to the Port of Lewiston, Idaho. In implementing these administrative missions the great Columbia River salmon fishery was practically destroyed. All mitigation measures taken proved failures primarily because these three federal agencies opposed sharing control of the river and its major tributaries. Together, with their traditional non-habitat constituencies, they normalized channels of access to Congress and the executive offices, typically thwarting opposition from other federal and state habitat agencies and citizen groups that protested their policies. With passage of the Endangered Species Act in 1973 some leverage for habitat protection at the federal level was acquired and soon was accompanied by state efforts.

The confluence of the public power movement, centered originally in Seattle, with the respective programs of the Corps and Bureau predated passage the EPA. Events of 1948 particularly favored the Corps: the sudden regional power shortage, the great "brownout" and the flood that wiped out VanPort. After 1948 these three federal agencies proceeded full speed ahead, with minimal resistance, to fulfill the Army Engineer Corps' ambition to dam the entire basin, based on the Corps' landmark 308 report of 1932.

The public power movement, which had been at the center of political controversy during the forty years before the war, was neutralized during the war. With creation of the Northwest Power Pool under BPA control, the movement lost its dynamism, largely because few PUDs were yet operating; the PUDs were still fighting in Washington state to buy out the private utilities. Meanwhile the private utilities tapped into the intertie, taking substantially more power than they contributed. Their overall financial condition was underwritten in the process by the federal intervention required for war production. The BPA favored industrial users of electrical power, aluminum and the secretive Hanford project primarily. While the Public Utility Districts continued to be stymied in their operations by the resistance of the private utilities, the public power preference clause in the BPA charter also was effectively circumvented during the emergency and gradually lost force thereafter. When Seattle City Light acquired Puget Sound Power and Light's city properties in 1952 PSP&L's future was strengthened by its linkage with the regional power grid and by the suburbanization that would spread over its territory after 1950. The irony, here, is that the BPA was substantially the product of the public power movement in Washington state, but in implementing its managerial objectives the BPA steadily undercut that movement as it pursued its own structural imperatives. As the BPA programs moved forward its decisions blurred the differences between public power utilities and the private power companies by serving both. As with other federal agencies BPA became obsessed with its own managerial objectives, producing and distributing electric energy, and subidizing energy costs for pumping water to irrigate farms in the Columbia Basin Project, while ignoring how its preoccupation affected all else in the Columbia basin, most emphatically the salmon. [1]

Along with industrialization of the West Coast came irreversibly altered demographic characteristics. Metropolitan areas took on more the character of upper midwestern and northeastern metropolises. In Seattle as elsewhere in the coast's metropolitan centers, African Americans became the largest nonwhite part of their respective populations. African Americans in Seattle numbered only 3,789 in 1940, but by 1950 they had more than quadrupled to 15,666. By 1960 11,135 more Blacks joined their numbers. Employment insecurity and restrictions on their housing mobility obstructed their integration with majority society. Mayor William F. Devin's Civic Unity Committee mediated these problems and reduced developing tensions. The CUC joined with various social agencies and key legislators in efforts to bring about enactment of a State Fair Employment Practices Committee in 1949. This committee's mission was to remove employment barriers to their employment. The most rigid of these obstacles to fair employment lay in the AFL construction and metal trades unions and the Teamsters union. The steady atrophy of the CIO's original prewar militancy during the war, that led to its later merger with the AFL, meant that Blacks and other nonwhites could no longer look to unions for employment assistance. The minorities were on their own, until mobilized by the civil rights movement in the 1960s. Then, minorities found the AFL-CIO unions in blatant opposition to their integration.

Associated with continued widespread job discrimination was persistent residential segregation practiced by the real estate operators. Realtors remained unfazed by the US Supreme Court's decision in 1948, *Shelley vs. Kramer*, which struck down restrictive covenants. Without residential desegregation there was no school desegregation. The defeat of a Seattle open housing ordinance in 1964 stymied attempts to desegregate the city's public schools. Seattle proved no different from other major cities in this respect. Not, however, through the fault of the mayor or his CUC. Historically rooted racism proved too hardy to alter quickly. And, when we consider the alternative to the Republican Devin, the Democratic party offered outright racists beginning with Mayor Earl Millikin during the war, and the region's congressional delegation, led by Mon Wallgren and Warren Magnuson, all with strong ties to the racist AFL and the Teamsters union. [2]

The status of organized labor also was abruptly altered during the period. Militancy, as manifested early in the organizing drive of the Congress of Industrial Organizations, practically ground to a halt during the war. Correspondingly, anti-union employers gained political advantages which they built upon after the war, in an effort to return to the days of the open shop. Foreshadowing the postwar open shop drive was the Smith-Connally Act in 1943, and President Truman's threat to draft strikers into the army during the May 1946 railway strike.

Undeterred and strengthened by the 1946 election, congressional allies of the open shoppers returned in force in 1947 and passed the Taft-Hartley Bill, then overrode President Truman's veto. Taft-Hartley became the open shoppers' charter. As such it underpinned the left-wing purges occurring within the CIO, which took shape in Seattle in 1940-1941, during the CIO's organizing drive at Boeing. What had been cumulatively taking place, step by step, was the steady removal of federal safeguards for organized labor, protections that had contributed mightily to the New Deal political coalition. The CIO reciprocated for its federal protection during the war by restraining its militants and by contributing decisively to FDR's reelection drive in 1944. How far the CIO moved toward accomodation can be measured by its reconciliation with the conservative AFL in 1955-56. Taft-Hartley played to the AFL craft unionists by incorporating changes in the Wagner Act favored by the AFL and Teamster union leaders. Not only did this reconciliation signal how far the CIO had grown into a bureaucracy like the AFL, but it meant organized labor no longer was at the cutting edge of social reform, a role that the CIO had played in the late 1930s when the National Labor Relations Act was passed, along with the Social Security Act and other key pieces of social legislation that needed and won the support of organized labor. That organized labor had revived as a political force in the late 1930s is attributable to the rise of the CIO, thereby making it the main target of the anti-New Dealers.

It was against this nationwide backdrop, transforming industrial relations, that the great Boeing strike of 1948 and the Pacific Coast maritime strike that fall, spun their contrasting outcomes: Taft-Hartley favoring Boeing as it succeeded in defying the NLRB's rulings, and ILWU winning its contest by successfully challenging the shipowners' confidence that Taft-Hartley guaranteed them victory. The future, however, lay with Boeing and the aircraft industry. Seattle's maritime trade steadily deteriorated until the 1960s, when it finally adapted to the containerized cargo mode of ocean shipping, as Seattle shipping tried to catch up with other Pacific Coast ports. While the Aero Mechanics Union was rebuilding, consistent with the now, flaccid AFL-CIO leadership, the ILWU gradually abandoned its militant ways just as did the shipowners; the two resorted to simple collective bargaining to accomodate to containerized cargo. Labor unions struggled to maintain membership, not by aggressively organizing the unorganized as the CIO had done in the 1930s. To have done so would have forced the national leadership to seek social/political remedies for the unorganized in the process, as with clerical and agricultural workers for example. This they were not prepared to do, choosing instead to oppose such ameliorative measures as "affirmative action". [3]

Alan Brinkley observed in his *The End of Reform* (1995) that organized labor no longer looked toward restructuring capitalist economy or forming a third political party with that end in view. As the war was drawing to a close labor leaders were appealing for full-employment as an economic goal. Full-employment meant steady wages; a "guaranteed annual wage" proposal was even floated by the United Auto Workers in its contract negotiations to end cyclical capitalism. Since substantially full employment seemed achievable in the early postwar years reform appeared unnecessary as long as consumption levels could be maintained or improved through traditional collective bargaining. In this process New Deal liberalism had undergone a dual transformation. One, the ranks of organized labor returned unionism to bread and butter issues, job security and maintenance of the union wage scale. "Consumer liberalism" is its character. It is essentially conservative. The second transmutational form taken by New Deal liberalism became what Brinkley terms "rights-based liberalism". The two tend to run in opposition to one another...a legacy of the 1940s. This impetus toward consumer liberalism further diverted vital elements of the New Deal coalition away from pathways leading toward extension of social reforms in which the once militant CIO played such a crucial formative role. Reflected here is the weakening of the countervailing power that took form under the New Deal.

Compared to the widespread violations of civil liberties during World War I and its aftermath, with two major exceptions, civil liberties were generally respected. Most flagrant, one that had no counterpart during the Great War, was the deprivation of all constitutional protection for resident alien Japanese and citizens of Japanese ancestry. California racist organizations had since early in the century propagandized against Japanese migrants to its shores. Their propaganda reached nascent anti-Japanese organizations in the Pacific Northwest. This propaganda prepared the nation to accept the notion of "military necessity" as justification for removal and internment of people of Japanese ancestry when it did occur. In this view, since Japan was the enemy, all US residents of Japanese ancestry, potentially, must also be the enemy. The War Department's suppression of evidence led to their evacuation and internment, and led the US Supreme Court to uphold the policy during the war. Redress of this unprecedented miscarriage of justice did not occur until set in motion in the 1980s, when critical suppressed documentation was uncovered under the Freedom of Information Act. There is no guarantee whether the constitution will be abrogated similarly in the future.

What part did that pre-eminent civil rights organization, the American Civil Liberties Union, play locally during the evacuation period? The ACLU initially announced its opposition to President Roosevelt's Executive Order 9066 after its 2 March 1942 board meeting. This decision provoked a bitter dispute within its governing board that forced a modification: "military necessity" must be proven; there must be civilian control over any prospective evacuation but should be on an individual basis; and evacuees should be at liberty outside declared military zones. Disappointed in the national board's vote (52 to 26) the Northern California ACLU branch pursued its own policy and took control of the Fred Korimatsu case. In Seattle ACLU's liaison, Mary Farquharson, also acted independently, choosing to work with Arthur Barnett in defending Gordon Hirabayashi. They also had the backing of the Church Council and the American Friends Service Committee.

According to ACLU historian Samuel Walker not until early 1943, under new ACLU leadership, did the organization belatedly file an *amicus* brief for Hirabayashi.[4]

The other major abandonment of constitutional protections of civil liberties in Seattle lay in the work of the Canwell Committee and the administration of the University of Washington, acting in the wake of the Canwell hearings. These events took place under cover of the early stages of the Cold War and would contort political life in the region and nation for another three decades. These early actions underscored their significance, locally as well as nationally. The UW's reputation was severely damaged by these transactions. It was further diminished in February 1955 when President Henry Schmitz rejected the UW Physics Department's proposal to appoint J. Robert Oppenheimer to a week-long Walker-Ames lectureship at the university. Oppenheimer, as chair of the Atomic Energy Commission, had recently had his national security clearance revoked for resisting development of a hydrogen bomb. Schmitz's predisposition against hiring controversial figures was indicated by his rejection of another Walker-Ames nominee, Kenneth Burke in 1952. Burke's left-wing proclivities and iconoclastic reputation brought fear the UW would meet public and legislative disapproval. And, as in January 1949, when the university administration dismissed three faculty, two for being Communists, there was the intimidating threat of the legislature avenging itself on the university. On campus the Oppenheimer rejection quickly became an academic freedom issue, a view that Schmitz refused to concede. Contributing to the accumulating tensions at that time was the state legislature, in session, and the Seattle hearings being conducted by the House Un-American Activities Committee. The legislative response to a UW student protest march to Olympia was introduction of a bill on 18 February, outlawing the Communist Party in the state; it required a disclaimer oath from state employees. With Governor Langlie's backing it passed and was signed into law 21 March.[5]

In such times of widespread public hysteria, when the true mettle of constitutional protections is really tested, they have been practically shredded. In the case of the Nisei their citizenship was simply withdrawn from them as a societal class on the basis of their racial affinity with the Japanese enemy. They were denied the opportunity to face charges of disloyalty on an individual basis. In the other category it was intolerance for advocates of social, political, and economic reform on the ground that such advocacy smacked of incipient socialism, or communism at worst. The liberalism of the New Deal was really at issue. We have reviewed how it was consciously eroded by its opponents through the defense buildup period, during the war and postwar periods, climaxing during the Cold War, with only occasional relaxation, most notably with the spate of social/civil rights legislation during the early period of the Lyndon Johnson administration. This was before his commitment to the war in Vietnam when protest against it absorbed national attention. Following the precedent set by the 1947 Congress, that of the 1994 Congress proceeded with even more revolutionary fervor, determined to eliminate the remaining legacy of the New Deal and its extensions made in the first two years of the Lyndon Johnson administration. Liberalism as a political force has clearly been decimated, whether eliminated remains to be seen. What is significant historically, is that the attacks on it gained sustenance and momentum under the cloak of wartime emergency, to be succeeded by more than three decades in the fog of an alleged "world wide communist conspiracy" and the Cold War. Now, instead of being disparaged as the opening wedge for socialism or communism, liberals and liberalism are politically castigated simply for being what they are and what they advocate. Red-baiting is irrelevant with the ending of the Cold War. Being merely liberal is taint enough.

# ARCHIVES AND MANUSCRIPT COLLECTIONS

*University of Washington Manuscript Collection and University Archives*

Carstensen, Vernon *Papers*
Church Council *Records*, Accessions 1358-7 and 479
Cornish School *Records*
Devin, William F. *Papers*
Farquharson, Mary *Papers*
Houghton, Cluck, and Coughlin (law firm) *Records*
Ichihara, Kaoru *Papers*
Inlandboatmen's Union *Records*
Japanese American Citizen League *Records*
Magnuson, Warren G. *Papers*
Matsushita, Iwao *Papers*
Millikin, Earl *Papers*
Mitchell, Hugh B. *Papers*
Myers, Guy C. *Papers*
Puget Sound Power and Light Co. *Records*
Ring Family *Papers*
Sakamoto, James Y. *Papers*
Seattle Art Museum *Records*
Seattle Civic Unity Committee *Records*
Seattle Lighting Department *Records*
Seattle Repertory Playhouse Records
University of Washington. Medical School. Dean *Records*,
    Accessions 81-96, 87-77 and 91-63
University of Washington. President *Records* Accessions 70-29 and 71-34
University of Washington. Regents *Records*
Urban League of Seattle *Records*
Washington State Federation of Labor *Records*

*Other Archival Holdings*

Seattle Public Library
    Seattle Chamber of Commerce *Minutebooks*
    Seattle Civilian Wartime Commission *Scrapbooks*
Seattle City Archives
Museum of History and Industry.
    Ladies Music Club *Scrapbooks*
Seattle Public School Archives
Louis Fiset Collection of Nisei recorded interviews

# CHAPTER ENDNOTES

## POLITICAL HISTORY OF THE 1940S

1. Irving Bernstein, *A History of the American Worker, 1933-1941: The Turbulent Years*. (Boston: Houghton Mifflin, 1970), pp. 252-298.

Philip Taft, *Organized Labor in American History*. (New York: Harper & Row, 1964), pp. 416-423, 471-483, 503-516g.

Walter Galenson, *The CIO Challenge to the AFL: A History of the American Labor Movement 1935-1941* (Cambridge: Harvard University Press, 1960), pp. 3-31.

Alan Brinkley, *The End of Reform: New Deal Liberalism in Recession and War* (New York: Alfred Knopf, 1995),pp. 201-03.

Richard C. Berner, *Seattle, 1921-1940: From Boom to Bust*. (Seattle: Charles Press, 1992), pp. 333-335.

Nelson Lichtenstein, *Labor's War at Home: A Study of the CIO During the Second World War*. (New York: Cambridge University Press, 1982), pp. 10-18.

Harvey A. Levenstein, *Communism, Anticommunism, and the CIO* (Westport, Conn.: Greenwood Press, 1981), chapter 2.

For workers in the aircraft industry see Jacob A. Vander Meulen, *The Politics of Aircraft: Building An American Military Industry* (Lawrence: University Press of Kansas, 1991), chapter 6.

John Kenneth Galbraith, *American Capitalism: The Concept of Countervailing Power* (Boston: Houghton Mifflin Company, 1962).

2. Charles P. Larrowe, *Harry Bridges: The Rise and Fall of Radical Labor in the United States*. (New York: Lawrence Hill, 1972), pp. 46-54.

Berner, *Ibid.*, pp. 339-343.

Bernstein, *Ibid.*, pp. 265-268.

Taft, *Ibid.*. pp. 435-444.

Jonathan Dembo, *A History of the Washington State Labor Movement, 1885-1935* (Unpublished Ph.D. dissertation, University of Washington, 1978), chapter 9.

3. Lichtenstein, *Ibid.*, pp. 16-23 (quote from p. 19)

Taft, *Ibid.*, pp. 516-522.

Galenson, *Ibid.*, pp. 31-32.

Alan Brinkley, *The End of Reform: New Deal Liberalism in Recession and War* (New York: Alfred Knopf, 1995). For extended discussion and analysis of the conflicts within liberal circles of the Roosevelt administration that resulted in FDR's tardiness in responding to the 1937-38 recession until it was too late for deficit spending, for example, to be effective. See especially chapter 5 "The Struggle for a Program".

4. Melvyn Dubofsky, *The State and Labor in Modern America* (Chapel Hill: University of North Carolina Press, 1994), pp. 152-161.

Levenstein, *Ibid.*, pp. 83-91.

James C. Foster, *The Union Politic: The CIO Political Action Committee* (Columbia, MO: University of Missouri Press, 1975), p. 8 footnote 10.

Galenson, *Ibid.*, p. 41.

5. Eugene V. Dennett, *Agitprop: The Autobiography of an American Working-Class Radical* (Albany: State University of New York Press, 1990), pp. 116-121.

Albert A. Acena, *The Washington Commonwealth Federation: Reform Politics and the Popular Front* (Unpublished Ph.D. dissertation, University of Washington, 1975), pp. 356-357. Acena (p. 375) quotes Francis's opinion of the WCF: "[it is] a certain rather minor pressure group masquerading as representing the CIO and its political program".

Lichtenstein, *Ibid.*, pp. 32-36.

Galenson, *Ibid.*, pp. 606-608.

Acena, *Ibid.*, pp. 386-96 outlines events following the WCF's February convention. At its convention the State CIO set out a definite anticommunist line after 140 leftist delegates walked out. The remaining delegates defeated a resolution supporting Harry Bridges against deportation, and barred Communists, along with Fascists from membership. Responding to the recent wave of anticommunism (concurrently, the CIO was being thwarted from organizing at Boeing) the WCF staged a "People's Rights" conference 7 June to defend those leftist organizations and individuals under attack, and to criticize FDR's policies. This all changed abruptly, when Germany attacked the Soviet Union 22 June 1941. The WCF thenceforth endorsed the President's domestic policies and made opening of a Second Front in western Europe its primary foreign policy goal. See also endnote 12 below.

Inlandboatmen's Union. *Records*, Accession 1615, Box 4 re Stimson's notification. UW Libraries Manuscript Collection.

Nancy Quam-Wickham, "Who Controls the Hiring Hall? The Struggle for Job Control in the ILWU During World War II" in Steve Rosswurm, editor, *The CIO's Left-Led Unions* (New Brunswick: Rutgers University Press, 1992), p. 50. It is uncertain how effectively Stimson's order was enforced, but the "Bridges Plan" for the West Coast - discussed below - seems to have prevailed. Cf. Howard Kimeldorf's *Reds or Rackets*, cited in endnote 12 below.

6. Lichtenstein, *Ibid.*, chapter 4.

Taft, *Ibid.* pp. 546-554.

Brinkley, *Ibid.*, pp. 180-81, 220-21.

7. Lichtenstein, *Ibid.*, chapter 4 (quotation is from p. 66), pp. 69-70.

Brinkley, *Ibid.*, pp. 210-11. Brinkley points to maintenance of membership as a concession by the federal government to business opposition to the closed and union shop agreements. Therefore, it could be taken away by federal authority as well as given.

8. *P-I*, 26 January 1941; *Times*, 4 February, 2 March 1941. "Cincinnatans" refers to the New Order of Cincinnatus, a conservative reformist organization of the mid-1930s to which Langlie owed his election, along with city councilmen David Lockwood and Frederick G. Hamley. See Richard C. Berner *Ibid.*, pp. 329-31; 349-55.

9. Earl Millikin *Papers*, file 15-8,9.

10. MacGowan to Magnuson, 6 March 1941, Magnuson *Papers*, Acc. 3181-2, file 49-18. At this time MacGowan was a partially employed newpaper man and a political "eyes and ears" for Magnuson. In February 1942 he would join the Office of Emergency Management as an information specialist; was transferred in 1943 to the Office of War Information in San Francisco; and returned to Seattle in February 1944 to a position in the Region 13 office of the War Production Board. He had long been urging Magnuson to press for a Northwest district office of the WPB in Seattle to free the four Northwest states from dependency on the Bay City.

11. *Times*, 4,6 March 1941. MacGowan to WGM, Magnuson *Papers*, file 49-18.

Albert Acena noted an "absence of an interest in the [1941] city election." pp. 383-84 of his dissertation on the Washington Commonwealth Federation.

12. *Times*, 28 May, 6,22 June, 7,17 July 1941. Beck's protection of Boeing would climax during the 1948 strike of the Aero Mechanics Union, when William Allen brought in the Teamsters Union to break the strike and the union. Cf. John McCann, *Blood in the Water*...pp. 95-148. The strike is covered below in greater detail in the chapter "1948: Liberalism in Disarray".

13. *Times*, 31 July, 2,7 September 1941.

Paul de Barros, *Jackson Street After Hours: The Roots of Jazz in Seattle* (Seattle: Sasquatch Books, 1993), pp. 76-77, 164-65.

14. Millikin to Hattie Williams, 6 March 1942, Millikin *Papers*, file 15-15. See also the chapter on the Japanese evacuation.

15. Fussell to WGM, 18 February 1942, Magnuson *Papers*, file 50-3.

16. *P-I*, 2 March 1942.

17. *P-I*, 4,7 March 1942. The *P-I* of 7 March quoted Devin: "My idea of labor's proper representation in city government is for all groups of organized labor to be properly represented...but in the past year only those whom Dave Beck said should have a voice have had a voice." See also a copy of Devin's speech before the Church Council, in Millikin's *Papers*, file 15-17. *Times*, 4,8 March 1942.

18. *P-I*, 6-8 March 1942; and Teamster's full page advertisement of 9 March.

19. *P-I*, 11,12 March 1942.

20. Acena, *Ibid.*, pp. 412-15.

Bruce Bartley, writing to Congressman Magnuson 18 March 1942, commented on Millikin's failure to mount a campaign: "I didn't know a single person in the Millikin campaign". Magnuson, *Papers*, Acc. 3181-2, file 49-55.

## Evacuation and Internment of Japanese Americans: "The Domination of Politics over Law"

1. The following sources were used for this section:

Shotaro Frank Miyamoto, *Social Solidarity Among the Japanese in Seattle* (Seattle: University of Washington Publications in the Social Sciences, 1939).

Louis Fiset, *Imprisoned Apart: The World War II Correspondence of an Issei Couple* (Seattle University of Washington Press, 1997), pp. 9-11, 15-21 for an intimate portrait of Japantown.

Roger Daniels, *Asian America: Chinese and Japanese in the United States Since 1850* (Seattle: University of Washington Press, 1988), chapter 4, pp.160-85, 2 36-38.

\_\_\_\_*The Politics of Prejudice* (New York: Atheneum Press, 1962), chapters IV-VI.

\_\_\_\_*Prisoners Without Trial: Japanese Americans in World War II* (New York: Hill and Wang, 1993), chapter 1.

Bill Hosokawa, *Nisei: The Quiet Americans* (New York: William Morrow, 1969), pp. 182-84, chapter 13.

\_\_\_\_ "The Uprooting of Seattle" in *Japanese Americans: From Relocation to Redress* edited by Roger Daniels, Sandra C. Taylor, and Harry H.L. Kitano (Seattle: Univeristy of Washington Press paperback edition, 1991), pp. 18-19.

Robert E. Ficken and Charles LeWarne, *Washington: A Centennial History* (Seattle: University of Washington Press, 1988), pp. 70-73 on local anti-Chinese movement.

On enactment of the state Anti-Alien Land Law in 1921 see Berner, *Seattle, 1921-1940...*, pp. 35-37; chapter 8 "Seattle and its Agricultural Hinterland" and chapter 12 on Japantown.

2. Louis Fiset, *Ibid.*, chapters 2 and 3. See pp. 28-30 re ABC list; pp. 78-79 for his release from Fort Missoula.

3. Examples of this kind of reporting follow.

Of critical importance related to these reports of suspected "fifth column" activities and alleged "attacks" off shore and in the air were their prewar simulations. Roger W. Lotchin covers these war games in his *Fortress California, 1910-1961: From Warfare to Welfare* (New York: Oxford University Press, 1992), pp. 76-82. Promotion of air races by Southern California boosters in 1919 led to collaboration of the Army Air Corps and Navy in the 1920s and 1930s in simulations of enemy attacks that assumed realistic proportions. The respective services were anxious to demonstrate the effectiveness of air power while the boosters aimed to concentrate the aircraft industry in Southern California. These exhibitions turned into a spectator sport attracting sometimes over 100,000 civilian watchers. The prospective enemy was inevitably Japan. These simulations must be linked in context with the endless anti-Japanese propaganda directed at the resident West Coast Japanese population. Southern Californians seem hardly to have missed a beat when war came on Pearl Harbor Day. The rumor mill was already in place, the citizenry conditioned for its propaganda barrage. Seattle newspaper reports of roundups and alleged fifth column activities usually came from California sources and the Presidio.

4. Hosokawa, *Nisei*...pp. 191-98.
Vernacular newspaper clippings in JACL, *Records*, University of Washington Libraries Manuscript Collection.

5. Louis Fiset's interviews with Sharon Aburano, Kenji Okuda, Shigeko Uno, and Jim Akatsu.

6. Monica [Kazuko Itoi] Sone, *Nisei Daughter* (Seattle: University of Washington Press, 1979), chapter VIII.

7. Louis Fiset interview with Bill Hosokawa.

8. Roger Daniels, *The Decision to Relocate the Japanese Americans* (New York: J.B. Lippincott, 1975).
Peter Irons *Justice at War: The Story of the Japanese American Internment Cases* (New York: Oxford Univeristy Press, 1983).
*Personal Justice Denied* was reissued by the University of Washington Press December 1998 with a forward by Tetsuden Kashima. Its original report was issued in 1983.

9. Irons, *Ibid.*, pp. 64-70 for proclamations, PL 503, and planning.

10. Louis Fiset, "Redress for Nisei Public Employees in Washington State After World War II", in *Pacific Northwest Quarterly* (88:1, Winter 1997), pp. 21-32. Sally Shimanaka Kazama was interviewed by Fiset 16 August 1995. She was one of the clerks who was forced to resign. From this interview and others recorded by Fiset it is apparent internal divisions within the Japanese community had developed, but seem to have been held in check principally by Sakamoto and Arai. Fiset is producing a study of Camp Harmony.

11. US. Congress. House. Select Committee on National Defense Migration. Hearings, pp. 11400-11572.
*Times* and *P-I* 28 February, 1,2, March 1942.
Mayor Millikin boasted to Hattie Williams 6 March 1942, during his mayoral campaign, that he was the only one who came out "flat-footedly" for mass evacuation in the course of the Tolan Committee hearings. While not true his view is clearly expressed, although allegedly he apologized to Sakamoto for all the burdens imposed on the Japanese, but he was only following Army orders.

12. Besides the newspapers see Tolan Committee hearings, page 11552 for Gill letter.

13. Some of the Japanese-operated farms were leased in 1942 to Western Farms, Inc. by the WRA. The "Willows" was one of them. By December 1943 it was $1,000 in arrears on its rent and was consequently trying to settle its debts for 20 cents on the dollar after convincing the FSA of its case. Bruce Bartley, the company's president and law partner of Congressman Magnuson, had refused WRA's access to company records to determine the fairness of its offer. Complicating

the matter further the FSA had "lost" the original contract and no copies were available. *P-I*, 7 December 1943 column by Doug Welch. In light of Magnuson's racial bias, by which he never distinguished the US Japanese from the Japanese enemy raise some doubt about the honesty of Bartley at least.

With respect to Congressman Magnuson's attitude during the evacuation his pencilled instructions for reply to a letter from Mrs. L.H. Duvall 10 October 1944 are indicative. At the top of her letter he wrote: "Pronto. Answer tell her my long opposition to Japs shot at them". She had complained about all the Japanese whom she observed returning. In his *Warren G. Magnuson and the Shaping of Twentieth-Century America* (Seattle: University of Washington Press, 1997), p. 119 Shelby Scates passes too lightly over this negative feature of Magnuson's career. Quotation is from Magnuson *Papers*, Acc. 3181-2, file 7-44.

On the Uno family Louis Fiset's interview with Shigeko Uno is the source. The family was approached by several dairies but found the offer by "Mr. Forrester" of the Alpine Dairy the only fair one. Alpine had hoped to expand its business during the war but gasoline shortages proved an impediment.

14. Baldwin to Farquharson 13 March 1942; in a copy of a letter from Baldwin to Edward Ennis of the Justice Department Baldwin wrote: "we are not interested in contesting any cases involving enemy aliens. Our sole concern is with the the evacuation of citizens and in those cases only where we are convinced that the order is unreasonable." Farquharson *Papers*, Acc. 397, file 3-4.

15. Peter Irons, *Ibid.*, pp. 154-59. The trial before Judge Black began 2 October 1942.

Samuel Walker, *Ibid.*, pp. 137-44. He covers the split within the ACLU's Board of Directors on the evacuation issue.

Hirabayashi kept up a regular correspondence with the Ring family, mainly with Eleanor - "Ellie". Letters quoted from here: 16,29 May, 1 July. One to Mrs. Ring (18 August) expressed his dismay at conditions at the Tule camp; another to her thanking her for Ellie's visit to those at Tule. And please thank F.O.R for the "financial lift". (16 September). This is a very rich collection of letters, referring to many other Nikkei inside and outside internment camps.

## The Wartime Economy: Introduction

1. Gerald D. Nash, *The American West Transformed*, chapter 2, pp. 38-39, table on p. 233.

Richard Lowitt, *The New Deal and the West* (Bloomington: Indiana University Press, 1984), Chapter 10.

Howard A. Droker, "The Seattle Civic Unity Committee", pp. 1-3.

Thomas R. Cox, *Mills and Markets: A History of the Pacific Coast Lumber Industry to 1900* (Seattle: University of Washington Press, 1974), chapters 5 and 6.

Robert E. Ficken, "Weyerhaeuser and the Pacific Northwest Timber Industry", *Pacific Northwest Quarterly* 70 (October 1979), pp. 146-54.

Carey McWilliams, *Southern California: An Island on the Land* (Salt Lake City: First Peregrine Smith Edition, 1983), chapters VII-XII.

Robert M. Fogelson, *The Fragmented Metropolis: Los Angeles, 1850-1930* (Cambridge: Harvard University Press, 1967), chapters 5 and 6.

William Issel and Robert W. Cherny. San Francisco, 1965-1932: Politics, Power, and Urban Development (Berkeley: University of California Press, 1986), chapter 2.

Carlos A. Schwantes, "The Pacific Northwest in World War II", *Journal of the West* (July 1986), pp. 4, 11.

Roger W. Lotchin W., *Fortress California, 1910-1961: From Warfare to Welfare* (New York: Oxford University Press, 1992), chapter 1.

Paul C.Pitzer, *Grand Coulee: Harnessing a Dream* (Pullman, WA: Washington State University Press, 1994) is the most recent and definitive volume on the Columbia Basin project.

For an overall perspective on the colonial aspect of western development see William C. Robbins, *Colony and Empire: The Capitalist Transformation of the American West* (Lawrence: University Press of Kansas, 1994).

Indicative also is a 12 September 1945 resolution of the Seattle Chamber of Commerce's Pacific Northwest Oriental Airline Committee: "Whereas, the western states are on the eve of a great industrial era which has been advanced by war-time needs...[the committee sees opposition from] some selfish and short-sighted eastern interests [in] attempts to thwart this natural and necessary development." Warren G. Magnuson Papers, Acc. 3181-3, box 41. UW Libraries Manuscript Collection.

Leonard Arrington, "The New Deal in the West: A Preliminary Inquiry", *Pacific Historical Review* (August 1969), pp. 311-16. The funding agencies listed were: the Reconstruction Finance Corporation, Federal Emergency Relief Administration, Civil Works Administration, Public Works Administration, Works Projects Administration, Civilian Conservation Corps, and Rural Electrification Administration. Of the 11 Far Western states Nevada, Montana, Wyoming, Arizona, and New Mexico benefited most, with Nevada receiving $1,130 per capita, ranging downward to New Mexico's $528. Washington's distribution was $375, Oregon's $355, California's $266.

Donald Worster, *Rivers of Empire: Water, Aridity, and the Growth of the American West* (New York: Oxford University Press, 1985) traces the federal role in developing the West.

Patricia Nelson Limerick, *The Legacy of Conquest: The Unbroken Past of the American West* (New York: W.W. Norton, 1987) pp. 87-88.

Michael S. Sherry, *In the Shadow of War: The U.S. Since the 1930s* (New Haven: Yale University Press, 1995), pp. 22-23, 71-72.


2. Clark Kerr, *Migration to the Seattle Labor Market Area, 1940-1942.* (Seattle: University of Washington Press. 1942), chapters I-III.

Karen T.Anderson, *Wartime Women* (Greenwood Press, 1981), chapter 1. Also her "The Impact of World War II in the Puget Sound Area on the Status of Women and the Family" (Unpublished Ph.D. Dissertation, University of Washington, 1975), pp. 16-18.

Seattle Lighting Department. *Annual Report, 1942.*

Millikin to Magnuson 22 June 1941, Magnuson *Papers,* Acc. 3181-2, file 49-26 and file 7-17.

*P-I*, 14 January 1943.

Schwantes, *Ibid.*, p. 5.


3. Nash, *Ibid.*, pp. 88-93.

Taylor, "Great Migration...", pp. 109-111.

Taylor, *Forging...*,pp. 160-62.

Art Ritchie and William J. Davis, *The Pacific Northwest Goes to War* (Seattle: Associated Publishers, 1944), pp. 33-34.

4. US Women's Bureau, Bulletin 209, *Women Workers in Ten War Production Areas and Their Postwar Employment Plans*, (Washington: US Government Printing Office, 1946), pp. 4-8 (quotation is from p. 8).

US Women's Bureau, Bulletin 211, *Employment of Women in the Early Postwar Period*, p. 1.

William H. Chafe, *The American Woman: Her Changing Social, Economic. and Political Roles, 1920-1970*, (New York: Oxford University Press, 1972), pp. 136-37, 140, 154-58.

Susan M. Hartmann, *The Home Front and Beyond: American Women in the 1940s* (Boston: Twayne Publishers, 1982), pp. 78, 82-87.

5. Taylor, *Forging...*, pp.161, 166.

Andrew F. Brimmer, *Some Economic Aspects of Fair Employment* (Unpublished Master's Thesis, University of Washington, 1951), pp. 80-82, 99-102.

Nash, *Ibid.*, pp. 91-92.

6. Anderson, *Wartime Women*, chapter 2; also *Impact of World War II...*, *op. cit.*, chapter 2, and p. 26 for the quotation

Droker, *Ibid.* chapter 1.

Seattle Lighting Department. *Annual Report, 1942.*

Kerr, *Ibid.*, pp. 132-33.

Schwantes, *Ibid.*, p. 11.

Frederic C. Lane, *Ships for Victory: A History of Shipbuilding Under the U.S. Maritime Commission in World War II* (Baltimore: Johns Hopkins Press, 1951), pp. 236-37, 261-65.

*Seattle Education Bulletin*, September 1941, January, February 1942. Copies in Seattle Public Schools Archives. The Board had estimated that $3 million was needed to accomodate the number of children who will live in defense housing projects.

Seattle Public Schools, *Annual Reports,* 1940-41 through 1944-45. SPS Archives. Pre-employment courses at Edison had been offered for aircraft and shipyard workers since 1939.

*Seattle Schools*, September, October 1942. Copies in SPS Archives. The WPB ruled in June 1942 that critical materials could not be used for permanent school construction; hence the Board's application for $1,264,000 for new school buildings was cancelled. Portables would be substituted. On curriculum changes see *Seattle Schools*, January-March 1943.

In a report of the Federal Regional Advisory Committee, "Composite Report on Puget Sound Area" dated 15 May 1944, the following statistics of federal civilian service employment were given for:

Sand Point Naval Air Station: 3387, including 71 nonwhites;

Naval Supply Depot: 2000, including 1150 women, 18 nonwhites;

Puget Sound Navy Yard: 30,057, including 5336 women, 1536 nonwhites;

Port of Embarkation: 7213, including 4150 women, 288 nonwhites;

Army Service Forces Depot: 2070, including 1187 women, 196 nonwhites.

Noted was no nonwhite employment after March 1944. Source: Wanamaker, Pearl, *Papers*, file 62-8. UW Libraries Manuscript Collection.

The *Washington New Dealer* for November 1941 carried a report about a Black, Eugene Beech, who was denied access to an aircraft training program of the Works Progress Administration. The

Washington Commonwealth Federation sought Congressman Magnuson's intervention. Magnuson *Papers*, Acc. 3181-2, file 5-5.

Referring to its labor recruitment efforts the Seattle Chamber of Commerce claimed that in 1943 it had brought in 9,000 additional workers for Boeing and 3,000 for the Puget Sound Navy Yard. Copy of letter to its D.C. lobbyist John Underwood, 18 April 1944. In Magnuson, *Papers*, Acc. 3181-2, file 7-60.

Katherine Archibald, *Wartime Shipyards: A Study in Social Disunity* (Berkeley: University of California Press, 1947). The author worked in Oakland's Moore Dry Dock Company shipyards, 1942-44. Convinced that her specific observations of social interactions were common to substantially all shipyards - since their workforces shared a common demographic and racial composition - she published this study. Indicative of her coverage and their relevance to the Seattle area operations are some chapter headings: "Women in the Shipyards", "Okies", "Negroes", "Lesser Minorities", "Unions", "Class Consciousness". With respect to Negroes Archibald contends that union resistance to their admittance to jobs that had been reserved by and for Whites might imply that Blacks could perform those jobs equally well for equal pay - if allowed to do so. This would undermine their fixation on White racial superiority, upon which Negrophobia was based. See especially pp. 79-98.

Schwantes, *Ibid.*, p. 11.

Magnuson, *Papers*. Acc. 3181-2, file 7-15. UW Libraries Manuscript Collection.

Chafe, *Ibid.*, pp. 139-41 for employment; 154-58 for equal pay.

Hartmann, *Ibid.*, ch. 4 and pp. 61-62 for equal pay; 80-82.

On women at Boeing: Times, 1 May 1942.

US Women's Bureau, Bulletin 209, pp. 14-15.

On Boeing's operations: *Pacific Northwest Industry*, 4:1 (October 1944), pp. 39-43.

7. This account is derived principally from the *Seattle Times*'s April 1941 coverage, supplemented by the following sources: Harvey Levenstein, *Communism, Anticommunism, and the CIO*, pp. 88-89, 148-49. John McCann, *Blood in the Water*, pp. 35-42. *Aero Mechanic*, 4,18 April 1941. On Beck and Sears *Times*, 28 May 1941. Inlandboatmens' Union *Records*, Acc. 1615, Box 4 for conflict within CIO. In IBU's Minutes for 7 May 1941 the police department was reported to have been urging hall managers to refuse use by CIO unions on grounds of potential "violence". UW Manuscript Collection. See also the influential *Argus*, 4 January 1941 for its account of the Civic Auditorium meeting and Lundquist's testimony that Boeing and Beck were together trying to break Local 751 and bring in the Teamsters as the company's union. See also *Argus*'s account, 19 April 1941 of the internal conflicts within the local CIO leadership and Mortimer's arrival on the scene. The *Argus*'s admiration for Dave Beck appeared in the hearing over the appointment of police chief Sears. Lundquist opposed Sears for his handling of the Boeing labor dispute, while Beck spoke for Sears. "Dave Beck is entitled to a respectful hearing. More than any other individual, he has thwarted the attempts of radical unions to control Seattle labor. He has never repudiated a contract with any employer...Labor is at the helm of Seattle as it is in every industrial center. The CIO followers of the Communist Party line have yet to break through in Seattle...due to one man - Dave Beck." 31 May 1941. The *Argus* regarded the New Deal as "socialistic", and the NLRB as dominated by Communists. 18 January, 1 March 1941. Whenever the *Argus* referred to "labor racketeers" - as it often did - it was careful to exclude Beck from that category. See also below, "1948: Liberalism in Disarray",covering the great Boeing strike of 1948.

Wyndham Mortimer's *Organize!: My Life as a Union Man* (Boston: Beacon Press, 1971), chapters 11 and 12 is the source for the Vultee strike, start of the North American strike, and his involvement in the Local 751-Boeing contest. Mortimer, an alleged Communist, is a casebook example of the symbiotic relationship established between President Roosevelt and the CIO leadership, and the preoccupation of the CIO leadership with defusing anything threatening that relationship; in this case interruption of aircraft production. An unpublished manuscript by Jacob Vander Meulen, "West Coast Aircraft Labor and an American Military-Industrial Complex, 1935-1941" covers this aspect of the Boeing-751 relationships. Copy is in the author's collection.

Taylor, *Ibid.*, pp.163-65.

McCann, *Ibid.*, pp. 32-42, 46-47, 86-87.

*Aero Mechanic*, 15 April 1943.

Droker, *Ibid.*, pp.11-13.

Weaver, *Ibid.*, pp. 116-17.

Nancy Quam-Wickham, "Who Controls the Hiring Halls" in Steven Rosswurm, ed., *The CIO's Left-Led Unions* (New Brunswick: Rutgers University Press,, c1992), pp. 49-59.

8. Jacob A. Vander Meulen, *The Politics of Aircraft: Building an American Military Aircraft* (Lawrence: University Press of Kansas, 1991), pp. 6-7; 211-217

9. Harold Mansfield, *Vision: The Story of Boeing* (New York: Popular Library, 1966), pp. 79-92, 104-06.

Ritchie and William Davis, *Ibid.*, pp. 13-16.

Peter M. Bowers, *Boeing Aircraft Since 1916* (London: Putnam and Aero Publishers Inc., Fallbrook, Calif., 1966), pp. 278-84.

Robert J. Serling, *Legend and Legacy: The Story of Boeing and Its People* (New York: St. Martin's Press, 1992), pp. 52-55; 59-61, 67.

Jeffrey S. Underwood, *The Wings of Democracy: The Influence of Air Power on the Roosevelt Administration, 1933-1941* (College Station: Texas A and M Press, 1991) chapters V-IX, esp. pp. 100-07, 110, 119-22, 130-31, 138-39, 150-52, 161-62.

10. Mansfield, Ibid., pp. 112-18, 119-24, 141-42.

Bowers, *Ibid.*, pp. 279-81.

11. Mansfield, *Ibid.*, pp. 112-24, 141-42.

Bowers, *Ibid.*, pp. 279-81.

Serling, *Ibid.*, pp. 64-65.

12. Magnuson to John Boettiger 29 August 1940 concerning shipyard expansions. Also a letter to Boettiger 1 July 1941 on Navy approval of a new forging plant for Isaacson Steel. Magnuson *Papers*, Acc. 3181-2, files 47-31 and 48-37.

Mansfield, *Ibid.*, 134-38, 143-46.

Bowers, *Ibid.*, pp. 279-81.

Schwantes, *Ibid.*, p. 5.

Serling, *Ibid.* P. 72.

Vander Meulen, Jacob, "West Coast Labor and the Military Aircraft Industry, 1935-1941", *Pacific Northwest Quarterly* 88:2 (Spring 1997), pp. 82-92.

Richard S. Kirkendall, "The Boeing Company and the Military-Metropolitan-Industrial Complex, 1945-1953". *Pacific Northwest Quarterly* (October 1994), p. 138.

*Seattle Times*, 19, 20 August 1943.

*New York Times*, 20 August 1943.
*Time [magazine]*, 2, 30 August, 6 September 1943.
*Newsweek*, 23 August 1943.

Associated Shipyards was formed from a merger of Puget Sound Bridge and Dredging Company and Lake Union Dry Dock and Machine Works.

13. Ritchie and Davis. *Ibid.*, pp. 19-33, 61.
The Black Ball Ferry Lines Purchased 17 surplussed San Francisco Bay ferries which doubled the number of round trips to and from Bremerton to 28 daily.
  Lorraine McConaghy, "The Lake Washington Shipyards: For the Duration" (Unpublished Master's thesis, University of Washington, 1987), pp. 56-62, chapter 3.
  US Women's Bureau, Bulletin 209, pp. 14-15 reported the NWLB considered $.50/hour as the dividing line between standard and substandard wages. Substandard wages were prevalent in the trades and service sectors.
  On the 48-hour week executive order see *P-I*, 10-13 January, 12 February 1943. In February it was extended to Auburn, Kent, Bremerton, Renton, Shelton, Everett, and Tacoma. While the AFL and CIO leadership applauded the edict the Seattle Chamber of Commerce objected to its application to retail, seasonal, and some small businesses. *P-I*, 13 February 1943.

14. McCann, John. *Blood in the Water: A History of District Lodge 751*. (Seattle: District Lodge 751, 1989), pp. 59-75.
  McConaghy, *Ibid.*, chapter 5, pp. 155-73.
  Magnuson *Papers*, Acc. 3181-2, file 7-16.
  Archibald, *Ibid.* pp. 193-96.
  See also Magnuson correspondence from December 1942 to March 1943 in Magnuson *Papers* Acc. 3181-2, box 40, which includes copies of *104 Reporter* 26 August 1943.

15. Vernon Carstensen, *Papers*. UW Libraries Manuscripts Collection.

16. Seattle Chamber of Commerce *Minute Books, 1942-1945*. In the Seattle Public Library. Only the 1943 volume indexed "E" winners; the entry for Western Gear (9 February) noted it was 6th such award. No such index entries were found in the other volumes.
  For newspaper accounts see *P-I*, 17,21 January, 7 February, 5 May 1943.

17. *Argus*, 4 January, 19 April 1941.
  Berner, *Seattle, 1921-1940...*pp. 50-55, chapter 29.
  See also "Energy for War", below.

18. *Argus*, 27 June, 14 November 1942, 5 August 1944.
  *P-I* 5 February 1943 on Colman.

19. *Argus*, 8 March, 27 December 1941, 18 July 1942, 23 January 1943.

20. *P-I*, 7,8,9,14,18 January, 4,5,9,11 February 1943.

# Endnotes

*Argus*, 29 January 1944.

"Spokane Viaduct " file in Magnuson *Papers*, files 7-17 to 7-20. See Magnuson to Maverick, 11 January 1943 asking for reconsideration of the steel request.

21. Shelby Scates, *Warren G. Magnuson and the Shaping of Twentieth-Century America* (Seattle: University of Washington Press, 1997), chapters 3-7.

Berner, *Seattle, 1921-1940*...pp. 77-94, chapter 3, pp. 354, 375, 412-13.

22. Hoffman to Senator Homer T. Bone, 23 September 1941. Seattle Lighting Department (hereafter abbreviated SLD). *Records*. Acc. 33-2, box 40.

For background on the controversy with PSP&L, and the "negotiation vs. condemnation" routes see Berner, *Seattle, 1921-1940...*, chapter 29, and George T. Melton The State Grange and the Development of Water Power Resources in Washington (Unpublished Master's Thesis, University of Washington, 1954), pp. 150-69.

Note should be taken that PSP&L charged its legal expenses of $670,000 to "operating expenses", which the Federal Power Commission ruled was illegal.

23. SLD, *Ibid.*, Box 44, PSP&L file; Box 21 for annual report of 1939. Notes of a conference on Ross dam, 15 May 1942, box 42.

Guy C. Myers, *Papers*. Box 4 for SLD annual report of 1941.

24. SLD, *Ibid.*, Copy of WPB order, box 21.

Melton, *ibid.*, pp. 182 ff.

PSP&L *Annual Report*, 1943.

PUD Commissioners *Newsletter*, 20 March 1944 in Houghton Cluck, and Coughlin, *Records*. E. Henry correspondence, file 2-4.

The crucial role of BPA is illustrated in the following: During the period 1 July 1944 to 30 June 1948 BPA provided 50.9 percent of all the electricity consumed in the 5 Pacific Northwest states. City Light took 6.45 percent of the BPA power while supplying the pool with 14.56 percent of its electricity. PSP&L took 8.81 percent of its power from BPA and supplied the pool with 30.4 percent of its electricity. From copy of *Watts News* (n.d.) in Magnuson *Papers*, Acc. 3181-3, file 50-30.

25. Melton, *Ibid.*, pp. 183-91.

Hoffman memorandum 1 July 1943 in SLD, *Records*, box 40 PUD correspondence and Referendum 25 files.

Mimeographed memorandum from Puget Sound Utilities Commissioners Association to Raver 18 March 1944, Guy C. Myers *Papers*, file 73-20.

PSP&L, *Annual Report*, 1944.

26. Melton, *Ibid.*, pp. 192-93, 195, 198-204, 207-11.

Myers to McLaughlin, 16 January 1945, file 72-14; Puget Sound Utility Commissioners Association to Mayor Devin and City Council 7 October 1945, file 73-20 and 73-4. Myers *Papers*.

PSP&L, *Annual Report 1946*.

PUD's Research and Information Service *Newsletter*, SLD, box 6.

R.W. Beck to Myers 6 June 1947, Guy C. Myers *Papers*, file 71-9.

On the Millard vote all the dissenting judges, plus William Steinhart, signed a statement rebuking Millard. *Argus*, 21 June, 13 September 1947.

## THE WARTIME ECONOMY: TRANSFORMATION OF WOMEN'S ROLES

1. Seattle Housing Authority, *First Annual Report* (January 1941), and *Second Annual Report* (February 1942).

Richard C. Berner, *Seattle 1921-1940: From Boom to Bust* (Seattle: Charles Press, 1992), pp. 183-84.

2. SHA, *First Annual Report* and *Second Annual Report*. According to the SHA's *Sixth Annual Report* (February 1946) the SHA accomodated 15,000 Boeing employees, 400 of Puget Sound Bridge and Drydock's, 800 of Todd Pacific's, 400 of Todd Drydock's, 400 of the Naval Air Station's, and 2,400 from all other employers.

On the Widmer trailer park see *Times*, 28 November 1943 in which some tenants are interviewed. One comment: "Everything we own is right here. We don't have any worries." A Brown family with 5 children: Mr. Brown sank $1,700 in a trailer and "nearly as much in the car, and while the war lasts it's going to be our home." It seems the hardships experienced during the 1930s prepared inmigrants, particularly, for those offered during wartime.

Seattle Civilian War Commission *Scrapbooks*, Seattle Public Library are especially valuable.

By October 1943 there were 5 canning centers operating. See *Times*, 14,15,17 October 1943. Photographs are in 17th issue: "Canning Centers Prove Success". During summer 1943 schools were used as canning centers. *P-I*, 28 August 1943.

On Victory Gardens registration see *P-I*, 28 February 1943. Cecil Solly's *Times* column "Garden Helps"; also comparable columns in the *P-I* ("Dig for Victory") and *Star*.

3. Karen Tucker Anderson, *The Impact of World War II in the Puget Sound Area on the Status of Women and the Family* (Unpublished Ph.D. Dissertation, University of Washington, 1975), pp. 129 for quotation, 131, 133, 135, 138.

Susan M. Hartmann, *The Home Front and Beyond: American Women in the 1940s* (Boston: Twayne Publishers, 1982), pp. 58-59, 82-86.

US. Women's Bureau, *Bulletin 208*, "Women's Wartime Hours of Work", pp. 3-5.

D'Ann Campbell, *Women at War With America: Private Lives in a Patriotic Era* (Cambridge: Harvard University Press, 1984), chapters 3,4, and 7 for general background.

William H. Chafe, *The American Woman: Her Changing Social, Economic, and Political Roles, 1920-1970* (New York: Oxford University Press, 1972), chapter 6 for general background.

*Seattle Schools*, February 1943. Copies in School Archives.

*P-I*, 23 November 1943 on Rainier Vista.

4. Anderson, *Ibid.*, 136-48, quotation from p. 138.

Hartmann, *Ibid.*, pp. 82-86.

5. *Aero Mechanic*, 17 December 1942, 14 January, 4 February 1943.

6. Anderson, *Ibid.*, pp. 149-51.

7. Anderson, *Ibid.*, pp. 149-57.

8. Anderson, *Ibid.*, pp. 157-67, quotation from pp. 166-67.
SHA, *Sixth Annual Report*.

9. Anderson, *Ibid.*, pp. 167-69, 177-79, 182-83.
*Aero Mechanic*, 2, 11 March 1943.
US Women's Bureau, *Bulletin 209,* Women Workers in Ten War Production Areas and Their Postwar Employment Plans", p. 56.

10. Anderson, *Ibid.*, pp. 39-48.
Hartmann, *Ibid.*, chapter 4, and for unions, employers, and women, pp. 63-67.
US Women's Bureau, *Bulletin 209*, pp. 4-5, 32.
US Women's Bureau, *Bulletin 211*, "Employment of Women in the Early Postwar Period", pp.2-6. 13.
Chafe, *Ibid.*, chapter 6.
For the Seattle area during the Depression see Berner, *Ibid.*, pp. 285-86.

11. Hartmann, *Ibid.*, pp. 55-56, 79.
Anderson, *Ibid.*, pp. 35-37, 52-56, 77-80.

12. *Aero Mechanic*, 23 July 1942.

13. Anderson, *Ibid.*, pp. 59-61.
Campbell, *Ibid.* chapter 4.

14. Anderson, *Ibid.*, pp. 61-66, 71-79.
*Aero Mechanic*, 16 July 1942 and for listing of course offerings in the Public Schools 26 November 1942, e.g., metal spinning, sheet metal layout and assembly, lofting, riveting, expediting procedure, inspection, etc. These announcements occurred regularly.

15. *Aero Mechanic*, 14 May, 2, 16 July, 3 September, 5 November 1942.
On loopholes in "equal pay for equal work" see Chafe, *Ibid.* pp. 155-58.

16. Anderson, *Ibid.*, p. 77.

## THE WARTIME ECONOMY: MILITARIZATION OF THE ECONOMY

1. Doris Kearns Goodwin, *No Ordinary Time: Franklin & Eleanor Roosevelt: The Home Front in World War II* (New York: Simon and Schuster, 1994), pp. 44-45, 259-261.

Isidor F. Stone, *The War Years, 1939-1945* (Boston: Little, Brown, 1988), pp. 78-87.

US Office of Price Administration, *First Quarterly Report for the Period Ended April 30, 1942* (Washington: US Government Printing Office, 1942), pp. 74, 133-134, 139. Hereafter cited as OPA.

Paul C. Pitzer, *Grand Coulee: Harnessing a Dream* (Pullman, WA: Washington State University Press, 1994), pp. 173-74, 249-250.

2. Ayers Brinser, *A History of the Administration of Rationing in the United States During the Second World War* (Unpublished Ph.D. Dissertation, Harvard University, 1951), pp. 62-63.

Goodwin, *Ibid.*, pp. 231-232, 314-315, 363.

John Kenneth Galbraith, *A Life in Our Times: Memoirs* (New York: Ballantine Books, 1981), pp. 157-158.

James MacGregor Burns, *Roosevelt, 1940-1945: The Soldier of Freedom* (New York: Harcourt Brace Johanovich, 1970), p. 118.

OPA, *Ibid.*, pp. 7-8.

Alan Brinkley, *The End of Reform: New Deal Liberalism in Recession and War* (New York: Alfred Knopf, 1995), chapter 8 in which Brinkley discusses the emerging flux of agencies to deal with production, allocation of resources, issuance of contracts, the dominating role of "dollar a year men" who preferred dealing with large corporations and conceded to the Army and Navy almost anything they wanted. The net effect was to contribute decisively to the undermining of New Deal liberalism.

3. OPA, *Ibid.*, pp. 8-14.

4. OPA, *Ibid.*, pp. 15-20, 27-34.
Goodwin, *Ibid.*, pp. 355-357.
Galbraith, *Ibid.*, pp. 153-158.

5. OPA, *Ibid.*, pp. 20-24.

6. OPA, *Ibid.*, pp. 24-42, 199-228.
Galbraith, *Ibid.*, pp. 163-173.

7. Brinser, *Ibid.*, pp. 2-4.
Victor A. Thompson, *The Regulatory Process in OPA Rationing* (New York: King's Crown Press, 1950), pp. 256-259.

8, OPA, *Fourth Quarterly Report for Period Ending January 31, 1943.* pp. 10-13.

[January 1943] news release of Office of War Information, Magnuson *Papers*, Acc. 3181-2, box 31.

9. OPA, *Third Quarterly Report for the Period Ended October 31, 1942*, pp. 2-6, 22-23.

## The Wartime Economy: OPA Implementation

1. Seattle Civilian War Commission, *Seattle Went to War: Final Report* (Seattle, 1946).

2. Copy to Magnuson of MAW letter to Henderson, 21 July 1942, Magnuson *Papers*, Acc. 3181-2, file 31/56. MacGowan to Magnuson 11 June 1942, file 50-13. *Argus*, 13 February 1943. See "The Wartime Economy" above on the ATS.
   *P-I* 14 January 1943 on the WLB.

3. *Seattle Schools*, January 1943, and scrapbook collection in School Archives.

4. I.W. Ringer, secretary of the association to Magnuson, 16 July 1942. Magnuson *Papers*, Acc. 3181-2, file 31-56.
   *Aero Mechanic*, 21 January, 11,18 February, 11,25 March, 15 April 1943.
   *Argus*, 23 January, 17 March 1943.
   How chronic was the meat shortage is attested by the meat status in mid-1945: Supplies were reported at an all-time low, expected to be worse. Packers had used up their May quotas. In July 7 large meat retailers closed for lack of meat while smaller ones opened intermittently. W.S. Greathouse of the Frye company blamed the black market. OPA raised the monthly quotas to increase supply. *Argus*, 2 June, 14 July 1945.

5. Carstensen to Magnuson 15 July 1942, *Ibid.* file 31-55, 31-56.

6. Hughbanks to Magnuson et al, 2 September 1942, Magnuson *Papers*, Acc. 3181-2, file 31-55; MacFarlane to Magnuson 23 October and Henderson to Magnuson 7 November; OPA press release [November] and Advance Release 6 November. *Aero Mechanic*, 29 October, 12, 19 November 1942. WVC report is referred to in 8 April 1943 *Aero Mechanic*. McKale ad is in *Aero Mechanic*, 1 July 1943. Hardy et al 18 November 1942 and Kennett to Magnuson, all in file 31-54. *Argus*, 22, 29 January, 4 March, 20, 27 May 1944
   *P-I*, 10, 14 January, 1943.

7. *Argus*, 29 November, 6, 20 December 1941, 10 January 1942.
   *P-I*, 12 January 1943. For gas shortage see 21 October and 31 December 1943.

8. *P-I*, 15 January 1943.

9. OPA regional office press release 6 June and clippings of Star and P-I in Magnuson Papers, Acc. 3181-2, file 31-57.

10. Letters and clippings in Magnuson *Papers*, Acc. 3181-2, file 31-57.

11. Roy W. Atkinson, State CIO director to Magnuson, 27 June; Gibson to Magnuson 1 July; Harding to Magnuson 3 July 1942, Magnuson *Papers*, Acc. 3181-2, file 32-1. *Aero Mechanic* 7 May, 4 June 1942.
    In June 1942 10,000 more workers were expected to arrive soon, according to War commission's registry office. Among the anticipated newcomers were 6,000 young women over the next six

months to replace men going into the armed services. More listings were needed immediately. *Argus*, 27 June 1942.

12. Oles to Magnuson 7 July 1942, Magnuson *Papers*, Acc. 3181-2, file 31-56.

13. Seattle Rent Division press release 29 September; Williams's letter of 1 October and Porter's letter of 12 October, both in Magnuson *Papers*, Acc. 3181-2, file 32-1.

14. Oles to Magnuson 21 October 1942, and copy to Magnuson of his letter to Byrnes, in Magnuson *Papers*, Acc. 3181-2, file 32-1.

15. *Aero Mechanic* 24 September, 22 October 1942.

16. Civilian War Commission, *Final Report*, pp. 24-28.
    *Times*, 15 August 1943.

17. *Aero Mechanic,* 7 and 21 January 1943. *Argus*, 7 March, 1 August 1942.
    *P-I*, 3,6 January 1943.

18. *Aero Mechanic*, 21 January, 11, 18 February, 11, 25 March 15 April 1943.
    *Argus*, 23 January, 17 March 1943.
    On the meat shortage see endnote 4 above.

19. *Aero Mechanic*, 25 March, 8 April, 20 May, 10, 24 June, 1 July, 12 August, 11 November, 2 December 1943.

20. *Aero Mechanic*, 25 March 8 April,20 May, 10,24 June, 1 July, 12 August, 11 November, 2 December 1943.

21. Jacob Vander Meulen, *The Politics of Aircraft*...pp. 165-66, 211-12. There were an estimated 150,000 aircraft workers in the IAM, and about 30,000 in the CIO's union. Douglas fought the IAM tooth and nail; after violating NLRB election rules in an earlier union representation vote, a second was held in August 1943, in which the IAM won collective bargaining rights. *Aero Mechanic*, 19 August 1943.

22. *Aero Mechanic*, 10, 17 December 1942.

23. *Aero Mechanic,* 9, 16 July 17,24 September.

24. *Aero Mechanic* 15 October 1942.

25. *Aero Mechanic*, 22, 29 October, 10, 17, 24 December 1942.
    *P-I*, 28 February 1943.

26. *Aero Mechanic,* 14, 21 January, 4 February, 4 March 1943.

On the Flying Fortress Committee see *P-I* and *Times*, 8,15,18,29 August and 22 September, *Star* 28 September 1943.

27. *Aero Mechanic*, 22 July, 5, 12, 26 August, 3 September 1943.
*P-I*, 16, 24 September, 7 October 1943.
*Times*, 3 October, 14 November 1943.
For national coverage see: *Time [magazine]*, 30 August and 6 September 1943; *Newsweek*, 23 August 1943.
Magnuson, *Papers*, Acc. 3181-2, file 7-15.

28. *Aero Mechanic*, 26 August, 9 September, 28 October 1943.

29. See for example: *Times*, 4 January 1943 photo of soldiers loading tin cans; 7 October 1943 on car shipments; 16 November 1944 "more tin cans..." *P-I* 7 August 1944 for "shipments up". For newspapers: *Star*, 14 November 1944; *Times*, 24 November 1944, 14 January 1945. For scrap metal: *Star*, 30 September, 5 October 1944 for photo of Blacks loading scrap metal, 13 November 1944,"collections in decline". For fats: *Times*, 18 November 1943; *Star*, 30 January 1945.

The Seattle Civilian War Commission scrapbooks at the Seattle Public Library are indispensable as a substitute for combing newpapers on microfilm. That clippings are included from neighborhood newspapers and other sources not usually collected makes this an invaluable source.

# The 1944 Elections, City and General

1. Albert Acena, *Ibid.*, pp. 429-31, 439.

2. Matthew Josephson, *Sidney Hillman: Statesman of American Labor* (New York: Doubleday, 1952), chapters 21-25.
Alonzo L. Hamby, *Beyond the New Deal: Harry S. Truman and American Liberalism* (New York: Columbia University Press, 1973), pp. 31-35, 53-55.
James M. Burns, *Roosevelt, 1940-1945: Soldier of Freedom* (New York: Harcourt, 1970), p 525.
James Foster, *The Union Politic...*(Columbia, MO: University of Missouri Press, 1975), chapter 2.

3. *P-I*, 2-4, 8,10-12 March 1944.
Howard MacGowan wrote Magnuson 27 March 1944: With Scavotto expected to win "Devin [fell back] on the very oldest campaign strategy...[in the] last days pulled out Beck, [Gottstein], Edris, Commonwealth federation [*sic*]...all the polls TURNED in his favor."
Vice operations continued to plague the city. A Municipal League report of 21 November 1942 noted: "Military, naval and public health authorities united this week to laud the closure of commercialized...prostitution...effected in October 1941 as a great step forward." Not for long: on 7 May 1943 the Air Force declared 74 square blocks off limits, and Mayor Devin threatened to fire the police chief, but the chief "stood firm against all official requests for prompt law enforcement." Devin ordered his dismissal, but the city council disagreed. Arrests were made and

Devin withdrew his order.

See also 8 July 1943 letter from Edwin Cooley of the San Francisco Federal Security Office to Eliot Ness, Director of social protection section of the Community War Services in Magnuson *Papers*, Acc. 3181-2, file 51-20. A "rest camp" for prostitutes was considered.

4. Acena, *Ibid.*, pp. 431-35.

5. Acena, *Ibid.*, pp. 435-37.
*Abstract of Votes for the Primary Election, July 11, 1944.*
*P-I*, 10 July 1944.

6. Acena, *Ibid.*, pp. 437-41; Harlin quotation is from p. 438.

In the *P-I*'s series of 4 November, the "Political Battleground", Harlin chose not to Red-bait DeLacy; instead he emphasized his long years as councilman, his blue collar roots in coal mining, and recently his service as director of the state department of labor and industry. Lindeman had been *P-I* publisher during the *P-I* strike of 1936; Hearst replaced him, after FDR's re-election, with John Boettiger, husband of Anna Roosevelt.

7. Acena, *Ibid.*, pp. 439-45.
*Abstract of Votes...*
*P-I* and *Times*, 8 November 1944.

8. Acena, *Ibid.*, pp. 443-47. CP leader Henry Huff thought the WCF "was not worth much". See Acena's p. 445, footnote 3.

## The 1946 City Election

1. *P-I*, 26,27 February 1946.
Berner, *Seattle, 1921-1940*...pp. 398-402.

2. *P-I*, 28 February, 9 March 1946.

3. *P-I*, 12,13 March 1946.

4. *P-I*, 1,13 March 1946.
Berner, *Ibid.*, pp. 77-94.

## Seattle Civic Unity Committee

1. Elliott M. Rudwick, *Race Riot at East St. Louis, July 2, 1917* (Cleveland and New York: World Publishing Company, 1966). Chapters 1 and 15.

St. Clair Drake and Horace R. Cayton, *Black Metropolis: A Study of Negro Life in a Northern City* (New York: Harper Torchbooks, 1962 revised edition), Pp. 3-29, chapters 1-4.

2. Richard Polenberg, *War and Society: The United States, 1941-1945.* (New York: J.B. Lippincott, 1972),pp. 99-101, 117.

Robert C. Weaver, *Negro Labor: A National Problem* (New York: Harcourt Brace Company, 1946), chapters II-VI.

Dorothy K. Newman, *Protest, Politics, and Prosperity* (New York: Pantheon, 1978), pp. 5-7.

3. Polenberg, *Ibid.*, pp. 100-10, 116-23; quotation is from p. 123.

The Four Freedoms was proclaimed by President Roosevelt in his annual message to Congress in January 1941: freedom of speech and expression, freedom of worship, freedom from want, and freedom from fear.

4. Polenberg, *Ibid.*, pp. 123-30.
Taylor, *Ibid.*, pp. 165-67.
Droker, *Ibid.*, pp. 33-34.
Weaver, *Ibid.* pp. 62-63.
St. Clair Drake and Horace Cayton, *Ibid.*, pp. 90-93.
Neil Wynn, *The Afro-Americans and the Second World War* (New York: Holmes and Meier, 1976),* pp.67-76..

5. Droker, *Ibid.* pp. 21-25, 36-38: quotation from p. 38.
Taylor, *Ibid. pp. 166-69.*
Seattle Civic Unity Committee (hereafter CUC), *Records* Accession 479 files 1-3 and 1-5 (UW Libraries Manuscript Collection)
Doris Pieroth, *Desegregating the Public Schools, Seattle, 1954-1968* (Unpublished Ph. D. Dissertation, 1979), chapter 1. The School Board acknowledged the need to introduce Black teachers, when it hired Thelma DeWitty and Marita Johnson in 1947, but later, when school segregation became apparent the Board insisted it was a housing problem, not their's.

6. Taylor, *Ibid.* pp. 169-70.
Droker, *Ibid.* pp. 18-21.
CUC, *Ibid.*, file 12-13.
In the Seattle Housing Authority's housing projects the percentages of Black occupancy as of 1949 were listed as follows:
In the permanent projects: Yesler Terrace 14 %, High Point 8.8%, Holly Park 9%, Sand Point .5% (due to segregation by the Navy).
In the temporary projects: Cedar Vale 8.1%, Delridge Way 40.8%, Duwamish Bend 27.7 %, Minor-Fir 28.2%, Holly Park Addition 19.2%, Rainier Valley Extension 20.7%, Stadium 30%, Taylor Avenue 19.8%. SHA "*Notebook*" in SHA Public Affairs office.
The Seattle Urban League reported in 1947 that while the non-white population increased by 60% from 1940 t0 1947 "dwelling units" for non-whites had increased by only 16%.

7 Taylor, *Ibid.* pp. 166-69, 171.

Droker, *Ibid.* pp. 21-22, 35.

In writing to Francis Johnson, manager of the Roller Bowl Skating Rink 4 February 1944 Johnson expressed his concern that ending this practice might "incite riots". The CUC urged the manager to deal with those who"tried to make trouble". CUC Accession 479, file 1-5.

For Harris article, *P-I*, 7 Apr. 1942.

8. Taylor, *Ibid.* p. 165-67.
Droker, *Ibid.* p. 36.
*P-I*, 26 January 1943 on snow shoveling by Black troops.

9. CUC. *Ibid.*, Paul V. Betters to Devin, 16 Feb. 1944, file 1-5. The CUC was formally established 18 Feb. 1944.
Droker, *Ibid.* p. 34.

10. Droker, *Ibid.* p. 34.
Taylor, *Ibid.* p. 170.
CUC. *Ibid.*, History, p. 5.; Greenwood to Haight 26 July 1944, file 1-5.

11. CUC. *Ibid.*, History.

The Seattle NAACP reported discrimination of two Chinatown reataurants that in effect amounted to denial of service to Blacks. In one instance, when a policeman was asked to intervene he said "we could not purchase a ticket".
CUC, *Ibid.*, 10 May and 10 June 1944, file 1-6.

12. Kaoru Ichihara, *Papers*, file 1-14 for copy of FDR letter to Stimson, in which FDR expresses - ironically in this context - that "no loyal citizen should be denied the democratic right to exercise the responsibilities of his citizenship, *regardless of his ancestry*...Americanism is not, and never was, a matter of race or ancestry." (Italics added). In light of the evacuation and the ongoing discriminatory treatment of African Americans at that time, this seems an incredulous statement.

John Underwood, Seattle chamber's Washington D.C. representative, to Magnuson, 6 May 1943. Magnuson, *Papers*, Acc. 3181-2, file 7-15.

Burrows to Magnuson, 29 July 1943. Magnuson, *Ibid.*

*P-I*. 23 and 25 Sept. 1943, p. 5

Boettiger to Magnuson, 5 Oct. 1943. Magnuson, *Ibid.* file 50-41.

Magnuson to Moffett, 3 Dec. 1943. Magnuson, *Ibid.*, file 36-34.

Atwood to Viola Churchill, 10 Nov. 1943. Same reply went to other correspondents. Magnuson. *Ibid.*, file 7-45.

From February through July 1944 Magnuson received many letters objecting to the WRA's policy and its handling of the relocation centers. Cf. file 7-45 in the Magnuson papers.

ACLU's Roger Baldwin wrote to "Our Friends in Oregon and Washington", 1 February 1943, that Senators Wallgren and Holmes had introduced a bill to "transfer control of evacuated Japanese and Japanese Americans from a civilian agency to the War Department" and the Senate's Military Affairs Committee had endorsed it. He writes the WRA is "doing an admirable job under great difficulties". Mary Farquharson *Papers*, Acc 397-5, file 1. UW Libraries Manuscript Collection.

The *Times*, 24 Aug. 1944 juxtaposed a photograph of General Mark Clark reviewing the 100th

Infantry Battalion at Leghorn Italy with an article about Grange masters in 5 western states urging exclusion of persons of Japanese ancestry from citizenship and for deportation at end of the war.

For a comprehensive overview of resettlement see also *Personal Justice Denied*...chapter 8 "Ending the Exclusion".

12. *Times*, 1 March 1942

Sueko Matsushima to "Father Murphy", 7 March 1943. Council of Churches. *Records*, Acc. 1358-7, file 15-25.

Report by Barnett, 26 Mar. 1942. *Ibid.*, file 15-5.

*Times*, 20 Sept. 1944, re Firlands and "Japs' Return To City Succeeding"; contrasted with *P-I* 20 Sept. 1944 re "Jap-Americans Filtering Back Into Seattle" and elsewhere. *Star* 20 Sept. 1944. *P-I* and *Times*, 5 Oct. 1944.

*Argus*, 28 October, 23 December 1944 on the opposition to return of the evacuees. In its 14 July 1945 edition its front page was devoted to "Enemy Agents At Work", in which it directed strong suspicion for the outbreak of forest fires upon Japanese returnees: "But how about the tens of thousands of Japs who have been 'screened' and released as 'loyal'?"

Howard A. Droker, "Seattle Race Relations During the Second World War" in *Pacific Northwest Quarterly* (October 1976), pp. 172-173.

For general coverage of the evacuees' return see Bill Hosokawa, *JACL: In Quest of Justice* (New York: William Morrow, 1982) chapter XVII.

13. *Star* and *Times*, 18 Dec. 1944.

*P-I*, 5 Oct. 1944 on league, and 23 Jan. 1945 on Wallgren.

Cf. E. Harriet Gipson of Seattle to Magnuson 13 Apr. 1945 about insulting behavior of US Attorney Charles Dennis toward a returnee, and her comment that "many other households have opened their doors to returning Issei and Nisei."

Cf. correspondence in Magnuson, *Papers*, Acc. 3181-3, file 40-41 A and B.

14. Interview of William F. Devin and Arthur Barnett, 14 Nov. 1972 by the author and Howard Droker. In Devin *Papers*, Box 14, University of Washington Libraries Manuscript Collection.

Droker, *Ibid.*, pp. 172-173.

Droker, *The Seattle Civic Unity Committee...*, pp. 48-52.

Fiset, *Imprisoned Apart: The World War II Correspondence of an Issei Couple* (Seattle: University of Washington Press, 1997), pp. 85-89. This is the correspondence of Iwao Matsushita whose papers are in the Manuscript Collection and University Archives of the UW Libraries.

Church Council *Records*, Acc. 479, file 11-17. A report in file 12-13, p. 10. reads: "Some of the more lucrative businesses in which Japanese had been fairly solidly entrenched are now partially or completely closed to them. The Teamsters Union and its closely affiliated organization of owners completely excludes them from the dry cleaning industry...and the potential competitors of the Japanese are able to reduce to a minimum their effectivenss in becoming established in the wholesale and retail produce business. Neither floor space nor materials can yet be secured for the reestablishment of many former lines of activity. Those businesses sold at the time of the evacuation have been found to be remunerative, and the present owners are not interested in relinquishing them."

Clifford Forster, the ACLU staff counsel, wrote Mary Farquharson 7 August 1945 asking her "to persuade Mr. [Ed] Henry to look into the question of bringing [an anti-trust violation suit] against the Teamsters Union and perhaps the Northwest Produce Association [for preventing] the Japanese from carrying on business." Farquharson *Papers,* Ibid.

The weekly *Argus* carried on a running battle against return of the Japanese. "It is our belief that all arguments for the return of the Japanese fall because of the *possibility* that some of them may engage in espionage, and that a single act by a 'disloyal' Jap...is sufficient cause to keep all Japs off the coast". 10 March 1945. It cited all the reports, that proved false, of sabotage and espionage circulated mainly by the Western Defense Command and the California press. Its 31 March edition featured an article, "Pampering the Nisei", in which it castigated the WRA for issuing a booklet, *Nisei in Uniform,* and describing the "takeover" of the Tule Lake by "treasonable" Nisei. In its 5 May number is a long article on Art Ritchie, of the Japanese Exclusion League, outlining his campaign in which the door prize is the above mentioned bust of General McArthur, "America's No. 1 Jap Hater". Its 2 June issue outlined the opposition on Produce Row, in which C.A. Adwen of the Northwest Produce Association objected to the WRA's intervention on behalf of the resettling Japanese. Its 21 July number brought readers uptodate on the "feud" between the WRA and NPA.

15. The survey text is spread over two accessions of Church Council *Records,* UW Libraries Manuscript Collection, Acc. 1358-7, file 15-23, and 1567-2, box 6.

16. The Joint Conference report was 5 June 1945. Church Council *Records,* Acc. 1358-7, file 15-6 and 15-29. Sally Kazama was interviewed by the author 23 August 1995.

17. Church Council *Records,* Acc. 1358-7, file 15-29.

18. Fiset, *Ibid.*, pp. 85-89.
Shiro Kashino had been a star athlete at Garfield High, class of 1940, universally admired at the school. See *Garfield Golden Grads [Newsletter],* 1996. He had been recommended for a Distinguished Service Cross, but he was denied it until one day before he died (9 June 1997) when a court martial conviction of him in May 1945 was overturned upon production of new evidence that cleared him of the charges. See Imbert Matthee article in *P-I* 9 February 1998.

19. *People in Motion...*(Washington, D.C.: Government Printing Office, 1946).

20. CUC. *Ibid.,* History.
   Taylor, *Ibid.* pp. 175, 178.
   Droker, *Ibid.* pp. 174 ff.
   CUC, *Ibid.,* file 12-3, 12-9, 12-13.
   Taylor, *Ibid.,* pp. 75-78.
   Joseph Zwirin of USES, in conference with the Metal Trades Council, urged passage of an FEPC bill in 1945 because employers refused to hire Blacks who were referred by the agency, *New World,* 8 November 1945.

21. CUC, *Ibid.,* files 1-7, 1-8, 12-4, 12-9, 12-10. Leading toward the formal institute was the sponsorship of interracial forums by three churches, which led Linden Mander to suggest introducing a "course of lectures" by the UW.
Irene Miller wrote to Greenwood 21 May 1948 about Weaver's "overwhelming" reception;

and to "Dear Bob" [Weaver] 10 February 1949 "You have many friends in Seattle". CUC, *Ibid.*, file 1-12.

22. CUC, *Ibid.* History.
CUC, *Ibid.*, file 12-4. The Urban League's N.P. Dotson, Jr. thanked the CUC for its VA investigation, adding, "I think I need to know more about the [CUC] and its work so that I can help as much as possible."

23. Miller to Reginald Parsons 7 June 1948, file 1-13; memo Miller to CUC's Helsell 30 October 1950 about progress since 1948, when all hotels except the Frye and Vance accomodated Blacks at the time of "the national Negro convention". File 13-9. Miller to Mrs. A.J. Fletcher 12 October 1949, file 1-

24. All references are from CUC *Records*, Accession 479.
Visiting Black jazz musicians as well as those in the classical repertoire could rely only on the hotels in "Chinatown" for public accomodations. Cf. Paul de Barros, *Jackson Street After Hours*...pp. 60-61, 78-79, and 174 for restrictions against Black bands playing north of the "color line", Yesler Way; also for mixed bands issue.
For an account of Roland Hayes's experiences see Doug Welch's article in the *P-I* 26 March 1942.

25. Taylor, *Ibid.*, pp. 171-72.
Droker, *Ibid.*, chapter 4.
CUC, *Ibid.*, file 1-3, "History of the State FEPC in the State of Washington".
On 9 March 1949 Henry Elliott wrote R.L. McGrath, managing editor of the *Times*, thanking him for its educational role on the FEPC legislation. He adds: "It is important to note that members of the extreme left-wing group actually opposed the legislation at the hearing before the House Labor Committee Feb. 25, 1949, suggesting some five amendments on the pretense of strengthening the law when the obvious result would have been to kill the bill". He wrote the same letter to Edward Stone of the *P-I*. CUC, *Ibid.*, Acc. 479, file 1-3.
The rigidity of the AFL's unions to acceptance of Blacks, quite apart from their union membership/employment, is indicated by the following case in the CUC's files for 1950-51. Lewis Watts reported to the CUC about the denial of dining room service to him at the Labor Temple, asking the CUC to inquire about the policy. The CUC's president Frank Helsell got an appointment with the Labor Temple's manager and board members in March 1951. Manager E.R. Kingsley claimed: "if negroes were admitted they [the club] would have no business within one week...[He was concerned about] girls working in the building...and they would not tolerate eating with negroes." Helsell: "I ran into a stone wall". CUC *Records*, Acc. 479, file 13-6.

## General Entertainment

1. Cf. *Star*, 25 September 1943.
Seattle NAACP to George Greenwood, chair of Civilian War Commission's War Services Division, 1 July 1942. File 174387 in Seattle City Archives.
Representing the Lewis Ford Post No. 289 of the VFW its Commander Henry Twaites ob-

jected to City Council President David Levine 30 May 1942, contending the Colman Club did not meet USO's general standards, was in a poor location relative to "safeguarding of health and morals of men in uniform", that the Federal Security Administration (which authorizes USO clubs) requires all buildings be open for the use of all men in uniform, and that a new facility should be provided. In City Archives under CWC reference.

*Times*, 28 November 1943. Groff concluded the facility was obviously inadequate, and if it had not been for the help of "many" lodges, churches, Seattle Repertory Playhouse, labor unions, the Wheatley YWCA branch, and Boys YMCA it would have been much worse.

On Service women *Times*, 7 November 1943 one week after the new USO facility opened at 1011 Second Avenue for "men only" they were asking for one of their own.

2. *P-I*, 9, 11 September 1943.

*Times*, 5 September 1943 and Sam Groff's article 3 November 1943 on Jefferson Park. Across the road from the cantonment was the 18-hole golf course.

*Star*, 25 Septmber 1943 and other Friday editions.

3. *Star*, 25, 30 October, 1 November 1943. 3,000 service men and women jammed the canteen opening night. Junior hostesses were out "in full strength".

4. Cf. *P-I*, 4 February 1944, *Times*, 2 February, 6 November 1944. Convenient general coverage is in the Seattle Civilian War Commission's Scrapbooks in the Seattle Public Library.

5. Scanning the theater sections of the daily newspapers.

6. See de Barros, *Jackson Street After Hours: The Roots of Jazz in Seattle* (Seattle: Sasquatch Press, 1993), pp. 58-59.

*Star*, 25 September 1943.

Civilian War Commission Scrapbooks.

7. De Barros, *Ibid.*, pp. 40-55.

8. De Barros, *Ibid.*, pp. 50-60. The author a 1939 graduate of Garfield High School remembers some of the African American musicians spawned there, whom de Barros writes about in some detail: impressario Robert "Bumps" Blackwell and drumming younger brother Charles, star athlete, trumpeter/saxaphonist Sonny Booker, saxaphonist Billy Tolles. In the next generation are Patti Bown, Ernestine Anderson, Quincy Jones, and the late Jimi Hendrix among others.

## CLASSICAL MUSIC/FINE ARTS

1. *Argus*, 5 May 1945, 16 December 1944.

On Schultz see Berner, *Seattle 1921-1940...*, pp. 263-64.

2. *Argus* for the period 1941-44.

*P-I*, 7,12 February 1943.

Inasmuch as Marian Anderson was scheduled to sing at the Moore on her yearly nationwide tour two sergeants at the First Avenue cantonment had been writing her letters that never caught up to her. As she was staying at the Olympic Hotel they frantically phoned there, talked to her agent, and ten minutes later she returned the call accepting the invitation. Writes Jack Jarvis of the setting: "In front of her were row upon row of wooden barracks. To the right was a busy highway. To the left lay the railroad tracks." *P-I*, 10,13 February 1943.

3. Esther W. Campbell, *Bagpipes in the Woodwind Section*...(Seattle: Seattle Symphony Women's Association, 1978), pp. 35-45. Campbell quotes Beecham differently: "Leave this hall. This is an insult to the audience" (p. 39). I have incorporated her second sentence.

Hans and Thelma Lehmann, *Out of the Cultural Dust-Bin: Sentimental Musings on the Arts & Music in Seattle From 1936 to 1992* (Seattle: Crowley Associates, 1992), p. 22.

*Argus*, 18 January 1941.

*P-I*, 3 November 1946 from Cecilia Schultz Scrapbooks in Special Collections Division, UW Libraries.

4. *Argus*, January 1944-September 1947, its music section.

Campbell., *Ibid.*, pp. 46-52.

Lehmann, *Ibid.*, pp. 29.

5. *Argus*, 4 October, 22 November, 20 December 1947, 10 January 1948. In its "1947's Best" musical fare only one concert of the symphony was cited, that for French pianist E. Robert Schmitz's performance of Prokofiev's third piano concerto. 3 January 1948.

Campbell, *Ibid.*, pp. 53-55. She mentions the arrival of Manuel Rosenthal as composer in residence at the College of Puget Sound.

For an appreciation of Linden see Lehmann, *Ibid.*, p. 30.

Hans Lehmann alludes to a key role played by Alexander Schneider in forcing Bricken out of the picture. *Out of the Dustbin...*,p. 30.

6. *Argus*, 1 January 1949.

Campbell, *Ibid.*, p. 57-59.

Lehmann *Ibid.*, pp. 30-31.

*P-I*, 17 April 1949. The musicians reserved the right to hire and fire orchestra members.

*Times*, 4 November 1948.

7. The above survey is derived from the Cecilia Scrapbook Collection in the Special Collections Division of the UW Libraries.

8. *Argus*, 12 September 1942, May 1943, 19 August 1944.

Ladies Musical Club Scrapbook Collection at the Museum of History and Industry. Whenever an African American was announced by either the LMC or Cecilia Schultz the publicity was consistently qualified by the term "Negro", accompanied by appropriate laudatory adjective conveying a genuine welcoming feeling expressing support for what their artistry signified: the equal or better of any, anywhere. The newspaper reviews seemed consistently to be genuinely praiseworthy of their performances, in no flagrant/intended way condescending. Probably the difficulty Roland Hayes encountered in gaining hotel accomodations is indicative of what other Black musicians confronted. Doug Welch reported in the *P-I* (3/26/42) no hotels would accomodate Hayes unless he would take meals in his room, and "to be seen as little as possible in the lobby." Hayes believed Nazi racist propaganda was adding to what was already deplorable enough in the US. Hayes stayed in a private home on Queen Anne Hill. In this connection see also Paul de Barros, *Jackson Street After Hours*..., who discusses the difficulties encountered by touring Black jazz musicians. Marian Anderson accepted the hospitality of jazz pianist Patti Bown, knowing the only hotel options open to her were those in "Chinatown", De Barros, *Ibid.*, pp. 60, 111. It seems Anderson eventually obtained accomodations at the Olympic Hotel, to judge from the account in endnote 2 above, when she was contacted there by the sergeants of the Black cantonment.

9. *Argus*, 11 July 1944, 22 December 1945, 22 June 1946 noting Ezio Pinza, Nathan Milstein, ballet dancers Svetlova and Dolin, as examples of signing up artists from LMC and Schultz series. Other such artists are Morini, Casadesus, and Menuhin. Alexander Schneider's entrance onto campus, infused it with his lively presence as instructor and performer. That, and Stanley Chapple's assumption of the school's directorship breathed fresh life to the university's music scene and the city's. In the 1960s it took an outside musical organization, New Demensions in Music under direction of composer/impressario Joan Franks Williams, to help reinvigorate the school. See also *Argus*, 11 January, 16 August 1947, 3 January 1948, in which David Pennell rates the best 1947 concerts, including: "The three Meany Hall recitals of Alexander Schneider - two in collaboration with Berthe Poncy Jacobson and one accompanied by the student chamber orchestra. The Paganini played with a set of Stradivari fiddles. Although short-lived (1946 to about 1952) the Paganini was recorded by RCA Records, and for some judges, excelled the Budapest Quartet, recorded by Columbia Records. Pennell also lists the Paganini's performance of Bartok's First Quartet as a highlight of the 1947 season. Bartok's six string quartets are considered by many musicologists as 20th century successors in line with Beethoven's.

10. *Minutes* for 1940-1941. Cornish School *Records*, Acc. 2654.

11. Cornish School *Minutes* for 1942-45. For\a list of the donors see *Minutes* for 17 October 1945.

For Nellie Cornish's fund raising difficulties see Berner, *Seattle, 1921-1940*...pp. 249-51. Also Ellen Van Volkenburg Browne and Edward N. Beck, editors *Miss Aunt Nellie: The Autobiography of Nellie C. Cornish* (Seattle: University of Washington Press, 1964), pp. 147-56, 161-63, 173-74.

12. Cornish School *Minutes*, 1946-1948. An outline of foundations Nichols contacted is in box 9 file 4. Paul Robeson paid the tuition of Edith Mary Bown (misspelled "Bowen" in Minutes), one of the three talented Bown sisters. Edith's debut was at Town Hall in New York, 1950; later she studied with Nadia Boulanger and Robert Casadesus. Her sister Patti became a famous jazz pianist. See de Barros, *Jackson Street After Hours*...p. 111. Indicative of the growing sensitivity on racial matters: "Due to race prejudice Mr. Foley thought it advisable not to present 'Little Black Sambo', but will present another dance program in its place." *Minutes*, 19 January 1948.

Browne and Beck, *Miss Aunt Nellie*...p. x. for the inability to raise matching money. They comment on the community's failure to fully appreciate the contributions the school had made and continued to make to the cultural life of the city and its environs. In 1954 the Music and Art Foundation of Seattle took over financial management of Cornish.

13. Martha Kingsbury, *Northwest Traditions* (Seattle: Seattle Art Museum, 1978), pp. 9-13.

William Cumming, *Sketchbook: A Memoir of the 30s and the Northwest School* (Seattle: University of Washington Press, 1984), pp. 129-40, "The Northwest School" Elsewhere he refers to it alternately as the "Callahan circle", pointing to the centrality of the Callahans' influence.

14. Kingsbury, *Ibid.*, pp. 36-46, and throughout the volume for her biographical essays on each of the artists and their milieus.

Tom Robbins, *Guy Anderson* (Seattle: Gear Works Press, 1965), [pp. 3-7].

William Cumming, *Ibid.*, pp. 49-63. On these "brainstorming sessions" see Kingsbury, *Ibid.*, pp. 21-22.

*Some Work of the Group of Twelve* (Seattle: Dogwood Press, 1937). The twelve were Callahan, Margaret and Peter Camfferman, Elizabeth Cooper, Earl T. Fields, Takauchi Fujii, Graves, Walter Isaacs, Kenjiro Nomura, Ambrose and Viola Patterson, Kamekichi Tokita. For a description of the Twelve and their arguments over "Realism" see Cumming, *Sketchbook...*pp. 21-26. He singles out Chinese-American painter Fay Chong as "solving" the "approaches to reality and painting it"...something Fujii, Nomura, and Tokita failed to do, in his estimate.

Frederick Wight, John Baur, and Duncan Phillips, *Morris Graves* (Berkeley: University of California Press, 1956), pp. 34-35.

Michael R. Johnson, editor, *Kenneth Callahan: Universal Voyage* (Seattle: University of Washington Press, 1973) At this time he was an assistant curator at the Seattle Art Museum. By 1944 his new style had taken shape, represented by "Vital Storm" and "Revolving World". His earlier more representational period may be readily seen in a mural on the ground floor of the Municipal Building. His mountain landscapes of the 1930s show the influence of Cezanne, an influence he shared in common with many among the "Group of Twelve". Cumming sets Callahan and Graves apart from the group, the former being clearly of the avant garde by 1937. *Sketchbook*, pp. 21-26.

On Tobey see: *Mark Tobey: The World of the Market* (Seattle: University of Washington Press, 1964); *Mark Tobey: a Retrospective Exhibition From Northwest Collections*. Catalog published by the Seattle Art Musuem for a showing of 244 of his paintings in fall 1959. His market paintings covered the years 1940-43. Some illustrate his incorporation of "white writing"; but "Gothic" captures it most fully at the end of the market series, 1943.

15. For Art Week see Seattle Art Museum *Records*, Acc. 2636, box 4 in UW Libraries Manuscript Collection.

George Nakashima, *The Soul of a Tree: A Woodworker's Reflections* (Tokyo: Kodansha International Ltd., 1981) Nakashima was born in Washington, worked as an architect in Japan, then to India, to Japan in 1939, returning to Seattle in 1940. Evacuated to Minidoka where he developed his woodworking skills.

16. Cumming, *Sketchbook...*pp. 11-144 for a vivid portayal of the artistic milieu of this early period.

Martha Kingsbury, *George Tsutakawa*, (Seattle: University of Washington Press, and Bellevue Art Museum, 1990), pp. 25-54. "Shouted down" quotation is from p. 53.

On Nomura see *Kenjiro Nomura: The George and Betty Nomura Collection* (Seattle: Wing Luke Museum, 1991). This collection of scenes from the Puyallup Assembly Center and Minidoka was discovered by the Nomura children after his death. Upon returning to Seattle after the evacuation Nomura ceased painting until Paul Horiuchi pulled him from this period of depression. Under Horiuchi's and Tsutakawa's influence Nomura's style became abstract, no longer representational.

17. In scanning the publications on the artists, Graves and Tobey in particular the patrons who

are mentioned most frequently are: Anne and John Hauberg, Mrs. Thomas D. (Emma) Stimson, Carolyn Kizer, Mr. and Mrs. Charles Laughton, Wesley Wehr, the Eugene Fuller Memorial Collection of the Seattle Art Museum, Berthe Poncy Jacobson, Mr. and Mrs. Ralph Nicholson, Elizabeth Bayley Willis, and Joanna Eckstein. One man shows for the younger painters in the constellation at the Art Museum: Cumming 1941, Richard Gilkey 1960, Leo Kenny 1949, Tsutakawa's sumi paintings 1978 (long after he had established a worldwide reputation for his sculptures, particularly for the fountains in many US cities and in Japan).

Fuller employed Callahan until 1953, shorter periods for Anderson and Graves.

18. SAM *Records*, Acc. 2636, box 4.

19. SAM *Records*, Acc. 2636, box 24

20. *Star*, 6 May 1942.

The most comprehensive listing of events occurring at Victory Square is to be found in the indexes to the Seattle Chamber of Commerce *Minute books*, 1942-1945. In the Seattle Public Library.

21. *P-I, Times, Star*, 14-15 August 1945.

# THE UNIVERSITY OF WASHINGTON:
## INDESPENABLE TO CITY'S ADAPTION TO MODERNITY

1. Charles M. Gates, *The First Century at the University of Washington, 1861-1961* (Seattle: University of Washington Press, 1961), pp. 193-94.

Eric Barr to Chief of Naval Personnel, 17 February 1943 concerning conversion of the UW's quarter system with the semester system employed elsewhere. Also, his 16 March 1943 letter. An undated memorandum about housing of V-12 students. And letter from Chief of Naval Personnel to President Sieg, 30 november 1945 about terminating the program. In UW President *Records*, Acc. 71-34, box 110.

*P-I*, 7 January 1943.

2. Gates, *Ibid.*, pp. 165-78.
Berner, *Ibid.*, pp. 37-39, 64-65, 131-39, 371, 448-49, chapter 14.

3. Clement A. Finch, *Fulfilling the Dream: A History of the University of Washington School of Medicine, 1946-1988* (Seattle: Medical Alumni Association, University of Washington School of Medicine, 1990), chapter 1.

*King County Medical Society, 100 Years* (Seattle: King County Medical Society, 1988) p. 20.

Hilding H. Olson, *A Retrospective View of Northwest Medicine: The Early History of Surgery and the Health Sciences of the University of Washington* (Seattle: UW Department of Surgery, 2nd edition, 1993) pp. 61-63.

Payton Smith, *Rosellini: Immigrants' Son and Progressive Governor* (Seattle: University of Washington Press, 1997), pp. 31-34.

5. Finch, *Ibid.*, chapter 1.

Memorandum, 10 May 1944, American College of Surgeons and the American Medical Association, in UW President *Records*, Medical School file, Acc. 71-34, box 110, University Archives.

On 24 May 1945 Sieg wrote to Dr. B.E. Anderson, Secretary of the State Dental Association to correct a "misconceptions", about the UW's role in getting passage of the legislative bill; Sieg disclaimed any active role for the UW, and asked that the dental association accept the school "as an established fact, and cooperate with the University authorities on the operation of the school..."

In a retrospective letter, 15 May 1953, UW Vice-President H.P. Everest to Governor Langlie, relating to founding of the medical school, Everest pointed to the skepticism on campus: "They were concerned as to whether or not the state could afford a medical school at that time and whether or not a good, sound staff could be developed...It was the Legislature and then the administration in Olympia which actually made the decision." In future discussion with Turner the WSMA and "particularly the Legislature and the State administration [assured Turner] not to worry about the financial support necessary...It was on that basis...that he accepted [the deanship]." In this letter Everest also referred to the 1950 failure to get the teaching and research hospital that was so important to Turner. Letter is in UW Medical School Dean's Office, *Records*, Acc. 87-77, box 40, University Archives.

Cora Jane Lawrence, *University Education for Nursing in Seattle, 1912-1950: An Inside Story of the University of Washington School* (Unpublished Ph.D. Dissertation, 1972), pp. 213-14.

Hilding Olson, *Ibid.*, pp. 65-70.

Payton Smith, *Ibid.*, pp. 31-34.

6. UW Medical School, *First Annual Report*, 18 June 1947, in UW Medical School Dean's Office *Records*, Acc. 81-96, box 17.

Hilding Olson, *Ibid.*, pp. 71-72.

The Bureau of Business Research had been publishing *Pacific Northwest Industry* which included "Indexes of Business Activity" and producing research through some of its faculty to aid in postwar planning. The UW's Institute of Labor Economics produced a study in 1948 on job opportunities for racial minorities that influenced passage of the state Fair Employment Practices Act. Responding to Seattle's radically altered demography the UW sponsored an Annual Institute on Race Relations.

7. Finch, *Ibid.*, pp. 107 ff. for photographs of graduating classes.

UW Medical School Dean's Office, *First Annual Report*.

8. UW Medical School Dean's Office, *First Annual Report*, and *Second Annual Report*, 15 June 1948.

Turner to President Allen, 9 January 1947, explaining the reorganization of the K.C. Hospital, in UW President *Records*, Acc. 71-34, Medical School file, box 106.

In a letter to state Senator Alfred J. Westberg, 9 December 1948, one month from start of the 1949 legislative session, about funding for the teaching and research hospital, Turner indicated "[It] must be a referral hospital to which patients can be referred by physicians throughout the state regardless of their ability to pay, therefore, they are largely problem cases." To handle them there must be a minimum of 400 beds. UW President *Records*, Acc. 71-34, Medical School file, box 106.

Getting the chamber of commerce to predictably support legislative funding of the medical school was a problem. When the chamber failed to lobby the 1947 legislature for medical school funding Kenneth Schoenfeld complained to E.L. Skeel, president of the chamber, of the dispersal among five chamber committees paralyzing effective chamber action, thereby contributing to the unfortunate outcome. He urged Skeel to establish one committee for UW affairs. Carbon copy in UW President *Records,* Acc. 71-34, box 97.

Friction with COH occurred early on. Dr. Herman Smith of COH wrote President Allen 3 February 1949, expressing uneasiness about the UW's setting up a "pediatrics teaching facility" inasmuch as he was under the impression that COH would be the "main pediatric hospital". Later, 16 April 1951, Turner complained of COH's narrow focus, attributing it to the Orthopedic Hospital Guild, "a society issue". The women in it are "suspicious" of the UW, but over the past two or three years the affiliation relationship had improved, no longer the "least satisfactory". UW Medical School Dean's Office, *Records,* Acc. 94-20, box 1.

For classroom space at Harborview the UW acquired one of the former mess halls from Paine Field, that had been declared surplus at war's end. Medical School Dean's Office, *Records,* Acc. 87-77, box 15.

9. Lawrence, *Ibid.*, pp. 215-22. Civil service examinations soon were required for nursing positions in federal and state government. She notes that 90 percent of public health nurses were then employed by tax-supported agencies. Public health nursing, thereby, became part of the curriculum. Passage of the Mental Health Act led to incorporation of a master's degree program in psychiatric nursing.

10. *King County Medical Society, 100 Years...*p. 23.

11. Walt Crowley, *To Serve the Greatest Number: A History of Group Health Cooperative of Puget Sound* (Seattle: GHC in association with University of Washington Press, 1996), chapter 5 "Group Health versus King County Medical Society".

Contract medicine had been practiced in one form or another since at least 1891, when the St. Paul and Tacoma Lumber Company contracted with the Fannie Paddock Memorial Hospital. The same is true for prepaid medical care. Cf., Nancy Rockafellar and James W. Haviland, eds., *Saddlebags to Scanners: The First 100 Years of Medicine in Washington State* (Seattle: Washington State Medical Association, 1989), chapter IV.

12. Turner to Senator Clinton Harley 24 March 1949, Medical School Dean's Office *Records,* Acc. 87-77, box 40.

Turner to President Allen, 23 April 1949, in advance of Wednesday meeting with Governor Langlie about financial solvency. UW President, *Records,* Acc. 71-34, box 106.

Turner to Riley, 31 January 1949, and to Harley 7 February 1949. Medical School Dean's Office, *Records,* Acc. 91-63, box 2.

*Third Annual Report*, 1 July 1949, Medical School Dean's Office, Acc. 81-96, box 17.

13. Turner to Allen 16 April 1950, Medical School Dean's Office *Records,* Acc. 87-77, box 40 crediting the "profession" and for his disappointment with the Alumni Association's opposition to Referendum 9.

*Fourth Annual Report,* Medical School Dean's Office, *Records,* Acc. 81-96, box 17.

14. "Labor at the University" *Pacific Northwest Industry*, January 1947, pp. 69-72.

Institute of Labor Economics, *Job Opportunities for Racial Minorities in Seattle* (Seattle: University of Washington Press, 1948)

Seattle Civic Unity Committee, "History".

15. Jane Sanders, *Cold War on Campus*, pp. 86-90.

On the American Legion's part of the protest see Allen's correspondence with Stephen F. Chadwick, former national commander of the legion. UW President *Records*, Acc. 71-34, box 97.

## SEATTLE PUBLIC SCHOOLS: VITAL COG IN WARTIME, TURN TOWARD FUTURE

1. See sections above on the wartime economy and the role of women.

On day-care nursery schools see School Board *Minutes*, 16 and 23 May 1947. (Hereafter, *Minutes*)

2. George D. Strayer, *Public Education in Washington: A Report of a Survey of Public Education in the State of Washington*, (Olympia: State Printer, 1946), pp. 152-53.

*Seattle Schools*, January and March 1946.

*Minutes*, 2 May 1947.

Seattle Public Schools Archives, E4, box 22 on bond drive..

3. *Seattle Schools*, March 1946.

*Minutes*, 20 September 1946 on evening classes.

*Minutes*, 23 May 1947, 13 February 1947 on religious education.

4. *Minutes*, 7 October 1946, 2 May and 12 September 1947, 16 January 1948.

Quintard Taylor, *Forging of a Black Community*, p. 175.

5. *Minutes*, 6 and 20 September 1946.

6. *Minutes*, 9 April 1947. At the hearing Edna Breazeale, president of the Seattle Association of Classroom Teachers, contended overcrowding was the main source of the problem. She contended that smaller size classes would alleviate it, but to do so the tax base would have to be raised, something the League had historically resisted. Cf., Berner, *Seattle, 1921-1940...*p. 233.

7. *Minutes*, 6 August 1948.

*Abstract of Votes for the 1950 General Election.*

## Postwar Economy: Introduction

1. US Bureau of Labor Statistics, *The Impact of the War on the Seattle-Tacoma Area*. (Washington: Government Printing Office, 1946)
Karen T. Anderson, *The Impact of World War II on the Puget Sound...*, pp. 188-91.

2. *Pacific Northwest Industry* (hereafter abbreviated *PNI*) July 1945, September 1945. And May 1949 for Nathanael Engle, "The West as a Market", pp. 144-47, 151-52.

3. *Argus*, 14 July, 18,25 August, 22 September, 10 November 1945.
*Times*, 16 August 1945.
*P-I*, 16-18 August 1945.

4. Nathanael Engle, "1946 Business Outlook for Western Washington" *PNI*, December 1945, pp. 46-51.
Loutitt, *PNI*, December 1949.
*P-I* and *Times*, 16-18 August 1945.

5. Indexes of Business Activity, *PNI*, May, August, November 1946, January-March 1947, February 1949, March 1951.

6. PSP&L, *1948 Annual Report*.

7. *PNI* December 1949.
State Employment Security Department, monthly reports for King County (it was no longer singling out Seattle): February and July 1948, February and July 1949.

8. Seattle Chamber of Commerce, *The Postwar Labor Market in the Seattle Area* (Seattle: Chamber of Commerce, 1946). The data was gathered by the chamber staff; Engle, Director of the UW's Bureau of Business Research, did the analysis. 7708 workers from 32 employers were questioned. For any one question about 1,600 responded.

9. Karen T. Anderson, *The Impact of World War II on the Puget Sound...*, pp. 192-93, 201-02, 205-07 (quotation is from p. 207). For employment opportunities affecting African Americans specifically see the chapter on the Seattle Civic Unity Committee, above.
John McCann, *Blood in the Water...*, p. 48 on Blacks in Local 751.
The monthly reports on the local job markets of the State Employment Security Department indicated in February 1946 that returning veterans mainly accounted for the increase in size of the labor force. Employment gains were chiefly at Boeing (about 12,000), while "substantial" losses were recorded for shipyards, government installations and offices, and the iron and steel industry. These trends would continue. "Lack of materials" was often cited as a cause for delays in production/construction in the early postwar period. Accounting for the delays, its July 1946 report judged: "Really substantial employment gains in basic industry will not occur until the supply of durable and consumer goods improves." High labor turnover was characteristic early in this transition period.

**292**  Endnotes

10. Anderson, *Ibid.*, pp. 192-95, 201-13. Black women suffered discrimination on both sex and racial grounds as employers reestablished prewar discriminatory practices, according to Anderson (p. 212). She cites A.F. Hardy, manager of WSES, for the observation that men were replacing women throughout the state by 1946.

The State Employment Security Department noted in April 1947: "Replacement of Women Workers Continues", especially in manufacturing, while "employment in the trades and services continues to be predominantly women". Preferance among employers for veterans was true for most establishments. It also noted employment was upward as supply of materials improved.

11. Anderson, *Ibid.*, p. 222. Her figures for decreases in employment by age category are: 49.7% for age 14-19; and those age 20-24, 25-34, 35-44 and 45-54 experienced declines of 40.7%, 24.2%, 18.0%, and 5.6% respectively. In the age 55-64 group there was an increase of 21.8% in employment.

## OPA, Postwar

1. See chapter above on OPA during the defense/war mobilization period.
   OPA, *16th Quarterly Report for Period Ending December 31, 1945*, pp. 1-3.
   OPA, *18th Quarterly Report for Period Ending June 30, 1946*, pp. 1-5.
   See Roger W. Lotchin, *Fortress California, 1910-1960: From Warfare to Welfare*(New York: Oxford University Press, 1992), pp. 156-69 for the early postwar planning of California cities.
   Michael P. Malone, "Toward a New Approach to Western American History", in Patricia Nelson Limerick, et al, *Trails: Toward a New Western History* (Lawrence: University Press of Kansas, 1991), chapter 10, especially pp. 147-57.
   Carl Abbott, "Planning for the Home Front in Seattle and Portland, 1940-1945", in Roger W. Lotchin, ed., *The Martial Metropolis: U.S. Cities in War and Peace* (New York: Praeger, 1984), pp. 163-89.
   U.S. Office of War Mobilization and Reconstruction, *First Report, January 1, 1945* and *Second Report, April 1, 1945.*
   U.S. War Manpower Commission, Washington State, *Post-War Employment in Washington State and Puget Sound Area*, ([Olympia, 1944]).
   On postwar planning see Alan Brinkley, *The End of Reform*...chapter 10, "Planning for Full Employment". The focus of liberalism changed in emphasis from anti-monopoly and regulation at the producing end to achieving full-employment. By this change of focus it was hoped sustained consumer demand would in turn maintain production, hence jobs. See his discussion of the Defense Plants Corporation role in disposing of its properties after the war as quickly as possible, which meant sales to the large corporations almost exclusively, to the neglect of small businesses (pp. 240-45).

2. OPA, *16th Quarterly Report...*, pp. 5,8, 100-102. Quotation is from p. 5.
   *P-I*, 14-10 August 1945.

3. OPA, *Ibid.*, p. 7.
   *P-I*, 17-19 August 1945.

4. OPA, *Ibid.*, pp. 7-10, 27-32. Quotation is from p. 27.

5. OPA, *Ibid.*, pp. 41-42.
   In the Warren G. Magnuson *Papers*, Acc, 3181-3 , Box 52 are several file folders of correspondence relating to the OPA. Senator Magnuson's office consistently responded to each correspondent, whether it be the Chamber of Commerce or individuals asking for the help he might supply. He seemed most often to supply it.

6. OPA, *Ibid.*, pp. 13-17.
   Reportedly "the biggest black market in the history of the OPA" for meat was broken the last week in February 1946, when federal agents raided operations in Seattle, Tacoma, and Yakima. *Argus*, 2 March 1946.

7. OPA, *Ibid.*, pp. 24-25.

8. OPA, *Ibid.*, pp. 30-38.
   On the 1946 strikes, see for example, David McCullough, *Truman*, pp. 493-506. Notably, McCullough has no coverage of OPA for the postwar period.

9. OPA, *Ibid.*, pp. 39-46.
   *Argus*, 29 June 1946.

10. OPA, *Ibid.*, pp. 77-82.

11. OPA, *18th Quarterly Report for Period Ending June 30, 1946*, pp. 1-3.

12. OPA, *Ibid.*, pp. 5-10.
    OPA, *19th Quarterly Report for Period Ending September 30, 1946*, pp. 1-2, 11-13.
    Syndicated columnist David Lawrence blamed the White House for encouraging the "unparalleled wave of inflation" and growth of the black market, by its new wage policy of February. To save OPA he insisted upon a wage freeze. Truman had promoted wage increases as a catchup measure, which led to the new wage policy. That real wages actually decreased during the period seems not to have been considered by Lawrence. His argument was not unique among OPA critics. *Times*, 28 June 1946. Indicative of the black market in Seattle was a front page report in the *Times* 10 June issue: "One third of Seattle's meat markets will be closed all this week or longer...because of declining supply of meat and black market activities, the Seattle Retail Meat Dealers' Association reported today".

13. *Times*, 8,9,27-30 June 1946.
    Alonzo L. Hamby. *Beyond the New Deal: Harry S. Truman and American Liberalism* (New York: Columbia University Press, 1973), pp. 79-80.
    Later that month the *P-I* reported: "Magnuson Hits OPA for Injustice to Business", accompanied by a photograph picturing him in action. *P-I* 27 March 1946. Box 52 in the Magnuson *Papers*, Acc. 3181-3, has six bulging file folders on the OPA, mainly constituents seeking exceptions or pleading for abolition of price controls altogether. Mitchell's appearance on the Forum was 7 March. Robert Nathan and Associates prepared a report for the CIO in 1949 commenting

**294**    Endnotes

on the abandonment of OPA: "The major catastrophe in the postwar period was the premature termination of price controls", and "failure to reinstate the excess profits tax...Taxes should have been increased in 1946 to stem the tide of inflation and remove the incentive to keep boosting prices." Copy in Mitchell *Papers*, Acc. 281-2, file 4-32.
*Congressional Quarterly*, vol. 1, pp. 393-406.

14. OPA, *18th Quarterly Report...*, pp. 5-10.
OPA, *19th Quarterly Report*  , pp. 1-2, 11-13.
*Times*, 19-26 July 1946. Quotation is from 22 July issue.
*Argus*, 6, 13 July 1946.
*Congressional Quarterly*, vol. 1, pp. 578-79.

15. OPA, *Ibid.*, pp. 1-5, 13-16, 29-30.
Alonzo Hamby, *Beyond the New Deal*, p. 136.

16. OPA, *Ibid.*, pp. 70-72.
The *Times* 24 July issue carried the front page column heading: "RISING COST OF LIVING JOLTS MARRIED VETS ATTENDING UNIVERSITY". Dean Newhouse reported there was a time when the university was "in the business of teaching...but now we are in banking, real estate, transportation and nursery schools". The *Times* for 21 October 1946 carried a front page column head : "U.W. Plans New Homes for Faculty", noting the UW will add $200,000 of its own funds to a grant of $350,000 from the State Development Board for housing 100 faculty and their families. These were prefabricated duplexes to be built in Union Bay Place.

17. *Times*, 15-17, 21,23,30 October and 8 November 1946.
*P-I*, 1,10 November 1946.
Nathanael Engle, Director of the UW's Bureau of Business Research, reported in 1947 that it would cost a typical family 74% more in 1947 than in 1939 to maintain the same level of consumption. He noted food prices had risen 96%, clothing 72%, housing 50%, furnishings 82%, taxes 300%, savings 76%. *Pacific Northwest Industry,* November 1947, pp. 27, 31-32.

18. Bayard O. Wheeler, "Housing Need in the Pacific Northwest", *Pacific Northwest Industry*, August 1947, pp. 180-85.
Mike Caraher, secretary of the Seattle Veterans' Association, wrote Senator Hugh Mitchell 22 July 1946, that homes were too pricey for vets, "ranging around $10,000... Most of us who are looking for homes - and that includes most of us - would like to rent...But rental property is practically unobtainable. [A]lmost half of the FPHA units ...are being occupied by one-time war workers...We believe these one-time war workers should be replaced by veterans in all FPHA units." Mitchell *Papers*, Acc 281-2, file 1-16.

19. Seattle Chamber of Commerce, Housing Committee "Outline of the Housing Situation in Seattle and Washington State". Copy in Magnuson *Papers*, Acc. 3181-3, file 42-16.
According to the 1947 *Census of Manufactures* the value of new residential construction in Seattle from 1945 to 1948 was:
1945   $11,077,969   2,827 dwelling units
1946   $19,765,325   3,364 dwelling units

1947  $23,301,787  3,346 dwelling units
1948  $26,690,110  2,860 dwelling units
Clearly the average value of individual dwelling units was increasing dramatically.

20. SHA, 6th-10th *Annual Reports*, (1945-49). At SHA's Public Relations office.
SHA, Notebook "Chronology of SHA History". At SHA's Public Relations office.
*Argus*, 17 November 1945, 26 January, 13 April, 11 May 1946.
" Clement A. Finch, *Fulfilling the Dream: A History of the University of Washington School of Medicine, 1946-1988* (Seattle: Medical Alumni Association, University of Washington School of Medicine, 1990), p. 17.
*Times*, 21 October 1946. See endnote 17.
During the congressional hearing Ross conducted the members on a tour of the projects in Seattle and Kirkland. Ross succeeded Jesse Epstein as director when Epstein was appointed Western Regional Director. See Mitchell *Papers* , Acc, 927, file 10-47.

21. See Droker, *The Seattle Civic Unity Committee...*pp. 158-71. In 1968 the state Legislature passed a "fair housing" bill following the asassination of Martin Luther King, Jr.

## Labor in Early Postwar Period

1. OPA, 17th *Quarterly Report for period Ending March 31, 1946.* pp. 1-12.

2. *Argus*, 29 September, 8 December 1945.

3. Melvyn Dubofsky in *The State and Labor...*,pp. 192-95, writes on the significance of the 1946 strike wave: As to the steel strike settlement, "[it] set in motion a wage-price inflationary spiral that cost consumers dearly and also damaged union prestige."
David McCullough, *Truman*, pp. 480-81 on steel strike; and pp. 492-506 on this "greatest" strike wave in US history.
*Argus*, 21 February, 22 March, 6,19 April, 17 May for updates on local labor scene.

4. *Argus*, 29 September, 8 December 1945.

5. *P-I*, 1,2,12,16,18 November 1946

6. *Argus*, 17 November, 8 December 1945; 5,19,26 January 1946.
In March 1945 the Washington Machinists Council had sent AFL William Green copies of telegrams complaining about Taylor's ineffectiveness and loss of union affiliations. They noted loss of the Teamsters and Taylor's refusal to accept the per capita taxes of the Aero Mechanics Union because they would vote for Weston. Washington State Federation of Labor, *Records*, Acc. 301, file 22-11.
See also Hugh B. Mitchell, *Papers*, Acc. 927, file 4-14.

296   Endnotes

*P-I*, 14, 28 October 1945.
*Times*, 28 October 1945.

7. Jackson to Weston 17 January 1947, WSFL, *Records*, Acc. 301, file 20-11. Jackson had kept in touch with Weston about anti-labor legislation, noting his opposition to the Smith-Connally Bill (1943) and the Case Bill (1946). See Jackson to Weston 7 February 1946, file 20-10.

## Boeing and the Postwar Economy

1. U.S. Office of War Mobilization and Reconversion. *First Report, January 1, 1945* and *Second Report, April 1, 1945*.
   U.S. War Manpower Commission. Washington State. *Post-War Employment in Washington State and Puget Sound Area* ([Olympia], 1944).
   Puget Sound Power and Light Company. *Annual Reports*, 1945-1947.
   Magnuson *Papers*, Acc. 3181-3, Box 41.

2. Lotchin, *Fortress California*..., chapter 1.
   Richard S. Kirkendall, "The Boeing Company and the Military-Metropolitan-Industrial Complex, 1945-1953" in *Pacific Northwest Quarterly* (October 1994), pp. 137-49.
   In a telegram, 10 September 1945, to Charles Clise, president of the Chamber of Commerce, Senator Magnuson assured him everything possible was being done to sustain B-29 production, and that the Air Force leaders realize Boeing's situation, and its critical importance for future heavy bomber production. Magnuson *Papers,* Acc. 3181-3, file 41-16. The Boeing file in Box 40 of this accession relates mainly to efforts in August and September, at protecting the company from cutbacks in bomber contracts. The Seattle chamber's Washington D.C. manager wrote on 7 Sept.: "Please thank Senator Magnuson for his prompt action in the Boeing matter...Kindly tell Warren...it would be a good idea if he would send a telegram to President [of the national] Chamber [of Commerce] outlining his efforts in Washington on Boeing situation."

3. Kirkendall, *Ibid.*, pp. 138-40.
   Robert Serling, *Legend and Legacy*...pp. 142-43 for Allen's testimony before the House Armed Services Committee in February 1956.

4. Kirkendall, *Ibid.*, pp. 140-43.
   John McCann, *Blood in the Water: A History of District Lodge 751 of the International Association of Machinists & Aerospace Workers* (Seattle:District Lodge 751, 1988), pp. 98-108.

5. Symington to Mitchell 5 May 1949; carbon copy, Hayes to Symington, 4 August 1949, Mitchell *Papers*, Acc. 281-2, file 5-2.

6. In summer of 1943 the chamber established a "Flying Fortress Committee" to divert employment to Boeing, which was experiencing a labor turnover of about 100 percent. This is covered above in the chapter on the OPA.

Kirkendall, *Ibid.*, pp. 143-47.

Lotchin, *Fortress California*...pp. 13-17.

Hugh B. Mitchell, *Papers*, Acc. 927, files 3-11 and 3-13. Congressman Mitchell wrote Carl Vinson, chair of the Armed Services Committee, 11 October 1949: "Our whole defense system is called into question by this Air Force decision [to disperse production inland], which rates Seattle as a 'vulnerable' area [and that this is due to] the weakness of our Alaska defense [as a result of the Soviet's atomic bomb threat]." Mitchell *Papers*, Acc. 281, file 19-8. In file 5-2 are: Mitchell to "Mr. President" 24 August 1949, and Symington to Mitchell 31 August 1949. In the latter letter Symington volunteered: "It is our understanding that Boeing anticipates little additional commercial business in the near future, necessitating cutting back the labor force engaged on commercial work to a negligible number". Shelby Scates interviewed Mitchell 11 January 1994, when Mitchell alleged the critical role played by Magnuson. See his completed a biography of Magnuson, *Warren G. Magnuson and the Shaping of Twentieth Century America* (Seattle: University of Washington Press, 1997), pp. 124-26.

An undated 8 page file memorandum in the Magnuson Papers is: "THE BOEING SITUATION". Excerpts: "Air Force officials refute emphatically reports that Boeing's Seattle operation will be abandoned or removed to Witchita..." This is contradicted by the following: "[The Air Force] declares that strategic and defense policies are cogent reasons for scheduling major aircraft production at inland, less vulnerable plants, and that important military contracts such as that on the B-47, probably will not be handled in the future at exposed sites, including Seattle." The memo continued, indicating Boeing could subcontract for some parts manufacture, and it miight consider returning to fighter aircraft production. Acc. 3182-2, file 44-4.

7. Kirkendall, *Ibid.*, pp. 147-49.

Serling, *Ibid.*, p. 159 for quotations.

During the defense mobilization period historian Michael S. Sherry notes the "institutional machinery of national security" was put into play, step by step. And: "The period before Pearl Harbor was also a new age of national security, an unwitting rehearsal for the Cold War." *In the Shadow of War: The United States Since the 1930s* (New Haven: Yale University Press, 1995), pp. 43-46. Quotations are from p. 43 and 44 respectively.

## LIBERALISM IN DISARRAY

1. Alonzo L. Hamby, *Beyond the New Deal: Harry S. Truman and American Liberalism* (New York: Columbia University Press, 1973), pp. 70-85, 123-34, 140-45, 205.

Alonzo L. Hamby, *Man of the People: A Life of Harry S. Truman* (New York: Oxford University Press, 1995), ch. 20.

Curtis MacDougall, *Gideon's Army* (New York: Marzani & Munsell, 1965), pp. 762-63.

Richard Neuberger, "Curtain Raiser for '48", *Nation*, 7 June 1947.

*Times*, 3,6 November 1946.

2. *P-I*, 3 November 1946. In August the Washington Pension Union led a march to Olympia, only to be told by Gov. Wallgren that he could not spend money not appropriated by the legislature. *P-I*, 14 August 1946.

*Times*, 6 November 1946.

Writing in the *Nation* of 7 June 1947 Richard Neuberger attributed DeLacy's disastrous loss for having "carried down the whole Democratic ticket". This was true only of the New Dealers or leftists.

3. Hamby, *Beyond the New Deal...*, chapter 6.
MacDougall, *Ibid.*, 102-27.
Harvey A. Levenstein, *Communism, Anticommunism, and the CIO* (Westport, Conn.: Greenwood Press, 1981), pp. 219-22.
Richard C. Berner, *Seattle, 1921-1940: From Boom to Bust* (Seattle: Charles Press, 1992), pp. 370-77.

4. Hamby, *Beyond the New Deal...*, p. 168: "The ADA's program was bringing it literally against its will, into identification with the administration". Also pp. 173-86, 196-98, 202-03.
David McCullough, *Truman* (New York: Simon and Schuster, 1992) pp. 562-65.
Hamby, *Man of the People...*, pp. 394-403.
MacDougall, *Ibid.*, chapter 7 for Wallace's European trip in spring 1947 and its significance in forming his foreign policy in relation to Truman's.

5. McCullough, *Ibid.*, pp. 551-53.
Hamby, *Beyond the New Deal...*, pp. 204-08.
Hamby, *Man of the People...*, 428-29.
Samuel Walker, *In Defense of American Liberties: A History of the ACLU* (New York: Oxford Univeristy Press, 1990), pp. 176-85.

6. Hamby, *Beond the New Deal...*, pp. 209-30.
Hamby, *Man of the People...*, pp. 446-49.
*P-I*, 13 December 1946.

7. Vern Countryman, *Un-American Activities in the State of Washington* (Ithaca: Cornell University Press, 1951), pp. 10-20.
Jane Sanders, *Cold War on Campus: Academic Freedom at the University of Washington* (Seattle: University of Washington Press, 1979), pp. 14-15.
Walker, *Ibid.*, pp. 180-85.
Berner, *Ibid.*, pp. 414-15.
Albert Acena, *The Washington Commonwealth Federation: Reform Politics and the Popular Front* (Unpublished Ph.D. Dissertation, 1975), pp. 275-80.
The purpose of the legislation revising Initiative 141, was to change old age assistance from a pension to a relief program. The lien clause transferred responsibility for supporting aged people from the state to heirs who were capable of supporting them. Need replaced age as qualification for state assistance. *Argus*, 15 March, 3 May 1947.

8. Countryman, *Ibid.* pp. 26-31.
Walker, *Ibid.*, pp. 180-81.
McCullough, *Ibid.*, pp.550-52.

Washington State Oral History Program, *Albert F. Canwell: An Oral History* (Olmpia: Secretary of state, 1997), pp 173-74. Hereafter referred to as *Canwell Oral History*

9. Countryman, *Ibid.*, pp. 17-18.
Sanders *Ibid.*, pp. 21-22.
William L. Dwyer, *The Goldmark Case: An American Libel Trial* (Seattle: University of Washington Press, 1984), pp. 33-34, 42-44.
Carey McWilliams, *Witch Hunt: the Revival Heresy* (Boston: Little, Brown, 1950) p. 141 for quotation.
*Canwell Oral History*, pp. 151-60.

10. Sanders, *Ibid*, pp. 23-24.
Dwyer, *Ibid.*, pp. 34-37.
Melvin Rader, *False Witness* (Seattle: University of Washington Press, 1969), pp 47,48.
Washington State Legislature, Joint Fact Finding Committee on Un-American Activities. *Second Report* (Olympia: State Printer, 1948), p. 1 Hereafter referred to as Canwell Committee, First or Second Report.
*Canwell Oral History*, pp. 195-96.

11. Canwell Committee, *First Report*, pp. 1-60. Note: Beginning with Budenz's testimony of all "expert" witnesses was from prepared notes. When Rader spoke from his own notes investigator Houston challenged the procedure and Canwell asked that he not use them.
Countryman, *Ibid.*, pp. 25-71 covers the first hearing in detail.
Rader, *Ibid.*, pp. 47,48, 68-72, 95-105.

12. Berner, *Ibid.*, p. 445.
Acena, *Ibid.*, pp. 360-61.
George W. Scott, *Arthur B. Langlie: Republican Governor in a Democratic Age.* (Unpublished Ph.D. Dissertation, University of Washington, 1971), pp. 118-20, 195-205.
Canwell Committee, *Ibid.* pp. 61-83.
*Canwell Oral History*, pp. 160-61. Ed Guthman replaced Ross Cunningham at this time. Cunningham professed not to know the reason for his replacement by Guthman whom he referred to as a "commie".

13. Canwell Committee, *Ibid.* pp. 61-76 for Sullivan; pp. 133-34 for Fletcher; p. 365 for Costigan; p. 427 for Armstrong; pp. 202-55 for Nat Honig, who at this time was on the payroll of Hearst's *Los Angeles Examiner*.

14. *P-I*, 1-4 March 1948.

15. *Times*, 2,6 March 1948. In the primaries Pomeroy raised $22,765 for his campaign, Devin $10,572.

16. *P-I*, 1-7 March 1948. By the new city charter police chiefs were to be appointed by mayor with council approval, but removal could be at mayor's discretion.

17. *Times*, 3,4 March 1948. City Council members were Mildred Powell, Frank Laube, Alfred Rochester, Robert Harlin, David Levine, and M.B. Mitchell. Fussell made only slight reference to prostitution and police protection. Portland was most "wide open", allowing both dog racing and nightime horse racing.

18. *Times*, 7,8 March 1948. Powell alleged she had only once before endorsed a mayoral candidate, Arthur Langlie.

19. *Times*, 9,10 March 1948.

20. John McCann, *Blood in the Water: A History of District Lodge 751* (Seattle: District Lodge 751, 1989), pp. 98-108.
  *New World* 20 May 1948 has a full page ad of Local 751's outlining the history of events leading to the strike. Allegedly, both the *Times* and *P-I* refused to run it. For the hesitancy of these two dailies to criticize Beck see William E. Ames and Roger A. Simpson, *Unionism or Hearst: The Seattle Post-Intelligencer Strike of 1936* (Seattle: Pacific Northwest Labor History Association, 1978), pp 150-52.
  *Aero Mechanic* 11,25 March, 1,8,22 April 1948.

21. *P-I*, 18,19 April 1948.
  *New World*, 22,29 April 1948.

22. *Aero Mechanic*, 6 May, 24 June 1948. In the latter issue is a section devoted to praise of the late Philip Johnson, Allen's predecessor. See also 6 May and 22 July issues.
  *Times*, 21 May 1948.
  *P-I*, 21,22 May 1948.
  *New World*, 6,20 May 1948.

23. Charles P. Larrowe, *Harry Bridges: The Rise and Fall of Radical Labor in the United States.* (New York: Lawrence Hill and Co., 1972), p. 293.
  Berner, *Ibid.*, 336-47.
  *New World*, 27 May, 17 June 1948.

24. *New World*, 8,15,22 July 1948.
  *Aero Mechanic*, The 3 June issue carried the headline: "Teamster Effort to Organize Scabs Is a Miserable Failure". Its 10 June issue notes the start of a petition campaign seeking President Truman's intervention, fully expecting a large sign up of businessmen, where Local 751 expected to tap into a reservoir of "anti-labor racketeering", which Beck seemed to epitomize among a large segment of the community. See also 8 July 1948 issue,...and that for 19 August which noted the withdrawal of four Retail Clerks Unions from "Teamster domination"..

25. McCann, *Ibid.*, pp. 114-39.
  *Aero Mechanic*, 24 June, 1,22,29 July, 5,19 August 1948 which noted "60,000 Lumber and Sawmill Workers" (AFL) pledged aid to 751 and demanded Beck's ouster as UW regent.

26. *Aero Mechanic*, 13,19 August, 16 September 1948.
   McCann, *Ibid.*, pp. 114-39.
   *Times*, 3 September 1948.
   Mrs. P. Favro to Congressman Hugh Mitchell, 29 March 1949. Mitchell promised to bring the matter to the attention of Air Force Secretary Symington. On 22 June 1949 Arthur C. Gerber urged Mitchell to press the NLRB for a "prompt election" because postponement "works to the decided advantage of the company-favored union". Mitchell replied he was working toward that end with 751's president Harold Gibson. Mitchell *Papers*, Acc. 927 Box 3-11.

27. McCann, *Ibid.*, pp. 150-53.

28. Larrowe, *Ibid.*, pp. 293-94.
   Howard Kimeldorf, *Reds or Rackets: The Making of Radical and Conservative Unions on the Waterfront* (Berkeley: University of California Press, 1988), pp. 148-49, 151.
   *P-I*, 2 September 1948.
   *Times*, 2,3 September 1948.

29. Larrowe, *Ibid.*, p. 294.
   *P-I*, 2,3-5 September 1948.
   *Times*, 3,4 September 1948.

30. *Times*, 7,10 September 1948.
   *New World*, 23,30 September, 14,28 October 1948.
   On 8 July 1949 Congressman Hugh B. Mitchell complained to Ralph Trigg, administrator of the Production and Marketing Administration that the loss to Tacoma during the strike emergency had never been regained by Seattle. He argued that Seattle's "rightful portion of government dry cargo" be restored. Objections to Mitchell's letter came from Tacoma's Mayor Fawcett, the Central Labor Council, and the International Longshoremens' Association. Mitchell *Papers*, Acc. 927, file 5-14.

31. *New World*, 28 October 1948 issue has full text of Murray's statement.
   Larrowe, *Ibid.*, Quotations are from p. 297.

32. Larrowe, *Ibid.*, pp. 297-99.
   *New World*, 11 November 1948.
   *Times*, 4 November 1948.
   A parallel with the WEA's conceding to finally negotiate once the election returned a Democrat to the presidency is to be found in Hearst's decision to seek an end to the 1936 *P-I* strike once FDR was re-elected. See Berner, *Ibid.*, pp. 368-69.

33. McWilliams, *Ibid.*, p. 146.

34. Sanders, *Ibid.*, pp. 19-22.
   McWilliams, *Ibid.*, pp. 148-49.
   Charles M. Gates, *The First Century at the University of Washington, 1861-1961* (Seattle: Uni-

versity of Washington Press, 1961), pp. 196-98.

Berner, *Ibid.*, pp. 283—85.

Ellen W. Schrecker, *No Ivory Tower: McCarthyism and the Universities* (New York: Oxford University Press, 1986), pp. 94-110.

*Canwell Oral History*, pp. 197-98.

35. Sanders, *Ibid.*, pp. 24-26.

36. *Times*, 20-22 July 1948.

37. Canwell Committee, *Second Report*, pp. 334-37.

Chief investigator William Houston was dismissed - given an "indefinite leave of absence" - by Canwell, and replaced by John Whipple. *New World*, 9 September 1948. The *New World*, 30 September 1948, reported that Mayor Devin had assigned former head of Seattle's "Red squad", Charles Neunser, to work full time for the Canwell Committee, while remaining on the police department's payroll.

*Canwell Oral History*, pp. 188-89. Canwell remained certain that Rader and Cohen were Communists.

38. Canwell Committee, *Ibid.*, p. 332.

39. Sanders, *Ibid.*, pp. 25-26.

Countryman, *Ibid.*, chapter VII.

*Times*, 21,22,27 October 1949 for the Guthman report pointing to the truth of Rader's account and to the falsity of Hewitt's testimony. New York Supreme Court Judge Aaron Levy had refused to extradite Hewitt for a perjury trial on the ground that it would be like sending him "to eventual slaughter". Levy added "I am wondering, genuinely wondering, what the civilization of that area [Washington] is." The *Times* had not yet declared an opinion on the Rader case, so Levy's refusal to extradite Hewitt, coupled with his intemperate remarks about the status of civilization out here, prompted the assignment of Guthman to the case. Besides vindicating Rader Guthman found that Canwell had not only prejudged Rader but he had ignored facts that contradicted his charges, and he had suppressed evidence that would disprove the charges against Rader. The latter related to the Lodge register which Canwell investigators had removed from the Lodge two days after Hewitt had testified. At the meeting with Rader and Allen on 20 October 1949 Canwell refused to cooperate in search of the files which he allegedly transferred to the Legislature's jurisdiction.

40. Lorraine McConaghy, "The Seattle *Times*'s Cold War Pulitzer Prize", *Pacific Northwest Quarterly* 89:1 (Winter 1997/98), pp. 21-32. Todd quotation is from p. 26.

41. Berner, *Ibid.*, pp. 256-61 has an account of the SRP's early career, and aspirations of Hughes and his ensuing rivalry with the Jameses.

42. Ronald Oakley West, *Left Out: The Seattle Repertory Playhouse, Audience Inscription and the Problem of Leftist Theatre During the Depression Era* (Unpublished Ph.D. Dissertation, University of Washington, 1993), pp. 159-66. Quotation is from p. 166.

Burton James to Sawyer Falk, president of the National Theatre Conference, 2,28 September 1948, and 3 February 1949. Seattle Repertory Playhouse, *Records* files 75-7,8,9. Manuscript Collection, UW Libraries.

*Times* and *P-I* 20-23 July 1948 cover the hearings.

*New World,* 22 July 1948.

See lengthy testimonies of Sarah Eldridge, Howard F. Smith, Isabel Costigan, Ward Warren, and George Hewitt, which appear in Canwell Committee, *Second Report.*

43. *Times* and *P-I* 3,4 November 1948.

44. *New World,* 11 November 1948.

Washington Secretary of State, *Abstract of Votes, 1948 General Election.* (Olympia: State Printer, 1948). The vote in King County on 172 was 93,815 For 129,706 Against. This contrasted sharply with voting in the more rural counties. Examples: Pierce 47,480 For 31,290 Against; Snohomish 24,546 For 15,998 Against; Whatcom 15,150 For 10,083 Against; Yakima 20,049 For 15,654 Against; Clark 17,810 For 9,456 Against; Grays Harbor 15,332 For 6,150 Against; Walla Walla 7,263 For 6,812 Against. What this seems to indicate is that the Canwell hearings on the Washington Pension Union turned King County voters against the WPU. King County was the operational base of the WPU, the source of its strength. Apparently the outlying counties were substantially less affected by the hearings. In Seattle, however, the local press was hostile to the WPU and supportive of the Canwell Committee. Their news coverage reflected this bias and seems to have affected voter opinion substantially. The final vote tally for the state was 420,751 For 352,642 Against.

See *Times,* for 18 January 1949 for Langlie's proposed budget, most elements of which were taxes to be passed on directly to consumers.

45. Sanders, *Ibid.*, pp. 23-28, 43-46. Quotation is from p. 43.

Countryman, *Ibid.*, pp. 188-94.

Gates, *Ibid.*, pp. 198-99.

46. Countryman, *Ibid.*, pp. 193-203.

Sanders, *Ibid.*, pp. 48-49. On p. 86 Sanders quoted from a letter, 11 February 1949, that Allen addressed to Columbia University provost A.C. Jacobs regarding a prospective faculty exchange between Rader and Herbert Schneider, " Our friend here [Rader] is going to be in trouble before long, trouble of his own making." As this was nine months before Rader was finally vindicated there persisted that condescending tone of Allen's with respect to faculty liberals, particularly those who collaborated with organizations identified as front organizations by federal authorities.

See also correspondence between Rader and Dean Guthrie in which Guthrie rejected Rader's request that the university demand that Canwell submit his evidence to the university, including the Lodge register. Guthrie contended the UW was not an "interested party" in a "legal sense". Rader was advised to pursue the matter himself. Rader to Guthrie 19 August 1949, and Guthrie to Rader 13 September 1949. UW President *Records,* Acc. 70-29 file 5-7.

Gates, *Ibid.*, 199-203, 210-11. Quotation is from p.199.

47. Countryman, *Ibid.*, pp. 199-204 for Kornfeder questioning; p. 241.

Gates, *Ibid.*, pp. 202-03.

Sanders, *Ibid.*, pp.44-46, and p. 49 for Kornfeder and the Hilen quotation.

48. Countryman, *Ibid.*, pp. 244-63, 356-57, 372-73, 388-90. Quotation is from p. 250.
Gates, *Ibid.*, 205-08.
Sanders, *Ibid.*, p. 54.

49. Sanders, *Ibid.*, pp. 51-54.
Countryman, *Ibid.*, pp. 186-90.

50. Allen's Report of 17 January 1949 is in UW President. *Records*. Acc. 71-34, box 107.
Gates, *Ibid.*, pp. 207-08.

51. The *P-I*'s front page column head of 20 January 1949 read: "Regents To Act On Teachers In Red Quiz"...[The legislature] "awaits the outcome". Its headline of the 23rd ran: "Regents Oust 3 U. Teachers in Red Probe". Photographs of the three professors accompanied the article, which continued alone on page 2, followed on page 12 with photographs. Niendorff reminded readers that this was the culmination of a "Full decade" beginning with President Sieg, "who sought justification for ousting Communists". And the Regents credited the Canwell Committee for "unflagging digging" to get justifying evidence.

52. Sanders, *Ibid.*, chapter IV.
Countryman, *Ibid.*, pp. 264-85.

53. Schrecker, *Ibid.*, pp. 94-112.

54. Schrecker, *Ibid.*, pp. 106-07, 94.
Sanders, *Ibid.*, pp. 148-49.

55. Countryman, *Ibid.*, p. 391.

56. Robert MacIver, *Academic Freedom in Our Time* (New York: Columbia University Press, 1955), p. 120. MacIver was director of the American Academic Freedom Project of Columbia University. The first volume published in this project was *The Development of Academic Freedom in the United States* by Richard Hofstadter and Walter Metzger.

## 1950: End of an Era

1. *Times*, 8-11 November 1950.
*Abstract of Votes for 1950 General Election*. (Olympia: State Printer, 1950).

2. Albert Acena, *The Washington Commonwealth Federation...*, pp. 419-23 on Initiative 151.
*Times*, 1,8,10, November 1950. Roderick Olzendam, Director of Social Security, outlined some of the "adjustments" to be made by passage of 178. He planned to review the eligibility of 141,967 persons on the rolls. Those living on a public transit line, who owned an automobile, would be eliminated; also those who owned a house above a mininmum value would be eliminated. The

*Times*'s Ross Cunningham defended 178 (16 November), expressing the hope that recommendations of the Seattle-King County Health and Welfare Council would be appended to it. The Council distinguished between need among old age pensioners and those who could continue supporting themselves. Would there be a backlash; if so, who would lead it?
*Abstract of Votes...*

3. PSP&L *Annual Report for 1947*.
Note to "Hugh" of 3 May 1949 in Hugh Mitchell *Papers*, Acc. 281-2, file 4-12. UW Libraries Manuscript Collection.
On the conflict between Bone and Ross see Berner, *Seattle, 1921-1940*...pp. 429-30.
For previous attempts to put the state into the electric business see Berner, *Seattle, 1900-1920*...pp. 203-04. Also, Berner, *Seattle, 1921-1940*...p. 40.

4. William F. Devin *Papers*, PSP&L negotiations file, in box 10.

5. *Times*, 1,8,10,17-21 November, 6 December 1950.
PSP&L *Records*, Acc. 2250, box 95 contains substantially complete records of the transaction.
PSP&L, *Annual Report, 1950* for "final" vote count.
In the congressional races in the Seattle district, Hugh Mitchell defeated Mrs. F.F. (Mildred) Powell Seattle's leading "vote getter" by about 6,000 votes, losing in the city by a slight margin, but winning in Kitsap County, where there was a concentration of unionized shipyard workers. Henry Jackson overwhelmed his opponent 73,296 to 45,537.
Senator Magnuson defeated his challenger, Walter Williams 397,718 to 342,464 votes. *Abstract of Votes...*

## Postscript

1. Cf. Keith C. Petersen, *River of Life Channel of Death: Fish and Dams on the Lower Snake* (Confluence Press, Lewiston. ID, 1995) pp. 15-19, 129-31, 140-46, 167-69, 180-84. Lisa Mighetto and Wesley J. Ebel, *Saving the Salmon: A History of the U.S. Corp of Engineers' Efforts to Protect Anadromous Fish on the Columbia and Snake Rivers* (Prepared for the Corps, published by Historical Research Associates, Seattle, 1994) pp. 65, 71, 85, 119, 127. Mary E. Reed *A History of the North Pacific Division* (U.S. Army Corps of Engineers North Pacific Divsion, 1991) pp. 116-17 for overuling by the Corps in 1947 of a proposed moratorium on dam construction until a study of the potential affect on the salmon was completed. The Corps objected that the moratorium would interfere with its projected dam construction program. See also Mighetto and Ebel, p. 71. and Roy W. Scheufele *History of the Columbia Basin Inter-Agency Committee* (Prepared for the Pacific Northwest River Basins Commission, successor to the CBIAC, [1970]), pp. 22-23; Scheufele of the Corps served as executive secretary for most of the life of this administratively powerless agency composed of volunteers representing mainly a variety of federal and state agencies; he occasionally referred to salmon issues as the Corps' "nemesis" as on pp. 27, 107, suggesting the bias of the Corps. For the effect of postage stamp rates on north central Washington and disap-

pointment among the dam's chief promoters see Robert E. Ficken, *Rufus Woods...*, pp. 176, 192-93, 212; Woods and his allies had wanted to industrialize the area with cheap rates established at "its" dam site. For the most thorough analysis of Grand Coulee in relation to the irrigation project see Paul C. Pitzer, *Grand Coulee...*, chapter 18 and pp. 357-70 and 224-25 on the 308 report. For a challenging overview see Richard White, *The Organic Machine: Remaking the Columbia River* (Hill and Wang, New York, 1995) chapter 4, "Salmon". On the competition between the Corps and Bureau cf. Keith Petersen and Mary Reed, Controversy, *Conflict and Compromise: A History of the Lower Snake River Development* (U.S. Army Corps of Engineers, Walla Walla District, [1990?]), p. 81 and Mary Reed, Ibid., p. 117. For a blistering account of their often destructive rivalry see Marc Reisner, *Cadillac Desert: The American West and its Disappearing Water* (Penguin Books, New York, 1993), chapter 6, "Rivals in Crime". Signifying the emerging strength of the environmental movement was the signing of a treaty between City Light and British Columbia in December 1983 that prevented the City of Seattle from raising Ross Dam, whose Skagit River reservoir stretched into to B.C. For a convenient summary of the dispute see *The Wild Cascades* (Published by the North Cascades Conservation Council, Fall 1985, Spring 1986). The NCCC was the point organization leading toward establishment of the North Cascades National Park in 1968 through which runs the Skagit. When Ross was fired as City Light superintendent in 1931 FDR, then New York's governor, hired Ross as an advisor on the St. Lawrence project; as president FDR appointed Ross to the Securities and Exchange Commission, then to head the BPA.

For the most recent and succinct view of federal hydropower and the Columbia River Basin project, see Paul Dorpat's and Genevieve McCoy's *Building Washington: A History of Washington State Public Works* (Seattle: Tartu Publications, 1998) pp. 239-251 on the Columbia Basin Project and pp. 293-309 on federal hydropower.

SPECIAL NOTE: The first two volumes of this history traced the origins of the regional conservation movement which climaxed with the successful legislative struggle establishing the Olympic National Park (ONP). Conservation policy matters were substantially ignored while attention focused on winning the war. Nevertheless the fate of the ONP was jeopardized by the unrelenting pressure of the lumber industry to exclude the old growth timber in the Bogachiel, Hoh, and Queets river corridors from the ONP boundary. Former US Forest Service director William Greeley, in his capacity as director of the West Coast Lumbermens' Association, led the industry strategy to log this timber. His lobbying efforts won over ONP superintendent Preston Macy and the National Park Service leadership itself to sacrifice these forested areas. Only the determined resistance of Interior Secretary Harold Ickes and the Emergency Conservation Committee restrained what logging was permitted. Locally these unrelenting attacks on the ONP's integrity led to formation in 1947 of the Olympic Park Associates by Irving Clark, Sr. to protect the park. Clark had been the primary local contact of the ECC The fullest account of these events is found in Carsten Lien, *Olympic Battleground: The Power Politics of Timber Preservation* (San Francisco, Sierra Club Books, 1991).

2. On job discrimination see William A. Little, "Community Organization and Leadership: A Case Study of Minority Workers in Seattle" (Unpublished Ph.D. dissertation, University of Washington, 1976). On housing discrimination see Howard A. Droker "The Civic Unity Committee and the Civil Rights Movement, 1944-1964" (Unpublished Ph.D. dissertation, University of Washington, 1974). On school desegregation see Doris H. Pieroth, "Desegregating the Public

Schools: Seattle, Washington, 1954-1968" (Unpublished Ph.D. dissertation, University of Washington, 1979). For an overview see Quintard Taylor, *The Forging of a Black Community*...chapters 6 and 7.

3. On containerized cargo and its revolutionary impact on labor management relations in the Pacific Coast maritime industry see *Men and Machines: A Story About Longshoreing on the West Coast Waterfront* (ILWU and the Pacific Maritime Association, San Francisco, [1961]); on the Mechanization and Modernization Agreement that recognized their shared interest in accomodating to handling such cargo. An early example in the early postwar period of unionization leading to social reform is the ILWU's organization of Hawaiian agricultural workers in the course of organizing the Hawaiian longshoremen out of which emerged a huge umbrella union covering all of them. See *The ILWU Story: Three Decades of Militant Unionism* (ILWU, San Francisco, 1963), pp. 30-44; for Mechanization Agreement see pp. 62-66. Note: the ILWU was expelled from the CIO in 1950, along with other left-wing unions.

4. Walker, *Ibid.*, pp. 139-42 on the split within the ACLU.

As a state senator Farquharson had pushed through a bill in 1937 abolishing the 1919 anti-syndicalism act. She also had been instrumental in freeing Ray Becker the last of the "Centralia massacre" prisoners.

5. Jane Sanders, "The University of Washington and the Controversy Over J. Robert Oppenheimer" *PNQ*, 70:1 (January 1979), pp. 8-19. Sanders, *Cold War on Campus*...pp. 109-25 and chapter VI, "The Oppenheimer Controversy".

# INDEX

## Symbols

100th Battalion 127
442nd Regimental Combat Team 127, 129
48 hour work week 58

## A

ABC list 21, 22
Aburano, Sharon 35
*Academic Freedom in Our Time* 241
Acena, Albert 111
ACLU. *See* American Civil Liberties Union (ACLU)
Adams, Joseph P. 113
*Aero Mechanic* 55, 78–79, 90, 92, 93, 220
Aero Mechanics Union, Local 751 50–55, 78, 92, 96, 99, 110, 113, 176, 199, 215–222, 252
"Aero Woman's Page" 77, 78
Aeronautical and Warehousemen's Union 220
Affirmative action 252
African American
 teachers 164
African American soldiers
 recreation for 136–139
African American women 55
African Americans 10, 49, 70, 118–122, 206. *See also* Employment of African Americans
 at Boeing 50-51, 54, 222
 demographic statistics 251
After-school programs 74
Air raid wardens 27, 86
Aircraft decentralization issue 197–198
Aircraft industry 248
*Aircraft Organizer* 53
Aircraft production 46
Akutsu, Jim 25
Alaska shipping 59–60
Alaska Steamship Company 193
Alien Property Custodian 149

Alien Registration Act 10
Allen, Edmund "Eddie" 57
Allen, Edward W. 33
Allen, Raymond B. 132, 157, 161, 227, 240
Allen, William 198, 198, 215, 218, 220, 221
Allis-Chalmers 7
Alpine Dairy 35
Aluminum Company of America (ALCOA) 80, 249
Aluminum industry 9, 249
Aluminum production 80
American Asociation of Social Workers 34
American Association of University Professors 240–241
American Civil Liberties Union (ACLU) 40, 123, 253
American College of Surgeons 155
American Council on Race Relations 122
American Federation of Labor (AFL) 4–6, 19, 131, 193, 252
American Friends Service Committee 24, 33, 123, 253
American Intelligence Service 211
American Legion 29, 39, 126, 127, 161
American Medical Association 155, 157, 160
American Plan 4
American Power and Light Corporation 66
Americans for Democratic Action 204
Anderson, Guy 147
Anderson, Karen 49, 72, 74, 76, 77, 79, 175–176
Anderson, Marian 140
Andrews, Emery 128
Andrews, Frank 55
Annual Institute on Race Relations 132
Anti-Alien Land Law (state) 23
Anti-Defamation League 123
Apartment Operators Association 93
Apel, Gertrude 125, 128
Arai, Clarence 23, 25, 27
Archipenko 148
Army Transport Service. *See* US Army: Transport Service

311

## Index

Arnold, Henry "Hap"  55
"arsenal of democracy"  80
Art Week  148
Associated Shipbuilders  46, 49, 59
Associated Women Students, UW  140, 145
Association of Medical Colleges  160
Athletic leagues  137
Atkinson, Roy  108, 123
Auburn, Washington  138
Austin Company  60
Automobile production  80–81, 183
Avalon (dance hall)  138
*Aviation Week*  220

### B

B-17 ("Flying Fortress") planes  55–57, 79
B-29 ("Super Fortress") planes  55–57
Bader, Barney  51
Bailey-Gatzert Elementary school  19
Bainbridge Island Japanese  37–39
Baldwin, Roger  40
Barnett, Arthur
    40, 113, 123, 127, 133, 253
Bartok, Bela  146
Bassett, Samuel  220
Bayley, Frank Jr.  133
Bayne, Stephen  217
Beal, Maude  228, 229
Beal, Walter  67
Beall, Wellwood  57
Beck, Dave
    5, 6, 12, 14, 54, 63, 107, 109, 124, 203, 213, 215, 218, 219, 228
Beecham, Sir Thomas  141
Bendetsen, Karl R.  29, 30, 36, 39
Benson, Elmer  217
Bert Lindgren Band  138
Bienz, Thomas  210, 228, 236
Bird [Gundlach], Bonnie  146
Black and Tan (club)  139
Black Ball ferries  213
Black, Lloyd  42
Black market
    meats  87
Black Musicians Union, Local 493  139
"blueprint for victory"  82
Bobrow, Norm  139
Boeing  8, 10, 46, 49, 74, 121, 153

African American workers  50–55
B-47 contract  200
B-52 contract  200
collaboration with Teamsters Union  218–219
Communist issue  51–55
employing women  78
government contract cancellations  176
labor recruitment  103–104
labor turnover  102
postwar  174, 196-197
Save Boeing Committee  199
wage scales  99–104
wages  58–59
Boeing Strike of 1948  218-222
Boettiger, Anna Roosevelt  110, 125
Boettiger, John  110
Boilermakers Union, Local 104
    49, 51, 59, 76, 78, 173, 176
Bomber, Harry  52
Bone, Homer T.  110, 245
Bonneville Power Administration. *See* US Bonneville Power Administration
Bothell Way Pavilion  138
Bowles, Chester  181, 202
BPA. *See* US Bonneville Power Administration
Bremerton  46
Bremerton Navy Yard  46
Brewster, Frank  14
Bricken, Carl  141–143
Brickey, W.L.  66
Bridges, Harry
    5, 7, 10, 51, 53, 194, 224
    as issue  222–226
    Harry Bridges Defense Committee  231
Brinkley, Alan  252
Broadway High  19
Broadway High School  25, 165
Brown, Harvey  52, 217
Brown, Prentiss  94
Budapest String Quartet  140
Buddhist temple  28, 29
Budenz, Louis F.  212
Building construction  184
    lumber shortage, postwar  189
Building Service Employees Union, Local 6  110, 212

Building Services Employees' International Union, 131, 208
Bullitt, Dorothy (Mrs. A. Scott) 85, 123, 146
Bullitt, Scott 63
Burke, Kenneth 255
Bush Hotel 139
Business failures 175
Butterworth, Joseph 228, 237
Byrnes, James F. 84, 93, 179, 202

## C

Cage, John 146
Cain, Harry P. 32, 111, 204
Callahan, Harlan 125
Callahan, Kenneth 147
Callahan, Margaret 148
Camp Harmony 23
Canwell, Albert F. 208, 235
Canwell Committee 219, 220, 235
  investigation of Seattle Repertory Playhouse 233
Canwell Committee Hearings
  on University of Washington 227-234
  on Washington Pension Union 208-212
Canyon Creek Lodge 232
Carpooling. *See* Ride sharing
Carroll, Charles 246
Carroll, John 108, 109
Carstensen, Henry P. 67, 88
Carstensen, Vernon 60
Catholic Charities 35
*Catholic Northwest Progress* 72, 73
Caughlan, John 133, 212, 228
Central School 25
Chapple, Stanley 143, 145
Child care 72–75, 73–74
Children's Orthopedic Hospital 157
Chinatown 18, 21, 25
Chittenden, Hiram Jr. 25
Christian Friends for Racial Equality 121, 123, 127
Church Council of Seattle
  15, 34, 40, 74, 113, 123, 125, 164, 253
  Civic Rights Committee 213
  Joint Conference on the Future of Japanese Church 127
  Nisei Steering Committee 127
Church-State issue 164
CIO. *See* Congress of Industrial Organizations (CIO)
City charter, 1946 114
City elections, 1942 14–16
City elections, 1944 107–112
City elections, 1946 112–114
City elections, 1948 213
Civic Auditorium 144
Civic Housing Association 92, 179
Civic Unity Committee. *See* Seattle Civic Unity Committee (CUC)
Civic Unity Committee Movement 120
Civil liberties 253
Civil Service Commission 31
Civilian War Commission 8, 68–71, 70, 85, 114, 151
  Day Care Committee 71
  Salvage Committee 104
  Seattle Homes Registration Bureau 92
Clark, Tom 206
Clifford, Clark 205
Cline, Walter 37
Closed shop 55, 223
co-option of CIO leadership 4
Coal strike 193
Cochrane, Edward L. 59
Coffee, John 102, 111, 204
Cohen, Joseph 228, 229–234
Cold War 10, 254, 255
Cole, Merwin 208
Colemen, Aaron 229
Coley, Ward 208
Collective bargaining
  resumption postwar 182
Colman, Clarence 110
Colman Club 136
Colman, Kenneth B. 61
Colman Pool 121
Columbia River Basin Project 45, 250
Columbia River salmon fishery 249
Columbia Valley Authority 245
Columbus Hospital 131
Commission on Wartime Relocation and Internment of. *See* US Commission on Wartime Relocation and Internment
Communist issue in CIO 204

## 314    Index

Communist Party and communists
    6, 10, 40, 52, 210–212
  CP outlawed, 1949  254
  hardliners in Party  230
  Issues at Boeing  51–55
  Non-Communist affidavits  223
  party membership at issue  236–240
company unions  4
Comparative wage scales  57–59
Concentration camps  29
Congo Club  139
Congress of Industrial Organizations (CIO)
    4-7, 10, 131, 215, 251, 253
  bureaucratization of CIO  251
  Communist issue  204–205
  Communist purge  52
  intervention in 1948 maritime strike  226
  Political Action Committee  108, 109, 187
Connelly, Edward  67
Conscientious Objectors Group  39
Construction industry
  postwar  174
"Consumer liberalism"  253
Consumer price index  174
Containerized cargo  253
Cooper, Carl  11, 108
Cooper, Felix  123
Cornish, Nellie  146
Cornish School (College of the Arts)  146–147
Cost of living  98, 100
  in 1946  192
Cost-plus contracts  49
Costigan, Howard
    109, 110, 203, 211, 212
Cotton, Gary  52
Coughlin, Paul  212
Council of Churches. *See* Church Council of Seattle
Council of Social Agencies  120
countervailing power  5
Countryman, Vern  209, 241
Coupon rationing  84
Cowley, Malcom  161
Craft unions  4
Crescent (dance hall)  138
CUC. *See* Seattle Civic Unity Committee (CUC)

Cumming, William  148
Cunningham, Ross  22, 161, 227, 236

### D

*Daily Worker*  211
Daniels, Roger  29
Daughters of the American Revolution  161
Davis, F. Benjamin  123, 133
Day care centers  71, 163
Day Care Committee  71
Day nurseries  73–74
de Barros, Paul  138
Decontrol of prices, postwar  188
DeGrief, Roy  131
DeLacy, Hugh
    12, 15, 109, 110, 111, 202–204, 212
Democratic Party  63, 109, 114
Democratic party  11
Demographic changes  250
  Chinese population  18
  Japanese population  18
Dennett, Eugene  7, 52
Department store sales  46
Devin, William F.
    9, 11, 14, 15, 61, 62, 103, 107, 112, 114, 125, 126, 127, 151, 172, 188, 213–214, 218, 245, 251
  racial issues  120, 122–123
Dewey, Thomas E.  219, 226
DeWitt, John L.  29, 36
Dewitty, Thelma  131, 164
Dick Parker's  138
Dies, Martin  108
Discrimination
  African American soldiers  122
  against African Americans  130–132
  against Nisei, 1945-46  127–130
  by hospitals  131
  in public recreation facilities  136–139
  in UW Medical School  156–157
Discrimination of the job  77–79
Dobbins, William  208
Dormitories  70
Douglas Aircraft  55
Douglas, William O.  206
Dreamland (dance hall)  138
Droker, Howard  120, 122, 133

Drumheller, Joseph  228
Dunbar, Grant  125
Duncan, James  164
Duncan, Todd  140

# E

"E" for Efficiency Awards  60
Eastman, George  214
Eastside Journal  58
Eby, Harold  229, 239
Economic Stabilization Office  180
Economy
   Wartime  44-106
   Postwar planning  171–174
Edison Technical School  50, 78, 165
Education. *See also* Seattle Public Schools
   evening school enrollment  164
   public funding  153
   University of Washington  153–158
Eisenhower, Dwight  206, 236
Eisenhower, Milton S.  37, 42
Elections. *See also* City elections
   general, 1944  109–112
   general, 1948  234–235
Electric energy consumption  174
Elementary schools  166
Elks Club  139
Ellington, Duke  138
Elliott, Henry Jr.  91
Elshin, Jacob  146
Emergency Defense Council of JACL  23, 27, 28, 29
Emergency housing committee  187, 189
Emergency Price Control Act  83
Emergency Price Control Bill  81, 82
Employment of African Americans  8, 48, 49, 50–55, 119, 130–131, 175–177
Employment of service veterans  175–177
Employment of women  8, 10, 47–48, 48–50, 60, 68–79, 175–177
   recruitment of  76–77
Endangered Species Act  251
Energy production
   top priority of Columbia dams  249
Engle, Nathanael  173, 175
Epstein, Jesse  120–122

Ernst, Charles F.  211
Ethel, Garland  228, 238
European Recovery Plan  205
Evacuation of Japanese  8–9, 15, 18–21, 253. *See also* Executive Order 9066 (Japanese Evacuation)
   Japanese farms  36–39
   newspaper coverage  27–30
   panic selling  35–36
Evening school enrollment.  164
Eviction rate  184
Excess profits tax  182
"Exclusion orders"  37
Executive Order 8802 (FEPC). *See* Fair Employment Practices Act (FEPC)
Executive Order 9066 (Japanese Evacuation)  29–30, 253
Executive Order 9835 (Loyalty/Security)  208

# F

Faculty rights to free speech and association  227
Fair Employment Practices Act (FEPC)  119, 130
Fair Rents Committee  85, 186
Fairless, Benjamin  192
*False Witness*  232
Family Life  74, 75
Family Life courses  163
Family Society of Seattle  33
*Far Eastern Review*  27
Farquharson, Burt  39
Farquharson, Mary  33, 40, 113, 253
FBI. *See* US Federal Bureau of Investigation (FBI)
Federal Arts Project  148
Federal Bureau of Investigation. *See* US Federal Bureau of Investigation (FBI)
Federal Housing Authority  188, 190
Federal Works Agency  73, 74
Fellowship of Reconciliation  39
Ferries  45, 62
"Fifth column"  30, 35, 42
Finch, Clement  154
Firlands Sanitarium  125, 157
First Avenue Cantonment  140
Fitz, Norman  235
Fleming, Samuel  31, 164

# Index

Fletcher, Frank  59
Fletcher, Jess  208, 212
Fluent, Russell  111
"Flying Fortress".  *See* B-17 ("Flying Fortress") planes
Flynn, Leo  214
Foisie, Frank  193, 222
Ford, Leland  29
Ford Motor Company  180
Forschmiedt, Rachmiel  164
Fort Missoula  21, 22, 25, 29
"Four Freedoms"  119
France, fall of  81
Francescotti, Zino  140
Francis, Richard  7, 52, 53
Frank, Robert  59
Frankensteen, Richard  53
Franklin High School  19, 23
Frederick and Nelsons  25
Free speech  227
Freedom of Information Act  29, 253
Freeman, Miller  34, 39
Frozen food storage lockers  88
Fuller, Richard E.  149
Fussell, Ed  14, 214

## G

G.I. Bill of Rights  155, 183
Galbraith, John K.  5
Gandy, Joseph E.  181
Garfield High School  26, 165
Gasoline rationing  83, 84, 89, 180
Gates, Charles M.  236
Gaylord Jones jazz band  139
General Electric  4
General Maximum Price Regulation (GMPR)  83, 179
General Motors  4
Georgetown area  95
Gibson, Harold  92
Goldmark, John, libel trial  210
Goodyear  4
Gottstein, Joe  12
Government contracting for aircraft  55–57
Government contracts
 role  46
Grand Coulee Dam  249
Grange, State  64–65
Granger, Lester  122

Graves, Morris  147
Great Depression  45, 76, 80, 171
*Great Northern Daily*  21
Great Northern Railway  18, 24
Greenwood, George  122, 131–132
Griffin, Eldon  22
Griffin, Tracy  237
Grocery stores  61
Groff, Sam  136
Group Health Cooperative  158
"Guaranteed annual wage"  252
Gullion, Allen  30
Gundlach, Ralph  228, 237
Guthman, Edwin  232

## H

Hall, David  155
Hampton, Lionel  138
Hanford project  9, 249
Harborview Hospital  121, 157, 159, 160
Harding, A.E.  53
Hardy, A.F.  59
Harlan, Kenneth  245
Harley, Clinton  160
Harlin, Robert  110
Harper, Paul C.  141
Harris, George B.  219
Harris, Helen  121
Harrison, Gregory  222
Harsch, Alfred E.  86, 92
Hart, Dean  131, 133
Hayes, Roland  121, 140
Health care  244
Heggen, Bert  245
Heilman, Robert  161
Henderson, Leon  81, 92, 94, 180
Henry, Ed  212, 237
Hewitt, George  210, 231
High Point housing project  70
High schools  19
Hill, Matthew  67
Hillman, Sidney  7, 52, 107, 110
Hirabayashi, Gordon  39, 40–42, 253
Hiring hall issue  224
Hockett, A.J.  155
Hodson, James  133
Hoffman, Eugene  64, 245
Hoffman, J.S.  87
Holly Park housing project  70

"Hollywood Ten" 206
Homemaking 68–71
Hook, Sidney 240
Hoover, J. Edgar 29, 206
Hopkins, William 161
Hori, Fukashi 125
Horowitz, Vladimir 140
Horr, Ralph 12
Hosokawa, Bill 19, 26, 33
Hosokawa, Robert 37
Hospital affiliation agreements 157
Hostels for Nikkei, 1945-46 128
Housing 46, 68–71, 94–95, 188
   emergency housing committees 188
   for African Americans 120, 190–191
   for veterans 190–191
   open housing 191
Housing projects 68–71
Houston, William 211, 229–231
Hughbanks, C.F. 89
Hughes, Glenn 139, 233–234
Hurley, George 204
Huson, Homer 211
Hysteria, wartime 22–28, 30

## I

Ichihara, Kaoru 125
Ickes, Harold 202
ILWU. *See* International Longshoremen's and Warehousmen's Union
Immigration 48
Independent Citizens Committee of the Arts and Sciences 202
Industrial Union of Maritime and Shipbuilding Workers 51
Industrial unionism 55–57
Industrial unions 4
Industrialization of the West Coast 248
Inflation 7, 82, 83–84
   postwar 165–166, 181–186
   wartime 179–180
Initiative 141 (state) 211, 235, 244
Initiative 151 (state) 244
Initiative 157 (state) 110
Initiative 166 (state) 66
Initiative 172 (state) 159, 160, 234, 235
Initiative 176 (state) 244
Initiative 178 (state) 160

Inlandboatmen's Union 7
INS. *See* US Immigration and Naturalization Service (INS)
Institute of Industrial Relations 161
Institute of Labor Economics 161
International Association of Machinists 50–55, 217
International Association of Machinists, Local 79 192
International League for Peace and Freedom 121
International Longshoremen's and Warehousemen's Union 5, 10, 51, 76, 193, 219, 222–226, 252
International Longshoremen's Association (ILA) 5, 51
International Machinists Union 52
International Typographical Union, Local 202 194
International Woodworkers of America 194, 217
Irons, Peter 29
Isaacs, Walter 148
Isaacson, Henry 123
Issei 9, 19, 21, 23–25, 27, 29
Ito, Kenji 28, 34, 36, 37
Itoi family 31–32
Itoi, Henry 26
Itoi, Kazuko 26. *See also* Sone, Monica

## J

Jackson, Henry 194, 235, 245
Jackson Street 138
Jacobs, Melville 228, 229, 238
James, Burton 233
James, Florence Bean 107, 228, 233
Japanese American Citizens League (JACL) 19, 23, 30, 39
   Emergency Defense Committee. *See* Emergency Defense Council of JACL
*Japanese American Courier* 21, 23, 27, 33
Japanese Association of North America 21
Japanese Chamber of Commerce 19, 22
Japanese Consulate 27
Japanese Exclusion League 126

318  Index

Japanese Hotel Owners Association 19
Japanese Language School 19, 22
Japantown 18
Jazz 139
Jefferson Park Recreation Center 137
Jensen, Harold V. 34
Johnson, Lyndon 254
Johnson, Marita 131, 164
Johnson, Philip 103
Joint Anti-Fascist Refugee Committee 231
Jones, Homer 203
Jones, Jesse 65
Jones, Robert 62
Journalism 22–23, 27, 233
Junior high schools 166
Junior Red Cross 74

**K**

Kaiser Shipyards 45
Kashino, Shiro 129
Kay, Lew G. 123
Kazama, Sally 128
Kechley, Gerald 145
Kent, Washington 125, 138
Kerr, Clark 45
Kibei 21
Kimsey, Herbert D. 13
King County Hospital System. 157
  *See also* Harborview Hospital
King County Medical Society 154, 158
King County War Chest 137
KING Radio 218
Kirkendall, Richard 197
Kirtley, W.B. 12
Kiwanis Club 34
Knudsen, William 7, 81
Korean War 200, 248
Korimatsu, Fred 253
KRSC radio 96
Krug, Julius 180
Kruger, Karl 141
Kyle, Henry 212

**L**

Labor Consumers' League 96, 179, 222
Labor force recruitment 8, 45–46, 47–48, 103–104

Labor turnover 55, 58, 102
Labor's Non-Partisan League (LNPL) 6
Ladies Musical Club 139–140, 144–145
Lake Union Dry Dock 59
Lake Washington Shipyard 46, 58
Langlie, Arthur B.
  11, 31, 32, 64, 110, 111, 113, 126, 134, 156, 199, 211, 234, 245, 254
Lanham Act 73, 94
Lapham, Roger 5
Larrowe, Charles 223
Laube, Frank 15
Laucks, I.F. 60
League of Women Voters 164
Left-wing purges in CIO 251
Lehmann, Hans 141
Lend-Lease Act 81
Levine, David 13, 15, 74
Lewis, John L. 4, 6, 52, 192
Liberalism. *See also* Rights-based liberalism and consumer liberalism
  in Aero Mechanics union 222
  liberals denigrated by Raymond Allen 235–237
Lichtenstein, Nelson 6, 8
Lindeman, Charles 111
Linden, Eugene 142
Lindgren, Bert 138
Lippman, Walter 30
Litchman, Mark 212
Little Steel companies 6
Little Steel Formula 98, 100, 181, 192
Longacres racetrack 63, 91
Lotchin, Roger 197
Lovejoy, Arthur 241
Lumber production 174
Lumber shortage, postwar 189
Lumber strike, 1945 193
Lundin, Alfred 11
Lundquist, Hugo 51

**M**

MacFarlane, Robert 89, 123
MacGowan, Howard 11, 86
Machinists' Union, Local 79 110, 176
MacIver, Robert 241
Mack, Russell 236
Magnuson, Warren G. 11, 14, 46, 47, 59, 62, 87, 89, 90, 92, 93, 110–

112, 173, 181, 199, 204
  opposition to Japanese return
  124, 126
Mallery, James A. 67
Manufacturers' Association of Washington 86
Manufacturing employees 46
Manzanar 30, 37
March on Washington Movement 119
Marine Cooks and Stewards Union 219, 223
Marine Engineers Beneficial Association 219, 224
Maritime strike, 1945 193
Maritime strike, 1948 222–226
  CIO intervention 226
  effect of Truman's re-election 226
Married teachers ban 164
Marshall, George C. 57, 205
Marshall Plan 205
Marshall, Robert 131
Martin, A.E. 123
Martin, Clarence 5
Martin, Suzanne 141
Maryknoll Catholics 129
Master Builders Association 186
Masuda, Thomas 26, 28, 34, 36
Matheny, David 155
Matsushita, Iwao 21, 128
Matthews, Mark 25
Maverick, Maury 62
McArthur, Douglas 127
McBride, Philip 219
McCaffrey, Frank 113
McClure, Worth 31, 164
McConaghy, Lorraine 59, 233
McDonald, D.K. 33
McGrath, Russell 233
McLaughlin, Frank 65, 244
McNutt, Paul 58, 100
McWilliams, Carey 229, 236, 239
Meharry University 156
Melton, George 66
Metropolitan Theatre 139, 144
"metropolitan-military complex" 196
Meyers, Victor A. 113
Michener, Lewis 53
Military contracts 45
Military labor battalions 7
Military production 81
Military-industrial complex 175

Military-metropolitan-industrial complex 3
Millard, William J. 67
Miller, Irene 132
Millikin, Earl 11-12, 13, 14, 15, 27, 32, 47, 54, 86, 91, 107, 110, 121, 215, 251
Mimbu, William 29
Minidoka 22
Minidoka Reclamation Project 25, 39, 40
Mitchell, Hugh B. 186, 197, 203, 235, 245
Mitchell, Mike 15, 186
Mitsui and Company 21
Miyamoto, S. Frank 123, 129
Mizumo, Chuck 26
Monsanto Chemical Company 182
Moore Theater 139, 140, 143
Morris, Bobby 14
Morris, Robert 247
Morse, Wayne 103
Mortimer, Wyndham 52, 53
Movie theaters 138
Muirhead, William 53
Municipal League 11, 15, 63, 164, 165, 214, 243
Municipal Transit Authority 76
Murphy, Richard 204
Murray, Philip 6, 52, 107, 204, 206, 224
Museum of Modern Art 149
Myer, Dillon S. 42

# N

NAACP. *See* National Association for the Advancement of Colored People
Nakashima, George 148
Nash, Gerald 48
National Association for the Advancement of Colored People 122, 136
  Seattle chapter 123
National Association of Manufacturers 186
National Chamber of Commerce 187
National Citizens Political Action Committee (NCPA C) 109, 202
National Council for Art Work 148

National Defense Advisory Committee (NDAC)  7
National Housing Act  68
National Housing Agency  94
National Industrial Recovery Act  4, 80
National Institute of Real Estate Brokers  186
National Labor Relations Act (NLRA)  4, 6, 252
National Labor Relations Board  4, 52, 54, 215, 220, 221, 223
National Maritime Union  219
National Meat Packers Association  98
National Retail Dry Goods Association  185
National Urban League  122
Nazi-Soviet Pact  7
"Negro Battalion"  51
Neighborhood cooperatives  75
Nelson, Donald  81
New Deal  3, 10
New Deal coalition  5, 7, 107, 204
    splintering of  251
New Deal liberalism  253
*New Dealer*  107. *See also New World*
New Order of Cincinnatus  11
*New Republic*  236
*New World*  219
Newspaper drives  106
Newspaper strike, 1945  194
Nichols, J. Byron  147
Niendorff, Fred  67, 110, 207, 227, 236, 239
Nikkei
    return of evacuees  124–130
    social survey  127–130
Nikkei (refers to both Nissei and Issei)  9
Nippon Kan Theater  18
Nisei  9, 19, 254
    100th Battalion  127
    442nd Regimental Combat Team  127
    servicemen  125
*Nisei Daughter*  26
Nisei in
    public schools  19, 31
Nisei Steering Committee  127
*No Ivory Tower: McCarthyism and the Universities*  240
"no.strike" pledge  7
Nomura, Kenjiro  147, 149

Non-Communist affidavits  223
North American Aviation  7, 52
*North American Times*  21
Northwest Annual Art Exhibitions  149
*Northwest Enterprise*  120, 122
Northwest Power Pool  45, 65, 246, 249, 250
"Northwest School"  147–148, 149
Northwest Steel Rolling Mill  105
Nursery schools  163, 166
Nursing schools
    African Americans  121

## O

O'Brien, Robert  37, 129
O'Connell, Jerry  108, 113, 203, 213, 217, 228
Odets, Cifford  233
Okuda, Kenji  24
Okumura, Tao  37
"Old Left"  244
Oles, Floyd  32, 92, 93
Olympic foundry  130
"only for the duration"  76
OPA. *See* US Office of Price Administration
Open housing  192
Open shop  4
Oppenheimer, J. Robert  254
Organized labor
    status in 1950  251
Osawa, Yoshima  28
Owen, Henry B.  86
Owen, Mrs. Henry B.  123
Ozawa, Ed  26

## P

Pacific Car and Foundry  46, 121
*Pacific Fisherman*  34
Pacific Huts  60
*Pacific Northwest Industry*  174
Pacific Northwest Symphony Orchestra  142
Pacific Power and Light  66
Paganini String Quartet  146
Palmer Johnson Sextet  139
Palomar Theater  138
Parents and Teachers Association (PTA)  72–73, 164, 243

Parker, Dick  138
Patterson, Ambrose  148
Pauley, Ed  202
Peace celebration  151
Pearl Harbor Day  15, 21–28
Pellegrini, Angelo  228
Penthouse Theater  139
Pennell, David  143
Pennock, William  204
Pennock, William  210, 212, 235
*People in Motion: The Postwar Adjustment of the Evacuees*  129
Permanent Exemption Plan  125
Pettus, Edward  210
Pettus, Terry  34, 107, 109, 210
Phillips Gallery  148
Phillips, Herbert J.  228, 238
Pike Place Public Market  35
Pitter, Marjorie  122
"point rationing"  84
Polenberg, Richard  118
Police department
  election issue, 1948  213
  vice operations  13
Police harassment
  of African Americans  122, 124
Pomeroy, Allan  213
Population
  migration  8
Port of Embarkation  47, 60, 224
Port of Lewiston  249
Port of Seattle  174
Porter, Paul  93, 100, 187
"postage stamp" rates  249
Postwar planning  171–173
Powell, Mildred (Mrs. F.F.)
  108, 109, 214
Pratt, Dudley  148
Price ceilings
  enforcement  96
Price Control Extension Act  187
Price controls  182
  decentralization by commodity/industry  83
  food  95–104
  postwar decontrol of prices  188
  retail prices  87–89
  wholesale prices  87
Price Decontrol Board  187
price schedules  83
Pro-America  113, 161

Progressive Citizens of America
  205, 206
Progressive Party  203, 204, 213, 234
Progressive Party of Washington
  217, 228
Propaganda  22–23, 30, 33
Proposition C, (City)  243, 244, 245
Providence Hospital  131, 154, 160
PTA. *See* Parents and Teachers Association (PTA)
Public dance halls  138
Public housing  94
Public Law 503  30, 36
Public Market  19
Public power movement  112, 113
  weakening  250
Public transportation  60–62, 91
Public Utility Districts  9, 64
Puget Sound Bridge and Drydock
  59, 173
Puget Sound ferries  214
Puget Sound Naval Shipyard  3
Puget Sound Navigation Company  213
Puget Sound Power and Light Company
  9, 12, 15, 64–
  66, 109, 113, 172, 196, 249, 250
  city franchise termination  243, 244
Puget Sound PUD Commissioners
  Association  245
Puget Sound Traction, Power and Light
  Company  61
Puyallup Assembly Center.  39
  *See also* Camp Harmony

# R

Rabbitt, Tom  110, 112, 204, 212
Race relations survey, 1944  123
Race riots in
  Detroit  119
  Harlem  119
  Los Angeles  119
Rachmaninoff, Sergei  140
Racism  9, 19, 42, 55, 118–122, 251
  in Aero Mechanics union  54, 222
Rader, Melvin  210, 220, 230–232
Railroad strike, 1946  192
Railway Express Agency  89
Rainier Brewing Company  12
Rainier Vista housing project  70, 72
Randolph, A. Philip  119

Ration Book 2  85, 87, 88, 95
Rationing  95, 180
Rationing program  87
Raver, Paul  65
Raymond, Allen  235
Real wages  192
  postwar  185
Reconstruction Finance Corporation  61, 65, 80
Recreation for service personnel  136–139
Recruitment of women  76–77
Red Cross  121
Red-baiting  6, 107, 108, 110, 111, 223, 255
Referendum 25 (state)  66, 109, 112
Referendum 7 (state)  166
Referendum 9 (state)  160, 243
Reichhold Chemical Company  181
Remember Pearl Harbor League  125
Rent controls  84, 91, 183, 187
  evasion of rent ceilings  93
  "Fair rent" committee  186
  rent ceiling  83
Rent profiteering  92
Renton, Washington  138
Rents  70
Republican Party  114
Residential construction  189
Residential segregation  251
Restrictive covenants  19, 132
Retail Grocers and Meat Dealers Association of Washington  87
Retail sales  176
Return of Japanese
  opposition to  124–125
Return of Nikkei evacuees  124–130
Reuther, Walter  204
Reynolds Metal Company  80
Ride sharing  61
Riesel, Victor  220
"Rights-based liberalism"  253
Riley, Ed  160
Ring, Eleanor  42
Ringer, I.W.  87
Ritchie, Art  126
Rivoli Theater  138
Robertson, Orville  33
Robeson, Paul  140
Rochester, Alfred  108, 109
Rogers, Nat  218

Roosevelt coalition  6
Roosevelt, Franklin Delano  58, 80, 102, 107, 119, 249
  seven-point anti-inflationary message  83
Rosellini, Albert  156
Rosenthal, Manuel  143
Ross, Alice  246
Ross Dam  64
Ross, James D.  63, 246, 249
Ross, Nancy Wilson  149
Rosselini, Leo  156
Rovelle, Paul  219
Rubber conservation  89–91
Rubber supply  82
Rubenstein, Artur  140
Rushmore, Howard  227
Ryan, Joe  5

## S

Sailors Union of the Pacific  224
Sakamoto, James Y.  19, 23, 27, 29, 31, 33, 35, 36, 39
Salvage Committee  85
Salvage drives  104–106
San Francisco Ballet  143
San Francisco general strike  5
San Francisco Opera Company  141, 143
San Juan Story  233
Sand Point Homes  70
Sand Point Naval Air Station  47, 70
Sanders, Jane  237
Savage, Charles  110–111, 111, 235
Save Boeing Committee  199
Savoy (club)  139
Scavotto, James  107, 108
Schmitz, Henry  254
Schmoe, Floyd  25, 33, 39
Schneider, Alexander  145
School building construction  163, 166
School curriculum changes  50
Schrecker, Ellen W.  240
Schultz, Cecilia  140, 143–144
Seafarers International Union  194
Sears, William  11, 54
SeaTac Airport  196
Seattle Art Museum  148, 149
  war poster contest  149

Seattle Central Labor Council
  5, 54, 127, 224
Seattle Chamber of Commerce
  11, 19, 30, 33, 46, 47, 58, 62, 87,
  94, 103, 155, 172, 174, 181, 196
Seattle Charter Revision Committee
  131
Seattle City Council 12
Seattle City Light
  9, 31, 46, 61, 64, 65, 66, 112, 245, 249
Seattle Civic Unity Committee (CUC)
  9, 44, 161, 192, 251
  Annual Institute on Race Relations
    132
  combatting African American
    discrimination 130–131
Seattle Defense Housing Committee 86
Seattle General Hospital 131
Seattle Homes Registration Bureau 92
Seattle Housing Authority
  46, 68, 94, 120, 121, 190–191
Seattle Housing Center 190
Seattle Industrial Union Council 53
Seattle Landlords Association 92
Seattle Municipal Defense Commission
  28, 86
Seattle Park Board 75
*Seattle Post Intelligencer (P-I)* 22–
  23, 111, 206, 226, 234
  coverage of Japanese evacuation
    28, 30
  coverage of Japanese return 125
Seattle Progressive Citizens League 23
Seattle Public School Board 242
Seattle Public Schools
  19, 50, 72, 73, 78, 87, 163–
  165
  after-school program 74
  Family Life program 74, 75, 163
  first African American teachers 131
  married teachers ban 164
Seattle Real Estate Board 91, 132
  restrictive covenants 132
Seattle Repertory Playhouse
  10, 139, 208, 220, 228
  Canwell Committee investigation
    233–234
Seattle Revival Center 144
Seattle School Board 126
*Seattle Star* 126, 137

coverage of Japanese evacuation
  28, 30, 32, 39
"Service Men's Week-End Where to
  Go List" 136
Seattle Symphony 139–142
*Seattle Times (Times)*
  22, 52, 72, 136, 227, 228, 233
  coverage of Japanese evacuation
    28, 29, 35, 36, 37, 39
  coverage of Japanese return 125
Seattle Transit System 131, 214
Seattle Urban League 121
Seattle War Housing Center 68
Seattle Welfare Council Defense
  Committee 85
Seattle-King County War Chest 73
Seattle-Tacoma Shipbuilding Corpora-
  tion 46
Second Interceptor Command 22
Segregation 121, 251
Self-regulation of business 80
Service Men's Club 136
Service women 136
Severyns, William 13
Shannon, William 15
"Share the Room" campaign 94
*Shelley vs. Kramer* 251
Shemanski, Alfred 123
Sherman, Sarah McClain 146
Ship Scalers and Dry Dock Workers
  110
Shipbuilding 3, 10, 45–47
Shipyard investigations 103
Shipyard training classes 49
Shipyards 48
  wage scales 58
Shopping 61, 68
Showboat Theater 139
Shucklin, Gerald 28, 30
Sick, Emil 12, 187
Sieg, Lee Paul 155, 227
Skagit County PUD 66
Skilled labor shortage 188
Smith, T.V. 240
Smith, Ben 126
Smith, Tom 110
Smith-Connally Anti-Strike Act 192
  (refer from War Labor Disputes Act)
  107–108, 109, 172
Smullyan, Arthur 228
Sokoloff, Nikolai 141

# 324 Index

Sone, Monica 26
Soule, Elizabeth 155
Southern California Aircraft Industry (SCAI) 55, 58, 100, 102
Southern Pacific Railroad 48
Southern Regional Council 122
Soviet Union. *See* Union of the Soviet Socialist Republics
Spangler, James 32
Spanish Castle 138
Spokane Street viaduct 47, 61
Squires, Bernard 121
Steel industry 81
Steel strike 191, 192, 194
Stettinius, Edward 80
Stevenson, Faber 120
Stimson, Henry 7
Stockman, Lowell 124
Stone, Clifford 51
Strategic bombing 57
Stratocruiser 199
Streetcars 60–61
Strikes 5, 52
    in 1946 191
        coal strike 192
        railroad strike 192
        steel strike 191, 192, 194
Stuntz, George 228
Suburbanization 250
Sugar rationing 88
Sugimoto family 24, 35–36
Sullivan, James T. 211–212
Superintendent of Public Instruction 49
Surplus property disposition 173–174
Swedish Hospital 131, 154, 160
Symington, Stuart 197, 198

## T

Tacoma Philharmonic 142
Taffinder, S.A. 59
Taft-Hartley Bill 194, 205, 251
Taft-Hartley Bill (Law) 216, 219, 223
Tai Tung restaurant 24, 36
Takahashi, C.T.. *See* Takahashi, Charles T.
Takahashi, Charles T. 26, 28, 40
Tanabe, Taeko 26
Teamsters Union 5, 12, 14, 16, 62, 66, 76, 109, 113, 124, 127, 129, 203, 216, 251

collaboration with Boeing 218–219
    raids 220
Testu, Jeanette 107, 108
Textiles 182
The 411 139
*The End of Reform* 252
The Washingtonians 137
Thomas, Christy 46
Thorgrimson, Richard 166
Tibbett, Lawrence 140
Tobey, Mark 147, 148–149
Todd, Elmer 233
Todd Shipbuilding Corporation 46
Todd Shipyard 121
Tokita, Kamekichi 149
Tolan Committee 13, 15, 27, 29, 32–35
Tolan, John 15, 32
Tollefson, Thor 204
Tourtelotte, Mrs. Neal 85
Trade associations 4, 80
Trailer parks 70–71
Treat, Mrs. Harry 146
Trianon Ballroom 123, 138, 139
Troy, Smith 33
Truman administration 202
Truman doctrine 205
Truman, Harry 80, 185, 186, 191, 197, 199
Tryout Theater 139
Tsutakawa Company 149
Tsutakawa, George 148–149
Tudor, Anthony 146
Turner, Edward 156, 158, 160, 243

## U

Ubangi (club) 139
Underwood, John 46
Unemployment 175
Union Bay Village 190
Union of the Soviet Socialist Republics 8, 107
Unions 50–53
United Auto Workers 252
United Automobile, Aircraft and Agricultural Implements Union 99
United Automobile Workers (UAW) 4, 52, 184, 192, 204
United Electrical Workers 4
United Mine Workers 4, 6

United Nations Reconstruction and Relief Administration  182
United States Steel Corporation  4
United Steel Workers Union  4, 192
University of Washington
  10, 21, 22, 24, 31, 40, 78, 124, 127, 190, 208, 234, 235
  Associated Women Students  140, 145–146
  Canwell Committee hearings  220, 227, 254
  Japanese students  19, 39
  return of Japanese students  126
*University of Washington Daily*  27
Urban League  122, 131, 132
US Air Force  197–198
  B-52 contract  200
US Army  7–8
  100th Battalion  127
  442nd Regimental Combat Team  127, 129
  Air Corps  197
  Fourth Army's Western Defense Command  23
  Jefferson Park Recreation Center  137
  Permanent Exemption Plan  125
  Quartermaster Corps  78
  Quartermaster Supply Depot  59
  ROTC  153
  Transport Service  7, 51, 59, 87
US Army Corps of Engineers  249
US Bonneville Power Administration  9, 45, 64, 172, 246, 249
US Bureau of Reclamation  249
US Commission on Wartime Relocation and Internment  29
US Employment Service (USES)  127, 131, 176
US Farm Security Administration  37, 39
US Federal Bureau of Investigation (FBI)  21, 22, 23, 24, 25, 26, 31, 33, 36, 59, 108, 208
US Federal Works Agency  63
US House Committee on Un-American Activities  206, 254
US House Select Committee Investigating National Defense  15, 208, 254.  *See also* Tolan Committee
US Immigration and Naturalization Service (INS)  21, 22, 129

US Justice Department  28, 129
US Marine Hospital  157
US Maritime Commission  46, 224
US National Defense Mediation Board  8
US National Labor Relations Board
  *See* National Labor Relations Board
US Navy  47, 59
  Office of Public Relations  22
  ROTC  153
US Office of Defense Transportation  61
US Office of Economic Stabilization  84, 93
US Office of Emergency Management  86
US Office of Housing Expediter  188
US Office of Naval Intelligence  21, 22
US Office of Price Administration (OPA)  8, 44, 58, 81–106, 171
  extension controversy  185–186
  price controls  83
  price schedules  81
US Office of Price Administration and Civilian Supply  81, 202
US Office of Production Management  7, 80, 81
US Office of War Housing Expediter  94
US Office of War Information  76
US Supreme Court  253
US Veterans Administration  130, 132
US War Department  28, 42, 253
US War Labor Board  49, 58, 87, 104
US War Manpower Board  58, 58–59, 76, 87, 94, 104
US War Manpower Commission
  Wage Stabilization Board  99
US War Production Board (WPB)  15, 58, 62-63, 65, 81, 84, 99–104, 163, 180, 188
US War Production Transport Commission  61
US War Relocation Authority (WRA)  36, 123, 124, 126, 128
US Wartime Civilian Control Administration  39
US Women's Bureau  48, 75, 76, 78
US Works Progress Administration  61, 72, 73, 211
USSR.  *See* Union of the Soviet Socialist Republics

## Index

UW (abbreviation for University of Washington) 19
UW Administrative Code 237–238
UW Alumni Association 160, 244
UW Annual Northwest Institute on Race Relations 161
UW Applied Physics Laboratory 153
UW Board of Regents 155, 161, 227–228, 236, 239
UW Business Research Bureau 174
UW Drama School 233–238
UW Health Sciences building 156
UW Institute of Industrial Relations 161
UW Institute of Labor Economics 132, 161
UW Labor Economics Department 133
UW Medical School 154–160, 243
UW Music Hall 140
UW Nursing School 155
UW Physics Department 254
UW School of Music 143, 145
UW School of Social Work 132
UW Sociology Department 132, 161
UW Tenure and Academic Freedom Committee Hearings 235–240

## V

"V-12" program 153
VanderSys, Arthur 92, 94
Vaudeville 138
Veterans
  postwar employment 176–177
Veterans of Foreign Wars 127
"Victory Canteen" 136
"Victory Gardens" 70, 95
Victory Square 106, 151
Victory-Japan Day 151
Vietnam 255
*Vigilante* 210
Virginia Mason Clinic 158
Vocational training classes 165
Vocational training schools 49
"Voice of the Aircraft Builders" 98
Volunteerism 85–86
Volunteerism in industry 80
Volunteers Committee 85
Voter registration drives, 1944 108
Voter turnout 111–112
Vultee aircraft plant 52

## W

Wage controls 98–99
Wage scales 49
Wage Stabilization Board 99, 100, 191, 193
Wage-price policing, 1946 191–192
Wages at Boeing 58–59, 100
Wagner Act 4, 6, 252
Wagner, Robert 4, 185
Walker, Samuel 254
Wallace, Henry 202, 205, 219, 234
Waller, Fats 139
Wallgren, Mon[rad]
  66, 67, 103, 110, 111, 126, 151, 156, 160, 173, 203, 213, 219, 234
Walsh-Healy Minimum Wage Act 52
Walters, Frank L. 40
Wanamaker, Pearl 49
War Chest Fund 137
War Housing Center. *See* US Office of War Housing Expeditor
War Labor Disputes Act 10 *See also* Smith-Connally Anti-strike Act
War poster contest 149
War Production Board *See* US War Production Board
War Relocation Authority (WRA). *See* US War Relocation Authority (WRA)
Warner, B. Gray 53, 54
Washington (State) Defense Council 72, 91
Washington (State) Fair Employment Practices Committee 130–132, 251
Washington (State) Legislature
  intimidation of UW 239–240
Washington (State) Power Commission 245
Washington (State) Superintendent of Public Instruction 73
Washington Committee for Academic Freedom 228
Washington Commonwealth Federation (WCF)
  7, 12, 34, 63, 107, 108, 110–112, 203, 205, 207, 211, 244
Washington Federation of Butchers 88
Washington Gasoline Dealers Association 91

Washington Old Age Pension Union 211. *See also* Washington Pension Union
Washington Pension Union 10, 112, 154, 155, 159, 204, 205, 207, 208, 210, 234–236, 244
Washington Produce Packers Association 32
Washington Social Club 139
Washington State Employment Security Agency 176
Washington State Federation of Labor (WSFL) 5, 14, 194
Washington State Medical Association 155, 158
Washington State Nurses Association 131
Washington Taxpayers Association 92
Washington Water Power Company 66
Waterfront Employers' Association 51, 193, 219, 222–226
Waterfront strike of 1934 5
Watts, Lewis 132
Weaver, Robert 132
Webster-Brinkley Company 60
Weisfield, Leo 85
Welch, Douglass 121
Welfare issues 244
West, Ronald 233
West Seattle 61, 95
Westberg, Alfred 133
Western Gear 60
Western States Council 172
Weston, Evan (Ed) 194
Westover, Oscar 57
Weyerhaeuser Timber Company 66
Whatcom County PUD 64
Wheeler, Bayard 188
White River Dairy 26, 35
Whitney Art Gallery 148
Wholesale price structure 81
Widmer's Trailer Park 70
Willard, Marian 147
Williams, Walter 91
"Win the War" 81
Winther, Sophus 228
Women workers 8, 48–50. *See also* Employment of women
Women's University Club 74
Women's Victory Corps 85, 90, 94
Woodring, Harry 57

Workers Alliance 211–212
Workforce composition 47-50
World War I 4
WPA. *See* US Works Progress Administration
"Wyatt homes" program 188
Wyatt, Wilson 188

## Y

Yamagawa family 125
Yesler Terrace 68, 120
YMCA. *See* Young Men's Christian Association (YMCA)
Young Men's Christian Association (YMCA) 24, 40
Young Progressives of Washington 217
Young Women's Christian Association 136
Youth for Christ 164
YWCA. *See* Young Women's Christian Association

## Z

Zioncheck, Marion 63
"zoot suit riots" 119